THE OLDEST GUARD

Stanford Studies in Jewish History and Culture

THE OLDEST GUARD

Forging the Zionist Settler Past

LIORA R. HALPERIN

Stanford University Press
Stanford, California

STANFORD UNIVERSITY PRESS
Stanford, California

© 2021 by the Board of Trustees of the Leland Stanford Junior University. All rights reserved.

No part of this book may be reproduced or transmitted in any form or by any means, electronic or mechanical, including photocopying and recording, or in any information storage or retrieval system without the prior written permission of Stanford University Press.

Printed in the United States of America on acid-free, archival-quality paper

Library of Congress Cataloging-in-Publication Data

Names: Halperin, Liora R., author.
Title: The oldest guard : forging the Zionist settler past / Liora R. Halperin.
Other titles: Stanford studies in Jewish history and culture.
Description: Stanford, California : Stanford University Press, 2021. | Series: Stanford studies in Jewish history and culture | Includes bibliographical references and index.
Identifiers: LCCN 2020049182 (print) | LCCN 2020049183 (ebook) | ISBN 9781503628496 (cloth) | ISBN 9781503628700 (paperback) | ISBN 9781503628717 (ebook)
Subjects: LCSH: Zionism—Palestine—Historiography. | Jews—Colonization—Palestine—History. | Agricultural colonies—Palestine—History. | Collective memory—Palestine—History. | Collective memory—Israel—History. | Palestine—History—1917–1948. | Israel—History—1948–1967.
Classification: LCC DS149.5.P35 H35 2021 (print) | LCC DS149.5.P35 (ebook) | DDC 320.54095694/09034—dc23
LC record available at https://lccn.loc.gov/2020049182
LC ebook record available at https://lccn.loc.gov/2020049183

Cover photo: Avraham Shapira at a Convention of Guardsmen in Netanya, 1937. Zoltan Kluger, Courtesy of the KKL-JNF Photo Archive.
Cover design: Susan Zucker

For Rami

CONTENTS

Acknowledgments ix

Note on Transliteration and Translation xv

Map of "First Aliyah" Colonies xviii

Introduction: Mother of the Colonies   1

1 Private Farmers and the Origins of "First Aliyah" Claims-Making   39

2 Arab Labor and the Rhetoric of Hierarchical Coexistence in Mandate Palestine   67

3 The Old Guard on Display   114

4 The Colony and the Village: Constructions of Coexistence after the Nakba   151

5 Jewish Immigrants and the Politics of Settler "First Ones"   189

Conclusion: Thinking about the First Aliyah
after 1967   237

Notes   253

Bibliography   295

Index   325

ACKNOWLEDGMENTS

In the months before I completed these acknowledgments, the entire West Coast of the United States was smothered in a blanket of smoke from unprecedented forest fires and the world was in the midst of the COVID-19 pandemic; a deepening, unequally distributed economic crisis; and the upheaval of the 2020 U.S. election and its aftermath. All of this only enhances my recognition of the ever-increasing precarity of the academic and societal frameworks in which I completed this project. Nonetheless, I feel joy at the opportunity to express gratitude.

My research was made possible by the financial and institutional support provided by a 2016–2017 fellowship from the Frankel Institute for Advanced Judaic Studies at the University of Michigan and a 2016 visiting position at the Harvard Center for Jewish Studies. I was able to complete research-related travel and secure the support of research assistants thanks to a Hadassah-Brandeis Institute Research Grant, an Israel Institute Research Grant, and support from the University of Colorado (CU) Program in Jewish Studies, the CU History Department, the CU Endowed Professorship in Israel/Palestine Studies, and the University of Washington Jack and Rebecca Benaroya Endowment for Excellence in Israel Studies.

I want to thank the staff members at several institutions whose tireless but often invisible and undercompensated work enabled me to do mine: Sarah Zaides Rosen, Kara Schoonmaker, Emily Thompson, Alexandra

Colley, Tracy Machman Morrissey, Toni Read, and Kevin Swantek at the University of Washington; Ted Lytle, Kellie Matthews, and Meghan Perea at the University of Colorado; Rachel Rockenmacher and Sandy Cantave Vil at the Harvard Center for Jewish Studies; and Cheri Thompson at the University of Michigan. Several faculty program directors and chairs helped nurture the academic communities and institutions I benefited from while working on this book: David Shneer z"l, Elizabeth Fenn, Nan Goodman, and Susan Kent at the University of Colorado; Jeffrey Veidlinger at the University of Michigan; and Noam Pianko, Reşat Kasaba, Leela Fernandes, Selim Kuru, Arzoo Osanloo, Cabeiri Robinson, Anand Yang, and Glennys Young at the University of Washington. Nor could I have completed this project without the assistance of several brilliant students. Nancy Ko and Oded Oron provided invaluable research assistance; Hayim Katsman assisted with the difficult process of attaining image rights for the book; and Jacob Beckert read and offered feedback on the entire final manuscript and helped me prepare it for publication. The book came into the world thanks to the wonderful editorial staff at Stanford University Press, including Margo Irvin, Cindy Lim, and Tim Roberts; the expert copy editor Marie Deer; and the series editors of Stanford Studies in Jewish History and Culture, Sarah Abrevaya Stein and David Biale.

A project about local institutions' past attempts to preserve and shape history necessarily relies on the contemporary institutions that continue to engage in this work. Much of my archival research was done in local archives based in museum or city municipality buildings. Often, I was the only researcher present, sitting alongside local senior citizen volunteers and devoted local archivists who provided me not only with documents but also, sometimes, with tea and snacks. Many generously continued to correspond with me about sources once I was no longer local. Thanks go to Galia Duvidzon, Nati Malakhi, and Noni Yaron at the Oded Yarkoni Petah Tikva Archive; Hadas Avivi, Nili Cohen, Efrat Haberman, Adi Rubin, and Orit Sagi at the Rishon LeZion Historical Archive; Liron Gurfinkel at the Zichron Yaʻaqov Historical Archive; Levana Feldman and Riki Shapira at Beit Rishonim, Ness Ziona; Marion Freudenthal at the Aaronsohn House Museum, Zichron Yaʻaqov; Nurit Alfassi at the Yesud HaMaʻala Archive; and Shiri Gonen-Ben Shimon at the Bilu Museum in Gedera. I want to express sincere appreciation to Yaakov Abramovich, Ehud Ben-Ezer, and Gideon Makoff, all descendants of First Aliyah "First Ones," who generously arranged to meet with me to tell me about their families. Thanks also to Rochelle Rubenstein at the Central Zionist Archive and Helena Vilensky of the Israel State Archive; Vardit Haimi Samuels and Elizabeth Vernon at the Judaica Division of Harvard's Widener Memorial Library; César Merchán-Hamann at the Getzel Kressel Archive at Oxford University's Leopold Muller Memorial Library; Thea Lindquist and Megan Welsh at the University of Colorado Libraries; and Mary St. Germain at the University of Washington Libraries.

As this project took twists and turns and finally coalesced into its final form, I benefited from the feedback and wisdom of numerous colleagues. Particular thanks go to Orit Bashkin, Jacob Beckert, David Biale, Nahum Karlinsky, and Derek Penslar, who gave feedback on the entire manuscript; and Alon Confino, Hilary Falb Kalisman, Sherene Seikaly, Gershon Shafir, and Tamir Sorek, who generously offered feedback on late versions of chapters and provided me with valuable corrections and insights. My cohort at the University of Michigan Frankel Institute, as individuals and as a group, read my work at several earlier stages and provided the most wonderful collegial exchange and connections I could have possibly asked for during a residential fellowship. Thanks go to Naomi Brenner, Mostafa Hussein, Lior Libman, Aviad Moreno, Shachar Pinsker, Bryan Roby, Noah Rubin, Gavin Schaffer, Rachel Seelig, Jeffrey Veidlinger, Shayna Zamkanei, and Yael Zerubavel, as well as to Maya Barzilai, Devi Mays, Rachel Neis, and Anita Norich, who were integral to the inspiring and supportive Judaic Studies community I benefited from during my year at the University of Michigan. I also was fortunate to share my work in progress at invited conferences and speaking engagements at the College of Idaho, Goethe University in Frankfurt, the University of Göttingen, the University of Minnesota, and the University of Wisconsin.

Upon settling in Seattle and at the University of Washington, with the dedication and support of Reşat Kasaba, Joel Migdal, and Noam Pianko, I found many delightful friends and generous colleagues in both of my home departments—the Jackson School of International Studies and the Department of History—and in the larger University of Washington Jewish

Studies and Middle East Studies communities. I'm grateful to the members of the informal historians reading group I participate in at the University of Washington—Daniel Bessner, Arbella Bet-Shlimon, Vanessa Freije, James Lin, Laurie Marhoefer, Devin Naar, and Nova Robinson. This group read an earlier version of chapter 1, and have become close interlocutors. I also especially cherish my ongoing collaboration and exchange with Devin Naar and Mika Ahuvia, who are close colleagues, ongoing sources of insight, and dear friends.

Many other colleagues across the world and close to home offered me sounding boards or presentation opportunities, challenged me, shared their work, introduced me to or helped me understand sources, and offered me new ways of thinking about my project. These include, in addition to those mentioned above: Yoav Alon, Smadar Ben-Natan, Nimrod Ben-Zeev, Amos Bitzan, Matan Boord, Michelle Campos, Julia Phillips Cohen, Leena Dallasheh, Karam Dana, Arnon Degani, Yuval Dror, Arie Dubnov, Omri Eilat, Elia Etkin, Marco Di Giulio, Jonathan Gribetz, Sara Yael Hirschhorn, Elizabeth Imber, Adriana Jacobs, Alexander Kaye, Menachem Klein, Geoffrey Levin, Callie Maidhof, Fredrik Meiton, Yehuda Mirsky, Srimati Mitter, Tamar Novick, Iair Or, Josh Reid, Shira Robinson, Laura Robson, Orit Rozin, Suzanne Schneider, Hizky Shoham, Noam Sienna, Andrea Stanton, Refael Stern, Lior Sternfeld, Yair Wallach, Shayna Weiss, John Willis, and Alex Winder. David N. Myers, Derek Penslar, Naomi Seidman, and Sarah Abrevaya Stein were generous mentors during my PhD training and have remained invaluable sources of ongoing support and advice. David Shneer, my mentor and colleague at the University of Colorado and an enthusiastic supporter of this project, left this world far too soon, as I was completing this book. His memory will forever be a blessing.

This was a project of peregrination, and I couldn't have done it, at least not nearly as enjoyably, without the generous neighbors, friends, family, roommates, and hosts at my many destinations: Aviva and Craig Alpert, Alana Alpert and Justin Sledge, Seth Anziska and Tareq Baconi, Michal and Motti Bitton, Ayehlet Cooper, Daniel Estrin and Hussein Shakra, Elia Etkin, Sandy Fox and Amir Unger, Kathie Friedman and Reşat Kasaba, Amos Geva and Kathrin Schank, Doug Halperin and Sally Cohen, Yael Miller and Gideon Heineberg, Adriana Jacobs, Julian Levinson and Lisa

Makman, Melanie Lidman, Liatte Miller, Samantha Moddel, Leslie Rogers, Kate Rosenblatt, Joel Russman and Robin Springer, Tova Scherr, Elana Shohamy, Sue and Jim Stockard, Shayna Weiss, Naama Zahavi-Ely, and Naomi Zeveloff, as well as the 2016 residents of Common Place in Cambridge, Massachusetts, and the 2016–2017 residents of the Michigan Branch Telluride House in Ann Arbor.

A special thanks to other dear friends, near and far, who have been present, attentive, and generous over the years I spent working on this book: Rawan Arar, Cameron Bellm, Lauren Berliner, Tara Bognar, Amaranth Borsuk, Matthew Ellis, Hilary Falb Kalisman, Sarah El-Kazaz, Shira Kieval, Moshe Kornfeld, Sarah Crane O'Neill, Mihaela Pacurar, Nova Robinson, David Schlitt, Ilana Sichel, Andrea Soroko Naar, Ronit Stahl, Saul Zaritt, and Sarah Zarrow. My sister, Aviva Alpert, and my parents, Bob and Wendy Russman-Halperin, were often too far from me, especially as the COVID-19 pandemic forced us to cancel all our planned travel, but they remained just a phone call away. Their generosity, love, and support, has meant the world to me.

Final thanks go to Sasha Senderovich, who has supported me enthusiastically and devotedly across multiple geographies and life stages. I couldn't have done this without him. This book is dedicated to Rami, who arrived in the world midway through my work on the book and whose presence (including extra presence during a pandemic-era daycare shutdown) made this process and these strange times somewhat more chaotic but ultimately much more bearable.

NOTE ON TRANSLITERATION AND TRANSLATION

The term *moshava*, used for the Jewish agricultural colonies established before 1948 on privately (rather than nationally) owned land, was a direct Hebrew translation of the word "colony." The term *kolonyot* was used in the nineteenth century for these same Jewish agricultural colonies, and "colony" remained the accepted English translation of *moshava* through at least 1948. Since 1948, "moshava," along with its plural "moshavot," has typically been used in English, taken over untranslated from Hebrew. I use both "moshava" and "colony" when referring to events before 1948, so as to remind readers of their interchangeable use. In discussing the history of moshavot after 1948, I typically do not translate the term, in keeping with standard usage. I translate the term *ikar*, and its more common later equivalent *haklai*, as "farmer" or "agriculturalist." These terms are used here for those engaged in private agriculture as owners of capital, not those working in agriculture as wage laborers nor as participants in collective or communal agricultural projects. I translate the ubiquitous term *rishonim* as "First Ones" in order to capture its literal meaning and honorific quality, though the term can also carry the sense of "founders."

All translations of primary sources are my own unless otherwise indicated.

I use the Library of Congress transliteration systems for Hebrew, Yiddish, and Arabic terms and titles, with a few variations and simplifications. I spell names of Israeli cities and towns using the localities' official English spellings, even when those do not match my standard transliteration rules (e.g. Rishon LeZion rather than Rishon Le-Tziyon; Zichron Ya'aqov rather than Zikhron Ya'akov). For names of Palestinian villages destroyed in 1948, I use the spellings from Walid Khalidi's compendium *All That Remains*. I use conventional spellings of personal names and other familiar terms (in most cases omitting diacritics and apostrophes from personal names), while following the Latin spelling preferred by authors and historical figures when I have been able to discern it.

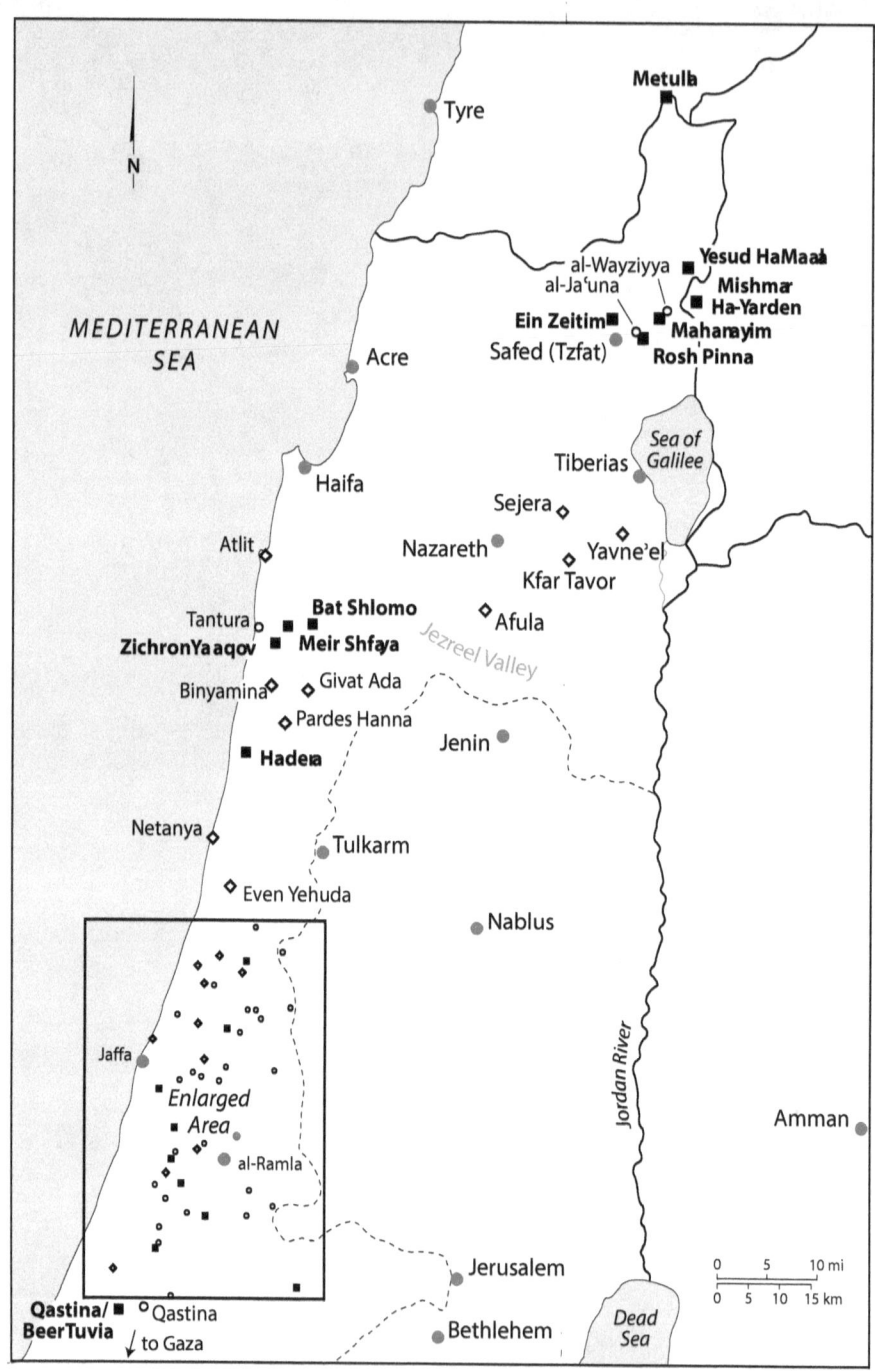

FIGURE 1. Early "First Aliyah" colonies and twentieth-century context.

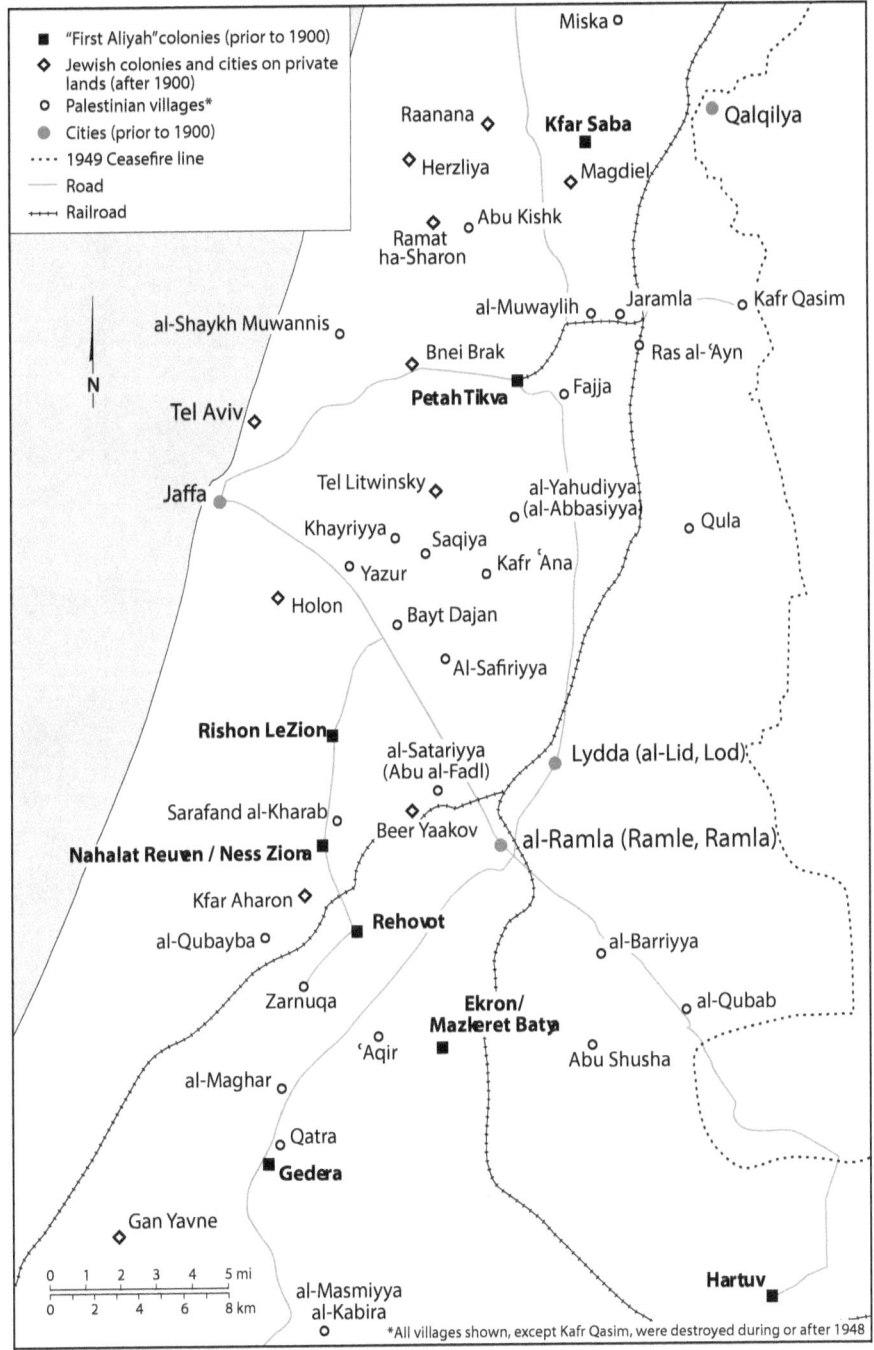

THE OLDEST GUARD

INTRODUCTION
Mother of the Colonies

In 1960, the Friedman and Sons Winery in Petah Tikva produced a new special edition liquor to celebrate the ninetieth birthday of Avraham Shapira, one of the last survivors of the city's first Jewish settler generation and a longstanding patron of the winery.[1] The Patron's Old Brandy featured Shapira's face on the front label and, on the back, a second image of Shapira on horseback overlooking a cultivated landscape. The act of consumption, the English-language text suggested to local and global consumers, "takes you back to the early years of the mother-colony and the foremost of its defenders, Abraham Shapira, who devoted himself to the defense of its fields and vineyards. . . . We now supply it to persons of discerning taste—for their exquisite enjoyment." The elderly Shapira personally handed out bottles of the brandy bearing his image to winners of an opening night raffle hosted by a Tel Aviv cinema—the man and his commemorative representation thus appearing on the same stage.[2] Consumers partaking of the spirits could simultaneously imbibe a past framed as a site of frontier heroism and successful agriculture, signal middle-class aesthetics, and understand their luxury consumption as a nationalist act.

Shapira was born in 1870 in a part of the Russian Pale of Settlement that is now southeastern Ukraine; he came to Palestine with his family in 1880 and, following stints in Jerusalem and Jaffa, came to Petah Tikva in 1883. Petah Tikva was a private Jewish agricultural colony founded in 1878

FIGURE 2. The Patron's Old brandy bottles, front and back (two bottle designs). Produced by Friedman & Sons Winery, ca. 1960 (courtesy of Hadi Orr).

by a small group of Ashkenazi Jerusalemites on lands purchased near the Palestinian village of Umlebes, northeast of Jaffa. Facing agricultural failure and inclement weather, its residents abandoned it in 1881, but it was revived two years later on a slightly different site by new settlers, including Shapira's older brother Michael, whom he soon followed to the colony.[3] Avraham Shapira became the renowned head of the Petah Tikva guardsmen and an owner of agricultural lands in the colony.[4] He died in 1965, at the age of 95, after living in Petah Tikva through periods of Ottoman, British, and Israeli rule.

Of the nearly sixty thousand residents of Petah Tikva in 1960, who might have seen The Old Patron's Brandy for sale, the majority had arrived after the establishment of the State of Israel in 1948, most of them from post-Holocaust Europe, the Middle East, or North Africa.[5] Some of them had been settled by the state in transit camps or government housing constructed on confiscated Palestinian lands and later incorporated into the municipality.[6] These newcomers, like several immigrant generations before them, would have become acquainted with Shapira mainly through stylized depictions and public performances that, like the brandy bottle, reliably featured his moustache, pipe, and Arabian horse. As he aged, he had become known by the moniker "the Oldest of the Guards" [*zekan ha-shomrim*] and remained a sought-after, if sometimes ridiculed, symbol of early Petah Tikva, of late-nineteenth-century private Jewish agricultural settlement more generally, and, most pertinently to those new immigrants, a symbol of the ongoing legacy of Zionism as a settler movement in which they themselves, willingly or not, were participants.

The period of settlement that Petah Tikva participated in and gave rise to is known retrospectively in Zionist discourse and Israeli historiography as the "First Aliyah," or first wave of Zionist immigration to Palestine (typically dated 1882–1904). Its iconic communities, distinguished by their ongoing private landownership even as the Zionist movement turned toward centralized national models of land acquisition and management, were initially known, in both Hebrew and Yiddish, as *kolonyot* (sing. *kolonya*). From the early twentieth century onward this term was replaced by the Hebrew word *moshavot* (sing. *moshava*), a translation of the word "colonies" and related to other terms meaning "settlement." The word "colony" continued to be used in European languages, including by Zionists, until after Israeli statehood, when the word "moshava" began to be used in those languages as well, borrowed from Hebrew untranslated.[7] Modern-day Petah Tikva, a bustling (and lovingly ridiculed) city in its own right, is still known by the moniker *Em ha-moshavot*, "The Mother of the Colonies."

Shapira's image—on brandy bottles and in person—evoked not only the 1880s or 1890s, however, but also the decades-long, twentieth-century history that is the subject of this book: the construction and deployment of the "First Aliyah" private colony as iconic place and the landowning farmer-settler-colonist-guardsman as iconic person against the political and cultural backdrops of the twentieth century. The "First Aliyah" emerged as a site of memory,[8] object of critique, and, specifically, symbol of private ownership and cultural conservatism. This happened in the context of the ascent and then reign of Labor Zionist leaders who considered the private farmers reactionary and anti-national; a growing Zionist partisanship within which private farmers were largely bit players; the arrival of waves of Jewish immigrants lacking familiarity with the early settlement past; and increasingly evident resistance among the Palestinian Arabs who found themselves displaced and had their national aspirations thwarted by the growth of the Zionist settlement project.

To their Zionist critics, the early colonies were discredited symbols of a failed first step at Jewish settlement. To Palestinian peasants, they were a source of employment within a Zionist ethnic labor hierarchy that exploited them and then increasingly, but never fully, excluded and displaced them. To Palestinian farmers and landowners, they were competitors within a growing export economy.[9] To local boosters and advocates of private farming, however, the most prosperous colonies were long-standing symbols of private enterprise, traditional Jewish attachment to the Land of Israel, pragmatic economic policy on behalf of the Jewish nation, and what they regarded as hierarchical coexistence between Jewish owners and the Arab workers they hired, against the protestations of Labor Zionists who insisted on the principle of "Hebrew Labor." Always celebratory, often counterfactual, highly selective, and sometimes—like the brandy advertising—apparently banal, evocations, re-creations, and constructions of the settler past concealed within themselves their own Zionist politics. The agriculturalist "ruling class" before World War I remained on "the fringes of the center in political and symbolic-value terms" under the British Mandate, but constituted a notable economic "elite" and "an alternative center" from a social standpoint.[10] The First Aliyah past—produced, cleaned, processed, and packed along with oranges and wine grapes—could also appeal to other groups outside the hegemonic Labor parties, including segments of the industrial capitalist, religious Zionist, religious non-Zionist, Revisionist, and Sephardi Zionist communities. The colony farmers are the often-disregarded precursors of and early, if ambivalent, participants in an emerging Zionist center-right politics, some of whose representatives would formally join with the militant right in 1965 to form Gahal, the predecessor to the 1973 Likud party.

Scholars of collective memory remind us that historical myths are created to serve the present and to help those in the present envision potential futures. Kristin Ross, writing about the protests and social upheaval of May 1968 in Paris, argues that the historical events themselves "cannot now be considered separated from the social memory and forgetting that surround them." Ultimately, she says, the problem of managing the memory of 1968 forms the "center of the historical problem of 1968 itself."[11] As Matt Matsuda has observed, "The past is not a truth upon which to build, but a truth sought, a re-memorializing over which to struggle."[12] Our concern, too, is not the period typically called the First Aliyah (1882–1904) but a later period during which the First Aliyah, as an amalgam, selection, and flattening of the stories of distinct late-nineteenth-century settlers and agricultural colonies, was truly constituted as a symbol in and object of collective discourse. The "First Aliyah" continued to reside spatially and symbolically in the nineteenth-century moshavot, particularly those on the Mediterranean coastal plain, well after the First Aliyah period had supposedly ended and been superseded. In presenting a foundational past in ceremonies, books, articles, interviews, and proclamations during the twentieth century—a modern nationalist variant of the "ritual and recital" that Yosef Hayim Yerushalmi associates with traditional Jewish memory[13]—the elites at the center of the moshava commemoration enterprise engaged in a dual project with a fundamental tension at its heart. On the one hand, they pushed for fellow Zionists to reintegrate the late-nineteenth-century Jewish colonies into the history of Zionism—indeed to place them, their commitment to private enterprise, and their status as "firsts" at its center. On the other hand, they endeavored to show that they represented a stage and phase of history that stood apart from Zionism as it had developed under the tutelage of Ben-Gurion's party Mapai (est. 1930) and Mapai's Labor Zionist predecessors and thus that it could model a path away from the movement's myriad ongoing difficulties and missteps. As commemorations of "firsts" became more formal parts of national commemoration after Israeli statehood, all manner of groups sought to insert themselves into or reframe the story of "firsts." As Jill Lepore has observed of the American Revolution, the foundational past, in this case a settler past that preceded statehood by more than half a century, exists outside the political dynamics of the present and is easily consolidated into a site of collective trans-political values that multiple groups can coopt.[14]

A History of Settlement

The First Aliyah agricultural colonies represented a numerically tiny phenomenon. By 1900, around fifty thousand Jews lived in Palestine, constituting about 10% of its population. Only around fifty-five hundred of them lived in rural Jewish colonies, most of them new immigrants but some of them former denizens of Palestine's urban Jewish communities.[15] The approximately thirty to fifty thousand Jews who had immigrated to Palestine within the previous quarter century had doubled Palestine's Jewish population but had overwhelmingly settled in existing urban Jewish communities. Moreover, like the similar number who followed them in the prewar twentieth century, they frequently didn't stay. Historians estimate that more than half left, usually either to join larger flows of immigrants to the Americas or to return to Europe. The total Jewish migration to Palestine around the turn of the twentieth century, moreover, represented a fraction of the 2.5 million Jews who sensed deteriorating economic and political horizons for themselves in the Russian and Austro-Hungarian Empires around that time and chose to emigrate (a group that, demographically, the Jewish migrants to Palestine mostly resembled). These Jewish migrations, in turn, occurred amidst much larger non-Jewish migration flows from Central and Eastern Europe and the Ottoman Empire.[16]

The instigators of rural Palestine settlement in the last quarter of the nineteenth century, a fraction within a fraction of the Jewish and non-Jewish migration that marked that period, included Jewish individuals with private capital and members of settlement organizations that had pooled personal and donor funds to purchase land in Palestine. Some of these bodies helped constitute, or emerged from, local Lovers of Zion (*Hovevei Zion*) chapters founded in the mainly Yiddish-speaking communities of Eastern Europe following the anti-Jewish pogroms of 1881–1882 in the Pale of Settlement, which followed the assassination of Tsar Alexander II.[17] Though settlement decisions were typically instigated by men, whole families traveled to Palestine, and women's journals and literary works convey the challenges of travel and settlement for women as well as their cultural lives and social aspirations.[18]

It was a time of intellectual ferment in Palestine, too, with religious modernist thinking expanding within the urban Jewish, Christian, and Muslim communities, in conjunction with the Jewish Enlightenment (Haskalah) and Arab Awakening (Nahda).[19] Urban Jews began to move outside the walls of Jerusalem and Jaffa and establish new neighborhoods beginning in the 1860s.[20] Agricultural settlement, however, was a significant step further. Rural Jewish settlers from abroad joined a small subset of these Ashkenazi Jewish religious modernists, most of them from families who had immigrated to Palestine only a generation or two prior. This group, including Yoel Moshe Solomon and Yehuda Raab, saw engagement in productive agriculture as a core part of Jewish modernization and a means of fulfilling the religious value of "settling the land of Israel" (*yishuv Eretz Yisra'el*). They faced profound economic, religious, and security concerns about land settlement from their communities, however.[21] While Jerusalemites made efforts in 1878 to establish Petah Tikva, religious Jews from Safed in the Galilee established Gei Oni (later, Rosh Pinna).[22] Both communities faced severe agricultural difficulties and abandonment but were bolstered in 1882–1883 by the influx of settler cohorts from the Russian and Austro-Hungarian Empires. These new settlers had been inspired by their own urge toward productivization and affinity to the Land of Israel after being steeped in the ideas of the Haskalah and having faced the same economic instability, increasingly illiberal politics, and anti-Jewish violence that encouraged many of their friends and neighbors to immigrate elsewhere. Petah Tikva, in particular, would retain its strong connection to the Ashkenazi community of Jerusalem (disparagingly called, along with other urban Jewish communities, the "Old Yishuv") even as it celebrated its role within a larger Zionist settlement narrative focused on immigration and settlement. But those who settled in other Jewish colonies during this period also tended to be and to remain religiously traditional compared to the activist Jewish worker factions who followed some decades later.[23]

Purchasers conducted their transactions, which were neither numerous, nor coordinated, nor well-organized, with the help of Ottoman Jewish, Christian, or Muslim brokers and translators. Sellers tended to be absentee landlords, urban notables in Palestine and other parts of the Ottoman Levant who had aggregated land from smaller holders as a consequence of the 1858 Ottoman Land Law, one piece of the empire's Tanzimat reforms aimed at centralizing imperial power, ensuring tax receipts, and stabilizing the economy through foreign investment.[24] As a politically disorganized community in a land with an existing imperial land regime, Jewish colonists relied on an active market in land sales. Even so, they were stymied and delayed by efforts on the part of the Ottoman Empire, which, fearing a new nationalist threat amidst rising ethnonational separatism elsewhere in the empire, tried to limit Jewish colonization in Palestine.[25]

The small clusters of Jewish colonists embarked on their projects amidst heightened European Christian interest in Palestine. As Palestine opened to the world economy and Ottoman capitulations agreements with European states continued to allow consular protections for foreign subjects, German Templers established agricultural colonies in Jaffa, Jerusalem, Haifa, and the Jezreel Valley. Christians from a variety of other origins, including the United States, established mainly urban Christian schools, missions, and businesses in the mid-nineteenth century.[26] Nineteenth-century Jewish colonists, too, typically maintained their European passports in order to secure the consular protection owed to foreign subjects, drew architectural influences in part from European colonies, dressed in European clothing, and, for the most part, had skin tones similar to those of European Christians. Yehuda Raab recalls the visit to Petah Tikva of an Ottoman Jewish trader, Da'ud Abu Yusuf, who did not initially recognize Raab and his fellow colonists as Jewish. Indeed, as Raab's story recounts it, Abu Yusuf had previously expressed surprise when a sheikh from the nearby village of Fajja told him that the colony was Jewish; Abu Yusuf explained to the sheikh that "he didn't see Jews, he saw *afranj* [European foreigners]."[27] Arab peasants, too, understood the new arrivals as participants in a broader European interest in Palestine, though some Muslim and Christian urban Arab intellectuals began to take interest in the specificities of the Jewish affinity to Palestine over the course of the 1890s and early 1900s.[28]

In the early 1880s, when Rosh Pinna and Petah Tikva were reconstituted, immigrant settlers also established Rishon LeZion, Ekron (later Mazkeret Batya), Nahalat Reuven (later Ness Ziona), and Gedera in a settlement bloc on the southern coastal plain (known at the time, though no longer, as Judea); Zichron Yaʿaqov on the northern coastal plain (known as Samaria at the time); and Yesud HaMaʿala and Mishmar ha-Yarden in an Upper Galilee bloc near Rosh Pinna and the city of Safed.[29] The Galilean colonies would remain demographically smaller and generate far less wealth than the coastal plain colonies, which participated most actively in Palestine's growing export market.

The aforementioned colonies initially attempted the grain and field-crop cultivation typical in Palestine at the time, but faltered and soon sought the support of the French Jewish philanthropist Baron Edmund de Rothschild, a supporter of Jewish productivization. He began to fully administer Rishon LeZion and Ekron/Mazkeret Batya and, through a Paris-based but locally staffed administration, provided farmers in other colonies with indirect subsidies, machinery, and French technocratic expertise, much of it gained in the French settler colony of Algeria.[30] The administration encouraged cultivation of and agricultural experimentation with wine grapes, which were the colonies' single largest crop in 1900.[31] Citrus cultivation, though not Rothschild's main area of investment, began to grow dramatically as the global market for the famous "Jaffa" oranges expanded.[32]

The later 1880s saw a settler society from Bessarabia establish Qastina (1887, later Beer Tuvia) northeast of Gaza and settlers from Zichron Yaʿaqov establish nearby Bat Shlomo (1889). During this period, the Lovers of Zion organization in Odessa sought permission from the Russian government to establish a settlement organization and, in 1890, founded the Society for the Support of Jewish Farmers and Artisans in Syria and the Holy Land, usually referred to as the "Odessa Committee." Vladimir Tiomkin, head of its Jaffa office, coordinated land purchases and dispatched agents, most importantly Yehoshua Hankin, to investigate and conduct transactions.[33] In the period that followed, Jewish settlement societies founded Rehovot (1890) and Hadera (1891), which remained independent of formal philanthropic support, though not of the technocratic expertise that also flowed to other colonies.[34] The late 1890s saw additional colony creation, including Metulla in the Upper Galilee, founded by the Rothschild administration; Kfar Saba, founded by settlers from Petah Tikva to its south; and Hartuv in the Jerusalem corridor, founded by Bulgarian Sephardi Jews.

It is worthwhile to dwell for a moment on the population numbers in individual colonies at this time. In 1900, the largest Jewish colonies were Zichron Ya'aqov, with 871 residents; Petah Tikva, with 818; Rishon LeZion, with 626; and Rosh Pinna, with 512. Rehovot, Metulla, and Yesud HaMa'ala, which had 200–300 residents each, were considered mid-sized, and a dozen more had 150 or fewer residents each—some as few as two dozen.[35] Only some of these residents, moreover, were landowners. By 1905, Rehovot had 425 residents, of whom only 56 were landowning farmers, and Hadera had 140 residents, of whom 36 were landowners.[36]

Colony landowners hired a combination of landless Muslim Arabs and poor Jewish immigrants to labor in their fields, typically favoring the former for unskilled work because of the lower wage they commanded and their greater experience doing similar work, usually on the lands of absentee owners, sometimes administered by local tax farmers.[37] Residents of nearby villages—and sometimes of improvised housing within the colony itself—had historically engaged in subsistence farming but increasingly sought wage labor in the growing export economy. Jewish farmers thus participated in and expanded a market that predated their arrival on the scene. These labor arrangements generated quotidian contact between owners and workers that would lead those commemorating the past to construct memories of "hierarchical coexistence," as we will explore. At the time, however, observers noted the harsh and often cruel treatment of peasant workers by Jewish employers and the hostility that changing land tenure created among Palestinian peasants who had their grazing and cultivation rights abrogated by new Jewish owners. Some of these peasants, Yuval Ben-Bassat has shown, appealed to the Ottoman sultan for his intervention to prevent these deleterious effects. Others attacked or directly confronted the colonists.[38] Arab rural space persisted in the colonists' psyches, however. Many continued to refer to their colonies by the names of the Arab villages where their lands had been purchased and whose denizens they encountered and employed: 'Uyun Qara/Rishon LeZion; Umlebes (sometimes Melabes)/Petah Tikva; Wadi Hanin/Ness Ziona. The use of Arab workers in the earliest private colonies became a particular bone of contention between landowners and the ideological cohort of settlers who would come to be known as the "Second Aliyah" and who, as we will discuss below, first constructed the private landowners as a discrete—and discredited—settler cohort.[39]

Arabic-speaking Jews—North African Sephardi, Mashriqi (Oriental), and Yemenite—also played notable roles in the establishment and labor economy of the colonies. Sephardi and Oriental Jews facilitated land purchases as financiers, translators, and intermediaries—and sometimes as settlers themselves, as Yuval Ben-Bassat has shown.[40] When Zalman David Levontin, the founder of Rishon LeZion, came to Palestine as an emissary of the Lovers of Zion, he gained introductions to several Sephardic dignitaries, including the British vice-consul in Jaffa, and several Jerusalem bankers, including Avraham Moyal and Haim Aharon Valero.[41] Some less prominent Arabic-speaking Jews were hired as guards, and many sold goods and services to the colonies nearest to their cities.[42] Yemenite Jews arrived in Palestine in several waves beginning in 1881, and while the first of them tended to settle in Jerusalem, from 1908 some secured agricultural work in the colonies, encouraged by Labor Zionists and the new Palestine Office of the Zionist Organization, who saw this population as an ideal work force: Jews who could be paid an "Arab" wage. The internal Jewish ethnic and racial labor hierarchies of the late Ottoman and mandate periods are thus an important precursor to the better studied dynamics associated with the post-1948 Jewish migrations from the Arab and Islamic world. As Nimrod Ben-Zeev has compellingly shown in his work on race and labor in the construction industry of Palestine/Israel, intra-Jewish dynamics intersect with and are sometimes concealed by the Jewish/Arab (implicitly Ashkenazi Jewish/Arab Muslim) ethnic hierarchies that Zionist (and British) discourse often referenced and reproduced.[43]

The earliest rural colonies, it should be noted, preceded the efforts by the Budapest-born Viennese journalist Theodor Herzl to unify Jewish fundraising, political advocacy, and settlement action through the Zionist Organization. Having articulated this call in his book *Der Judenstaat* (The State of the Jews), in 1896, Herzl convened the First Zionist Congress in Basel in 1897, at which point the oldest colonies were a decade and a half old and being buffeted by accusations of corruption and mismanagement. Though the "First Aliyah" became a part of Zionist settlement history, its constituent communities were appropriated into the Zionist narrative only ambivalently and in retrospect, and have appropriately been called "proto-Zionist."[44]

In 1900, the Rothschild administration turned over its Palestine colonies to the Jewish Colonization Association (JCA), founded by the German-Jewish philanthropist Maurice de Hirsch in 1896, initially around the idea of encouraging productive Jewish agricultural settlement in South America.[45] Soon, however, private owners in the first colonies took steps to ensure greater independence and control over their export operations. In 1900, citrus growers created their first marketing cooperative, Pardess, and in 1906 viticulturalists established the Vinegrowers' Association (*Agudat ha-kormim*) to take the place of the JCA in practice.[46] The JCA continued acquiring lands for colonization, primarily in the Lower Galilee, and in 1924 was reorganized as the Palestine Jewish Colonization Association under the oversight of Edmund de Rothschild's son James.[47] Though the colonies founded in the early years of the twentieth century under JCA auspices are typically regarded as part of the First Aliyah based on their year of founding and mechanism of purchase and ownership, the historical geographer Yossi Ben-Artzi has suggested that 1900 and the transfer of the Rothschild colonies to the JCA is the more appropriate cutoff point.[48] Some of the Lower Galilee colonies of the JCA period, most notably Sejera, became better known as organizing centers for Labor Zionist Second Aliyah activism than as ongoing exemplars of the First Aliyah.[49]

Though the nineteenth-century Jewish colonies represented a tiny and economically precarious phenomenon in their own time, their twentieth-century commemoration—and, I argue, their constitution as objects of memory—occurred in places that had been radically transformed. In the decade before World War I, the total colony populations grew by 60%, to around nine thousand inhabitants, and commenced growing again after the disruption of World War I. These later increases were thanks both to new British provisions for Jewish immigration in the context of their League of Nations mandate and to the prosperity created by the global demand for citrus in the 1920s and early 1930s, an industry that was centered in Petah Tikva, which the historian Nahum Karlinsky describes as "the cradle of Jewish citriculture as a private-initiative activity." Between 1922 and 1927, Petah Tikva's population nearly doubled. Rishon LeZion grew by 50%, and Rehovot by 40%. Despite the growing ideological importance of Labor Zionist settlements, 75% of Palestine's agricultural output by 1935 was from citrus, which was almost solely in private hands. Labor Zionists, too, were becoming much more tolerant of private enterprise in practice, though on the condition (rejected by many veteran farmers) that Arab labor be wholly excluded.[50]

The 1981 publication of *Sefer ha-'Aliyah ha-Rishonah* (The First Aliyah), a definitive collection of Israeli scholarship edited by Mordechai Eliav, proclaimed in its introduction that "Despite its importance in the history of the Yishuv [Jewish community of pre-1948 Palestine, literally "settlement"], the First Aliyah has not merited the appropriate place in the historiography of the Yishuv and the national movement."[51] That volume drew on and reflected a growing body of Israeli scholarship on the "First Aliyah" since the late 1970s that had revealed the constructed quality of the "Aliyot" paradigm; explored historical connections between the "First Aliyah" settlers and Palestine's Sephardi and Ashkenazi urban religious communities (the "Old Yishuv"); examined significant divisions within the period known as the "First Aliyah"; and placed immigration stories in their European imperial and East European Haskalah (Jewish Enlightenment) contexts. In the decades since, a significant field of largely Israeli scholarship, much of it cited along with earlier scholarship in the preceding paragraphs, has continued to illuminate the economic, social, and cultural life of the late-nineteenth- and early-twentieth-century colonies.

Despite the growth of nineteenth-century colonies during the British Mandate years, however, scholars often limit their interest in the "First Aliyah" per se to the period of the First Aliyah "itself," or, noting the artificiality of the First/Second Aliyah division at around 1904, the period ending in World War I. When early moshavot appear in the historiography of the Yishuv and Israel in the interwar and post-1948 periods, in contrast, they typically appear as centers of economic production led by ideologically disengaged farmers, sites of immigrant settlement and urban growth, or targets of criticism by Labor Zionist spokespeople and local Jewish workers.[52] Historians have continued to sidestep the ongoing cultural development of the colonies, the political stakes and utility of the "First Aliyah" framing, and the perspectives of increasingly well-established leaders and owners in the twentieth century. Few have explored processes of memory, though works by the historians Anat Helman, Yosef Lang, Billie Melman, and Nili Aryeh-Sapir are notable.[53] Karlinsky, in his notable history of the private citrus industry through 1939, notes the nearly wholesale exclusion of capitalists and private owners—industrial and agricultural—from the history of Zionism, a result of the historiographic assumption that the "capitalist plain," containing the most prosperous colonies, was defeated by the "socialist [Jezreel] valley," the area in the Lower Galilee targeted for collective and communal settlements on nationally owned land beginning in the early twentieth century.[54]

The capitalist plain, ultimately dominated by privately held Jewish lands, was the site of thriving agriculture, industry, and sizable communities of Jewish immigrants. It remains Israel's capitalist center today. Many of those whom we will encounter in the following pages saw the vitality of their communities as lying in private enterprise and individual landownership, even though in fact many survived their early years only thanks to external philanthropic support. They frequently cited the aspiration for "each man to sit at peace beneath his own vine and fig tree" (Micah 4:4), a verse that George Washington, in another context, considered a favorite because of its allusion to the agricultural idyll and the paradigms of private property and individual initiative so central to the vision of American settlement.[55]

As of the end of 1936, only 23% of the Jewish rural population of nearly a hundred thousand lived in "national" settlements. The remaining 77% lived on privately owned lands in cities and moshavot.[56] On the eve of Israeli statehood, private Jewish landownership in the part of Palestine that would become Israel was almost as common as national ownership: the Jewish National Fund owned approximately 1 million dunams, while 800,000 were in private Jewish hands (and a similar number were privately owned by non-Jews, mostly Arab Muslims and Christians).[57] The State of Israel, of course, was the inheritor of the pre-1948 Zionist national settlement project. When it appropriated Palestinian village lands, as well as British state-controlled lands, in and after 1948, it rendered them state lands. The combination of nationally owned Jewish lands purchased before 1948 and state lands nationalized during or after 1948 now forms 93% of Israeli territory, not including Gaza or the West Bank, though the state has moved to authorize limited land privatization in the past decade.[58] This statistic, however, obscures the centrality of private landownership to the pre-1948 Zionist settlement story and its exclusive role in Jewish land acquisitions before 1900.

Some scholars have erroneously suggested that discourses about private property and profit, so central to Anglophone settler societies, were absent from the Zionist case because they were replaced by a "pure settlement" model of Labor Zionism in which all land was to be owned by the national collective.[59] The tendency of both Zionist and anti-Zionist scholars to focus on Labor Zionists and national models of land acquisition while overlooking other earlier and ongoing private models—and the enduring influence of those who benefited from them—is, to use Dmitry Shumsky's phrase, "methodological rather than ideological."[60] If we shift our historical methods to acknowledge the "capitalist plain," its historical exemplars, and its ongoing centrality, we reveal a core component of the Zionist story.

The moshavot in the center of the country grew as rapidly as they did because these communities—like other privately held towns and cities founded later—nurtured middle-class Jews' desire to own property, allowed agricultural land to be subdivided for new residential areas as demand grew, and did not restrict Jewish settlement on ideological grounds, as some Labor Zionist settlements did. In 1924, Moshe Smilansky, the Rehovot agriculturalist and writer of fiction who also chronicled the history of the "First Aliyah" colonies, told Arthur Ruppin of the Zionist Organization's Palestine Office that middle-class arrivals specifically wanted to buy land in the moshavot, since "The type of people, the living conditions, and the economic conditions in the moshavot suit their taste."[61] The growth of population and industry in central moshavot led the British to invest in roads and infrastructure and connect central moshavot to the electric grid and railway lines before both smaller Jewish settlements and most Arab cities.[62] In general, the larger, more central, and better connected a colony was, the more new immigrants felt comfortable moving there, especially if the idea of pioneering self-sacrifice and geographic isolation didn't excite them. Many central moshavot, then, promoted themselves as symbols of settler identity and the rural frontier without demanding of immigrants the sacrifices that were associated with newer, more far-flung, or more overtly ideological rural settlements.

In the few years following the 1948 War of Independence/Nakba and Israel's declaration of statehood, Israel absorbed a mass immigration of Jews from Europe, the Middle East, and North Africa, doubling its population to 1.5 million, this after displacing and then preventing the return of around

700,000 Arab Palestinians who had lived in the territory that became Israel. Jewish immigrants, many of them survivors of the Nazi Holocaust or postwar ethnonational violence in Europe, the Middle East, and North Africa, were provisionally settled by the state near central moshavot, some in immigrant transit camps on the sites of Palestinian village lands that Israel or its pre-state Zionist militias had recently captured and confiscated.[63] These areas were initially outside the moshavot municipal boundaries but were sometimes later annexed into the jurisdictions of moshavot, and in either case provided much of their labor force. Between 1948 and 1972, the population of core moshavot exploded: Hadera's population went from 11,800 to 32,000; Petah Tikva's from 21,900 to 93,500; Rehovot's from 12,500 to 39,300; Rishon LeZion's from 10,400 to 53,000. Tiny Ness Ziona, between Rishon LeZion and Rehovot, grew from 2,300 to more than 12,000.[64] Population growth and growing Jewish diversity meant protracted challenges from Labor interests and the regnant Mapai party. Nonetheless, landowning elites continued to actively promote the commemoration of "their" past even when they didn't control municipalities. The private landowners of the moshavot, called "bourgeois" by their early detractors for their aesthetics and labor practices, evolved into one pillar of centrist politics in the Yishuv and Israel, even though urban capitalists and the professional middle class displaced them as the prime exemplars of the Israeli center and the icons of the twentieth-century Israeli bourgeoisie.

Aliyot and the Making of "First Ones"

The nineteenth-century Jewish colonies gained the mantle of modern Zionist "firstness" after the fact. By the later 1920s, the term "First Aliyah" had come to refer—simultaneously and often inconsistently—to a period of time (typically 1882–1904); a group of people (Jewish immigrants during this period); a set of associated places (privately owned agricultural colonies); a set of economic sectors (particularly citrus and wine grapes); and a set of ideologies or, as it often seemed to Labor Zionist observers and as we will address in a moment, non-ideologies.

The system of marking Jewish immigrations through numbered aliyot (first, second, etc.) emerged following the issuance of the Balfour Declaration in 1917, nearly forty years after the founding of Petah Tikva. A product of Britain's imperial aspirations during World War I, this nonbinding British statement of support for the establishment of a Jewish national home in Palestine became the basis for key terms of the League of Nations Mandate for Palestine. Granted in 1922 and applied in 1923 amidst a wave of postwar support for movement toward ethnonational state creation in the formerly Austro-Hungarian and Ottoman lands, the mandate obligated the British to facilitate Jewish immigration, establish an undefined "national home for the Jewish people," and protect the "civil and religious rights of existing non-Jewish communities." The term *aliyah*, "ascent," had been in use since the nineteenth century to describe delineated periods of historical Jewish migration to the Land of Israel. This modern usage derived from the ancient Jewish concept of ʽ*aliyah la-regel*, ascent to Jerusalem during the three yearly Jewish pilgrimage festivals. *Aliyah* had also been used more generally since ancient times to describe Jewish travel from the Mediterranean coast to the hilltop city of Jerusalem.

To Zionists perceiving modern history through the lens of trans-historical, symbolic Jewish time, the 1917 Declaration seemed to augur a mass return movement such as those that had transpired in ancient times: first, after 538 BCE, when the Persian potentate Cyrus invited exiled Judeans back to the Land of Israel following the Babylonian exile nearly a half century earlier, and second, the population movement from Babylon to Jerusalem described in the biblical books of Ezra and Nehemiah. If the Cyrus Decree had spurred the "First Aliyah" of the Jews and Ezra and Nehemiah had led the "Second," Balfour seemed to promise a modern "Third Aliyah." Some writers even imagined that this immigration wave could create a Jewish majority in Palestine, though such a large migration was not immediately forthcoming.[65]

As the terminology of a macrohistorical "Third Aliyah" caught on in Zionist circles in the post-Balfour years, Hizky Shoham has shown, activists in the ascendant Labor Zionist movement started to retroactively divide prewar Jewish settlers into modern "First" and "Second" Aliyot. Against an emerging left-wing Zionist ethos marked by affinity to socialism and commitment to Jewish-only ("Hebrew") labor, the private colonists of the nineteenth century were remembered, to varying degrees, as being economically reactionary, religious, Yiddish-speaking, dependent on philanthropic capital, and, because of their practices of both hiring Arab labor and refraining from partisan engagement, unsupportive of the Jewish national project.

Distinctions over labor and culture that had motivated local struggles before the war served, in the writing of Labor Zionists, to delineate which people, communities, and economic efforts belonged to the "First" Aliyah and which belonged to the emerging "Second." In setting themselves apart as the instigators of a Zionist vision, early-twentieth-century Labor Zionists distinguished between Jewish owners and class-conscious workers as they began to initiate new settlement, initially adjacent to moshavot and increasingly on lands acquired by the Jewish National Fund in the Lower Galilee and elsewhere.[66] The chronological division point between "First" and "Second" Aliyot, later set in 1904–5—just before the first major organizing of workers in the colonies—remained murky until the later 1920s. The temporal Aliyot divisions were then and remain today an arbitrary and imprecise periodization convention, ideological distinctions crudely mapped onto periods, people, and spaces during a period in which private land purchase initiatives continued.

Nonetheless, historians still conventionally divide the period between 1882 and 1948 into five waves of Jewish immigration to Palestine. The moshavot are firmly enshrined as the central accomplishment of the first of these waves—the term is used only for privately owned colonies. The second wave is marked by ongoing labor activism within the older private colonies; the establishment of kibbutzim (Jewish-only labor communes) and other labor settlements; and, come the 1920s, an infrastructure of workers' organizations including the Histadrut labor union, various social service arms, and a militia (the Haganah). The post-Balfour immigration, which proved to be much smaller (around 35,000 people) than the messianic wave some Zionists had originally forecast but whose leaders augmented many of the "Second Aliyah" labor institutions, became the "Third." The "Fourth" and "Fifth" Aliyot, significantly larger and named while they were still ongoing, followed in the later 1920s and 1930s, respectively, as a Polish economic crisis and then the Nazi takeover in Germany and Austria roiled Central and Eastern European Jewish communities. Though stereotyped descriptions of these later waves—for example of German Jews as snobbish—came from those Jews already in Palestine, the new immigrant groups themselves also adopted this periodizing language in understanding and commemorating themselves as a cohort.[67]

The periodization scheme was primarily directed internally. It provided Jewish settlers a way, albeit imprecise, to negotiate internal tensions along linguistic, cultural, and ideological lines. Debates over "firstness" didn't begin in the twentieth century, however. Jewish settlers who had arrived in the 1880s briefly described themselves as the "First Aliyah" in comparison to the arrivals of the 1890s, the so-called Tiomkin Migration (after the director of the Odessa Committee's Jaffa Office, mentioned above). Romanian Jewish founders of Zichron Yaʿaqov and Rosh Pinna (from the Austro-Hungarian Empire) claimed the crown of symbolic (if not chronological) firstness against the Russian Jews who had founded Rishon LeZion. Petah Tikva residents argued that their abortive 1878 founding made them the true settler "First Ones" (*rishonim*) but argued internally over which Petah Tikva settlers should be regarded as the true founders.[68] Unimpressed with the "firsting" claims of these relative latecomers, some Jerusalemite Jews referred to the early-nineteenth-century "First Aliyah" of the students of the Vilna Gaon, the rabbinic scholar and teacher who had encouraged his followers (known as the Perushim, or separatists) to go to the Holy Land.[69] These early squabbles over firstness suggest that the Zionist settlement periodization scheme that called the private agricultural colonists the "First Aliyah" emerged in a cultural climate already concerned with primacy, firstness, and the enumeration of waves of migration.

The first stage of private and uncoordinated land acquisition and its attendant difficulties led both to Labor Zionist settlement movements and, even more consequentially for the Zionist project, to coordinated land purchase efforts by the Jewish National Fund (1901) and the Palestine Office of the World Zionist Organization (1908).[70] Both Labor Zionists and Zionist Organization officials looked askance at the private landowners, albeit for different reasons. As Zalman David Levontin, founder of Rishon LeZion and, later, of the Jewish Colonial Trust and Anglo-Palestine Bank, wrote in 1924, "As is well known, the messengers of the [Zionist] Organization also dismiss the value of private initiative, as well as the [private] colonies that were founded before the Organization existed."[71] Meanwhile, driven as much by economic pressures as by ideological vision, local pro-Labor Zionist groups perceived—and wrote into their historiography—a battle between two settlement models that culminated in the victory of their own more deserving one.

Both their early economic difficulties and their distinctive (and, to Labor Zionist observers, aberrant) cultural features led early historians of Zionist settlement, most of them associated with the Labor movement, to present moshavot as epitomes of failure, undesirable continuity with the Jewish diasporic past, or, more charitably, as a first stage in an evolving process of Zionist colonization that took on a more collectivist cast with time. Shmuel Yavne'eli notably promoted negative assessments of these communities in his two-volume 1961 work on the "Lovers of Zion period," calling most of the settlers non-Zionist and the Lovers of Zion movement itself "bloodless, unenergetic, and lacking intimate connections to the project in the land."[72] More recent survey histories have by and large replicated these dismissive assessments. "The achievements of the first two decades of Jewish settlement were not impressive," writes Alan Dowty, explaining briefly that this immigration "failed to put the return to Zion on the world's agenda."[73] In the "clash of civilizations" between the First and Second Aliyot, "the Second Aliyah clearly won," writes Anita Shapira (no relation to Avraham), who also compared the earliest colonies to "a Lithuanian shtetl" or, in the case of Rishon LeZion, "a mix of a Jewish shtetl and quasi-French customs" because of the Rothschild influence.[74] As Zeev Sternhell writes, "Although the builders of the first moshavot, the people of the First Aliyah, had preceded them, the real founders were the members of the Second Aliyah."[75]

The Politics of Apoliticism

Moshavot between the 1920s and 1960s, the chronological focus of this study, produced commodities for export and housed immigrant Jews even as their leaders, like their founders, "lacked clear political goals for the Yishuv they were creating." Derek Penslar characterizes First Aliyah agronomists like Aaron Aaronsohn and Menashe Meirovitch as "apolitical Zionists" who forwarded a technocratic ideal of an "empowered, apolitical, and businesslike" expert.[76] Scholars have also overwhelmingly equated mandate and early state-era "Zionist culture" with Labor Zionist culture, asserting that the Zionists to be "credited with shaping the social, cultural, and political foundations of the New Jewish society" were secular, socialist, ideological, politically engaged, and devoted to Jewish-only labor.[77] Amir Ben-Porat acknowledges that landowners had a distinctive culture, created in contact with both the pre-Zionist religious communities of Palestine and the Arab majority but, "to their misfortune, their voice was swallowed up by that of the intellectuals connected to the workers' parties and it was not heard."[78]

Most moshava elites, to the extent that they held any institutional leadership positions beyond the local level come the mandate period, were affiliated with the Palestine branch of the avowedly "non-political" General Zionists within the World Zionist Organization or the Farmers' Federation, one of several non-aligned "Citizens Circles," groups organized around professional interests. Scholars who have written institutional histories of these bastions of the Zionist "center" have remarked on their lack of leadership, vision, unity, or commitment to engaging in Yishuv politics. If there was a political common bond among them, it was "not belonging to the Labor movement."[79] The Farmers' Federation, which evolved from several local and regional federations, joined other capitalist professional groups in 1941 to form the Civic Union (*ihud ezrahi*), which Orit Rozin has described as particularly inert: "their intellectual horizons extended no farther than their farms and towns."[80] Rozin's assessment of the private farmers, however, is exactly the point: their economic and commemorative vision, both before and after statehood, indeed focused on their farms and towns. For them, these locales' particular settlement histories, rapidly growing populations, and centrality to the overall economic growth of the Zionist project made them worthy of celebration and national recognition.

Zionism, as the term suggests, is an ideology, and Jewish Studies scholars have long studied it within a broader concern with Jewish intellectual history. Seeing a history still "caught in the webbing" of the Labor Zionist movement, as Eran Kaplan has put it,[81] important studies have revisited the intellectual histories of Revisionism,[82] religious Zionism,[83] Sephardi and Mizrahi Zionism,[84] and the non-socialist ethical Zionist visions connected to Brit Shalom and proponents of bi-nationalism.[85] But phenomena perceived as non-ideological have, until recently, been sidelined. Where Labor Zionists and their later rivals the Revisionists were highly politically engaged and well-published, the early private farmers associated with the "First

Aliyah," Anita Shapira writes, were "mute, or, at least, half-mute." Shapira attributes their muteness to "an absence of historical consciousness" and calls them a "people of action" who were "far from abstract thinking" and lacked "an ideological formulation of Zionism."[86]

Nonetheless, as Yael Zerubavel writes in her landmark 1995 study of Zionist collective memory, "As bits of the past are remembered, they seem to expand; when they are overlooked, they shrink."[87] And indeed, as bits of the first Aliyah past were remembered in and beyond the moshavot, they did in fact expand, becoming the subjects of study for a cottage industry of local historians, based in growing and prosperous towns, who were buoyed by the dominant, if ambivalent, periodization of the era as "First." The iconic cultural-economic combination represented by the owner class in the moshavot—private initiative, the use of Arab labor, tolerance for religiosity, and insistence on pragmatism and moderation—can be seen as a longstanding alternative, and interestingly mainstream, cultural discourse, one that was particularly powerful precisely because promoters and observers alike perceived it as "apolitical."

What I refer to as the "politics of apoliticism" presumes that nationalist economic activity, technological development, and the pursuit of economic growth undertaken outside of a partisan political structure are not political. The moshava politics of apoliticism in the twentieth century has echoes in the neoliberal idea that market-driven approaches, technology and technocracy are non-political "goods" that sit in a noble place above partisan rancor, but emerges more directly from a nationalist logic that sees the nation as natural and thus possessed of a set of inherently non-political features and from a colonial logic that regards economic development as an unqualified good.[88] Private agricultural producers thrived on the idea that the national collective could succeed only when rooted in private initiative and ownership. Sherene Seikaly has shown that Palestinian Arab businessmen during the mandate period, likewise overlooked by earlier historians, also felt that they were working for their larger national cause while "defin[ing] their work as 'non-political.'"[89] As John Breuilly has written, however, "nationalism is just one particular form of politics. Like all forms of politics, it is entangled in a world of material interests, of corruption, and self-seeking rhetoric. Like all forms of politics it has its symbols and ideals, its genuine believers. Like all forms of politics it can rise and fall and interact with politics that pursue other objectives than that of national self-determination."[90]

Today Petah Tikva, where Avraham Shapira lived, is the fifth largest city in Israel, with a population of over 230,000. In 2015 it was Israel's number one exporter (Tel Aviv was in fourth place that year).[91] Upon visiting, one may notice not only its historical moniker "The Mother of the Colonies" (*em ha-moshavot*) but also its new city motto, adopted in 2008, proclaiming that Petah Tikva has "the pace of a city, the heart of a colony" (*ketzev shel 'ir, lev shel moshava*). Rishon LeZion, established in 1882, is now Israel's fourth largest city, with a population of 250,000. Nearly 900,000 Israelis (10.5 % of the population and 13% of Jews) live in the "First Aliyah" moshavot—now municipalities—of Rishon LeZion, Petah Tikva, Rehovot, Kfar Saba, Hadera, and Ness Ziona combined. Another 370,000 (5% of Jews) live in Netanya, Herzliya, and Hod HaSharon (originally Magdiel), former agricultural colonies founded in the 1920s in a second wave of colony creation led by children of the First Aliyah colonies whose role in commemoration we will revisit. For comparison, only 117,000 (1.3% of the total population and 2% of the Jewish population) live in kibbutzim, the icons of twentieth-century socialist Zionist rural settlement that have become the most emblematic symbols of the early Zionist settlement enterprise.[92] But though this is in part a story of individual localities over time, we can also find contemporary echoes of "First Aliyah" discourses well beyond the historical moshavot—in a variety of Israeli communities defined in the public imagination by their lack of ideological zealotry and generally labeled either "center-left" or "center-right." Some live in towns and suburbs within Israel proper and others in so-called non-ideological or suburban West Bank settlements, which the anthropologist Callie Maidhof has studied as exemplars of the "anti-political middle ground of moderation."[93] Mapping the First Aliyah as a twentieth-century paradigm also helps us map the history of an ostensibly apolitical Israel, or an Israel "beyond politics," whose political importance is often hidden in plain sight.

As a temporal and symbolic bridge between the Jewish immigration and settlement that predated the Zionist movement and that which occurred under its auspices, the First Aliyah offered Zionist society a liminal space in which to scrutinize central cultural values and axioms.[94] Discussions about it focused and helped manage concerns about Jews' capacity for personal and collective transformation, the place of religious traditionalism and capitalism within the Zionist movement, and uncertainty about the implications of growing Palestinian opposition—but also contribution via labor—to Zionist economic growth.

Our task, then, is to interrogate how and why historical actors attempted to rehabilitate this particular past, to identify the implicit or explicit politics of their ostensibly apolitical undertakings, and to show how their commemorative discourses helped forge a settler past that also was and is an ongoing settler present.

Firsting

The periodization scheme of numbered Aliyot, even as it sidelined the "First Aliyah" at its very moment of discursive creation, also participates in deeper processes of erasure, albeit always incomplete. First, it frames Europe as solely a place to be escaped from and directs our focus toward Palestine settlement, even while Zionist and other Jewish institutions abroad remained central to both the settlement process and a diasporic project of Jewish modernity. Second, the framework wrongly imputes nationalist motivations of ideological "ascent" to all Jewish immigrants included in the scheme and simultaneously obscures the immigration history and ideological diversity of the Sephardi and Ashkenazi urban populations that constituted approximately 5% of Palestine's population in 1880. The bracketing of preexisting Jewish populations in Palestine as "outside" the settlement project also conceals the participation of urban religious modernists in early settlement and misrepresents the ongoing religious, educational, commercial, and familial connections between urban Jewish communities and new agricultural colonies.[95] Third, and farthest-reaching in its effects, the paradigm of rural land settlement as a process of re-creation ex nihilo obscures the Arabic-speaking, mostly Muslim Palestinians who constituted an overwhelming majority of Palestine's population, the bulk of the colonies' workforce for decades, and the majority of those who would confront and ultimately be violently displaced by the Zionist settlement project.

Jean O'Brien, a scholar of American settler colonialism, has coined the term "firsting" to describe the near-obsessive settler focus on chronicling firsts (first places, people, births, deaths, furrows, wells, houses of worship, roads, etc.). Such litanies assert settler primacy and reflect and reinforce concurrent denials of competing indigenous claims to place. Invocations of firsts, she writes in reference to nineteenth-century commemorative activities in New England colonies, constitute "a straightforward scripting choice" that subtly argues for the sole legitimacy of settler societies.[96] The 1948 commemorative volume for Petah Tikva's seventieth anniversary, titled *Reshit* (First/Beginning), contains ten pages of firsting that enumerate, among other things, "first manufacturing," "first houses," "first roads," "first granary," "first borders," "first budget," "first taxes" and "first casualties."[97] Firsting effaces existing and competing claims to space, but it also functions within an internal settler discourse to manage disputes between different waves and movements of settlers. As Massachusetts and Connecticut towns feared declining influence relative to the emerging manufacturing centers down the Atlantic coast, they turned with enthusiasm to commemorative activities, O'Brien observes.[98] Similarly, the moshava attention to memory in the mid-twentieth century stemmed from a fear of occlusion. The local can contain elements of resistance to nationalist elites while continuing to uphold other key features of hegemonic national narrative. The tensions between Zionists that we see when we train our eyes on local colonies are best conceptualized not as divisions "between patriotic and critical historiography, but between different versions of local patriotism."[99] To adapt Patrick Wolfe's insight, the discourse of "firstness" is not simply "misleading"; it is a "performative representation" that helps displacement to occur.[100]

We might describe the ideologically charged Second Aliyah discourses of "firstness" as supersessionist. Like the storied relationship of Judaism and Christianity (according to Christian narrative), the earlier phenomenon served a vital, sacred purpose in its time but was flawed and incomplete. Thus, it was inevitably replaced by a successor with the coherence, strength, and divine imperative to supplant its predecessor while fulfilling the essence of the original vision.[101] As in the case of the first monotheistic faiths, however, the ideology of supersession did not mean that adherents of the later movement lacked interest in or concern about their predecessor, in this case the "First Aliyah." On the contrary, just as the theological displacement of Judaism engendered deep and lasting Christian anxieties about both the persistence of Judaism and the rightness of the Christian theological tradition, the rhetorical displacement of the First Aliyah—at the very moment of its creation as a concept—took place amidst concerns about the persistence of private farming, driven by native Arab labor, as a leading economic force. Adam Katz and Eric Gans have discussed Christian anxiety and the tradition of anti-Judaism to which it gave rise in terms of "firstness," noting that "The first is always in a state of disequilibrium."[102]

But the Christianity metaphor works on another crucial level, too. Participants in the Jewish/Christian dialogue, both historical and contemporary, focus on tensions and divisions internal to the broader monotheistic system and take for granted that the polytheistic systems that preceded them (and that in practice influenced them and were coexistent with them) were their opposites, inherently retrograde, and in need of replacement.[103] Likewise, the twentieth-century discourse about "firstness" between First and Second Aliyah spokespeople not only took their own supersession of Palestine's existing communities and remaking of space for granted; that debate itself also produced and reproduced that supersession. Neither Christians and Muslims nor urban Jewish populations were polytheists, of course, but they, too, dwelt in Ottoman multiplicity: in a multiethnic, multireligious—if increasingly fractious—space that would be foreclosed by competing ethnonational movements and their anxieties about "idolatry" and loyalty.[104]

If the "first" is always in a state of disequilibrium, that which we might call the "pre-first," that which lies outside of or adjacent to the very temporality that generates claims to firstness, produces even more extreme unease. This is because those communities and their economic and cultural influences, which settlers see as subject to replacement, remain not only in the form of "spectrality" or "haunting," but through their ongoing, evident life-making, politics-making, and economic activity. Moreover, unlike in the North American case, Jewish settlers did not see Arab communities as assimilable into the settler community through education or marriage, nor as liable to disappear.[105] Regina Schwartz's comment regarding the Bible's construction of ancient Israel as the presumptive replacement for other Near Eastern groups can be cited as a comment, mutatis mutandis, on the creation of modern Israel in its relationship to its Palestinian or Arab "other": "Every effort to deny, repress, contain, and otherwise minimize how tentative the construction of Israel is has instead the effect of underscoring the vulnerability of that model."[106]

Moshava founding narratives often follow a script shared by later Zionist settlers of all stripes: the settlement of a barren "wasteland" (*shemamah*) and the creation of Jewish space, understood to be civilized space. In a special 1932 issue of *Bustenai*, the journal of the Farmers' Federation, Moshe Smilansky recalled that when European Jewish settlers came to the land that had been purchased for the establishment of Rishon LeZion in 1882, they found it full of "thorns and thistles" (*kotz ve-dardar*) and "many foxes in this desolate place." But the group was not in fact alone. "While I was diving into my thoughts," Smilansky remembered, "the translator who was with me, from among the natives of the land [*yelidei ha-aretz*] came to sit next to me and said, 'this place where you intend to found a colony is in great danger.'" Smilansky inquired as to the nature of the danger and was told, ominously, that "when you build houses and settle there, dozens of riders on horses will come in the middle of the night and they will plunder and murder." As the foxes "yelled bitterly," Smilansky lay his head on the translator's shoulder and fell asleep. The next morning, he rejoined his settler friends: "While singing, we set up two or three tents on the hill which we had sat on at night and we called the place 'Rishon LeZion' [The First to Zion]."[107]

Two sorts of natives appear in this memory, the proximate and the distant. Smilansky has an intimate relationship with his native-born, Arabic-speaking, probably Jewish translator, enough that he is comfortable falling asleep on the man's shoulder. This translator figure is absent from the desolate scene, however, until he surfaces to provide useful information about the landscape, specifically, information about the second category of native: the Bedouin thief who will emerge out of the darkness and wreak destruction on the future colony. This paradigm of friendly native intermediaries (including Jews) and shadowy threats, both of which fade in and out of awareness, pervades Zionist settlement discourse across political lines. But private colonists experienced a particularly permeable barrier between colony and Arab or Palestinian space as peasant laborers moved in and out on a daily basis not simply to "help" or "hurt" the colonies but as part of an economic relationship of capital and labor. These racialized economic relationships and geographies of contact offered grist for colonists' narratives of "hierarchical coexistence," ones that would persist even after 1948 when many of these villages were marked by their absence. As the Smilansky episode reminds us, too, the racialized hierarchies at issue were not simply Jewish/Muslim, or colony/village, but also Ashkenazi/Sephardi or Ashkenazi/Oriental Jewish.

Narratives of colonies' relationships to nearby villages—and the geography of these relations—remained part of local settler memory even after the villages' destruction, sometimes as sites of new racialized hierarchies that were constituted as Jewish immigrants from Arab and Muslim lands were settled or settled themselves on these lands. Zionist memory does not fully erase the reality of non-Jewish, non-Zionist, and non-Ashkenazi communities; it selectively sees them. As Kevin Bruyneel defines the term, settler memory is "the capacity to see and not see Indigenous people as contemporary subjects."[108] The "seen and unseen" Jewish populations in question in our context included relatively recent migrants to Palestine from within the larger Ottoman empire or Islamic world as well as those who had been in Palestine for generations and were often known among Ashkenazi settlers as "natives of the land" (*yelide ha-aretz* or *bnei ha-aretz*). The term "Mizrahim" for Jews from Arab and Islamic lands emerged following Israeli statehood. Palestinian rural populations, likewise known among Jewish settlers as "native born," were also called Arabs, peasants (*fellahin*, Arabic), Bedouins, neighbors, or "Semitic brothers," depending on context. This last term reflects a discourse of affinity to rural Arabs informed in part by European race science. These communities' particular forms of presence (and absence) in First Aliyah commemorative discourses recur throughout our exploration. They, like the moment of settlement itself, are "remembered and forgotten," to cite Chris Healy's work, "through a variety of institutional and habitual practices."[109]

Settlers and Memory

My references to Zionist settler memory in comparative perspective do not negate the fact that Zionist memory is also a variant of modern ethno national memory. The movement began in late-nineteenth-century Central and Eastern Europe, in an era and context of multiple ethnolinguistic nationalisms. It was premised on deep cultural and linguistic roots in a national territory, and its adherents, most of whom initially had no intention of emigrating, also sought to claim space and rights from and within empires that were simultaneously facing other ethnonational movements. Core aspects of Zionism, including Jews' historical experiences of discrimination and violence, engagement in minority politics within multinational empires, efforts to modernize and teach Hebrew as a national language, and affinity with but also ambivalence toward imperial powers, cannot be appreciated outside an ethnonational framework. Some have been central to my own research.[110] But Zionist memory also has a core feature that is not especially amenable to these comparisons: its emphasis on histories of rural agricultural settlement in a distant and, despite its symbolic importance, unfamiliar land. The language of settlers (*mityashvim*), settlement (*yishuv/hityashvut*), and settlements (*yishuvim/moshavot/moshavim*) (initially also rendered using the language of "colonization") was and remains omnipresent in both internally and externally facing Zionist discourse. To understand and contextualize it, we need comparisons from other societies where settlers came to stay and build a new society for people like themselves in a place they regarded as desolate, neglected, and hostile, but ultimately authentically theirs and divinely ordained for their use.[111]

Whereas ethnonationalists rally for cultural autonomy and revival in their places of residence—something Jewish ethnonationalists, including many self-proclaimed Zionists, did in Central and Eastern Europe[112]—settlers recall the imperative of escaping cities and polities of origin to break free of persecution and physical and cultural degeneracy. The process of creating settler narrative "requires a series of creative acts of transmutation" that begins with the selection and "dramatic ordering" of events.[113] In the Zionist case, this transmutation required not only reordering and resignifying Jewish history but also deemphasizing alternative and ongoing expressions of Zionism overseas that neither emphasized settlement nor demanded a break from urban origin points. Settlers engage in identity building and collective awakening in an unfamiliar setting made hostile by harsh weather, disease, failing agriculture, and unfriendly native populations, a setting that they believe needs to be—and can be—(re)made familiar. According to the historian Richard Slotkin, the story of the American frontier myth typically begins with the settlers' journey from the metropolis to the wilderness, where they perceive stark oppositions between humans and nature and between settlers and natives. As they seek to overcome these dichotomies, the settlers also mediate them and move between them, eventually establishing a solid homestead.[114] The bicentennial celebration of Stamford, Connecticut, in 1842, for example, proclaimed: "They came and the wilderness was changed into the abode of civilized man."[115] Yael Zerubavel has more recently comprehensively catalogued how oppositions between wilderness and civilization are central to the Zionist settlement story as well.[116]

Settler memory, as a consequence, emphasizes survival over and above heroic death. Zerubavel's seminal work on memory, *Recovered Roots*, emphasizes that Zionist commemorations, across communities and parties, shared an emphasis on ancient Jewish heroes and the sanctification of land through the heroic death and blood of the fallen, both past and present.[117] This trope was particularly prominent in the cultures of the Labor Zionist ideologues of the "Second" and "Third" Aliyot and also influenced "First Aliyah" commemorations (as we will see in chapter 2). Nonetheless, Zerubavel's focus on symbols of national death and defeat (Masada, Bar Kokhba, and Tel Hai) as the wellspring of rebirth obscures the tendency of locals to celebrate and recruit living settlers from the modern past as markers of continuity.

Anglo-American settler colonies offer useful comparison cases of societies that sought and successfully gained independence from an imperial power.[118] However, they do not present the only possible comparative models or fully applicable ones, given the nineteenth-century European ethnonational and imperial context in which the Zionist project emerged and the developed Ottoman imperial system that Jewish settlers, including those who predated the formal Zionist movement, encountered upon arrival.[119] The Zionist desire to achieve an ethnonational project via settler colonization, in a territory controlled by an empire other than the ones most of them had left, is a distinctly late-nineteenth- and early-twentieth-century phenomenon. As Tara Zahra has recently shown, statements in support of purposeful "emigrant colonization" abroad proliferated in the late nineteenth and early twentieth centuries, and not only among Jews, in the wake of the mass emigrant departures from Central and Eastern Europe. Zionist settlement, Zahra notes, was the only successful scheme to come out of this context, but Jewish Territorialists during the same era explored colonization projects on several continents.[120] Memory discourses around Jewish colonization in Palestine, though they can be illuminated by certain features of faraway and contextually distinct Anglophone settler colonies, thus emerged out of a more proximate context in which residents of countries without overseas colonies considered emigrant colonization in South America, Asia, or Africa feasible precisely because—and only *if*—more powerful colonial empires could facilitate or approve of their colonization initiatives. In the early twentieth century, Laura C. Robson has revealed, the British Empire indeed attempted to harness existing ethnonational sentiment and encourage voluntary ethnonational migration, resettlement, and colonization—not only of Jews, but also of Armenians and Assyrians—for their own imperial ends.[121] In such settings, settlers' narratives of transformation are meant to appeal not only inwardly or to residents of the metropolises from whence they came, but also to larger imperial powers. When a drinker of brandy—or a consumer of educational curricula, a parade spectator, or an actor in a local play—recalled the past, they were celebrating both the "First Ones" (*rishonim*), as the settlers were commonly known, and the ongoing documentary process of commemorating settlement for both internal and external consumption.

While Western national movements in general have prized documentation and archiving, in the settler context this drive toward documentation first occurs in the immediate vicinity of non-literate local populations whom settlers understand to be transient, lacking in meaningful historical claims, and located outside the boundaries of the collective-in-the-making. In this context, writes O'Brien, "documentary records symbolize civilization," noting that they record evidence both of early settlement and of an ongoing process of commemorating that settlement: memory of memory itself.[122] Often erroneous from the standpoint of historical fact, the pamphlets, publications, ceremonies, and other memory documents became "locations of ideological production and consolidation."[123]

Mapping the First Aliyah

The map of "First Aliyah" settler memory, charted across decades and regimes, is a palimpsest with multiple distinct and conflicting maps layered within it. When I set about commissioning a map to assist and orient readers, I remembered maps of nineteenth-century Jewish rural settlement I'd seen in books about Zionism or the Israeli-Palestinian conflict. They typically showed early Jewish colonies alongside older, larger cities included for reference: implicitly, even if this was not the intention of the author, a network of Jewish colonies in a white space that was waiting to be filled—and which would in time be filled—by Jews.[124] But if we study twentieth-century memory, we see that the First Aliyah was made not against an expanse of possibility but amidst changing imperial circumstances, ongoing Zionist settlement, Jewish and Arab nationalist politics, and decades of relationships with Palestinian peasant laborers, whose villages became a core part of settler's cognitive maps. The map of First Aliyah memory that this book offers, both concretely on page xviii–xix and conceptually, is therefore a map of "First Aliyah" Jewish agricultural colonies flanked by rural villages, older urban centers, and later-established Jewish communities, including Tel Aviv (1909) and private agricultural colonies established in the twentieth century. Because our explorations of settler memory encompass the periods both before and after the Palestinian Nakba in 1948, the Palestinian villages marked on the map take on a spectral quality: except for those such as Kafr Qasim, which survived, they are both sites in a real landscape and sites that only exist in a memory landscape. The map also includes the ceasefire line of 1949 (the Green Line), which took shape around the significant economic, material, and Jewish residential infrastructure initiated and developed in "First Aliyah" colonies and which served as Israel's de facto eastern border until 1967.[125] These map layers reflect interlaced memory contexts for a past whose foundations were laid in the Ottoman late nineteenth century but whose cultural meaning evolved only later, over multiple stages and contexts.

The First Aliyah as Twentieth-Century History

As Michel-Rolph Trouillot has emphasized, we must not think of the past as something that simply happened, but rather as something created: those commemorating the past "do not succeed such a past: they are its contemporaries."[126] The co-creators of the past who are of greatest interest to us resemble a group that Alan D. Gordon, in his work on preservation and commemoration activities in early-twentieth-century Montreal, calls "heritage elites": middle-class residents who established societies for the preservation of the city's heritage.[127] The local quality of memory that we find in the moshavot also resembles the "interchangeable representation of the local, the regional, and the national community" that Alon Confino attributes to the German hometown (*Heimat*) historians after 1880.[128] Like them, moshava heritage elites engaged in a decentralized, highly localized process of gathering documents, taking oral histories, planning events, and building exhibitions. In the most prosperous moshavot, the heritage elites were often landed farmers descended from the settler "First Ones," but they could also be later-arriving farmers. In smaller or more peripheral moshavot with fewer economic accomplishments to confer status, family descent and a connection to the founding stories proved even more significant.

Though the oldest settlers relished telling of deprivation on the settler frontier and complained of exclusion from the Zionist collective memory, their lands and other assets often made them and their children some of the most rooted and financially stable members of the Yishuv and Israel, despite fluctuations in the export market. This remained true after 1948, the era of displacement of Palestinians and systematic discrimination against newer Middle Eastern and North African Jewish immigrants. This contrast became especially clear to me when, working with the Avraham Shapira papers in Petah Tikva, I found a warranty certificate for a new American-made Philco refrigerator that Shapira's wife Hana had purchased in December 1948.[129] In the midst of war, displacement, and early Israeli state formation, the Shapira family was doing well and, despite surely sharing in the anxiety of the political moment, was demonstratively not going anywhere. Elizabeth Furniss, who has studied the memory of frontier settlement in British Columbia, notes the flexibility of the notion of pioneer: "any number of individuals may be honoured as pioneers on the basis of a range of fluctuating criteria: their length of residence, their age, their adherence to a particular lifestyle."[130] The ability to contend with harsh circumstances became a mainstay of moshava memory, but it was by no means a requirement for the rememberers themselves.

Moshava elites, local leaders, and the family members of "First Ones" celebrated settlement anniversaries, published non-scholarly histories, and wrote newspaper articles about the past. They coordinated ceremonies that combined speeches and performances; participatory song or dance; special prayer services in the colony synagogues; and competitive games that evoked the heroic and "native" qualities of founders, often using Orientalist symbols, including a Bedouin-inspired horsemanship competition known as a *fantaziya*. Both before and after Israeli statehood, moshava elites and their allies retold and reinvented the stories that they had learned from parents, grandparents, and local elders about the groundwork that their towns and cities had laid for the national project, and in so doing they participated in processes of group formation and identity negotiation.[131] Living elders played important roles in these commemorative process. Avraham Shapira of Petah Tikva, whose prominence on a brandy bottle invited us into this topic, will be a recurrent figure. We will also get to know Menashe Meirovitch of Rishon LeZion, who spoke and presented frequently on his settlement experiences; Moshe Smilansky of Rehovot, who became a prolific chronicler of the First Aliyah as well as the president of the Farmers' Federation; members of the Aaronsohn family of Zichron Yaʿaqov, whose pro-British espionage work during World War I catapulted them, and Zichron Yaʿaqov, to symbolic prominence; the Jaffa-born David Tidhar, who took particular interest in commemorating First Aliyah figures; and Yitzhak Ziv-Av, who directed the Farmers' Federation in the first decades of Israeli statehood. Though we glimpse the lives of early settler women only fleetingly in many of the stock narratives about a masculinized colony past, female as well as male descendants took part in commemorative events and contributed ephemera to exhibitions.

Erving Goffman would call these people's staged and curated commemorative activities "performances" in that everyone involved was playing a part. Some really believed in the truth of the past they were performing, while others acted as "cynical performers" deluding audiences—in what they imagined to be good faith—"for [the audience's] own good, or the good of the community."[132] Before 1948, these embodied practices helped constitute, as H. V. Nelles writes about the 1908 Quebec Tercentenary, "a celebration of an imaginary country, one which the organizers hoped to create."[133] Streets, houses, irrigation, businesses, and governing structures could be imagined as independent settler spaces beyond the reach of the mandatory state or the majority Arab population even as political independence remained in the future and was not, strictly speaking, the priority of locally oriented Jewish landowners. After statehood, colony anniversaries could supersede Israeli Independence Day as opportunities to mark the moment of historical transformation.

Our explorations into these commemorative performances are grounded in archival and published documents. I found many of them in small archives housed in municipalities or local historical museums, which tend to rely on a limited staff and, sometimes, community volunteers. These institutions welcome local researchers and amateur genealogists more often than foreign scholars, and I regularly benefited from conversation as I worked. I also consulted files at larger Zionist and party archives and several periodicals, particularly those that served the political center and right (including *ha-Boker, Do' ar ha-yom, Herut,* and *ha-Mashkif*) and private farmers (*Bustenai*)—as well as Arab and British periodicals. Insights into the lingering resonances of the "First Aliyah" and its iconic colonies also emerge in the commemorative activities of later moshavot such as Binyamina (1922), Herzliya (1924), and Netanya (1929), which were founded or led by children of the "First Aliyah" moshavot and assumed central roles in organizations linked to private agriculture. While we can get the perspectives of urban, elite Palestinians through Arabic sources, the perspectives of peasant figures more central to moshava memory often have to be interpolated through imperial and Zionist sources. Though a reconstruction of peasant experiences in the First Aliyah colonies is not within the scope of this book, I strive to name and identify some of those experiences by reading my source material critically and against the grain.

Three broad-ranging, twentieth-century developments compelled moshava heritage elites to narrate their pasts and shaped the stories they told over the course of a period between the 1920s and 1960s that straddled the British Mandate and early Israeli statehood. First, growing political segmentation in the Zionist movement made the moshavot an object for intraparty discourse on the nature of Zionist "firstness" and encouraged farmers themselves to stress their detachment from political processes and ability to transcend partisan divides. Second, the intensification of Palestinian resistance to Zionism and, come 1948, growing regional conflict motivated nostalgic accounts of settler-native relations in the colonies' early years. Spokesmen for the First Aliyah colonies claimed that, because their communities predated the significant spike in tensions that followed the 1908 Young Turk Revolution and 1917 Balfour Declaration, and chose pragmatically to continue hiring Arab workers, they represented a Zionism characterized by positive relations and, evoking again the virtue of apoliticism, the absence of deleterious "politics." Third, rapidly increasing Jewish immigration from the mid-1920s through the late 1930s and again in the 1950s and 1960s swelled the mandate and early statehood-era Yishuv. Educational curricula, ceremonies, and other cultural events thus became opportunities for revisiting, reshaping, and constructing a story of Zionist beginnings that emphasized sacrifice, heroism, and "firstness."

Chapter 1 shows how farmers and their representative organizations evolved a politics of apoliticism both in their initial responses to Labor Zionist challenges in the first years of the twentieth century and as a mandate-era strategy employed amidst Labor-Revisionist strife. During this same period, chapter 2 shows, farmers developed the claim that they represented an earlier era and ongoing model of Jewish-Arab coexistence based on hierarchical employer-employee relationships combined with displays of Jewish force against those who would disrupt those relations, a discourse I describe critically as "hierarchical coexistence." Tropes of apoliticism, hierarchical coexistence, and frontier heroism, all of which presumed ethnic and civilizational hierarchies, converged in images of the past circulated to youth and immigrant groups. Chapter 3 looks at the promotion of the living moshava hero among immigrant youth through radio programs, school curricula, parades, and detective fiction, all produced by Zionist actors outside the labor movement for consumption by a "non-ideological" public.

Chapters 4 and 5 move through Israeli independence and the Nakba to the 1950s and 1960s, when moshava farmers continued to promote their settlement history through anniversary celebrations and commemorative institutions in a profoundly transformed local landscape. Chapter 4 is concerned with the evolution of the moshava hierarchical coexistence discourse following the destruction of most of the Palestinian villages that had provided them labor before 1948 and in the presence of a new Palestinian citizen minority under military government rule. I consider the Zionist memory politics around the Israeli-orchestrated 1957 sulha following the Kafr Qasim massacre of 1956, headed by Avraham Shapira, before turning to the treatment of four destroyed village sites within the post-1948 moshava memory landscape. These include two sites repurposed to explicitly honor settler icons of the First Aliyah past. Chapter 5 considers the new demographic and political landscape of Israel from 1948 to 1967, taking as its point of departure the Jewish immigrant transit camps established adjacent to moshavot, most of them on confiscated village lands. Moshava leaders and agricultural elites continued to promote their history, via ceremony, education, and commemoration, to mainly working-class immigrants, amidst challenges from Labor parties and derision from native-born youth. Ultimately, however, Zionist discourses of settler firsts, even if they took the "First Aliyah" as their reference point, were of utility to a range of Zionist political constituencies, from Labor Zionists to the Revisionist right to religious parties. These divergent interpretations were on display in 1962 when Israel organized events and a special Knesset session to mark "The Year of the First Ones," on the eightieth anniversary of the conventional start of the First Aliyah. Though it put Zionist division on display, the commemoration also worked, through a process of "firsting," to consolidate a shared Zionist settler memory narrative against the implied erasure of that which preceded the "first."

Agriculturalists in the "First Aliyah" moshavot, as exemplars of a growing, if inchoate, Zionist "center," gave expression to a desire, shared by multiple twentieth-century Zionist groups, for non-socialist origin narratives, Arab-Jewish harmony in the face of evident Palestinian opposition, and an "apolitical" national narrative of the frontier that could appeal to diverse new immigrants. The conclusion of this book moves past the fracture point of the 1967 war and the rise of Likud in 1977 to think about more recent manifestations of the discourses we have seen expressed in commemorations of the "First Aliyah." Late-nineteenth-century private colonists do not sit in a direct causal lineage with today's political moderates, "non-ideological" settlers, or owners of capital, but we can identify in these groups important resonances of the moshava landowners' and leaders' rhetorical commitments in generations past. Drawing on emerging scholarship on settlements, labor, and ethnic hierarchies in contemporary Israel/Palestine, the concluding chapter suggests the importance of exploring alternative through-lines in Zionist history connected by the bonds of capitalism, private enterprise, and the rhetoric of apoliticism and hierarchical coexistence.

An archival folder of materials related to Zichron Ya'aqov's eightieth-anniversary celebration in 1962 contains a surprisingly frank assertion from an unnamed writer: local celebrants were not so interested in the town's actual history. "When the historian comes in future generations," the writer surmised, "he'll certainly look back on the period with objective eyes, and will conclude whatever he concludes." But for now, "when we come to survey the past with its shadows and its light, we can proudly summarize it as a period that built the foundations of a Jewish homeland renewed through vision and faith along with suffering and limitless stubbornness and through devotion to the mission—something that can be a symbol and road sign for us today."[134] The job of local memory makers, this writer implied, was to be deliberately selective, to curate just those events or personalities that laid the foundations for a national project. To encase the colony's past in bottles as dignified as those that contained its famous wines.

Given the disjuncture between the documented history of the First Aliyah and its commemoration, it bears emphasizing that this book follows the local—and sometimes profession-, class-, or politics-specific—twentieth-century commemorative gaze. The documents at the heart of this project are saturated with omissions, misrepresentations, and self-aggrandizement, as well as with secondary discourses about the urgent necessity of correcting perceived omissions and misrepresentations by others. In our story, living individuals able to participate in and shape their own commemoration often eclipsed figures who had by all accounts been objectively more important during the "First Aliyah period" itself: bankers such as Zalman David Levontin, acquirers of land such as Yehoshua Hankin, and Baron Edmond James Rothschild. For historians of the pre-World War I period, these distortions—real and perceived, intentional and unintentional—should be approached as methodological challenges en route to understanding the true history of late-nineteenth-century Jewish rural settlement. As Michel-Rolph Trouillot argues, however, by the time historians appear, "someone else has already entered the scene and set the cycle of silences."[135] Heritage elites, elder settler exemplars, and eager publics doggedly insist upon finding "meaning in history," as Yerushalmi describes the central preoccupation of Jewish memory; and in seeking that meaning, they create it.[136] To cite Jean O'Brien, their writings and performances "formed a vernacular historical sensibility of enduring influence, as their work, however fanciful or downright erroneous, became blueprints for understanding the past."[137] The bright spots, the shadows, and the selective spotlights themselves are our primary sources. They reveal the twentieth-century forging of an oft-forgotten Zionist historical current whose echoes continue to reverberate in new forms today.

(CHAPTER 1)
PRIVATE FARMERS AND THE ORIGINS OF "FIRST ALIYAH" CLAIMS-MAKING

The first European Jewish agricultural colonies (moshavot) in Palestine, though founded in the late nineteenth century, developed their distinctive identity beginning in the early twentieth. As newcomers, socialist-leaning Zionists sought employment in the colonies, the most ideologically active of these aspiring workers built their political identity against the inefficacy, religiosity, and labor exploitation they perceived in the Jewish farmers who had hired them. Self-proclaimed advocates of the Jewish worker began to build the Labor Zionist organizations and parties that would go on to lead the Yishuv and Israel from the late 1920s through 1977.[1] While Labor Zionists, particularly in the Mapai party (founded 1930), increasingly tolerated private enterprise, the agriculturalists of the moshavot continued to appear as paragons of "those to whom money came easily and who could allow themselves to be idle" and who seemed to be using private capital to advance personal rather than national objectives.[2] These encounters, however, also led to a less acknowledged inverse outcome: as landowners confronted newcomers whom they saw as hyper-ideological, impractical, partisan, divisive, and irreverent, they articulated their own identity and historical legacy in distinctly laudatory terms: as an apolitical and pragmatic group committed to private initiative, traditionalism, Jewish unity, and Jewish-Arab coexistence achieved via hierarchical labor arrangements. Like the New Englanders who began to actively commemorate their colonies' founding moments in the nineteenth century as new American population centers grew and as they feared declining influence,[3] Palestine's first colonists began to devote energy to commemoration as they began to be eclipsed by more politically powerful groups.

The early colonies faced a strong internal challenge because of real early weaknesses: inability to make a profit; impractical agricultural choices; and reliance, to varying degrees, on the philanthropic intervention of the Paris-based Rothschild administration. Outside observers had noted these difficulties before Labor Zionists would define themselves in opposition to the colonies' practices. "As a man's capital increases, so diminishes his desire and ability to live a simple life of physical labor," Ahad Ha-'Am (Asher Ginzburg) wrote following a series of visits to the Jewish colonies in Palestine in 1891 and 1893.[4] To move from ideas to action, he thought, settlers needed to leave behind a set of unflattering diasporic attributes, proceed more slowly and conscientiously with their settlement program, and focus on the cultural dimensions of national revival rather than solely on economic gain. Labor Zionists, a tiny ideological cohort among the approximately thirty-five thousand Jewish immigrants to Palestine in the decade before World War I, would combine Ahad ha-'Am's critique with a call for an alternative labor policy.

As newcomers critiqued the use of Arab workers, revolted against the religiosity of the old guard, demanded that women be allowed to do agricultural labor, and established a culture of late-night club meetings, they sought inspiration and justification from Marxist Zionist Ber Borochov's insistence that "the class struggle can only take place where the worker toils" and Aaron David Gordon's romantic ethnonationalist maxim that "labor binds a people to its soil."[5] Materially speaking, however, these landless immigrants began to organize—starting in Petah Tikva in 1904—because they needed work and wished to attain "European wages" for it.[6] In 1905, the struggle for the "conquest of labor," which centered on the exclusion of Arab workers but also included wage demands and elements of collective transformation, commenced in earnest with the founding of the non-Marxist socialist labor organization *ha-Po'el ha-tza'ir* (the Young Worker). A 1907 article in one of the first issues of their journal of the same name criticized the Rishon LeZion winery for firing six Jewish employees who had gone on strike. While the head of the winery had chalked up the downsizing to a reduction in available work, those who were fired were sure that it was because of "their greater [class] consciousness."[7] The Labor leaders Eliezer and Yisrael Shochat, Yehezkel Hankin, and David Ben-Gurion began their leadership careers in Petah Tikva, which has been called "the crucible [*basis yetzirah*] for the Second Aliyah." Farmers, in turn, organized a "boycott" against organized Jewish workers in 1906, which was ended when the World Zionist Organization, which shared the interest of securing employment for Jewish workers, intervened.[8] Jewish workers were replicating patterns typical of labor conflicts in multiethnic societies, Gershon Shafir has argued. Capital naturally wants to hire cheaper labor, so higher-paid workers protect themselves by struggling against the lower-paid workers while couching their demands vis-a-vis employers in ethnonational terms.[9]

As they undertook to change the labor relations in the existing colonies, these workers and labor leaders employed a militant rhetoric of "conquest" (*kibush*). Labor Zionists initially focused on market conquest, transferring unskilled agricultural labor from the hands of Arabs to the hands of Jews; later, they framed Jewish work as skilled work that should command a higher wage.[10] While the term *kibush* in Hebrew typically refers to territorial conquest (and later referred to the Israeli military's conquests and conquered territories in the 1967 war), here the term described persuasion and economic transformation. The "conquest of labor" paradigm ushered in a related vocabulary of conquests: the conquest of guarding jobs from Arab workers (*kibush ha-shemirah*); of nature (*kibush ha-shemamah*, conquest and civilization of the wilderness); and of culture (*kibush ha-lashon*, conquest of language: the movement for modern Hebrew and away from diasporic multilingualism that had begun in late-nineteenth-century Jerusalem). As landowners proved resistant to these demands and as new land acquisition opportunities emerged with the opening of the Palestine Office of the Zionist Organization in 1908, the newcomers began to establish separate labor collectives (*kibbutzim*, originally *kvutzot*) and labor colonies (*moshavei 'ovdim* or *moshavei po'alim*).[11] After World War I, some advocates of this nexus of programs and ideologies began to call themselves the Second Aliyah and see that wave of immigration, implicitly represented by a tiny elite, as the exemplar of dedicated, ideologically pure, successful Zionist settlement.

By the 1920s, the Zionist labor movement had founded a powerful workers' union (the Histadrut), a sick fund, soup kitchens, a consumer cooperative, clubs, and several newspapers and political parties, achieving a level of political and institutional coherence that the landowning colonists never attempted. Shmuel Noah Eisenstadt, the noted sociologist and founder of the Histadrut Labor archive (now the Lavon Institute for Labor Movement Research), wrote in 1959 that the motivation to collect a labor archive emerged in the 1920s from the fear that "with its continual striding forward from stage to stage, [the Labor movement] doesn't guard the events of its life and struggles."[12] Driven by the fear of loss, said Yaakov Tzidkuni, a folklorist involved in the project, "young people, half-unemployed" in the 1920s, developed a "deep spiritual relationship to any printed object, any document or certificate" and "tried not to miss a single scrap of paper."[13] The archive itself was founded in 1932 and housed in 1934.[14] It would be not only a record of Labor's history, but an archive of its ideology's victory over the supposed cravenness of earlier, but still ongoing, Jewish practices of private enterprise in Palestine. In addition to their other metaphorical conquests, then, Labor Zionists also elevated their own history above competing settlement pasts, while joining with their rivals in elevating Jewish Zionist pasts over competing non-Jewish Palestinian pasts. We might call this process *kibush ha-historyah*, the conquest of history.[15]

The personal accounts in collected labor archives repeatedly contrast the revolutionary Second Aliyah with the retrograde First, starting with the encounter between the two groups in the colonies. Pinhas Spektor, who organized one of the first workers' colonies, Ein Ganim, adjacent to Petah Tikva, wrote of Petah Tikva in 1907 that "if we didn't know that we were standing in the Land of Israel, we would have definitely assumed that we had come to a typical Jewish shtetl in the diaspora in which people fight with each other like people do when their plates are empty." For Joseph Klausner, who first visited in 1912 as a Zionist (though not a Labor Zionist) activist, the way residents prayed in the big synagogue also evoked "a Lithuanian shtetl twenty or thirty years back." He asked: "is this a Hebrew colony?"[16] Both the Jewish employers and their Arab workers appeared to be backwards according to the new settlers' modernist sensibilities: the "hundreds of Arabs" who had come to Petah Tikva with their families generated "unbearable" noise and commotion, but the Jewish depravity was worse: Spektor was appalled by the overseers who would "ride expertly on their donkeys with a whip in their hand, speaking coarsely as they chose [Arab] workers from among the masses."[17] Shlomo Zemach, one of the founders of the Labor newspaper *ha-Po'el ha-tza'ir* (The Young Worker) and the workers' organization *ha-Horesh* (The Ploughman), recalled that he expected to find a home in the existing Jewish colonies after he arrived in 1904, but was disappointed to find that the existing Jewish colonists practiced a religious lifestyle and were lazy, dependent on outside support, and unconcerned with independent labor—they reminded him of "the French colonist in Algeria." From a great desire to emulate them, he said, emerged the imperative "*not* to be like them."[18] David Ben-Gurion later wrote that without the efforts of the Second Aliyah and its victory, the Yishuv as a whole, and not just Petah Tikva, would have become an "exilic, atrophied community, subjugated to others and dependent on the magnanimity of the Arab majority," just like the First Aliyah colonists.[19]

Mordecai Reicher, who would later edit the workers' paper *Petah Tikva ha-'ovedet* (Working Petah Tikva), described the 1905 interaction between owners and Jewish workers as "a meeting between two distant worlds that barely had a bridge between them." The employers "were the conservative, religious ones, disappointed after years of assaults by nature and distress, broken in both body and soul." The workers "were the invigorated, active ones, lifted up on waves of desires and new ideas about building the land and society, a working nation, and love of man."[20] Arthur Ruppin, head of the Palestine Office in Jaffa, wrote in 1913 rejecting the private enterprise model and calling the colonies "an aging organism" that needed to be reinvigorated by "introducing new enthusiastic young elements from Europe."[21] Even if the colonies were turning a profit, "any enterprise in Palestine that generates a large profit for the merchant is usually the least profitable of all for our national goal, and vice versa."[22] Zionist historiography would largely record the conclusion that the Second Aliyah activists militated for Jewish immigration and the Jewish national project, while the private farmers were in a state of "ideological retreat" into their own walls with no national consciousness at all.[23] It would also maintain the belief that the Second Aliyah's supersession of the First Aliyah brought an end to both "diasporic" and "colonial" features of land settlement.[24]

This discourse elides the fact that the private farmers' motivation to engage in Jewish agricultural settlement dated back less than a century and had marked a significant modern development inspired by ideas of Jewish "productivization"; that the Zionist Organization abroad maintained a central role in the movement; and that the exclusion of Arab labor represented an alternate form of Jewish settler colonization, not its absence. Over time, moreover, the labor movement itself became far more inclined toward private initiative. "Private capital was no longer perceived as the epitome of evil," and the Labor Zionist language of pioneering stretched to accommodate the idea that national goals could be served through private capital, so long as it hired only Jewish labor. In the telling of ex post facto chroniclers, however, the desired socialist ideology was set against a non- or pre-ideological combination of avarice, incompetence, and traditionalism, and colonies continued to be branded as "antisocial and antinational."[25]

When Labor-oriented chroniclers and historians wanted to redeem the First Aliyah as a category, they elevated one tiny and essentially uninfluential group: Bilu. Bilu, a student organization whose acronymic name referenced Isaiah 2:5, "House of Israel, Come Let Us Go," was founded in Kharkov in January 1882 by Israel Belkind. Its establishment followed anti-Jewish violence in the southern Russian Pale of Settlement after the assassination of Tsar Alexander II. This upheaval also produced a much larger wave of out-migration to the United States. Six months after its founding, a first Bilu group left Kharkov for Istanbul, but did not immediately succeed in sending a settler detachment to Palestine. On July 6, 1882, a group of fourteen, led by Belkind, finally arrived in Jaffa and sought work in Mikveh Yisrael, the agricultural colony associated with the Alliance Israélite Universelle, an organization devoted to the regeneration of Jews across the Middle East and North Africa but not to Jewish nationalism per se. In early 1883, the group moved on to Rishon LeZion, which had been established on the basis of private capital the previous year. By 1884, a small group founded Gedera on land that had been purchased by Mikveh Yisrael. After a brief period of self-governance according to collectivist principles, Gedera quickly came under the management of the Rothschild administration. Because the Bilu members (known as Biluim) were ideological young people who had come without their families, who attempted (but failed) to live cooperatively, and who championed the idea of self-sacrifice for an ideal, the Zionist activist Joseph Trumpeldor praised the group as "the first Hebrew pioneers." In

1939, the Labor Zionist leader Berl Katznelson called Bilu "the type of first *oleh* [Jew ascending to the Land of Israel] who laid the foundations for settlement," while clarifying that the members of the First Aliyah as a whole "were not Biluim." The historian Shulamit Laskov emphasizes that, "in the eyes of the pioneers of [First Aliyah] settlement," the Biluim were "foreign and strange." Though the group failed to achieve any significant settlement program outside of Gedera, which itself was not especially economically successful, "over time the image of the First Aliyah got blurred" and was remade by Labor Zionists who had become disappointed in their conservative predecessors and employers and found in Bilu an alternative model that fit their notion of Jewish settler pioneering.[26]

The Colonists Reply

The private farmers, though disorganized, far less vocal than their rivals, and dogged by real economic and organizational failures, did not keep silent. As they shared a perception of the newcomers as overwrought, hotheaded ideologues, they began to present themselves as principled moderates who had a foundational, apolitical commitment to the land and to Jewish productivity. Gershon Shafir calls their stance the forerunner of a "moderate Israeli nationalism" that saw the profitability of the Zionist enterprise as the most important national goal and Arab labor as a necessary, if not necessarily desired, means to this end.[27]

As *ha-Po'el ha-tza'ir* and other labor newspapers debated the appropriate models of labor organizing, owners published their views in more established newspapers such as those founded in Jerusalem by the noted supporter of Hebrew vernacularization Eliezer Ben-Yehuda—*ha-Zvi* (the Gazelle), *ha-Or* (the Light), and *Hashkafah* (Outlook). These newspapers, sometimes called the "general" press (as opposed to the politically aligned press), reflected the concerns of the moshava agriculturalist class, modernist elements of the Ashkenazi community in Jerusalem, and Sephardi businessmen and intellectuals. All of these were elements of the diverse non-socialist communities that would continue to develop into the mandate and statehood periods and that is obscured by artificial divisions between the "Old Yishuv" (i.e. "pre-Zionist" community) and the "First Aliyah" (i.e. presumptively "Zionist" settlers).[28] Ben-Yehuda, though he was receptive to workers' demands, had an emotional attachment to the First Aliyah colonies. His son Ben-Zion (later called Itamar Ben-Avi), dubbed the "First Hebrew Child" for having (ostensibly, though not in fact) been raised entirely in Hebrew, was born in Jerusalem on the same day that the Rishon LeZion colony was founded: July 31, 1882. Ben-Yehuda's second wife Hemda wrote in 1931 that Eliezer "considered himself the father of twin children." "What name," Hemda remembered Eliezer asking, "should be given to the first Hebrew child and its twin sister, the first colony?" "So the boy was called Ben-Zion [Son of Zion] and the twin sister was called 'Rishon LeZion' [First to Zion]."[29] Ben-Avi would go on to ally himself explicitly with private farming interests.

In the years before World War I, as workers' demands grew and owners' opinions fractured, Ben-Yehuda's newspapers hosted debates among farmers about the legitimacy of the Hebrew Labor movement, its ideological valence, and its effects on the Yishuv economy.[30] Part of their unease came from the fact that the community of capitalist farmers was indeed fraying. The takeover or subsidizing of most colonies (except Rehovot) by the Rothschild administration in their early years and then by the Jewish Colonization Association in 1899–1900 raised significant doubts about the independence of the "independent initiative" that characterized the moshavot in their idealized form. Moreover, the children of the moshavot were leaving in droves, many for overseas.[31] As they articulated their own stances about future economic and labor policy, the farmers also referenced their own origins, ostensibly prior to politics, and accused workers of not properly comprehending the settlement project that had preceded them.

In 1908, a writer signing his name as "Young Farmer" (*Ikar tza'ir*) responded to the accusation that farmers like himself were trying to get rid of Jewish workers and hire cheaper Arab workers. There are two kinds of workers, he wrote in *ha-Zvi*: "If you are talking about real workers, who get up in the morning and go home at night and don't read monthly or daily newspapers and don't know what *ha-Po'el ha-tza'ir* is, then there are no conflicts between workers and farmers. But if you are talking about members of the editorial board [*hevre ha-ma'arekhet*], eaters of vanilla ice cream fighting the war of the workers, if there's a division between that group and the people of the Yishuv, what's the big shock?" He cites an example where a certain Mr. Feigelzon hired Jewish workers to weed his orchard but found that only one in ten did the job correctly. Feigelzon then had to hire a second round of workers to get the job done. "Young Farmer" lambastes the new workers for being lazy, for spending time talking about labor rather than actually doing it and thus giving employers no choice but to find other workers. There's a certain irony here: farmers also read daily and weekly newspapers, and at least a few (including this one) considered them a forum in which to spend time arguing the merits of employment policies. But the national community he imagines is a non-ideological one, for whom intellectual discourse is secondary to action. "Give us workers for the sake of work, not for the sake of conquest."[32] Egalitarian classlessness routinely characterizes representations of settler colonial social orders, argues Lorenzo Veracini. In this case, farmers understood organized Jewish workers as rebelling against the proper order, one in which Jews at any level of the economy shared in their commitment to an ethnonational project without regard to class. They, like some on the political right, would repeat this assertion when they saw class struggle seem to threaten nationalist unity.[33]

The Jaffa journalist and industrialist Mordechai ben Hillel Hacohen, who participated in founding Tel Aviv, joined farmers in emphasizing the poor quality of the Jews who were seeking work. "For the money that an employer gives, he wants work, not theories and phrases. He wants the work of muscles." He doesn't want the kind of workers who get together on Saturday night until after midnight, when they have to get up early for work the next morning. Hacohen compares them to more docile Jewish workers, whom he presents as more nationally committed. "Say what you will about Petah Tikva, but lots of Hebrew workers are working there."[34]

Hacohen was right: many or most of the newer Jewish workers in Petah Tikva were not socialist ideologues. In 1904–1905, some of them were fleeing Russian conscription into the Russo-Japanese war, assumed they would return to Russia, and wanted a day's work more than they wanted to agitate for social change.[35] Even later, as Gur Alroey demonstrates, most "Second Aliyah" immigrants preferred to live in cities and those who did land in moshavot saw it as a last resort after not finding urban labor in their professional fields. As Zeev Smilansky found in a 1912 survey, "one can consequently find among agricultural workers not only weavers, brushmakers, confectioners, etc., whose professions are still unknown in Palestine, but also locksmiths, shoemakers, house-painters, bookbinders, etc."[36]

"Building the house of Israel in the Land of Israel," Hacohen continues, "requires mortar and bricks for now, simple materials and tools, not bells and whistles [*pe'erim ve-tza'atzu'im*]."[37] In making a basic capitalist argument that docile workers are preferable to those who resist or make demands, he joins farmers in taking a step toward articulating a public image for the moshavot as communities of owners *and* workers more committed to action than to discussion, more to labor and productivity than to ideology. If "conquest" was an inherently divisive political program and ambition that set one group of Jews (workers) against another (owners), "work" was the broader national project rooted in inherent values of productivization and national unity. Labor Zionists would have surely felt, not unreasonably, that such "simple" Jewish workers lacked the appropriate class consciousness and were being exploited, if they were hired at all, by profit-hungry landowners. Hacohen and "Young Farmer," in contrast, attempt to present ideological simplicity as an ideal expression of national commitment.

As the farmers berated ideological newcomers, they were not only addressing the present and future, they were making claims about the past. In 1912, Menashe Meirovitch, a Bilu member who became a Rishon LeZion landowner and agronomist, berated the labor newspapers. Accusations that owners were appropriating land meant for workers and denying workers access to socialist publications weren't just words of criticism, he wrote; they were words of "desecration" (*hilul*) against people "who suffered nearly their whole lives in wind and rain until they managed to see the fruit of their labors." "Don't blaspheme [*teharef*] them," he continued, using a biblical verb for non-Israelites who blaspheme God or defy Israel,[38] "because the First Ones [*rishonim*] have already done something lasting and the later-comers [*aharonim*] have not done anything yet." In using the talmudic terms for different generations of commentators to characterize the different waves of agricultural settlers, Meirovitch is adapting the interpretive principle of *yeridat ha-dorot*, the diminution of the generations since the revelation at Mount Sinai, wherein earlier sources take precedence over later ones. Those who disregarded this divinely ordained hierarchy could be accused of a kind of heresy: inappropriate innovation.[39] Meirovitch implies that the criticism of Zionist "*rishonim*" by later generations was a similar kind of heresy.

Meirovitch echoed this accusation of disrespect in 1914 when he commented on workers who had disrupted a speech by the head of the Rehovot colony committee. "Who are these cries directed against?" he asked rhetorically. They are directed against "a man who has been doing the work of revival for twenty-five years and has devoted so much labor and effort to the Yishuv in general and to Rehovot in particular. Is there no gratitude or respect for the first pioneers?!"[40] The command to respect the owners came not only from economic imperatives or even commitment to the future of the national project, but also from the sacred imperative to properly honor the leaders of the past. The past becomes a cudgel used to silence political dissent while promoting a particular "apolitical" politics of its own.

Generations of farmers, *ikarim*, would pit non-ideological "doers" against Labor ideologues. During Hanukkah 1934, the farmer Zvi Horvitz wrote an appeal for unity "to the people of Gedera" saying that "just as the Hasmoneans fought, the Biluim fought, and we need to fight against the multiplicity of gods, the multiplicity of political currents."[41] A 1936 article by the archeologist and Zionist activist Nahum Slouschz, a supporter of the First Aliyah colonies, reviewing Menashe Meirovitch's 1936 memoir *From the Trail to the Road* [*Meha-shevil el ha-derekh*], admiringly described "these First Ones" [*rishonim eleh*] as "literalists" [*pashtanim*] who

> understood life as it simply was, without adornment, decisively. Because there are really two types of Jews: Jews who are smart alecks and Jews who are not. The former always want to be petty and delay . . . and don't do anything themselves, but through their oversight also bother others and prevent them from doing anything. The latter, on the contrary, don't philosophize and don't ask questions, but are always ready to act, to do and fulfill the Torah that they have received.[42]

Meirovitch, he wrote, was among the latter type. Organized, ideological workers, he implied, were of the former.

Such discourse about apolitical moshava founders continued after statehood as well. Speaking in the 1950s, David Smilansky of Rehovot, brother of the aforementioned Zeev Smilansky, described Hayim Ettinger, chairman of the Geulah Land Development Committee in Odessa, as "not one of the speechifiers and babblers but one of the activists and doers."[43] When I met in June 2016 with Gideon Makoff, the grandson of one of the founders of Rehovot (Batya Makoff) and the former CEO of the Pardess Citrus Cooperative, he differentiated the farmers from the people of Mapai, the dominant Labor Zionist party from the 1930s to the 1970s, saying that the farmers "didn't have time to write" because they were hard at work.[44] The common bond in this rhetoric is that the demands of ownership created national and ethnic stability and precluded philosophizing and leftist political organizing. As the American builder William Levitt was said to have put it in 1948, employing similar rhetoric in a different context, "no man who owns his own house and lot can be a communist. He has too much to do."[45]

As Labor Zionists built both their political strength and a commemorative apparatus that would consign moshava farmers to the past, second-generation farmers found new ways to promote capitalist Zionist agriculture and defend the historical legacy of the moshavot. In 1921, a group of moshava sons, many of them of the same chronological generation as the socialist ideologues of the "Second Aliyah," founded Bnei Binyamin (Children of Benjamin), named for both Binyamin (Edmond James) de Rothschild and Binyamin Zeev (Theodor) Herzl. Its slogan proclaimed that the organization supported "preserving what exists and building what has been destroyed" (*shemirat ha-kayam u-vinyan he-harev*). Through youth organizing, sports teams, and cultural activities, they encouraged their counterparts, particularly in smaller moshavot, not to leave agriculture and to stay in Palestine, this at a time when many of their peers were leaving for Europe and the colonies were still rebuilding after World War I. They also took a more supportive line toward Hebrew labor, without committing to the removal of Arab workers entirely. Their first president was Alexander Aaronsohn, of the notable landowning and agronomist family of Zichron Yaʿaqov, whose siblings Aaron and Sarah were known for their leadership of the pro-British espionage organization Nili during World War I. Itamar Ben-Avi (né Ben-Zion Ben-Yehuda, son of Eliezer Ben-Yehuda), served as vice president. Eitan Belkind of Rishon LeZion was secretary.[46] Bnei Binyamin was instrumental in initiating the first round of agricultural colony construction after World War I, particularly in the region north of Tel Aviv known as the Sharon. Netanya (est. 1929, now the seventh largest city in Israel) became the most prominent of its colonies and an exemplar of private initiative: its residents knew "that they had no one to rely on except themselves," remembered General Zionist activist and journalist Yaakov Groman.[47]

Bnei Binyamin operated near the margins of the Zionist movement and sometimes directly at odds with its establishment, but with private capital at its disposal. Its 1921 regulations stated that it aimed "to promote and develop agricultural local economies and build a rural Yishuv on the basis of national economic foundations, in the spirit of practical commerce and the freedom of private initiative," while also extending the reach of Hebrew labor and the promotion of Jewish-grown goods.[48] Alexander Aaronsohn reached out to Louis Brandeis in the United States, encouraging Americans to support investment and oppose Labor settlements, which he claimed were living off the largess of diasporic Zionist philanthropy in a way that resembled the *halukah* (charitable donations) system that had supported the urban religious "Old Yishuv."[49] This is a particularly notable claim given that Labor Zionists had long criticized the moshava farmers for their relationships of dependency with the Rothschild administration and the Jewish Colonization Association. Indeed, the rhetoric of Jewish independence would remain interwoven with realities of dependency on other actors.[50] Following initial internal conflicts, the leadership of Bnei Binyamin shifted into the hands of Oved Ben-Ami and Gad Machnes, also sons of Petah Tikva colonists, who established a settlement arm called Hanotea (The Planter) in 1924. In his June 1926 speech to the fourth congress of Bnei Binyamin, Ben-Ami said that the goal of the organization had been "to defend the honor of the agricultural Yishuv which was being desecrated by crude attacks on the economic projects and settlements of our fathers, founders of the first colonies."[51]

The organization, like all settlement organizations, was explicitly forward-looking, but drew legitimation and sustenance from emphasizing its links with the First Aliyah colonies. After Bnei Binyamin founded the Binyamina colony in 1922 on the Mediterranean coastal plain south of Haifa, children of Zichron Ya'aqov's founders and representatives from other colonies participated in its dedication ceremony in 1923. It was held on Tu Bishvat, the rabbinic new year of the trees, re-envisioned as the Zionist holiday of tree planting. Baruch Raab (Ben-Ezer), son of Yehuda, known for plowing the "first Jewish furrow" in Petah Tikva, spoke in the name of Bnei Binyamin. Those reclaiming land, he said, were following in the civilizing footsteps of the founders of Zichron Yaʿaqov and Hadera before them: "before we came, these places were desolate and destroyed. The Arabs said that every bird who drank water in this place would lose its feathers. Only Jewish sacrifices turned these valleys of death into blessings."[52] The Jewish reclamation of territory from the state of desolation that had been enabled and tolerated by Arabs had, he implied, begun with the first settlers and would be continued. The language of sacrifice and blessing conferred a sacred mission and divine imperative on the process.

When Herzliya (also named for Theodor Herzl), north of Tel Aviv, hosted a groundbreaking ceremony two years later, in 1925, with the participation of members of Bnei Binyamin, the organizers invited 88-year-old Leah (Haya Rachel Leah) Gissin to lay the cornerstone. Gissin (nee Krokin) had been a Lovers of Zion activist in the Mohilev region of the Russian Pale of Settlement when she met Efraim Gissin. Their sons Moshe, Shlomo Zalman, and Aryeh Leib would migrate to Palestine in the early 1890s and become some of the most important landowners in Petah Tikva and employers of many of the men who later became Second Aliyah leaders and critics of the moshavot.[53] As Leah, who by that point had more than sixty descendants, bent down to place the stone: "a great cry burst forth from the mouths of those assembled: 'Mazel tov, to the life of the land!'" As the band began to play, "song was heard on the hills, the creation song of the new builders. Groups of people sat on the hills, enjoying themselves with memories, telling stories of fortitude [gevurot] and wonders on the fields of the new Herzliya."[54]

Nahum Slouschz claimed in his speech that "This city [Herzliya] belonged to our people in the Second Temple period," making the jump from antiquity to the 1920s that Yael Zerubavel has shown was iconic to Zionist memory. But the founders of Herzliya, Slouschz continued, weren't simply picking up where the ancient heroes had left off. They were "the sons of the first pioneers who dedicated the cornerstones of the Yishuv with their blood and suffering. There are lots of partners here. The first pioneers were the First Ones. Today you are a great people." It was up to those in attendance, moreover, to continue a process of settlement expansion. "And on the day that you expand outwards to the north up to Haifa and to the south down to Tel Aviv, the great plan of Herzl will have been fulfilled."⁵⁵

A year later, Bnei Binyamin founded Kfar Aharon (named for the Zichron Ya'aqov planter Aaron Aaronsohn) near Ness Ziona. Aaronsohn, born fifty years prior, had disappeared in 1919 in an airplane over Europe as he participated in negotiations on behalf of the Yishuv during the Paris Peace Conference. Feige Lehrer, the 93-year-old widow of Ness Ziona founder Reuven Lehrer, laid the first cornerstone and Fishel Aaronsohn, Aaron's 87-year-old father, laid the second. Ben-Ami opened, explaining that "today we are establishing a living memorial to one of the best and most excellent of the Yishuv, our great teacher, Aaron Aaronsohn," who, he said, "symbolized the type of the new Jew." What did it mean to Bnei Binyamin to be a "New Jew," a term omnipresent in Labor Zionist rhetoric? In this context, it wasn't about loyalty to the working class or physical regeneration, but rather engagement in private initiative and technological innovation, which Aaron typified through his discovery and development of ancient wheat. The initiators of Kfar Aharon, Ben-Ami said, were "the descendants of the first pioneers" and continued the legacy of two older, nearby moshavot, Ness Ziona and Rehovot. Though "the founders of Ness Ziona are absent . . . their spirit floats over their sons, the pioneers of Kfar Aharon."⁵⁶

Performing Firstness for the British

The audience for these displays was, in the first instance, Jewish. Moshava heritage elites, to use Alan D. Gordon's term for nonprofessional guardians of local memory, wanted to show colony residents, potential residents, and other Zionist onlookers that the history of settlement stretched back to the nineteenth century and that moshava founders should be regarded as the "firsts" in an emerging nationalist lineage. But after the British conquest of Palestine in late 1917 and their assumption of the League of Nations mandate in 1923, the target of these displays also included a far more powerful spectator. The British had taken up the dual obligation to modernize their newly held territory while also bringing benefit and not harm to the land's mainly Arab Muslim inhabitants. Jewish settlers, armed with scientific knowledge and the motivation to develop the land, seemed to be exactly the right emissaries.⁵⁷ British Colonial Office correspondence from 1923 mentioned that "Jews are the only people capable of rebuilding [Palestine]."⁵⁸ Secretary of State for the Colonies, The Duke of Devonshire (Victor Cavendish), said that same year that by giving Jews the opportunity to develop Palestine, "we are serving the interests of civilization as a whole, quite apart from any sentimental considerations about restoring a scattered people to its ancient fatherland."⁵⁹ Consequently, the British supported Jewish investment in Palestine from whatever political corner it happened to come from. In practice, it came primarily from private enterprise, initially agricultural and later also industrial. Reminding the mandatory officials of the ongoing economic contributions of the Jewish colonies to the development of the country became a key plank in local commemorative efforts.

Arthur James Balfour's visit to Palestine in March and April 1925 provided a high-profile opportunity to show off the colonies' achievements. Setting foot for the first time in the land that he had set onto a new course with the issuance of his eponymous declaration in 1917, the former British foreign secretary traveled on a rail line that reflected a history of imperial capital investment in Palestine. He rode the Ottoman Jaffa-Jerusalem line from Jaffa to Lydda (al-Lid) and transferred to the Ottoman World War I-era Eastern Railway Line, north to Ras al-'Ayn. From there he made his way to Petah Tikva on the Zionist-financed rail spur completed in 1921, which would become self-financing by the end of the 1920s thanks to Petah Tikva's prodigious citrus exports.⁶⁰ A short film clip by the French filmmaker Camille Sauvage shows banners and decorative greenery hung along newly swept streets, massive crowds, and more than a hundred men arrayed on horseback to greet him.⁶¹ Balfour was also taken on a tour of the colony and its citrus groves. He received a similar welcome during visits to Rishon LeZion to the south and Rosh Pinna in the Upper Galilee, both founded in 1882, and the new Bnei Binyamina colony.⁶² While he also visited the cities and Jewish communities of Haifa and Tiberias and the 16-year-old city of Tel Aviv, recently assigned municipality status by the British, records do not suggest that he visited Labor settlements, like kibbutzim. For all their symbolic value for Labor Zionists, they were not at the forefront of agricultural or industrial production.

We might be inclined to view celebratory accounts of Balfour's visit simply as evidence that the Yishuv of the 1920s was overjoyed about the Balfour

Declaration, which many saw as the dawn of a messianic era, "the first shofar blast of our freedom," as Mordecai ben Hillel Hacohen wrote.[63] But precisely because of the changes that followed the declaration—the rise of Labor Zionism as a hegemonic force in the Yishuv and the intensification of Palestinian Arab resistance—memories from before Balfour also became spaces for the agriculturalists of the early colonies to make claims about the past. As claims about the past always are, these were claims about the present: that they, a non-socialist, pragmatic, and "apolitical" cohort, had the experience and tools to ensure the Yishuv's economic productivity while minimizing conflict with Arabs. As they arrayed themselves to greet Balfour, the young men and elder statesmen of the moshavot were signaling their own firstness against the upstart Labor leadership. They were constructing themselves as the appropriate objects of Zionist memory.

When they welcomed Balfour to town in 1925, the moshava representatives were eager to show him evidence of their agricultural successes, the rapidity with which they had rebuilt after the devastation of World War I, and, more symbolically, the depth of their rootedness in an era of increasing Jewish immigration under the mandate. Dr. Chaim Weizmann and Nahum Sokolow of the Zionist Organization in London accompanied Balfour in Petah Tikva, joined by the head of the newly formed local council and "Oldest of the guards" Avraham Shapira, wearing his riding boots. Shapira was not only a relic of the settlement past but a symbol of ongoing settler vitality. A photograph shows Balfour and Shapira touring some of Petah Tikva's citrus groves in business attire.

Just four years earlier, in 1921, Shapira had led Petah Tikva's defense against an attack that occurred amidst larger anti-British and anti-Zionist riots in Jaffa and that killed four local Jewish guardsmen. Anat Helman suggests that Petah Tikva's attention to commemorating these as heroic deaths, an initiative led by Bnei Binyamin members, eclipsed the story of "its unstable foundation in 1878 in the days of the 'Old Yishuv.'"[64] There is no doubt as to the rhetorical value to Petah Tikva of this memorial ritual in the 1920s and 1930s given that Labor activists continued to accuse its ruling elites of reactionary politics. But the prominence of Shapira and the Bnei Binyamin riders around Balfour's visit also communicated pride in the colony's founding as a symbol of both early and ongoing settlement and defense. In a 1960s

FIGURE 3. Avraham Shapira (right) accompanies Arthur James Balfour (center) on a tour of Petah Tikva orange groves during Balfour's 1925 visit (courtesy of the Historical Archives of Petah Tikva).

interview, Shapira also recalled traveling to meet Balfour in London and telling him, 'I'm happy to shake the hand that signed the Balfour Declaration to establish a national home for the Jewish people.'" Balfour, he remembered, chuckled and replied, "I am happy to shake the hand that protected the lives of the settlers more than once."[65]

This was not the first time that Shapira had served in such a dignified role or that the colony had been proud to show itself off to governmental representatives. During World War I, Shapira had also accompanied the Ottoman governor Jamal Pasha on a visit to Petah Tikva and attempted to intervene with him to prevent the conscription of some of Petah Tikva's youth into the Ottoman army.[66] In 1917, two Ottoman Arab intellectuals were sent on a mission to Palestine to report on its material and cultural conditions. While they visited multiple religious and ethnic communities, Rafiq Tamimi and Muhammad Bahajat were particularly enthralled with the Petah Tikva and Rosh Pinna colonies, which they regarded as models of cleanliness, modern technology (including streetlamps and running water), and cultural elevation for the country as a whole. The visitors painted an idealized image of a Jewish landowning class that spent its leisure time writing letters to send around the world, reading European and Jewish newspapers, having intellectual conversations with family members, and playing the piano: "a cultural life like in the most advanced countries of the world."[67] These Ottoman visitors had come with fixed conceptual dichotomies between civilized and uncivilized, modern and premodern in mind, not unlike the Jewish colonists and the British imperial representatives who followed. The bourgeois qualities and leisure-time activities that impressed the cultured Ottoman visitors were, notably, the very same ones that appalled Labor Zionist activists in the colony. The latter saw it as leisure earned on the backs of Arab labor and enjoyed by a group lacking strong ethnonationalist ideological commitments; they also considered cultural affinities with French elites to be distinct marks of shame. For a community that relied on the good grace of and ongoing patronage relationships with imperial rulers, however, the attention and positive evaluations were welcome.

In November of the same year, Lord Herbert Plumer, new High Commissioner of Palestine (1925–1928), visited Rishon LeZion. It was another occasion to impress upon a local British official the contributions of a colony to the overall development of Palestine. Here, too, the colony was decorated for the occasion, with a flower-covered gate of honor set up close to the synagogue and riders from Bnei Binyamin ready to greet the distinguished guest. Where in Petah Tikva the orchards were the spectacle, Rishon LeZion showed off its winery and presented its founders as the enablers of an economically prosperous business enterprise. "These men with white hair who sit here around the table," said winery manager Yaakov (Jack) Shapira (no relation to Avraham Shapira) in a speech, "were the First Ones who grazed the lands of Rishon LeZion, neglected for 1,000 years. And now Rishon LeZion sends its wines to all five continents! Rishon LeZion, without any exaggeration, is now to the East what Bordeaux is to France."

This history of economic development by Jewish settlers, Jack Shapira suggested, placed upon the British the "great obligation to revive a dead land." He hoped that "under your government farming in Palestine will flourish." Mayor Dov Lubman (Haviv) emphasized that the founders were the "first pioneers" who roused this land from its slumber to join the ranks of "cultured nations" and in the process provided work for "thousands of the [Arab] neighbors, natives of the land, who make a living" here, adding that "this example should be a model for the entire land."[68] Menashe Meirovitch emphasized the international prominence of the colony, noting that "it is recognized by the various classes of people visiting our villages." He used the opportunity to call for several specific policy changes for the benefit of agriculturalists: the extension of greater credit, protections against theft, the creation of favorable conditions for export through tariff and tax policy, new road infrastructure, and the recognition of Rishon LeZion colonists' legal rights to their land holdings.[69]

The Arab press, published and read by urban notables engaged in their own competing agricultural export activity, also picked up on the praise British officials were heaping on the colonies for their economic contributions. In 1931, *Filastin*—using the Arabic name, ʿUyun Qara, for the village where the colony of Rishon LeZion was established—reported on High Commissioner John Chancellor's visit to the area during the grape harvest and his praise of the Jewish settler celebrants. "Wine and oranges are the spine of Palestine," Chancellor said, and he hoped that "the colonists [would] increase the economic resources of the country so it gets to a better position than it is in today." He even went so far as to predict that America would "come back from its dryness" and repeal prohibition, creating an even larger market for the colony's wines. *Filastin* also picked up on the claims to "apoliticism" and direct patronage relationships with the British that the colonies touted. "Work alone, not politics, is what illuminates the path of life," Chancellor was quoted as saying, before attending a dinner with Avraham Shapira, Menashe Meirovitch, and a variety of winemakers. No doubt pleasing themselves with a glass or two of the local vintage, these colony elites "asked His Excellency the High Commissioner that he lessen the financial burdens that the makers of wine are suffering under" and received a vague promise from Chancellor that he would look into these demands.[70] A year later, when Rishon LeZion celebrated its fiftieth anniversary, *Mirat al-sharq* reported that ten thousand people attended its celebration. It also presumed that its readers were familiar with the colony's significance: "the Rishon colony, as readers know, is famous for its wine and exports large quantities to Europe."[71]

Though the leaders of the "Second Aliyah," the Labor Zionist elites, would place their settlement starting point in 1904, a decade before the war, the pre-World War I agricultural history of the Yishuv was in fact overwhelmingly a story of the privately owned moshavot. So it was not without cause that moshava leaders imagined that it was their own network of colonies, for all their struggles in the early years, that had encouraged Balfour to issue his declaration in the first place. Over the decades that followed, they continued to insist that they were the primary but too often ignored sources of the Jewish agricultural sector's economic vitality.

Competing Commemorations

The desire of the colony elites to claim a noble origin point grew as representatives of the newly self-appointed "Second Aliyah" cultivated and burnished their own image, with the private colonies as their foil. David Ben-Gurion, Histadrut secretary and future prime minister of Israel, talked about the colony farmers with a mix of praise and denigration in the remarks he gave at the twenty-fifth-anniversary celebration of the Second Aliyah, in 1929. He acknowledged "the First Ones [*rishonim*] who preceded us: the members of the First Aliyah," saying that their "path-breaking [*nahshoni*] enterprise educated us from our youth." Nonetheless, he offered the First Aliyah as a cautionary tale: "we need to also appreciate the failures of our First Ones . . . from whom we learned how not to go and what kind of Yishuv not to create in the land." Whatever their lofty ambitions, he lamented, they "lost all will and inclination for great action," thanks to their dependency on foreign philanthropic aid. When the "son of the Second Aliyah" came to the land, he found "foreignness, alienation, and moral decline."[72]

Leaders in the moshavot did not acquiesce, however, in the face of the supersessionist narrative, by Ben Gurion and others, of weak founders who needed to be displaced. The journal of the Farmers' Federation, *Bustenai* (founded 1929), occasionally took time out from discussing advances in seeds and plowing methods, shifting markets for citrus or other commodities, or the impacts of British government policies to speak about more symbolic or commemorative matters. In a 1929 article, Joseph Sapir, General Zionist leader, owner of citrus orchards in Petah Tikva, and son of First Aliyah financier Eliyahu Sapir, critiqued the commemoration of the "Second Aliyah" in which Ben-Gurion had participated. First of all, he said, this very periodization flattened all the predecessors into one group, ignoring divisions between those who came in 1882 and those, like the founders of Rehovot, who arrived in the early 1890s with more substantial private capital and might be thought of as the true "Second Aliyah." All of this "has been erased from the history of the Yishuv." Moreover, he added, the Aliyah distinction suggested that those who immigrated during the "Second Aliyah" were all Labor Zionists, coming to supersede their predecessors. In fact, the great majority of the rural settlers of the "Second Aliyah" (counted according to the chronological years of their arrival) became involved in the quintessential profession of the moshavot—citriculture—some of them indeed as owners. For all intents and purposes, those settlers became part of the economic patterns and ideological dynamics considered typical of the First Aliyah. Though the citrus growers had become the largest exporter in the Yishuv, somehow Labor Zionists chose to overlook that: "who mentions any of them [*ve-khol eleh, man dekar shemam*]?" Sapir asked rhetorically, using talmudic language.[73]

Sapir alleged that the demarcation and commemoration of the Second Aliyah introduced divisions where there should have been apolitical national unity. "This time of happiness," he said, "which should have been dedicated to bringing hearts together, to forgetting the bitterness of the past, and to uniting around that central idea of building the land" was instead deployed "to pour oil on the bonfire of hatred." But Sapir vowed that the moshavot would not remain silent, despite being declared "rotten" by the Labor establishment: "That which is planted in the ground won't be uprooted so easily." The First Aliyah was not a once-and-done phenomenon, it was an ongoing vital process with its own waves, development, and complexity, and, he thought, it represented the ongoing essence of the Yishuv: settlement and economic development on behalf of Jews.[74]

In August 1932, the Farmers' Federation designated a week for a period of education about and celebration of the fiftieth anniversary of the arrival of the Bilu group in 1882. Unlike Labor Zionists, who celebrated Bilu as an exception to the general First Aliyah trends, *Bustenai* took Bilu to be the crème de la crème of an honorable movement. Hayim Ariav, General Secretary of the Federation, put out an announcement indicating that the goal of the event was to "explain the value of the shining era of the Bilu group, *and the farmers who came after them*, to the building of the moshavot and the Yishuv in general."[75] Zvi Butkovsky from the Hadera colony emphasized the individual initiative that underlay Bilu's contributions to the national project. In addition to initiating agricultural labor and introducing scientific developments in agriculture, they pioneered the idea of "Hebrew property" (*rekhush 'Ivri*, i.e. proud Jewish ownership and defense of property) and inaugurated the idea of a growers' cooperative, a mode of organization that Labor Zionists later began to adopt as well: "the big cooperatives today are thanks to them." And finally, they mastered self-defense against the "half savage" with their "*nabout*" (club) and "*tabandzi*" (tabanjah—gun) to defend their "families, houses, lives, and property."[76]

In Labor settings, Bilu would become "laborized" and read as the first quasi-socialist pioneers set against a broader wave of immigration generally presumed in Labor circles to have lacked these features. Here, however, Bilu is recruited as a model for the kind of settlement values embodied by the Farmers' Federation: scientific research and development, the protection of private property as a national resource, and the idea that the cooperative of private owners, not the socialist collective, was the ideal mechanism for supporting economic development.[77] By emphasizing the continuity between the founders' values and the ongoing progress, farmers sought not only recognition but also markets and investments. As Arthur Ruppin wrote in 1936, a new immigrant who "arrived at the Jewish moshavot and saw only old people totally dispirited, he would be seized by a terrible disappointment and he would immediately scurry back."[78] If the moshavot were to prevail, boosters knew, they had to parlay their origin stories into ongoing investment by sons and new immigrants alike.

They would do so by walking the line between defending their central role in the Zionist settlement story and claiming to exist outside politics. It was the same careful line that industrial business ventures walked. Palestine Potash Ltd, given a concession in 1930 to extract an essential fertilizer component from the Dead Sea, alternated between describing their business as "a full-fledged Zionist project" and as a "private, profit oriented firm that shunned all things political."[79] The moshavot, too, had a strong interest in being recognized not only as Zionist but as the wellspring of the Zionist settlement enterprise. At the same time, they sought both operational independence and the perception of a nationalism elevated above politics: bringing benefit to the Jewish economy—and to all of Palestine's inhabitants—without any partisan allegiances.

Moshava anniversaries provided additional opportunities for local leaders to characterize their colonies as originators and bastions of an "apolitical" or "simply national" space that could provide a counterexample to both the array of Labor Zionist parties and the acrimony between these and the rising militant Zionist right wing. Speeches, readings, and performances emphasized that founders were apolitical, traditional Jews who were committed to the land and Jewish practice, embraced private enterprise as an engine for national growth, and believed that an authentic connection to the nation sat above party loyalty or ideology.

Following Rehovot's fortieth anniversary in 1930, Tel Aviv's General Zionist mayor Meir Dizengoff recalled the "pioneering work" of the founding settlers Eliyahu Zeev Levin-Epstein and Zeev Gluskin and wished for Rehovot that it "bloom and develop . . . together with all the Jewish cities and villages in the land," as we look ahead "for our complete redemption."[80] If some of these sentiments were generically nationalist, others took the opportunity to specifically allude to successes in the capitalist sphere. The colony council received a letter from a woman claiming to be "the first natural [born] resident of Rehovot." Her parents had celebrated the distinction by naming her Rehavia, which comes from the same Hebrew root as the colony's name. Rehavia Kantorovitz was proud to be the namesake of the first moshava "to be founded and to stand until today through independent means [*kohot 'atzma' iyim*] without any support from anyone." But Rehavia's pride didn't satisfy her: she wanted documentation of her role in local "firsting": a certificate proving that she was the first child to be born in the colony.[81]

Rehovot's particular pride in private initiative, as a colony that had not come under the control of the Rothschild administration, motivated a letter from Yehudit Levin-Epstein, the widow of the Rehovot founder Eliyahu Levin-Epstein. She wrote from Detroit for the moshava's fiftieth anniversary to say that she hoped she would eventually be able to return to "our land" and "see the progress of our colony."[82] Levin-Epstein had moved to the United States with her son, also named Rehavia, who in 1936 had been appointed director of the American Economic Committee for Palestine. The organization, founded in New York, focused on promoting the economic development of Palestine by "stimulating safe and profitable private investments in Palestine, assisting small investments, attracting large capital for industrial enterprises, and concessions, and long-term credits, organizing the marketing of Palestine products and manufactures, and the examination of opportunities for opening new fields of industry." A Jewish national home, the organization believed, needed to be economically self-sustaining, a goal they felt was best achieved through private investment.[83] Rehavia Levin-Epstein had returned to Tel Aviv to be the head of the Palestine Office of the organization. Yehudit, his mother, though not personally involved with the organization, was wrapped up in the transatlantic movement of capitalist business leaders between the Yishuv and the United States. In evoking "the progress of our colony," Yehudit was surely speaking of the growth of individual initiative and economic cooperation that her son was promoting back in Palestine. Private investment would remain both a bedrock of the relationship between the United States and Israel after 1948 and a goal and object of pride for those American Jews who would come to call themselves Liberal Zionists.[84]

The Politics of Apoliticism

Moshava farmers gathered into new organizations later in the mandate period to insist that their commitment to land and nation stood outside politics and that they had been sidelined for that very reason. By "politics" they meant not the project of ethnonationalist settlement and society-building—which they supported and participated in—but rather partisan fracturing, which they claimed to eschew and avoid. For its part, the Farmers' Federation believed that its work was non-political but disagreed as to the necessity of engaging in partisan structures nonetheless. Moshe Smilansky, its president and later the editor of its journal, *Bustenai*, took a more absolutist stance: that its members were united not by political views but by professional ambitions. Moreover, unlike "political questions like Hebrew labor," professional questions "have answers that can be solved without politics." Smilansky even saw "politics" as "a fatal drug."[85] Joseph Sapir, on the other hand, argued that farmers must engage in Yishuv partisan politics if they were to defend their interests and not cave to the left. Sapir believed that "politics are the economics of tomorrow," that is, that political decisions made today shape future economic conditions. He became a key figure in the Citizens Circles and General Zionist party, both of which claimed to be "non-political" while engaging in partisan political races.[86]

On May 26, 1940, one hundred and fifty delegates from twenty-three moshavot gathered in Tel Aviv for the "Conference of Moshava Youths." Ezra Ichilov, son of the citriculturalist Moshe Ichilov, declared in his opening address that "We are the generation that learned Zionism not from pamphlets and declarations, but through actions and sacrifice. It is not all right that they continue to ignore us and to push us to the sides." Avraham Tehomi from the Maccabi club (best known for his involvement in the 1924 murder of the anti-Zionist Dutch Jew Jacob Israel De Haan) called for fighting against "the unfettered partisan urge." Representatives from other sympathetic organizations, including the Farmers' Federation, agricultural syndicates, the Revisionist organization Beitar, and the General Zionists, concurred that not only did the lack of Zionist movement support for non-politically aligned individuals engaged in private agriculture fail to serve the economic interests of the Yishuv, it constituted a slight against the fathers. Indeed, Moshe Uzieli of the General Zionists thought that supporting young farmers would mean supporting "a mix of vibrant youthful energy and the good conservatism of the fathers."[87]

In July 1939, another new organization called the Union of Sons of the Yishuv had convened for the first time. Comprised both of moshava farmers and urban religious interests, it claimed to be a non-political organization that aimed "to weaken as much as possible the partisan hatred that is poisoning the life of the Yishuv," to "unify the children of the Yishuv and youth from all communities and classes, to involve them in building the land, and to get involved in matters related to the Yishuv."[88] Zerubavel Haviv of Rishon LeZion spoke at a 1942 meeting of the organization, as did Hayim Ariav, who, though not a farmer himself, became secretary of the Farmers' Federation in 1931 and participated in the founding of the Farmers' Bank (Bank Ikarim) and the agricultural school in Pardes Hanna in 1936.[89] The organization published, among other volumes, the biographies of the Petah Tikva veteran Zerach Barnett and the Rishon LeZion veteran and Bilu member Israel Belkind. The founder Israel Ben-Zeev (Wolfensohn), a scholar of Arabic and a native of the Jerusalemite Ashkenazi community, claimed in January 1940 that the organization "had more members than Mapai" and was working to elevate the voices of "the tens of thousands of people who don't have a voice or representation."[90]

Among the issues they focused on, the Union of Sons of the Yishuv supported a single unified Zionist educational system and opposed the division of Jewish education into ideologically structured streams. By the 1930s, the Zionist educational system had split into three "streams" (*zeramim*, sometimes translated "trends"). The original Hebrew-language Zionist school system, founded in 1913, came to be known as the "General Trend" when a Religious trend and a Labor Zionist trend joined the mix in 1920 and 1926 respectively. Yuval Dror, scholar of the Labor Zionist stream generally and kibbutz education in particular, writes that the General Trend "did not have an ideology of its own" and was weakened by its lack of party ties and deficient organizational system.[91] This assessment, however, could also be framed in positive terms. General Trend educators and supporters, Zionists who tended toward centrist or right-wing stances but denied the presence of any associated "ideology," "favored an apolitical stance, allowing them to pursue the goals of strengthening national unity and creating a new Jewish culture."[92] Again, centrist and right-wing Zionism were hardly apolitical: theirs was a nationalist ideology that privileged erasing political distinctions *within* the Zionist movement so as to ensure national unity and achieve political objectives in relation to the British and Arab Palestinians.

Some of the opposition to the Labor stream schools focused on the Labor schools' secular orientation; religious voices in the group said that secular education was an "idol in the sanctuary." But the more prominent thread included a demand for a nationalism that transcended partisan politics. At its Hadera meeting, the organization called for "preferring the interests of the nation over the interests of the party," stating that "the school is the place where the soul of the nation is created, not the party. We strongly oppose an educational system built on streams that exploit education in schools for the interests of political parties."[93]

Moshava farmers constructed themselves as the originators and maintainers of a loyal, nonpartisan nationalism, even though—and indeed because—they never formulated concrete political ideologies or established functional political parties. This process of articulating a national identity that transcended (what they understood as) politics was arbitrated through the periodical press and continued in response to Labor Zionist efforts to canonize the "Second Aliyah" as the standard-bearer of the Zionist settlement effort. The moshava farmers sought—and won—the admiration of British Mandate officials who were eager to support Jewish settlers as their agents in developing the land economically, and established patronage relationships with the British that allowed them to circumvent emerging Zionist political institutions. Over the course of the 1930s and 1940s, the farmers emphasized a further rhetorical strand in their historical narration: that they adopted pragmatic economic practices that allowed for ongoing "hierarchical coexistence" with the very Palestinian workers whom Labor Zionists witnessed them exploiting. We turn to this topic in the following chapter.

(CHAPTER 2)

ARAB LABOR AND THE RHETORIC OF HIERARCHICAL COEXISTENCE IN MANDATE PALESTINE

In 1940, Petah Tikva celebrated the seventieth birthday of Avraham Shapira, the colony's former head guardsman who had become known as "The Oldest of the Guards" (*zekan ha-shomrim*). Guests from Petah Tikva, other Jewish colonies, Jaffa, and Palestinian villages attended a gathering where they heard speeches that praised Shapira as both a relic of a bygone past and an inspiration for the present. Shapira was the preeminent local model of an Ashkenazi Jewish colonist who had established positive relations with rural Arabs throughout the region from a position of uncompromising strength. At Shapira's seventy-fifth birthday party, five years later, Petah Tikva again convened a celebration, where it hosted thirty "Arab chieftains and sheiks from tribes all over Palestine" who, according to a *New York Times* reporter, arrived "in full regalia," brought their own sheep to be slaughtered for the feast, and spent several hours "listening to the encomiums and returning them before joining Jewish riders in feats of horsemanship."[1]

These encomiums came from several directions. The local archives contain a transcript of a speech delivered in Arabic by an unidentified Jew at the 1940 gathering who emphasized that "we are celebrating one of our men who became famous not only among Jews across the land but also among Arabs."[2] The event program, which included horse races and "Oriental accompaniment," also noted that Shapira was known colloquially in Arabic as "Sheikh Ibrahim Mikha," Mikha likely being a reference to his older brother

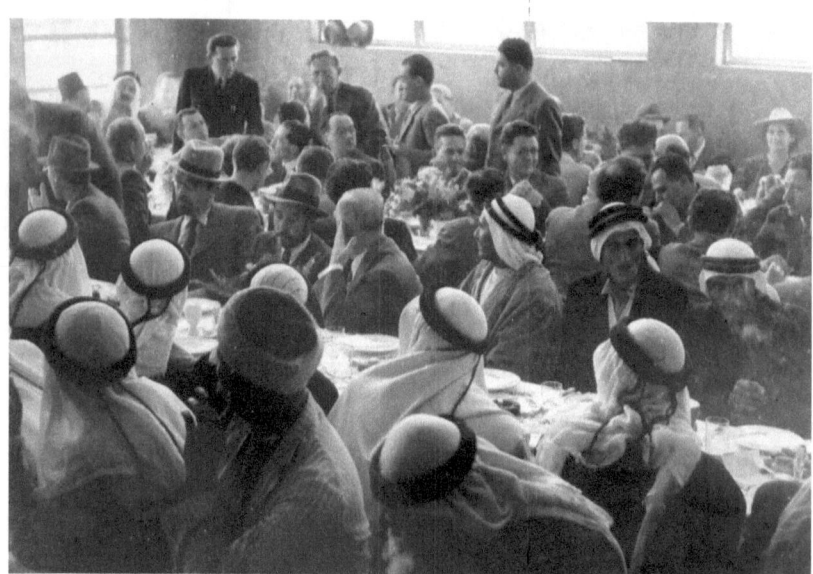

FIGURE 4. Guests gathered to celebrate Avraham Shapira's seventieth birthday, Petah Tikva 1940 (Zoltan Kluger, courtesy of the KKL-JNF Photo Archive).

Michael who had preceded him in Petah Tikva as a farmer.[3] Ali Mustaqim, a Jaffa landowner and politician, wrote after the event to the mayor of Petah Tikva, Joseph Sapir, with apologies for leaving the party early. He emphasized that he had been called back to Jaffa for business and assured Sapir that "our friendly relations have not been affected in the least."[4] In honor of the 1945 event, the Jewish Agency sent a letter to the Petah Tikva municipality noting that

> [Shapira's] name flutters over many pages in the magnificent annals of building and guarding our name and our honor—so great was his role in improving friendly neighborly relations. Proud and upstanding, he knew how to weave a web of good connections between the villages that border our points of settlement.[5]

Arab Palestinians, urban and rural alike, were self-conscious actors in a rapidly changing region. Notables protested British policy toward Zionists and, by the time of the Shapira celebration, peasants had undertaken armed rebellion against Zionist and British targets during the 1936–1939 Arab revolt.

Arab youth movements, unions, and peasant associations had begun to engage, though ultimately unsuccessfully, in what Charles Anderson calls "state formation from below."[6] While early Jewish settlers assumed and claimed that they had brought benefit to the rural Arabs of Palestine, Hillel Cohen has made clear that instances of friendliness or collaboration during the mandate period revealed Palestinian partisan divisions, familial dynamics, and economic interest, not blanket appreciation for Jewish settlers or their agricultural colonies.[7] Nonetheless, Zionists of multiple orientations persisted in their desire to see rural Arabs in particular as a locally oriented, non-ideological population, or at least one that could be productively tamed or redirected through effective policy and organizing. Displays of ongoing "good relations" in the present, understood to have been built on good relations in the past, offered curios of coexistence in the midst of an ever-worsening struggle over land and national futures. Remembering and reenacting camaraderie was a way to escape the darkness of contemporary politics by "knotting the [past and present] together in uncanny harmony," as Nisa Ari has characterized a distinguishing facet of Orientalist discourse.[8]

Moshava residents were certainly not the only Zionists to valorize an authentic European Jewish connection to the east achieved through personal and collective transformation. The "New Hebrew Man" in Arab garb or the Hebrew Bedouin, particularly as symbolic tropes, are most associated with Labor Zionists.[9] Shapira was also a useful propaganda tool for Labor Zionist outreach efforts: the Histadrut-published Arabic newspaper *Haqiqat al-amr* covered the Shapira seventieth birthday party, pointing out that "Jewish, Arab, and British leaders gathered under one roof" to celebrate him.[10]

But moshava elites, looking to establish settler primacy through claims about their close relations with rural Palestinians, held two cards that other Zionist groups did not: chronology and proximity. First, moshavot inarguably preceded the major outbreaks of intercommunal violence of the twentieth century, which increased following the Young Turk Revolution of 1908 and the accompanying rise of ethnonational movements in the Ottoman Empire and, even more intensely, after the 1917 Balfour Declaration and British assumption of an explicitly pro-Zionist mandate for Palestine.[11] Early settlers could thus appear to stand prior to, if not outside of, those developments. First Aliyah moshavot, landowners believed, invoked not only the imperative or at least possibility of Jewish-Arab coexistence, but also, in their minds, a history of such connection having already occurred. Second, to the ongoing chagrin of their internal and external Labor Zionist critics, the moshavot relied on proximity to Arab workers and villages. Whether it was a landowner hiring native agricultural workers or a head guardsmen overseeing native guards, the employer who defied the orthodoxy of Zionist national institutions by refusing to adhere to a pure Hebrew Labor agenda could be reconceptualized as one who maintained personal relations with hired laborers and local Bedouins and who could—and in practice did—informally resolve whatever local conflicts arose despite the close employer-employee relations. If Jewish settlers formed relationships with Palestine's Arabs and informally resolved conflicts during a period when Jews "did not encounter Arab nationalism,"[12] then it seemed to follow that more serious turns for the worse must have come later. Veteran farmers blamed this decline not only on simple misunderstandings, irrational transformations among the peasants, and pressure from Arab elites but also on Labor Zionist arrivals who had neither experienced nor created these supposedly harmonious relations. These formulations directly contradicted the dominant Labor Zionist claims and related historiography, which vilified the private landowners and assumed—though with little demonstrable evidence—that labor separation was inherently a path toward coexistence.[13]

Scholars of Zionist labor history note the rise of the principle—if not the practice—of Hebrew Labor and suggest that those who did continue to hire native Arab labor, such as in the citrus-growing colonies, rationalized its use as temporary. Gershon Shafir characterizes the First Aliyah as "an inhibited pure settlement drive that reconciled itself to a plantation-type economy."[14] Baruch Kimmerling reasons that where settler communities could not achieve "high frontierity," his descriptor for a large, sparsely populated space, they had to "supervis[e] a complicated and hierarchically structured population economy."[15] But Zionists in some of the most important "First Aliyah" colonies not only rationalized the use of Palestinian labor and the emergence of ethnic hierarchies, though they surely did that; some also elevated it, not as a goal in its own right but as a producer of interethnic harmony in practice. In this sense, the colonies echo settler discourses elsewhere that invoke "partnership" between settlers and natives and construct a division of space based not only on separation but also on hierarchical relationship.[16] The frontier, Penelope Edmonds argues in her work on nineteenth-century aboriginal laborers who lived in camps outside Melbourne, is "not an outward moving linear abstraction," like the lines on Zionist maps that show the limit of Jewish landholdings. Rather, the frontier "was often domestic, local, and personal."[17] Memories of hierarchical coexistence were not of a strict border traversed but of a contact zone inhabited.

Those whose grazing or planting rights had been disrupted when Jewish settlers initially purchased land sometimes ended up working as hired labor in those colonies. Villages became economically bound to the colonies closest to them. Many found themselves subject to cruel and abusive treatment, "as though they were animals," noted Ahad Ha-'Am on his second visit to Palestine in 1893.[18] Some protested, not only through the acts of violence that made their opposition most visible to settlers, but also through petitions sent to the Ottoman government. One sent from the Abu Hataba Bedouin in the Mazra'at Duran area in late 1890 noted that after Jewish settlers had purchased lands to found Rehovot, "they started to chase us away from our place of residence and to prevent us from cultivating our crops on the above-mentioned farm."[19]

Peasant fears grew after the British conquest of Palestine and the mandate's explicit guarantees to Jews. Elite Arab politics of protesting British policy and Zionist settlement gave way to more grassroots and episodically violent anti-Zionist resistance, particularly during the 1936–1939 Arab Revolt.[20] It was at this time that moshava leaders accelerated their narrative of "already achieved" and "pre-political" coexistence. Labor-oriented parties saw Arab opposition as essentially tractable through economic separation and labor organization. Revisionists regarded opposition as organic, decried as foolhardy attempts to placate this population through labor organizing, and encouraged the cultivation of Jewish military strength to ensure, down the road, a docile Arab population that would submit to Jewish rule. The older capitalist interests in the First Aliyah moshavot, though they had defined themselves in opposition to a small core of ideological socialists and often welcomed the economic liberalism within the Revisionist platform come the 1920s, sat outside the most ardent political discourse on the "Arab Question." Many shared the Revisionists' critique of Labor's collectivist ethos, separatist rhetoric, and efforts at intra-Jewish class struggle. Like the Labor parties, however, many were basically optimistic about the possibility of coexistence but saw this coexistence occurring at least in part through contact and the ongoing employment of rural Arabs (in addition to Jews). Above all, they insisted that in seeking out the most beneficial economic conditions for agriculture—and having already done so since their communities' founding days—they were working to promote the Zionist project while supporting those simple Arab workers who "took the high road to the Jewish colony," as Moshe Smilansky put it in 1939, and had little to do with elite politics.[21]

By the mandate period, the moshavot had become the iconic symbols (though not the sole employers) of "Arab labor" within the Yishuv and were the target of ongoing efforts by Jewish activists to get veteran landowners to replace those workers with Jews. But while "Hebrew Labor" gained traction as a shared Zionist value and informed labor practices in newer private colonies, older coastal moshavot, particularly those in citrus growing, failed to overhaul their hiring in practice.[22] As additional sites of "Arab labor" in Jewish-run enterprises have garnered academic attention, scholars have complicated what the sociologist Shmuel Noah Eisenstadt first called the "dual society" paradigm, which effectively implied that the only sphere of Jewish-Arab interaction was the sphere of political conflict.[23]

"Arab Labor"

The Mediterranean coastal plain region had been relatively sparsely populated in the early nineteenth century but became denser around mid-century, one to two generations before the beginnings of rural Jewish settlement, as peasants from the more populated highlands were drawn to villages on the coastal plain amidst improved security conditions and the growth of Arab-controlled commercial export agriculture. Jewish settlers did not purchase or settle on vacant land. Rather, Gershon Shafir writes, "the same processes which made Jewish settlement possible also strengthened the forces which stood to impede and oppose it." These preexisting populations also provided the first colonies a ready workforce.[24] Citrus, the most important export crop, was especially labor intensive and Jewish colonies continued to hire native workers, even as Jewish immigrant numbers increased, primarily out of simple capitalist logic: it was more flexible, more abundant, and commanded

FIGURE 5. Workers in the citrus groves of Rehovot, 1900 (courtesy of the KKL-JNF Photo Archive).

a lower wage. This logic also reflected and reinforced a racialized hierarchy that saw Arab Muslim peasants as docile and accustomed to the demands of unskilled agricultural labor.

Jewish workers from the Middle East also became part of the emerging hierarchies. Jews from Yemen had come to Palestine starting in 1881 due to religious affinities and then chain migration, and mostly settled in Jerusalem. A second wave in 1908, however, found its way to the colonies, particularly to Rishon LeZion, which had previously hired members of the Jerusalem community to work seasonally in its winery. Labor Zionists and the Palestine Office seized on Yemenites of a group as potential Jewish workers who could be paid an "Arab" wage.[25] In practice, however, Yemenite Jews aspired to be owners of their own lands rather than menial workers. They appealed to colony committees to this end, Bat-Zion Eraqi Klorman shows, but to no effect: the local elites did not consider them for anything other than manual labor and they did not become owners of private lands in their own right.[26] Tensions between Ashkenazi employers and Yemenite workers boiled over in 1913 when Yohanan Makoff, of one of Rehovot's founding families, beat three Yemenite Jewish women who were gathering branches from his land. When they tried to escape, he sent Arab workers after them to tie them to a donkey and drag them around the colony. The event caused an uproar in Ashkenazi Labor Zionist circles, amid calls to protect Yemenites from cruel owners.[27] Such moments of Jewish worker solidarity, however, obscure the tensions that arose due to the fact that Yemenite Jews garnered higher wages for unskilled labor than Palestinian Muslim Arabs but lower wages than Ashkenazim, and thus were more likely to displace Ashkenazi Jews than non-Jewish Arabs.[28]

The premise that immigrant Ashkenazi Jews and rural Arabs had once gotten along in Palestine thanks to settlers' paternalistic benevolence and local cultural knowledge, requires, like all collective memory, a selective reading of the past. Ahad Ha-'Am warned that the freedom wrought by colonization—"boundless freedom, wild freedom, that one can find only in a land like Turkey [the Ottoman Empire]"—leads to despotism, "as always happens when a slave comes to rule." The Palestine Jewish colonist, one might say in paraphrase, was liberated from subjugation but also feralized by the process of colonization. How, Ha-'Am asked, could colonists maintain that liberation without "raising the ire of the natives through disreputable acts"?[29]

Having witnessed instances of denigration and abuse, the most ardent promoters of Hebrew Labor saw in the moshavot an intrinsic system of exploitation rooted in a dependence on philanthropy and an absence of appropriate nationalist sentiment. They feared that this system of interethnic labor exploitation would endanger the security of the Yishuv as a whole, both by not providing work for Jewish immigrants and by encouraging Arab resistance. They thus proposed economic separation, primarily to ensure work for poor Jewish immigrants but also, as they saw it, to assure the security of settlements, eliminate labor exploitation from the Zionist program, and win back Arab support for the Jewish settlement project. At most, however, labor activism oriented toward Jewish needs succeeded in splitting the labor market and monopolizing skilled jobs, but never "conquering" the market. As such, unskilled Jewish workers continued to suffer from unemployment.[30]

Nonetheless, instances of Palestinian attacks on colonies that used non-Jewish guards seemed to affirm the Labor Zionist theory of class resentment. In 1910, *ha-Poʻel ha-tzaʻir* reported on an attack by Qalqilya-area villagers on the moshava of Kfar Saba, whose land had been purchased in 1898 adjacent to the similarly named Arab village (Kafr Saba). The villagers, it said, were avenging the killing of an Arab worker from Qalqilya by a farmer from Petah Tikva. They left in their wake "broken windows, broken dishes on the floor. Also, feathers in the air. Only small numbers of belongings were left unbroken. The appearance of the house was like after a pogrom." The Qalqilya man's murder and consequent retribution, the journalist stridently wrote, was wholly attributable to the inappropriate labor practices of Petah Tikva. The Jewish farmer, he said, "wanted to save a few cents [*bishlikim*]" so he hired an Afghani guard instead of a Jewish one. Thieves came, but the Afghani guard didn't intervene, "whether because he was asleep or because he didn't see." When one of the thieves tried to steal the guard's gun, the guard shot the thief. The circumstances of the incident and the identities of the particular protagonists mattered less to the writer than its implications for this model of colony guarding. "If many in the moshava had boasted that their *jedaʻ* [Arabic, "strongman"], the head of their guards [Avraham Shapira], with the help of his Arab and Bedouin [hired] guards, would show his strength to the Arabs of Qalqilya," now his whole model had been proven wrong: "Here, now, one can see all that is bad in the Petah Tikva style of guarding."[31]

Ha-Shomer, the Jewish self-defense organization founded in 1909 and associated with a small cohort of ideological Labor Zionists, prided itself on a new model of Jewish-only guarding combined with Arabic knowledge. In her retrospective essay about her role in the formation of ha-Shomer, Manya (Vilbushevitz) Shochat asked rhetorically, "how would a small group of Jews live among masses of Arabs, educated in the tradition of the desert, the rifle, and the knife, whose ethics are totally different from ours?" Her answer to this classically Orientalist conundrum was rooted in labor separation and cultural competency: the guard program pushed Jews "to learn the Arabic language and the customs and concepts of the Arabs, because for the project to succeed it was necessary to create neighborly relations based on mutual respect and in accordance with the people's psychology and its traditions."[32] Promoting coexistence though labor separation and education, not hierarchical employer-employee contact, became the hallmark of Labor Zionist ideology.

Farmers' Perspectives

As Jewish labor activists emphasized the exploitative nature of colony agriculture while lobbying farmers to discriminate in favor of Jews, farmers began to construct and emphasize narratives of hierarchical coexistence. Avraham Shapira reportedly was asked to consult with the founders of ha-Shomer on methods of engaging with the Arab population, given his recognized "expertise" on the matter, despite the fact that his ideology regarding labor differed from theirs. But when ha-Shomer asked him to employ only Jewish guards from their organization, he refused, saying that this step would harm Jewish-Arab relations.[33] The Labor Zionist axiomatic linkage between economic separation and security obscures an inverse discourse among First Aliyah descendants and private farmers. The latter held that they—and not Labor Zionists—had created Jewish-Arab harmony through job creation on Jewish-owned land, while also providing employment for Jewish immigrants.

The discourse we can observe among farmers and their representatives was not a full-throated defense of Arab labor. Some did voice concerns in the early days of settlement that Arab workers would negatively influence Jewish children, report Jewish building activity to the Ottoman authorities, or bring out bad qualities in landowners. Over time and under increasing pressure, many paid lip service to the importance of Hebrew Labor. Economic dependence on and contact with Arab labor, however, had also produced and continued to produce proximity and human contact. The agricultural colonies that were growing commodities for export turned to local Arabs to supply them foodstuffs, often sold by local women, for their own consumption.[34] Though native labor provided seasonal flexibility to employers, who could hire on a temporary basis because they felt no concern for the workers' year-round livelihood, farmers also had long-term relationships with Arab workers who came from nearby villages or lived seasonally near the colonies to support a growing export market. In 1889, a colonist in Rishon LeZion noted that forty Jewish settlers were surrounded by four hundred Arabs:

> The Arab village of Sarafand [al-Kharab] which stands to the south of [Rishon LeZion] used to be a complete ruin . . . Now it has become a big expan-

sive village, because many families who had deserted the village have settled in it [again], since [now] there is work for all of them . . . and for their wives, sons, and daughters.[35]

Some such workers were able to lease back land that they had previously worked under Arab landowners and continue to labor as tenant farmers. Owners saw these as stable relationships and often trusted Arabs to do security detail for the colony. As Yaacov Roi has shown, workers did field labor for Jews, harvested grapes and oranges, and transported Jewish produce to market. Guards and wagon drivers worked on fixed, often long-term contracts while others were day laborers: each morning in Rehovot, a workers' market would take place where the landowners would choose workers for the day.[36] In contrast, Jewish workers' relationships with their employers were increasingly made fraught by some workers' commitment to ideals of Hebrew Labor.[37]

By the 1920s and 1930s, farmers, facing ongoing pressure from Labor Zionists, began to express at least rhetorical support for the principle of hiring Jewish labor, but they continued to hire Arab workers well into the 1930s. British reports from 1932 indicate that male "European" (i.e. Jewish) orange pickers commanded a wage of 200 mils (1 mil being 1/1,000th of a pound), while an "Asiatic" (i.e. Arab, but also Yemenite Jewish) laborer doing the same job would earn 80–100 mils. This 2:1 ratio also obtained for "ploughing, reaping, threshing, harvesting," while fruit picking (olives, grapes) saw a 3:1 wage ratio. The wage spreads in the realms of construction and crafts were smaller, closer to 3:2 or 4:3.[38] Though the Farmers' Federation and most of its members spoke to the nationalist value of hiring Hebrew workers, they tended to advocate for a "mixed" (that is, Arab and Jewish) labor force. A 1935 Labor Zionist report on Hadera labor practices, during this period of booming citrus exports, suggested that 88% of the workers hired by farmers on the local council were Arabs. It commented on the "long columns of Haderan Arab women streaming in to weed farmers' fields" while Jewish women sat without work.[39] Though the overall ratio of Arab to Jewish workers declined over the course of the mandate, with a sharp drop during the 1936–1939 Arab revolt, the expansion of the Jewish economy meant that the proportion of Arab workers employed in the Jewish economy as a percentage of all Arab workers increased through the mid-1930s.[40] In the late 1920s and early 1930s, the "vast majority" of Arab villages in the Jaffa region were connected in one way or another to the citrus industry, whether as workers, suppliers, or managers. Urban Arab notables and businessmen, who controlled a vibrant Arabic press, saw the citrus growers of Petah Tikva or Hadera during the mandate as economic competitors to their own export operations. They rarely mentioned the nature of the Jewish farmers' labor arrangements which were, after all, similar to their own.[41] Moshava leaders and veteran residents, seeking to carve out a place for a moderate Zionism based on private agriculture, narrated a story of hierarchical coexistence enabled by settlers' personal virtue and economic wisdom that continued in the present, despite changing circumstances.

Yitzhak Epstein's 1907 essay, "The Hidden Question," might be seen as one origin point for the discourse of hierarchical coexistence. Epstein was one of the first early Zionist writers to reflect on the ethical and national problem of dispossessing Arabs in the course of European Jewish immigration and land settlement.[42] Some readers, therefore, regard him as a harbinger of an ethical critique that would later develop within bi-nationalist groups like Brit Shalom.[43] But it's more appropriate to see Epstein's utopian vision of Jewish-Arab coexistence, which the historian Yosef Gorny calls "integrationist" and "altruistic,"[44] as an early voice in a capitalist coexistence discourse premised on Jewish-Arab hierarchy.

Epstein, a Hebrew teacher who had immigrated to Palestine in 1886, warned that when Jewish colonists purchased land being worked by peasants, they left a festering wound in the peasants' hearts. He cautioned that even if workers seemed compliant "as long as the wages were good," they would protest later if they sensed that they were going to be removed from the land they held dear. Jewish colonists could mollify this protest, however, by committing to purchase only fallow lands and allowing peasants to remain on land that they had been working at the time of purchase, while instructing them in modern farming practices.[45]

Epstein celebrated the fact that "the situation of the [Arab] cities and villages near the colonies has been elevated" and specifically touted the fact that their population was employed in the colonies: "many craftsmen, stonemasons, builders, whitewashers, donkey and camel drivers, and thousands of workers find work in the colonies."[46] Moreover, his plan to purchase lands and allow peasants to stay, labor for the Jewish landowners, and be educated in modern farming practices explicitly ran counter to the emerging Labor ideology. For Epstein, however, both Jewish settlement and the hiring of low-wage Arab labor were justified so long as they were accompanied by modernizing and civilizing reforms. Agriculturalists who hired Arab labor and considered it wrongheaded to do otherwise would echo variants of this position in the decades that followed.

Palestinian observers, who began to articulate their own demands for self-determination, would not likely have accepted this arrangement over the long term. But some did note, in retrospect, their relative approval of the colony model as compared to the thoroughgoing displacement of Arab Palestinian labor by the Labor Zionist separation scheme.

As the historian Rashid Khalidi has written:

> The pragmatic and relatively unideological settlers of the first *aliya* (1882–1903) in effect came to treat the fellahin little differently than had their former Arab landlords. They disappropriated the fellahin but in most cases they did not fully dispossess them, as they integrated them into plantation-style colonies, characterized by a large number of Arab laborers and a few Jewish overseers. This uneasy, but at least temporarily manageable situation changed definitively with the second *aliya* starting early in the twentieth century.[47]

Private Jewish farmers both accepted and promoted this assessment, even as the holistic consequences of Jewish settlement for the Palestinian peasantry made what was once "manageable" increasingly intolerable.

In 1913, Moshe Smilansky, the Rehovot agriculturalist and farmer leader who wrote prolifically about the First Aliyah in both nonfiction and fictional works, was chastised by the Labor Zionist critic Yitzhak Vilkansky (later, Volkani), the manager of the Ben-Shemen training farm (est. 1907), one of the first settlements on Jewish National Fund land. Vilkansky charged moshava farmers with both exploiting Arabs and failing to learn from them. Smilansky, however, replied that Vilkansky was "breaking down open doors." Learning from Arabs was not a Labor Zionist innovation. Quite the contrary: "the sons of the moshavot sensed this naturally and learned from the Arabs." Collaboration was intuitive, and ultimately mutually beneficial, he said. Jews took the nail plow (a simple, commonly used plow in Palestine) and improved it, "and now the Arabs are buying the improved plow from us." Arabs and Jews traded expertise about olives and vegetables. Those contacts, established because of pragmatic economic choices, had led farmers to insights and positive interactions that newcomer workers later claimed to have invented. Though Smilansky admitted that the Rothschild administration had made errors in their agricultural policy, he argued that private initiative remained at the heart of the moshava enterprise and was its essence, even in colonies that received part of their land or capital from philanthropic sources.[48]

Menashe Meirovitch of Rishon LeZion also spoke about the mutual benefit he believed derived from hiring Arab workers. Writing in 1914 in the Jerusalem newspaper *ha-Herut*, he contended that the Laborites' methods of advocating for "Hebrew Labor" would be dangerous to relations between settlers and peasants. Not only was hiring Arab workers necessary from a practical standpoint, since "there is work that can't be done by Hebrew workers," it was an appropriate strategic move. While "most of the workers should be Jews . . . we should be forbidden from removing our neighbors, citizens of the country, among whom we live, from this work."[49] Zionists claiming to be nonexploitative, he implied, were in fact complicit in the displacement of and resulting violence from Arab workers.

Moshava landowners also suggested that the ongoing relationships with Arab workers and guards could help rather than harm the colonies' security. In October 1909, the Jerusalem newspaper *ha-Zvi* (*The Gazelle*) published a special article from Petah Tikva that lauded the fact that twelve Jews ('*Ivrimz*) had accepted jobs as guards in the orchards and critiqued Avraham Shapira, the current head guardsman, for refusing to institute Jewish-only guarding. The hiring of the new Jewish guards inspired the writer, under the pseudonym "ha-Tziyoni" (The Zionist), to extol the virtues of Hebrew guarding and the inherent weakness of a mixed force.[50]

But replying in *ha-Herut* a few weeks later to defend Shapira, a writer calling himself "Dover Emet" (Truthteller) countered that security in the colony was excellent thanks in large part to Shapira. Shapira, he insisted, had investigated the theft of a horse and cow, captured an Arab perpetrator, interrogated him, and gotten payment for the stolen goods. "The acts and bravery he showed then are known to everyone." The people who "scorn a man when they should thank him for all his great acts that he did for the moshava" did not understand that Shapira's decades-old relationships with local Arabs helped him assure the security of the colony.[51]

Indeed, Gur Alroey has found that colony farmers often felt that the new regime of "Hebrew guarding" being promoted by ha-Shomer hurt rather than helped their relations with nearby Arab peasants. Their accounts contradict the self-congratulatory, ex post facto testimonies that comprise most of the recorded "history" of that Labor-affiliated guard organization. The landowner accounts tell a story of young ha-Shomer men eager to abuse Arab workers and guards and stir up trouble. Sami (Shmuel) Tolkowsky from Rehovot even wrote a letter to the colony committee claiming that one ha-Shomer guard regularly beat Arabs and imposed roadblocks to monitor their movement. Tolkowsky, an agronomist whose family was in the Antwerp diamond trade, considered this behavior tantamount to "crimes against humanity" [*pesha'im hamurim neged ha-enoshut*] and worried that this behavior would ultimately harm the moshava and lead to conflict. Tolkowsky's critique of ha-Shomer joined a broader pre-World War I pattern of farmers praising their own (relatively) better relations with local Arabs in polemics with early Labor Zionist critics. Tolkowsky would go on to serve as a partner in the Pardess citrus syndicate and as the chair of the Jaffa Fruit Company.[52]

Eitan Belkind, a nephew of the Bilu member and Gedera founder Israel Belkind and son of the Rishon LeZion founder Shimshon Belkind, later echoed this assessment in his 1972 history of Rishon LeZion, where he framed the early settlement past as an era before conflict: "In the period of Turkish rule, there were no violent incidents [*me'ora'ot*] between Jews and Muslims." He blames not only "Arab incitement" for the later deterioration but also ha-Shomer, which "communicated with . . . non-Jewish workers with force [*be-yad hazakah*]." Crude physical force had replaced understanding as the primary mode of Jewish engagement with Arabs, he suggested: they didn't know Arabic or the customs of the *fellahin* (peasants, Arabic), said Belkind, and "the result was the arousal of hatred toward the Jewish settlers [*mitnahalim*]."[53]

The farmers thus anticipated a line of reasoning that continued to unfold following the 1917 Balfour Declaration, the British conquest, and the British assumption of the Mandate for Palestine in 1923. The process of separating the Jewish economy from the Arab one would not lead to two independent, class-conscious working populations; it would create an economy and society of Jews that was increasingly built on and despite the unemployment and thwarted aspirations of Arab Palestinians whom Zionists neither knew nor understood. Even in these early exchanges we can identify a contending if inchoate capitalist coexistence rhetoric that assumed that Jews and Arabs would necessarily be intertwined in Palestine, that hierarchical relations between employers and employees were not ipso facto a bad thing, and that attempts to unduly interfere in the market for reasons of ideology were ultimately bad for Jews and bad for the country as a whole.

The discourse of hierarchical coexistence, initiated before the war to defend the labor status quo in the moshavot, later became a way both to defend the continued use of Arab labor and to narrate the moshava as having "always" been peaceful. In his December 1929 testimony to the Shaw Commission of Inquiry, convened after the riots and reprisals that had spread around the country earlier that year, Shapira emphasized his own role in local coexistence. By this point, Shapira had been in Petah Tikva for nearly a half century. Lord Erleigh, council for the Jews before the commission, asked Shapira to clarify the colony's practices of hiring Arab workers. He replied that six hundred Arabs worked in citrus and were "permanently resident in the orange groves." The week preceding the outbreak of violence, he acknowledged, many of the workers' family members had left, followed by the workers themselves, but he insisted that political upheavals did not generally affect the good relations in the colony. "It is a most uncommon practice for them to leave the place," he noted, saying that this happens "only in abnormal conditions." Moreover, Shapira confirmed that even after the outbreak of the disturbances, he had gone with two others to al-Yahudiyya, the nearby Arab village. "Is it a village with which you yourself have always had friendly relations?" Lord Erleigh asked. Yes, Shapira replied, "always friendly relations except in 1921." He went on to explain that after leading the charge against an attack on Petah Tikva that year, he had helped mediate peace agreements (*sulhas*) with the villages. He asserted that since March 1922, "we have been living in perfect amity and peace with them." "I hope nobody will succeed in disturbing the peace," he added.[54]

So positive were Shapira's relations with al-Yahudiyya, he claimed, that he had learned of the disturbances in Jaffa while socializing there. "When I was sitting there drinking coffee and smoking the narghileh as is the Arab custom, I saw a car coming from Jaffa, three gentlemen were in the car, two of whom I knew." A crowd of four to five thousand people gathered around the car as they learned from Khalil Bayud of Kafr Amr (probably Kafr 'Ana) and Hussein Abd Ulal of Sayket [probably Saqiya], "that troubles had broken out in Jaffa and Moslem blood was being sacrificed." But when asked whether they indeed responded to this call and went to Jaffa, Shapira replied, no.

The commission spent a few minutes trying to determine the cause of the relative harmony. Was it indeed the local peace agreements, or was it the Collective Punishment Ordinances imposed by the British in 1921? Shapira acknowledged that punishing offenders was appropriate, but he insisted that it was the personal relations that made the colony unique. These relations were not just between villages, they were between employers and workers. "We have never had any trouble with Arab labour ourselves," he said, and while he denied that he "prefer[red] to employ Arab labour to Jewish labour," he stressed that he refused to abide by the Labor Zionist principle of hiring Jews in place of Arabs: "I will not agree to a workman being replaced by another." This arrangement, he stressed, could occur because the colony was "not under Zionist control," that is, the control of Zionist institutions, but rather was a privately held economic operation where "everyone is his own landlord."[55]

In his own testimony to the Shaw Commission, the former mayor of Nablus, Hajj Tawfiq Hammad, reflected this perception of relative (though not outright) approval of the "First Aliyah" colonies. He noted that

> in the early days, the Jew who came worked on his land and employed Arab labour. Since immigration commenced in larger numbers these Jewish employers have turned away the Arab labourers and have employed Jews in their place thereby throwing out of work a large number of Arabs. . . . I understand that the Zionist policy is to dispose of the Arabs in every possible way and to replace them with Jews."[56]

While Shapira and other veteran colonists did continue hiring Arab workers,

Hammad's assessment of the general trend was accurate. Some farmers in newer colonies in the Sharon region, including Raanana (est. 1922) and Magdiel (est. 1924, later part of Hod HaSharon), expressed dedication to the Hebrew Labor ideal.[57] In 1934, a Farmers' Federation faction that was supportive of 100% Jewish labor broke away to form a new organization of "nationalist farmers." The Labor Zionists, meanwhile, had warmed to the idea that, as Ben-Gurion wrote in 1933, "private capital serves the Zionist cause if it functions as an instrument for Hebrew labor."[58] Until the mid-1930s, however, the private farmers who were most active in commemorating the "First Aliyah" echoed Shapira's assertion that a wholesale rejection of Arab workers would be inappropriate. Moshe Smilansky, the most prominent advocate of this position, called a Hebrew Labor policy akin to a boycott and stated that unless Jewish farmers wanted to prompt a retaliatory boycott against themselves, farmers were obligated to hire some Arabs: "We live among them and we neither want nor are able to erect a Chinese wall between us."[59]

By the mid-1930s, however, Arab opposition to the now rapidly increasing Jewish immigration had become more organized and, in 1936, sparked what would become known as the Arab Revolt, which commenced with an Arab boycott of Jewish businesses and continued with a broader popular uprising against British and Zionist infrastructure and Jewish settlers. In response, the British cracked down hard, deported many of the revolt's organizers, and convened a further commission, led by Lord William Peel. The commission proposed a partition for Palestine that, though never adopted, paved the way for the better-known 1947 United Nations partition plan. Partition plans reflected the theory that ethnic mixing inherently created ethnic conflict. Labor Zionists promoted a variant of this theory on the level of labor policy and supported both partition plans, at least provisionally.[60]

In 1936, Gershon Shafir has shown, five Zionist opponents of partition offered a model of capitalist bi-nationalism based on the ethnic labor hierarchy that still characterized the moshavot and parts of the industrial sector. One of these opponents was Moshe Smilansky, representing the Farmers' Federation. The others were Moshe Novemeysky, head of Palestine Potash, whose charter stipulated 50% Arab workers; Pinhas Rutenberg, who employed Arab workers at the power stations of the Palestine Electric Company and insisted on the apolitical nature of this Jewish-run enterprise in the face of Arab protests; Gad Frumkin, a judge born into the community of religious Jerusalemite Jews that had also spawned Petah Tikva; and Judah Magnes, the American-born chancellor of the Hebrew University, who supported binationalism from a stance of Jewish ethics. These men represented distinct lineages that converged around the discourse of hierarchical coexistence.

Their resulting plan, finalized on May 31, 1936, began by stating that "the classic Zionist approach of promising indirect economic benefits and concessions lost its effectiveness with the rise of Arab nationalism."[61] The only solution, they thought, was offering direct benefits through employment. Their multipronged plan included encouraging the immigration of Jewish capitalists while limiting general Jewish immigration, restricting Arab sales of land to Jews, helping Arabs develop the remainder of their land, and, most pertinently, committing to hire Arabs in the Jewish economy. As Shafir writes, they believed that "Two national communities cannot be connected solely at their political apex; socioeconomic integration has to be part of their members' everyday lives."[62] The report, though never adopted at any level of the Zionist administration or the Yishuv, offers an explicit vision of hierarchical coexistence. The Farmers' Federation ultimately accepted the Peel partition plan out of a belief that political compromise was no longer possible, but did not abandon the principle that "the basis for cooperation is economic, not political."[63]

Hierarchical Friendship

Rising Jewish immigration numbers and the Arab boycott of 1936, the opening stage of the 1936–1939 Arab Revolt, made it easier for Jewish employers to turn to a more fully Jewish labor force. It was at this time, however, that moshava founders and commemorators particularly idealized past relations between owners and workers and recalled specific personal relationships that gave color to more abstract claims of hierarchical coexistence as a distinct feature of the First Aliyah colonies.

Scholars have emphasized the tendency of employers across diverse spaces, time periods, and economic settings to idealize their relationships with hired labor and deploy a rhetoric of friendship that obscures realities of economic hierarchy. Friendship has been conceptualized in the West as occurring in a "disinterested" space separate from the "interested" sphere of the market. "We can understand ideal friendship," the literary scholar Ivy Schweitzer writes in her study of the concept since ancient times, "as a deep-seated *fantasy* of similitude, even merging, and a desire for a realm free from the commercial relations of exchange."[64]

The fantasy persists across cultures. White housewives in 1970s Atlanta, the historian Premilla Nadasen records, created a Maids' Honor Day to celebrate largely black domestic workers whom they considered part of the family and to whom they felt connected by "an emotional bond, mutual obligations, and a relationship separate from the marketplace."[65] The *New York Times* critic Wesley Morris discusses a particular twentieth-century American narrative of interracial friendship generated by a white person's employment of a black person. This economic arrangement, he argues, produces a "conditionally transactional" friendship, "possible only if it's mediated by money" and "entirely conscripted as service and bound by capitalism."[66] As Nadasen incisively writes, however, "employer claims to kinship were rarely genuine, and in any case were not reciprocal." The rhetoric of friendship and family obscured "what was in fact a market relationship."[67] Jewish agricultural colonists likewise instrumentalized individual economic relationships as evidence of hierarchical coexistence.

As Zionists butted heads over the increasingly intractable "Arab Question"—how to interpret and respond to evident Arab resistance to Zionist immigration and settlement—moshava leaders and veterans recalled specific past relations. In 1938, Yaakov Bendel, head of the Rosh Pinna colony committee since 1920 and a regular writer for the agriculturalist journal *Bustenai* and the General Zionist *ha-Boker*, wrote of a recent encounter with a longtime Arab acquaintance, Abu Hamdan, who had visited him at home. He described it in terms that illustrate both Bendel's nostalgic memory and the gap in perspective between the two men.[68]

After Bendel greeted Abu Hamdan with the Arabic *Ahlan wa-sahlan! Itfadal* (Welcome, please come in), Bendel writes, Abu Hamdan was soon relaxing in Bendel's one easy chair, "as is appropriate for an acquaintance and friend and in particular for a 'partner [*shutaf*]' of over 35 years." This was a true friendship, Bendel suggests, but he begins to explain that in fact the two were never partners: "we never engaged in business together or plowed together." Instead, "*Ya shariki*," my partner, was just a nickname Bendel had given to Abu Hamdan, who had come to Rosh Pinna from the Beqaa Valley (between Beirut and Damascus) around the turn of the century. Abu Hamdan lived with his own family in al-Wayziyya, just outside Rosh Pinna, and tended the flocks and did other work for Jewish farmers who had settled in the area. Bendel recalls the warm relationship between the two families: "my family would offer his children leftovers from our meal and slices of bread and sometimes clothing or a pair of worn-out shoes." Occasionally, Abu Hamdan would help himself to some of Bendel's property—eggs from his hens or, one night, tiles from his roof. But Bendel took this in jest, calling him "my partner" because he "shared" in his property. This relationship of a landowner and a poor Arab worker seemed to him to be one of friendship— years later they would meet when Abu Hamdan came through Rosh Pinna "remembering those good years when we were young and strong."

This time, however, Bendel felt a strain in the relationship. "I can see that you are self-absorbed and pensive," Bendel told his guest, "What are the thoughts that disturb you?" At first Abu Hamdan was elusive: "Time," he groaned. Bendel didn't understand: "Time? But what's the problem with time? As far as I know your situation is strong. You have flocks of sheep and cattle on your property, your children are like olive saplings around you, you have a noble horse and you've surely amassed enough to feed your family for the whole year." Bendel assumed that Abu Hamdan's only possible concerns could be personal and material. But times had changed, and Abu Hamdan was not satisfied with personal stability. Now, national concerns, of which Bendel feigned ignorance, troubled his friend. "It seems that you haven't paid attention," Abu Hamdan told his Jewish friend/employer, "to what's going on in *Filastin*." He made his meaning clear: he was stewing over bombings and murders in the streets "in the middle of the day": massive British reprisals against the Palestinian Arab community following the assassination, in late 1937, of the known Zionist sympathizer Lewis Y. Andrews, the British Commissioner for the Galilee. Bendel was still optimistic, but Abu Hamdan was unsure, "and he parted ways from me depressed and angry [*'agum u-merugaz*]."[69] Bendel was clearly nostalgic for his long-standing relationship with Abu Hamdan, one that had seemed to exist outside and beyond politics. He wanted their visits to continue to transcend conflict, even as the Arab

Revolt unfolded around them. But current events, which to Bendel took place wholly outside the men's flocks and coffee dates, had intervened. The column simply ends with Abu Hamdan's angry departure; Bendel doesn't reckon with it. Is he troubled by the insertion of politics, or does he simply continue to hope for more sessions of reminiscing about a period in which politics were somehow absent?

Jewish agricultural colonies hired Arab peasants not only as field laborers and guards but also in other service roles. Stories of these individuals' loyalty to their Jewish employers and willingness to defend them against hostile Arabs (often from rival family clans) are marshalled as further evidence of hierarchical coexistence. One such story pertained to the Aaronsohn family of Zichron Ya'aqov, several members of whom had founded the World War I-era Jewish espionage organization, Nili, which relayed Ottoman intelligence to the British.

From the perspective of the British, Aaron Aaronsohn was notable for his commitment to agriculture. "No man had greater faith in the possibilities of Palestine from an agricultural point of view," said the Zionist sympathizer Captain William Ormsby-Gore soon after Aaronsohn's death in a plane crash en route to the Paris Peace Conference.[70] The *Times of London*'s obituary called him "a strong broad-shouldered man of the best type of open-air Jew."[71] But moshava sources, while emphasizing these professional and personal talents, also cited the good relations he enjoyed with subservient Arab employees. His agricultural work, wrote his brother Alexander, "also provided a living to many Arabs, neighbors of Zichron Ya'aqov. Common needs created friendship between these Jews and Arabs, and not a single conflict disrupted the development of this little Jewish village surrounded by Arab villages. The good relationship of the simple Arab peasants to the first simple pioneers was to their credit."[72]

In 1939, twenty years after Aaron's death, the religious Zionist newspaper *ha-Tzofeh* celebrated him as "a son of generations of farmers" and thus a "son of the land": *ben ha-aretz*, a term also used at the time for native-born Sephardi and Oriental Jews. His native status seemed to be reflected in his connections both to the land and to local Arabs: "every evening, after his work in the vineyard, he would seat himself on a horse and take in the blue expanses. He'd absorb the view, the climate, he knew every hill and valley, every wadi and channel. He'd visit the Bedouin tents [*oholei kedar*] and make bonds of friendship with their residents. He'd learn the language of their customs and the sources of their livelihood."[73] Mastery of the landscape and elevation over it, along with personal relationships with Bedouins and command of their culture, cemented (or co-created) his "nativeness."

A year later, still in the midst of the Arab revolt, the General Zionist newspaper *ha-Boker* published an interview with Nasser Ghanem Abu Farid, a Christian Arab who had served as a personal guard for the Aaronsohns in Zichron Ya'aqov.[74] Abu Farid's interlocutor was Herzl Hayutman, whose father Yitzhak had been involved in founding both the far north Metulla colony (1896) and the city of Tel Aviv (1909). Fluent in Arabic, Hayutman conducted an interview with Abu Farid that highlights the latter's love for Aaron Aaronson and, by extension, the pre–World War I Zichron Ya'aqov colony as a whole.

Abu Farid, as Hayutman encountered him in 1939, was the picture of old age, with weakened legs and thick brows that covered his eyes. He was sitting in a chair typical of "the period before modern furniture appeared." Abu Farid had worked for both Meir Dizengoff, later the mayor of Tel Aviv, and Hayutman's father, Yitzhak, in Baron Rothschild's glass factory in the coastal village of Tantura, producing wine bottles for nearby Zichron Ya'aqov. Later, he was hired to manage Baron Rothschild's horse stables in Zichron Ya'aqov. There, he also became particularly friendly with Aaron, worked at his experimental agriculture station, managed his family's stables, and served as his personal wagon driver: "From then on I didn't budge from the Aaronsohns' house." An earlier conversation between Abu Farid and Aaronsohn, recalled by Abu Farid, highlights the unusual relationship between them, one that exemplifies the paradoxical but iconic combination of Jewish-Arab economic hierarchy and supposed friendship and equality. "Listen, Abu Farid," he said Aaronsohn once told him, "if I made a pita we'd have to split it equally. If we sat down to eat, you aren't my servant—we are equal. Even if you wait for me at the entrance to the inn holding the reins of the two horses and help me get on the horse once we get to Jerusalem, here while we are on the road, without foreigners around [*be-he'adar ha-zarim*], we are brothers [*anashim ahim anahnu*] and so we will be always."[75] Abu Farid—via Hayutman—uses the phrase "we are brothers" in evocation of the phrase Abraham uses to his nephew Lot in promising that there will be no conflict between them or between their servants (Genesis 13:8). Aaronsohn and Hayutman, then, seem to be promoting a specific kind of coexistence: the Arab is employed by the Jewish farmer, depends on him for his livelihood, and serves him. Nonetheless, the Jewish narrator characterizes them both as "natives" and as equals in an intimate and mutually respectful relationship. Abu Farid seems unbothered by the apparent contradiction; indeed, he seems grateful for the relationship and he may well have been. But we are reading Abu Farid through the translation and lens of Hayutman, son of the Metulla colony, for whom a hierarchical yet amicable Jewish-Arab relationship is part of a stock narrative about the Aaronsohns, Zichron Ya'aqov, and the First Aliyah colonies more generally.

Abu Farid, moreover, recalls warning the Aaronsohns about impending Arab attacks and trying to dissuade others from carrying them out. Hillel Cohen writes about Christian Arabs from the Mount Lebanon area whom Zionists encouraged to collaborate in such ways. This collaboration, Cohen argues, made sense to participants as a means of gaining leverage within local Palestinian conflicts. From the time that the Nili organization, founded by the Aaronsohns, came into being, Cohen writes, it drew on a robust network of "residents of the established moshavot," who "already had a comprehensive network of acquaintances among Arabs that allowed them to obtain considerable information."[76] These relationships, when recalled selectively and outside of their local social context, seemed to provide evidence that authentically good relations were an inherent outcome of the economic structure of the colonies.

As the mandate period wore on, colony farmers emphasized these positive hierarchical relations as a way of countering what they perceived as widespread neglect of moshava founders and leaders. The Union of Sons of the Yishuv, an organization of veteran Jews in Palestine that included both religious urbanites and moshava farmers, discussed marking the month of May 1944 in memory of Aaron's death twenty-five years earlier. "We have sinned an unforgiveable sin against our heroes and holy ones—and an even bigger sin against the fate of our nation, in adopting a conspiracy of silence around the glowing example of Aaron's activity," they wrote.[77] David Tidhar, head of the organization's commemorations committee, complained to the head of Tel Aviv's city education department, Dr. Eliyahu Rosenbaum, that "irresponsible organizations" were engaged in "distortion and the substitution of bad for good." In such a context, he felt, it was important "to present to the youth an example of supreme heroism."[78] As part of the commemorations, the organization would draft press releases, print large pictures and postcards of Aaron for display and distribution, offer prizes for the best student essays, and supply lecturers and educational materials to moshavot.[79] The Association of Vinegrowers (*Agudat ha-kormim*) wrote to Tidhar praising him for "fulfilling a sacred obligation" in promoting Aaronsohn's memory.[80]

Language Politics

These cases imply (and construct) close relationships between European Jewish colonists and Arab employees that were mediated by the colonists' knowledge of Arabic. In practice, "First Aliyah" Jewish agricultural colonists frequently knew only a little Arabic. When the American Yiddish writer Yehoash (Solomon Blumgarten) visited Palestine in 1914, he noted that most "know only sufficient Arabic to converse with their Arab *'Arbaji* (wagon-driver) or their Arab help. As to writing and reading Arabic, that is out of the question."[81] Various attempts had been made to teach Arabic in the colonies, including hiring a teacher in Rishon LeZion,[82] but new immigrants' knowledge of the language rarely improved. However, although Arabic knowledge was little more than a tool in employer-employee relations, the specific ability to converse with a wagon driver—a hired employee within a hierarchical relationship—was precisely the quality that Hayutman marshaled as evidence of close contact in his conversation with Abu Farid. Indeed, the limited Arabic abilities of Jewish riders in Arab-driven wagons at least exceeded those of the Zionist settlers who eschewed Arab wagon drivers altogether, even if the latter claimed to be doing so out of a desire to "escape the colonial settlement structure" and replace it with "social justice, brotherly love, and hope for peace."[83]

Labor Zionist organizations, when they promoted Arabic knowledge, did so from a place of labor separation. Mapai, David Ben-Gurion's party, founded in 1930, made its own efforts to encourage Arabic study within the Labor stream of the educational system. The Histadrut (General Federation of Labor) opened an Arab Department that same year. The Marxist-Zionist organization ha-Shomer ha-Tzaʻir, which supported binationalism in Palestine until 1947 and became part of the leftist Zionist party Mapam after 1948, created an Arab Department in 1940 to formalize the study of Arabic and Arab history and customs and to promote encounters between members of its kibbutzim and residents of nearby villages.[84] Members of the Zionist left, both Marxist and non-Marxist, branded themselves as the vanguard of outreach to and coexistence with Arabs, as against both the landowners, whom they believed to have exploited Arab workers, and the Revisionist right, who considered such outreach largely pointless and employed Arabic primarily for the purpose of intelligence gathering.[85]

Groups on the Zionist left sometimes acknowledged the tension at the heart of their endeavor: the act of striving for ideological closeness from a position of economic separation would render Arabic knowledge among Jews even weaker than before. In a 1942 memo to Moshe Shertok (Sharett), head of the political department of the Jewish Agency and later the second prime minister of Israel, Miriam Glickson, the deputy head of the Arab Bureau, commented that

> Today there is a lack of direct contact between Jews and Arabs such as existed in the first settlements [the First Aliyah colonies]. Then there were Arabs in every house and community and every resident knew how to conduct a conversation with them. But today the settlements are separate, most of their residents don't know Arabic at all and the work of spreading the language is only beginning.[86]

Though Glickson appears to be bemoaning the loss of Jewish-Arab contact that had supposedly occurred in the early Jewish agricultural colonies, she finds solace in efforts to replace it with structured language study opportunities.

While Yehoash critiqued colonists' Arabic usage for its instrumentality, others had expressed concern before World War I that excessive contact with Arabic in fact reflected the colonists' insufficient commitment to the Jewish nationalist cause. In 1908, the Jerusalem intellectual Josef Klausner (later to become a noted Revisionist) accused the moshavot of cultural corruption. While Labor Zionists had excessively adopted Arab cultural forms such as Arab clothing, horse-riding, guns, and abayas, he thought, the moshavot were especially compromised because they were filled with Arab workers and tenant farmers and maintained, at least colloquially, the Arabic names of the villages where they had purchased their land. Names like Qatara, Qastina, and Wadi Hanin [Hunayn], he wrote, "are victorious over the Hebrew names" of Gedera, Beer Tuvia, and Nahalat Reuven [Ness Ziona]. "So long as moshavot have Arabic names," he feared, "the name will always be a reminder that this is Arab land on which Jews are foreign."[87] Whereas in the case of nineteenth-century New England settler memory (and later in the Israeli state), native names reflected a "last" remnant of a people perceived to have been fully vanquished, in Palestine before 1948 they marked a landscape where Jewish settlers remained foreign and where daily contact with a majority, Arabic-speaking population persisted.[88] Later, a *chizbat*, a satirical anecdote from Labor Zionist culture "that is always a little bit true," pilloried a farmer from the northern Metulla colony for the persistence of such relations.[89] When the farmer is addressed in Hebrew, he turns to his Arab worker and asks in Yiddish "*Muhammad, vos zogt er?*" [Muhammad, what is he saying?][90] The joke, typically laconic, neatly encapsulates the stereotypical First Aliyah type in the minds of young interwar Labor elites: the farmer has Arab workers, having not taken upon himself the Labor Zionist imperative of hiring only Jewish ones. Moreover, he is a speaker of Yiddish, the principal linguistic symbol of the European diaspora and the Ashkenazi religious community of Palestine. Therefore, he relies on an Arab worker who assists him not only with labor but, ironically, with the Hebrew language itself, which the worker, apparently also a Yiddish speaker, understands better than his employer does.

Limited as the farmers' Arabic proficiency may have been, they became defined by their proximity to Arab workers, not only among their detractors but also in their own collective memory. As Labor Zionist organizations claimed to be promoting coexistence, the farmers presented themselves, however ineffectively, as people who created real (hierarchical) coexistence. Decades after Epstein had called for establishing a "covenant of peace" through "a proper understanding of the Arab nation, its characteristics, inclinations, hopes, language, and literature,"[91] Zerubavel Haviv (1894–1987), son of the early Rishon LeZion colony settler Dov Lubman-Haviv, called on fellow Zionists to renew their commitment to Arabic language instruction at the grade-school level. "Knowledge of the language of our neighbors is an elementary obligation," he wrote in the General Zionist *ha-Boker* in 1946, "and shared lives will not be possible in this land and in the vicinity without a common language." Haviv, a member of the conservative wing of the General Zionists that was also home to other Farmers' Federation affiliates, felt that Labor Zionists had systematically overlooked the achievements of their non-Laborite predecessors. Why, he mused, did later arrivals "never [stop to] wonder about the acts of the First Ones [*ma'asei rishonim*] and think that the entire Hebrew Yishuv was founded upon their own arrival?" They were forgetting a story of coexistence, he thought: "We should not forget that the first immigrants who came from the West to lay claim in the land of our fathers wandered its length and breadth and were received with love and friendship by the Arab residents of the land." With a claim to farmer apoliticism and a swipe at the deliberate, institutionalized politicking of Labor Zionism, he noted: "This was possible before the politics and before there was hatred between the peoples."[92]

This discourse on harmony between Ashkenazi Jewish settlers and rural peasants has intriguing similarities with a distinct but chronologically parallel phenomenon: calls for coexistence from Arabic-speaking Sephardi and Oriental Jews in Palestine. During the mandate period, Abigail Jacobson and Moshe Naor have shown, Jewish intellectuals from the Levant, Iraq, and North Africa formed political and cultural organizations in Palestine to promote a specifically Middle Eastern Zionism, one that they believed needed to be rooted in the organic connection among Jews, Christians, and Muslims who shared a knowledge of Arabic as well as Ottoman and post-Ottoman identities.[93] Like the Ashkenazi private colonists, Sephardi organizations tended to accept ethnically based labor hierarchies, operate outside the realm of Labor politics, and reject its associated Hebrew Labor program. "To say that one did not want Arab workers was in contradiction to wanting to bring [Jews and Arabs] closer together," the Sephardi Zionist activist Avraham Elmaleh (Elmaliach) remembered in a 1964 interview.[94] In the wake of the outbreak of the Arab Revolt in 1936, Sephardim active in the Pioneers of the East organization founded the Liberal Party (distinct from the party of the same name founded in 1961) to promote cultural, social, and economic contacts between Jews and Arabs and represent Sephardic Jews before the Peel

Commission.[95] While the Sephardi and Oriental Zionists' discourses about shared language and culture were distinctive to them, these communities' economic visions resembled those promoted by private Ashkenazi farmers in that they assumed a mixed labor economy, they were comfortable with hierarchical coexistence with rural Palestinians, and they, too, were accused by Labor Zionists of being "narrow-minded."[96] Members of the two groups both populated the capitalist-oriented General Zionist party and identified socialist or social democratic politics as "political" or "ideological" but, like conservative politicians elsewhere, saw their own endeavors as apolitical or non-ideological.[97] Moreover, both groups saw the late Ottoman era as a time of pre-political intra-religious coexistence and themselves as representatives of that exemplary past, albeit for different reasons and with a focus on different geographies (urban in the former case, rural in the latter). As Avraham Elmaleh wrote in a report in conjunction with the Peel Commission visit:

> Prior to the war [World War I], when the problem of Zionism had not yet emerged on the agenda in its full force, there was peace in the land and no man spoke ill of his fellow or sought to harm him, and the two peoples lived together in an almost idyllic atmosphere . . . In this idyllic era, not only were there no riots or attacks against the Jews, but the Jew and Arab lived in complete harmony, and this harmony was particularly noticeable given the persecution and oppression that faced the Jews in the Western countries.[98]

While Elmaleh was alluding to urban relations between Arabs and Jews, he did not believe that the scattered Ashkenazi colonies of the prewar era constituted a significant exception to this rule. These constituencies, along with urban Ashkenazi owners of capital, would form an emerging, if inchoate and disparate, non-Labor Zionist middle-class interest group. Noting these points of contact, Jonathan Gribetz has advised "caution against imagining a clear divide between Ashkenazim and Sephardim."[99] These Sephardi Jews wanted coexistence, Gribetz allows, but "it is important to recognize the terms on which this coexistence and cooperation were meant to be based": terms that meshed far better with the Zionist center and right than its left flank. Vladimir Jabotinsky would remark in 1928 on Sephardi and Oriental Jews' support for his Revisionist movement. Over time their children were more likely to join the Irgun militia than the Labor-aligned Haganah.[100]

These alliances and commonalities challenge assumptions that Ashkenazim who arrived in "numbered Aliyot" shared little with the Sephardi and Oriental Jews (or, for that matter, Ashkenazi Jews) who had lived in Palestine's existing urban centers. This assumption elides all European Jewish agricultural settlement into the orthodoxies associated with the Second Aliyah, understanding Sephardi and Ashkenazi communities as ipso facto older than Ashkenazi settler ones and part of a deep, timeless traditional past. In practice, much of the late-Ottoman urban Yishuv, Ashkenazi and Sephardi alike, dated back only to the mid-nineteenth century. Those who arrived during both the "First Aliyah" and "Second Aliyah" periods prior to World War I, whether Ashkenazi, Sephardi, or Oriental, were far more likely to want to join existing urban communities than fledging rural settlements.[101] "First Aliyah" arrivals who did undertake rural settlement relied on existing urban Jewish communities for quotidian and communal needs. But by the time the British took control of Palestine and made these communities, along with Jewish immigrant arrivals, Palestinian citizens, both the urban Jewish elites and the colony founders saw themselves, like Muslim and Christian Arabs, as veteran or "native" residents of Palestine in relation to waves of Jewish newcomers.

The Union of Sons of the Yishuv, whose efforts to commemorate Aaron Aaronsohn and defend "General Zionist" education we noted earlier, also united veteran Jewish communities, both "Old Yishuv" and "First Aliyah," around their purported familiarity with Arabic and local culture. At the national convention of the organization in May 1942, speakers emphasized that only those who had been in the country for a long time, whether part of the "Old Yishuv" or the older, religious elements of the "New Yishuv," should try to resolve the ongoing Jewish-Arab conflict. "In solving the Jewish-Arab problem, people are getting involved who have been in the country for a short time and don't know the language of the Arabs, their customs, or their ways of life." Yet in the same meeting, Dr. Yaakov Mikhlin, a native of Jerusalem and the head of the organization's Tel Aviv executive, compared his organization with analogues across the Atlantic working to elevate "the fathers of the settlement project in America."[102] The "Sons of the Yishuv" claimed authority on the basis of their nativeness, which they understood to encompass both Sephardi/Oriental and Ashkenazi, "Old Yishuv" and "New

Yishuv," Zionist and non-Zionist settlers one generation earlier, and settlers ten generations earlier, all of whom could could be compared to a long-standing settler project across the ocean.

Ultimately, these communities were united by their sense of contact with Arabs and ability to speak and understand at least some Arabic (though their ability to read and write varied considerably). Avraham Shapira first migrated to Jerusalem from the Russian Pale of Settlement in 1880 with his family. His family was originally from the northern (Lithuanian) Pale, but his father Yitzhak Zvi had moved south to Ukraine to experiment with farming, as he later aspired to do in Palestine. As new arrivals in Jerusalem investigating possibilities for rural settlement, the Shapira family quickly became connected to Jerusalemite Ashkenazi families, who knew some colloquial Arabic, in an urban setting where "the walls of language and culture were low."[103] Reuven Rivlin (grandfather of the contemporary Israeli president of the same name and husband of Avraham Shapira's sister Ita) learned Arabic more seriously than most: he studied in an Islamic school for a year. His son Joseph Joel Rivlin would research Islamic Studies at the Hebrew University and translate the Qur'an into Hebrew.[104] Eliezer and Yehuda Raab, early residents of Petah Tikva who came from this modernist Jerusalemite community, had functional colloquial Arabic. A man who began his journey within the Jewish communities of urban Palestine could, paradoxically, deploy his city-acquired Arabic knowledge to present himself as a "strong" rural figure rhetorically differentiated from the "diaspora," the very diaspora that some would accuse Palestine's urban Jewish communities of perpetuating. At the same time, an urban familiarity with Arabic was not sufficient to prepare Jewish settlers for their rural encounters. Yehuda Raab, who preceded Shapira in Petah Tikva, recounted learning about "the ways of the Arabs" from two Oriental Jews he hired as guards in the colony: the Baghdadi Da'ud Abu Yusuf and a Jaffan of North African extraction, Ya'qub Zirmati. Both had gained familiarity with the Ottoman hinterland as animal traders.[105] Abu Yusuf and Zirmati serve an ambivalent role in narratives about early Ashkenazi Zionists learning Arabic and Bedouin customs. They become conduits for specifically rural local knowledge that could transform their Ashkenazi counterparts into competent, Arabic-speaking, local defenders, but they also reveal a basic lack of confidence in the Ashkenazi settlers' ability to effect this transformation. But in these Ashkenazi Zionist texts, these figures are instrumentalized and then elided within a narration of a European Jewish return to the land.

Shapira portrayed himself as someone who served the cause of Petah Tikva and the Yishuv as a whole through his self-made personal contacts with rural Arab Muslims. These contacts, however, had actually begun in Jerusalem. Shapira had begun to learn Arabic, he explained in his 1939 memoirs, after encountering in Jerusalem what he described as Jewish cowardice that "turned a person's simple walk on the earth into a source of danger and bravery [*sakanot u-gvurot*]." The young Jewish children in his religious school in Jerusalem seemed "pale and bloodless." Shapira claimed that, unlike the rest of them, he was not afraid to walk in the "streets of the Goyim [non-Jews]" or to cross the fields between the Old City's Jaffa gate and Nahalat Shiv'ah, the new neighborhood outside the city walls. He had been fantasizing about transcending stereotypes of Jewish weakness since his early childhood in Ukraine. While in synagogue on the holiday of Shavuot, he said, he had dreamt of "Vassily and Ivan fleeing from him just as he and his friends had to flee from them."[106] According to Shapira, his transformation into a latter-day, Semitic version of the stereotypically Russian "Vassily and Ivan" began after his family left Jerusalem and relocated to Jaffa, a step on the way to purchasing lands in Petah Tikva.

Language would be the linchpin of his acclimatization to Jaffa, where Jews had lived since the 1820s.[107] In 1887, Jaffan Jews, like those before them in Jerusalem, started founding neighborhoods outside the walls: first Neve Tzedek and then Neve Shalom (1890). The Shapira family, however, lived within the Old City walls. While Avraham Shapira noted the "few orchards" around Jaffa, he echoed widespread Orientalist tropes in recalling a "desert of sand" beyond an ancient city that was "even more of a wasteland than in Jerusalem."[108] Such descriptions of the Jaffa region as "a desert of sand" or a "wasteland," commonplaces reiterated in commemorations of Tel Aviv,[109] obscured the expansive orchards to the city's east and south that European visitors described as "delightful" and blooming with many kinds of fruit trees.[110] Jaffa's hinterland, the heart of Palestine's emerging Arab-led export economy, would also become the center of the Jewish citrus enterprise.

As he began the process of gaining the Arabic skills to confront that "wasteland," Shapira recalled, he understood only curses such as *"yil' an dinak"* (may your religion be cursed), *"Yahudi kafir"* (Jewish infidel), and *"Shekenazi hanazir"* (Ashkenazi pig). But Shapira had been primed by the insults of Ukrainian goyim like Vassily and Ivan, and he pressed on "so he could respond." Israel Bartal has noted that aspirations to become like the mythologized Ukrainian Cossacks motivated "Second Aliyah" ha-Shomer guardsmen as well.[111] "Through this exchange of 'compliments,'" Shapira recalled with typical bravado, he came to realize that he knew how to speak Arabic, and within a few months could "quarrel and play" with them without inhibitions. He, too, had anxieties about the transferability of that experience to the rural context. Upon arriving in Petah Tikva, he heard about the Oriental Jewish guards who had mentored Yehuda Raab, and "the desire burnt in his heart to be a hero like them." But Shapira wondered whether his early acts of bravery really counted. "Is this really heroism? Is that it? . . . And they told tales about [Da'ud] Abu Yusuf and Ya'qub Zirmati, certainly they managed to do things greater than he, and still it wasn't true heroism. So, he continued striving for it."[112] Arabic, which by all accounts Shapira came to speak and understand fluently, became central to retrospective narratives of his renowned ability to charm, impress, and intimidate Arabs in Palestine and farther afield.[113] The actual life experiences and contacts that granted him this familiarity, however, were often obscured in commemorative documents.

David Yellin, the child of a long-standing Jerusalemite family, also praised the Rishon LeZion agriculturalist Menashe Meirovitch for coupling Arabic use with paternalistic benevolence. In 1911–1912, Yellin knew, Meirovitch had published a column called "Peasant Letters" (*Rasa'il fallah*) in the Arabic newspaper *Filastin*, under the pseudonym "Abu Ibrahim." Yellin admired the way Meirovitch used these columns to share agricultural expertise with Palestinians:

> He didn't only preach to his [Jewish] brothers, but also to our Arab neighbors. We all remember his writings in the Arab press, which he signed as "the Palestinian peasant," in which he always talked about practical, useful matters and, along the way, proved to [Arab] others the good that we [Jews] are bringing to the land through our work.[114]

What Yellin didn't mention was that Meirovitch did not in fact write the articles in Arabic. As Shay Hazkani and Samuel Dolbee have pointed out, he did not know the literary Arabic in which the columns were written and, like most Jewish landowners, spoke little more than "a few colloquial phrases." He wrote the columns, which called for peasants to modernize their agricultural and health practices and recognize the promise of Ottomanism, in French. They were then translated into Arabic by the Greek Orthodox co-owner of *Filastin*, 'Isa al-'Isa.[115] The nature of this relationship was intentionally concealed from *Filastin*'s readers, but it also seems to have been lost to Yellin two decades later. Whether or not Yellin knew that the columns were not written in Arabic, his admiring retrospective article suggests that they spoke to Meirovitch's ability, as a member of a founding settler generation committed to hierarchical coexistence, to speak to peasants and share his agronomic knowledge with them. Meirovitch himself would tout his generation's own good relations with Arabs in a speech delivered on the occasion of British High Commissioner Lord Plumer's visit to Rishon LeZion in 1925 (referenced in chapter 1): "we have struggled with our arms," which always were and are "the plough and the furrows and the most amicable relations to our neighbors—the inhabitants of the country."[116]

Jews on Horseback

Not only could some exemplary First Aliyah figures speak Arabic, according to commemorative narratives with varying levels of veracity, they also mastered another symbol of "nativeness": the ability to ride Arabian horses. Yaakov Bendel, whose visit with Abu Hamdan we discussed above, recalled in 1931 that two Rosh Pinna guards, Pesach Lieb Buksheshter and Menahem Grabovsky, won respect from the Bedouins, "who respect anyone who rides a noble horse." As a consequence, he said, they earned Arabic nicknames that grafted their Arabized status onto their typically Ashkenazi physiognomy: "Abu Musa Hayl al-Shaqra" (Moshe's father, the blond warrior) and "Abu Da'ud Hayl al-Zarqa" (David's father, the blue-eyed warrior). Both, Bendel recalled, were regularly invited to Bedouin weddings and horsemanship competitions.[117]

The horse was the quintessential nineteenth-century symbol of authentic Jewish entry into the mores of non-Jewish society.[118] Leo Pinsker evoked the elusive appeal of horses when he complained in his 1882 tract, "Auto-Emancipation," that Jews "at best . . . attain the rank of goats, which in Russia are mated with racehorses. And that is the highest reach of our ambition!" The true ambition, he implied, was to become racehorses or, at least, their masters.[119] During his 1898 visit to Palestine, Theodor Herzl stopped by Rehovot (est. 1890), where a group of Jewish riders approached him: "twenty young fellows who put on a kind of *fantasia* [Bedouin-style display of horsemanship, Arabic *fantaziya*], lustily singing Hebrew songs and swarming about our carriage." He added that "they reminded me of the 'Far-West' [in English] cowboys of the American plains whom I once saw in Paris."[120] Herzl was likely recalling Buffalo Bill's show at the 1889 Exposition Universelle in the French capital.[121] The Rehovot Jews, it seemed to him, had attained the level of the American settler colonists, or at least could act the part as well as those who did so on display in Paris. Commenting on Tel Aviv Purim parades and Zionist spectacles during the mandate period, Hizky Shoham notes that a rider's ability to control and maneuver horses "exemplified the new Jewish man's distinction from nature, and his ability to control and suppress the non-civilized elements, be they the desert, inner aggressive impulses, or human groups which resemble nature."[122] The symbol of the skilled Jewish horseman pervaded Zionist settlement organizations of all stripes during the mandate period and is closely associated with memories of the Labor Zionist ha-Shomer guardsmen.[123]

The "First Aliyah" colonists, however, did not ride horses only for their symbolism. In the late nineteenth century, as in the early twentieth when ha-Shomer got its start, horses were still a key work tool, not merely a nostalgic or ceremonial object. Before a system of paved roads existed, settlers got goods to market, supplies to the colony, and people from place to place by using horse-drawn wagons, which required the "social ability to establish a working relationship with horses."[124] The Jewish agricultural colonies emerged at a historical juncture when equine and industrial technology coexisted, and horses, trains, and ships (and sometimes also mules and camels) were all part of the transportation network. Horses, traded regionally between Egypt, Mesopotamia, and Greater Syria, could be a significant symbol of wealth and power, and that trade in horses was the industry that had drawn Ya'qub Zirmati, the Sephardi Jewish Petah Tikva guard from

Jaffa, to the Ottoman hinterland.[125] As the twentieth century wore on in Palestine and the horses and carriages were replaced by motorcars and public buses, those conveyances became objects of nostalgia, reminders of a lost settler childhood.[126] Zionist artists in Mandate Palestine, including Nahum Gutman, Ziona Tagger, and Reuven Rubin, included images of Jews on horseback among their nostalgic, idyllic, and Orientalist subjects.[127] David Shimoni wrote poetically in the 1920s about the wagon drivers of Rehovot plying the "unconquered, unpaved roads": "there is only one path for them, that is the path ascending forward."[128] Meir Dizengoff, mayor of Tel Aviv from 1922 to 1936, wrote an essay in 1934, "To My Mare," about acquiring a horse he named Mehira ("Quick One") from a Bedouin named Abdullah near Gaza. Hayyim Nahman Bialik immortalized Mehira in a 1934 poem in which he exhorted the horse to "run and fly, run and gallop, day and high, in the valley and on the hill."[129] The First Aliyah moshavot could claim to have been the first ones to use the now symbolic horse as both a quotidian work tool and a means of defending the colony.

Dizengoff is remembered more for his leadership of Tel Aviv than for his associations with First Aliyah places and communities. But he was an early member of the Lovers of Zion organization in Odessa and initially came to Palestine in 1892, hoping to develop a glass bottle-making factory to serve Baron Edmond James de Rothschild. Nasser Ghanem Abu Farid, whom we recalled earlier as a wagon driver, worked there for a time. Though he left Palestine soon after and returned only in 1905, Dizengoff fits into the symbolic narrative of the First Aliyah both in terms of the timing of his initial arrival and in his ongoing commitment to private enterprise. He, too, made claims to settler authenticity via his horsemanship and the relations with Bedouins that enabled it. Before bringing his beloved horse to the city, he claimed, he would ride with the sheikh's two sons, and he went on to win a variety of horsemanship competitions. Ultimately, Mehira didn't do well in the city. "She died," he wrote, "after she was disturbed by the telephone cables being laid on the sidewalk, and she whinnied, rose up on her legs, and a bus run by Ma'avir hit her. Then she got sick and died."[130] The quintessential Zionist urban space, Tel Aviv, apparently wasn't good for Mehira. Although in his telling it was Mehira who had catapulted this Eastern European Zionist into a position of native prowess, she then left him to continue on without her as mayor of the city figured as the typological opposite of the rural Palestinian landscape she had represented.

By the 1850s, railroads had become a national obsession in America and Europe alike. In 1892, the French-financed Jaffa-to-Jerusalem rail line was inaugurated; the Ottomans and then the British extended the network in the following decades. But if the railroad telegraphed power, horses symbolized daring and adventure. That the railcar was called an "iron horse" speaks to the lingering value of real horses, who were nimbler than railroads and, like the automobiles that followed, able to deviate from a set course.[131] Avraham Shapira tells a story in his 1939 memoirs about racing a train while on horseback. It communicates a sense of conflict between traditional and modern modes of economic power and harnesses the horse (literally and figuratively) as a symbol of Oriental authenticity. One day around the year 1900, Shapira writes, the agronomist Meir Apfelbaum discovered that his horses had been stolen. Apfelbaum, who had come to Palestine in 1882 and traveled to various colonies including Petah Tikva, dispatched Shapira and his guardsmen to hunt them down. As they followed the horses' hoofprints toward the nearby village of al-Yahudiyya, they approached the train tracks of the then-new Jaffa-Jerusalem rail line. (This was the line that Lord Balfour would ride en route to Petah Tikva in 1925.) A train then approached, full of European tourists who gawked at both the "exoticism of the landscape" and the group of five Jews "dressed as Bedouins." The posse of Petah Tikva riders noticed the train but "continued following the writing on the earth" in pursuit of the horse thief. Then, from the window of the train, Hugo Wieland, the German Templer owner of a flooring business in Jaffa, called to Shapira, urging him to race—he hoped to tell a story to the German tourists about the Jewish Sheikh who raced in competitions alongside Arabs. "The spirit of sport was aroused in Shapira," the narrative continues, and without ever losing sight of the hoofprints of the team of horses, he plotted his course and competed with the train for half an hour until he passed it. The train passengers burst into applause as the train turned to make its way up the Judean hills and Shapira and his riders continued southward.[132] Shapira, on horseback, had beat the slow-moving train, and proved his skills and bravado to his 1939 readers. The moshavot had helped bring economic progress to Palestine, according to commemorative narrative, but settler bravery on horseback could both outshine their modern features and imbue them with meaning.

Colony commemorations valorized figures on horseback in much the same way that American commemorative discourse aestheticized American frontier heroes whose significance lay not in their organizational memberships, ideologies, or partisan political work but in their individual self-sacrifice and ability to contend with natural and human challenges. As the American historian Frederick Jackson Turner put it in his influential 1893 article, written just five years before Herzl's encounter with the Rehovot horsemen, the frontier is productive of individualism and self-sufficiency. "It produces antipathy to control, and particularly to any direct control."[133] Turner argued that the frontier created the American as a species separate from its European origins, a uniquely American character defined by "that masterful grasp of material things, lacking in the artistic but powerful to effect great ends; that restless, nervous energy; that dominant individualism." The image of the cowboy became the symbol of American individualism in political discourse, advertising, and youth culture. Dramatic narratives, for example about settler battles with Native Americans, Joy Kasson has written, "blurred the lines between fiction and fact, entertainment and education." Spectators particularly enjoyed "performers who could claim personal experience in the West" but who could also offer depictions of the "real" West that evoked not necessarily the reality of that experience but rather "spectators' memories of the West as it had been portrayed for years in literature, art, and popular culture."[134]

The American paradigm of rugged individualism seems inapplicable to the Zionist case when Zionist society is understood through the lens of its collectivist features and ethnolinguistic national program. But an overemphasis on Labor Zionism and the kibbutz collective, on the one hand, and tropes connected to the ancient past and Hebrew cultural specificity, on the other, have obscured the concurrently central place of settler entrepreneurship, individualism, and private enterprise in Zionist history. American Zionists, steeped in the imagery of the Western frontier and often supportive of visions of Zionism rooted in liberalism and private enterprise, imagined the Zionist pioneer as a "Western cowboy" and commonly adopted cowboy imagery in their promotional material.[135] At the same time, the moshavot, whose leaders by the mid-twentieth century saw private ownership and economic productivity as the most important mechanisms of demonstrating national commitment, celebrated the Zionist rugged individual using American imagery: the Jew on horseback was the cowboy, the Arabs were hostile Indians, and the Jew's mission was to survive the harsh landscape and create a prosperous society on the Palestine frontier within a space unsullied by modern politics. At the same time, believing that they had (re)become the true natives, colonists would also compare settler "First Ones" to Native Americans. Referencing the title of James Fenimore Cooper's novel, first translated into Hebrew in 1896, a 1948 article reflecting on the death of the Petah Tikva settler Yehuda Raab proclaimed "the last of the Mohicans is gone," and a 1966 article called the recently deceased Avraham Shapira "the last of the Mohicans of the Yishuv veterans."[136]

Loss and Threat as Proving Ground

While local moshava commemorations elided the mistreatment of Arab employees, they did not ignore violent Arab resistance to Jewish settlement. In fact, colony commemorations regularly incorporated narratives about attacks but used these incidents as exceptions that proved the "rule," namely that conflict was purely localized and Jewish settlers were able to manage it through hierarchical coexistence and exemplary displays of Jewish heroism. The moshavot provide a nostalgic model within this discourse not only because of the purported absence of violence but because of the colonists' apparent ability to harness personal relations to contain it when it did occur.

Moshava commemoration evolved over the first half of the twentieth century, within an emerging Zionist "cult of the fallen." From 1908 onwards, Arieh Saposnik has argued in his study of Labor Zionist commemoration, deaths were taken as "signs of renewed life." The historians Gur Alroey and Muky Tzur have explored the extent to which settlers of the Second and Third Aliyot took their lives by suicide, seeing death as a heroic way—indeed the only socially acceptable way—to confront their feelings of despair.[137] The Zionist activist Yaakov Zerubavel, writing for the Labor publication *ha-Ahdut* in 1912, denounced the traditional Jewish memorial prayer, *Yizkor*, as the prayer of a passive people praying for miracles rather than defending themselves, and he called for a new Jewish heroism.[138] Whereas the diasporic Jew was posited as spiritually and nationally dead, an emerging Labor

Zionist discourse imagined a new national Jew who had an eternal life even after death. *Ha-Ahdut*, for example, mourned the death of a guardsman in a 1911 obituary, calling him "another hero [who] has quenched the soil of our land with his blood" and continuing, "may this blood become the dew of life, awakening new powers."[139]

In South Australian settler memory, Robert Foster, Rick Hosking, and Amanda Nettelbeck have shown, native attackers were regularly depicted as "depredators, marauders, and plunderers." These words, which suggest shadowy origins and irrational motives, resemble the Hebrew terms most commonly used to describe threatening natives (*shodedim, mitnaplim, homsim, gozlim*).[140] In New England settler chronicles, settler deaths indicate the victory of the wilderness over the settlement while providing sites of consecration and glorification of the founders that enable the future of the settlement enterprise. An 1855 history of Charlemont, Massachusetts (est. 1743), for example, recounts how the burial site of Moses Rice, who was killed and scalped by Native Americans, became a sacred spot, set apart as "the hallowed depository of his mortal remains and those of his children's children," which "shall be guarded by an appropriate enclosure from the intrusive plowshare, and the unhallowed feet of cattle and swine."[141] Adam J. Barker calls cemeteries, monuments, and burial markers "deathscapes," arguing that these sites play a key role in the settler colonial alteration of a landscape by filling it with "markers of settler society" that displace natural or indigenous markers.[142] In determining which bodies were to be seen, marked, and mourned (and, implicitly, which were not), these commemorative processes also enacted what Shaira Vadasaria has called "necronationalism."[143] The political and economic contexts of American, Australian, and Zionist settler deaths differ, but what rings familiar are the tropes and modes of commemoration, the way those looking backwards grant local, national, and spatial meaning to these incidents. Yael Zerubavel emphasizes the role of heroic death in Zionist master narratives of rebirth. The establishment of the cemetery and monument marking settler deaths at Tel Hai, "the first modern monument in the country," might be seen as a prominent early example of Zionist necronationalism.[144]

Those commemorating the "First Aliyah" colonies also saw attacks as intrusions of the wilderness into a space of civilization: "There were Arabs in

Umlebes [the site of Petah Tikva] who were jealous for [the Jews'] land, and whose wilderness had been chased away," wrote Moshe Smilansky in 1932.[145] In 1948, on the occasion of the seventieth anniversary of Petah Tikva, the agriculturalist Moshe Ichilov, born in 1903 in Petah Tikva and active in several agricultural cooperatives, remarked on his experience visiting the cemetery:

> Fate has brought me several times to the cemetery. I went after fresh souls that were snatched away before their time. And there, on the silent hill, at the moment that we laid to eternal rest the young bodies in the place where the bones of the founders lay, I thought to myself: was it not those heroes who gave birth to these recent ones? . . . Is it not the loyal spirit of the ones who went first that called out to all who came after them? It is worthwhile! [*kedai ha-davar*]! It's worthwhile to live and fight, to fight and die for the nation, land, and homeland.[146]

As Ichilov's reflections make clear, those who came to the cemeteries commemorated both the losses that had preceded them, a kind of ancestor worship, and the losses that they themselves had witnessed. "I, one of the remnants," said Menashe Meirovitch in 1942 on the sixtieth anniversary of the arrival of the first Biluim, "stand by the precious graves in Gedera, in Rishon LeZion, on the Mount of Olives in Jerusalem, and in Tel Aviv."[147] The state of being a "remnant" (*sarid*) marked certain older people as guardians of memory, who could act as a bridge between the necronationalist sites—whose buried dead they personally remembered—and those who had been born or had immigrated later and who could claim only to be the successors of those founders.

Moshava commemorators experienced their losses in the light of historic and ongoing contacts between Jewish colonists and native workers and a narrative of hierarchical coexistence. The same proximity that allowed or facilitated attacks (and which Labor Zionist leaders condemned) also created personal relationships that, as conceptualized in these commemorations, enabled key individuals to resolve conflicts, seek compensation, and restore relations to a purportedly stable status quo ante. Two murders of Jewish settlers by Arabs from the vicinity, one of a blacksmith in Ness Ziona in 1888 and one of a butcher in Petah Tikva in 1895, show these commemorative narratives in action. I share Robert Foster, Rick Hosking, and Amanda

Nettlebeck's aspiration (noted in their study of settler narratives of Australian frontier violence, briefly cited above): "not so much to uncover the 'truth' of the historical events—although what actually happened, as far as can be established, is important to our analysis—but rather to examine how the events have been mythologized."[148]

The earlier of these two casualties, Avraham Yalovsky, came to Palestine from Bialystok in 1883, at the age of 33, and became a blacksmith for the newly established Ness Ziona colony (also referred to among settlers by the site's Arabic name, Wadi Hunayn or Wadi Hanin, and by the name Nahalat Reuven, after its founder Reuven Lehrer). On December 25, 1888, Yalovsky was found murdered on the outskirts of the colony, near the main road, in the clay hut he had positioned to make himself easily accessible to passersby who needed their horses shod. Much remains obscure about the event and the man himself, but local accounts suggest that he was killed during a drenching rainstorm that filled his hut with water. His wife, visible in the story only through her absence, had taken their children away to the center of the colony to escape the flooding, but Yalovsky stayed, "to protect his work instruments." Moshe Smilansky would call him "the first Hebrew casualty in the Yishuv."[149] In 1994, Israeli Prime Minister Yitzhak Rabin also referred to him while signing the Cairo Accords with the Palestine Liberation Organization, citing him as the first Jewish casualty in the settlement history of Zionism. The man who forged horseshoes was also used to forge national memory.[150]

During the mandate period, several local writers remembered Yalovsky for his good relations with the rural Arabs whose horses he shod, though they never identified customers by name. Smilansky emphasized that "Yalovsky learned Arabic and in his nature loved joking and had lively, entertaining conversations and would draw customers both through his talking and through his work."[151] According to memories shared in 1926 by Ness Ziona resident Moshe Levanon, "Often Arab peasants and Bedouins from among his acquaintances [*maʿarufiyya*, Arabic] would meet in his house and he would chat with them about various matters." In Levanon's view, the blacksmith Yalovsky was killed despite his good relations with the peasants who would come to him.[152] This narrative combined several features that lent credit to Yalovsky and by extension to Ness Ziona. He was an entrepreneurial businessman, operating independently and drawing customers. He was intrepid, willing to set up shop outside the center of the colony. And he was jovial, building personal relations seemingly outside the realm of politics. He seemed to embody a kind of moderate, apolitical, personable character, which, though shattered by the seeming intrusion of ethnic strife, nevertheless proved that he and his colony stood above it.

The same personal relationships with Arab clientele that set Yalovsky apart in Levanon's mind also featured prominently in Israel Belkind's later memories of the search for the murderer(s). When Yalovsky was brought to nearby Rishon LeZion to be buried, Belkind recounted in his 1917 Yiddish memoirs, "the whole colony was shocked and all the colonists were ready to act to find the murderers." When the Ottoman police failed to produce leads, Belkind recalls, "a thought came to me." His personal connections with former Arab employees would perhaps lead to a breakthrough:

> I knew one Arab who was previously a guard in Gedera. He was a half-urban, half-Bedouin guard. Apparently, he was Moghrabi—from the Moroccan Arabs. I would often run into him in Jaffa. I invited him over and asked him whether he had heard anything about the murder in Wadi Hanin. He said he had heard about it. "Nu," I said to him, "you can have ten napoleons if you find out who was involved in it." The Arab took my offer.

Twenty-four hours later, Belkind recounts, the man returned with information that there had been three murderers: two peasants from the Sarafand al-Kharab village, and a Bedouin living nearby. He knew their names but wouldn't reveal them before getting the money. Nonetheless, he promised to testify against them if he received payment. Belkind recalls rushing to Rishon LeZion to gather the ten napoleons and agreeing to hand the case over to Joshua Ossovitsky, a clerk for the Rothschild administration who had arrived in Palestine in 1882. For some reason, however, the case was dropped and never brought to trial. Belkind's implication is clear: authority figures from abroad, whether Ottoman or Parisian, simply did not have the capacity to resolve conflict. Only personal dealings between Jewish landowners and Arabs, greased with money, could bring perpetrators to justice. The non-Jewish guards appear here not as a security hazard, as they would appear in the classic Labor Zionist discourse, but as connections that, because of their economic dependency on the colonies, are central to the resolution of conflict.[153]

Another murder seven years later in Petah Tikva provided the impetus for Avraham Shapira—and his mandate-era biographers—to assert the value of personal economic relations, when combined with settler heroism, in investigating crimes against Jewish colonies. On the night of September 12, 1895, the butcher of Petah Tikva, Shalom Yaakov Rosenzweig, was killed in the street after leaving the home of Rabbi Aharon Orlovsky, whom he had visited to verify whether a slaughtered animal was kosher. The fatal shot was fired from within a group of Arabs from Nablus, led by the tax collector Salim bin Amin al-Qasim, who had stopped in town for some libations. One of al-Qasim's horsemen, Ahmad Khalil, was ultimately deemed the responsible party and convicted of manslaughter on March 24, 1896, according to accounts by the Jerusalem-born journalist and educator David Yellin (mentioned earlier in connection with his praise of Menashe Meirovitch's relationships with Arabs.)[154]

Yellin's account is concerned with the mechanisms of the Ottoman state in Jerusalem. He emphasizes the "excellent" judges who "know how to distinguish between truth and lie" but reveals relatively little about the local events other than the fact that the colony men "hastened and rode on their horses and chased after [the perpetrators] and caught them."[155] This sort of praise for Ottoman processes, however, was not the typical view of the colonists themselves. When local accounts mentioned the Ottoman state at all, they presented it as hostile, endemically corrupt, and incapable of delivering justice—if anything, simply a system to be evaded and outsmarted through settler grit.[156] Shapira likewise reverses the emphasis in his 1939 memoirs, which offer a locally generated, heroic narrative focused not on the Ottoman state but on the local, extra-legal process his men used to chase down and capture the murderers. Offering a story of bravery, cunning, and horsemanship, he tells of colony residents capable of besting locals through intricate local knowledge and himself as the individual hero who does not wait for external approval before acting. This narrative is the instantiation of a frontier, which the literary scholar Mark Rifkin has called a space "in which the juridical structures of the state are suspended."[157]

Al-Qasim, Shapira said, had come to Petah Tikva while collecting taxes in villages nearby. Shapira indicates that al-Qasim and his entourage encountered one particularly recalcitrant peasant and that, unable to extract payment of taxes through persuasion, al-Qasim had his gendarmes tie him and his wife to two trees in the sun in the hope that this torture, especially when inflicted on the wife, would compel them to pay. But "Salim [al-Qasim] couldn't put up with watching the two suffer," said Shapira, so he went with some of his entourage to the Jewish village of Umlebes (Petah Tikva) to pass the time at Katz's tavern. They "enjoyed themselves, with intoxicating beverages—which Allah forbade. And thus they spent the time in the company of bottles and glasses until sunset and even after it got dark." Sometime after (either "in the moonlight" or "at daybreak on Friday"; the text is contradictory), the shots rang out in the street and Rosenzweig the butcher was killed.[158]

Shapira, who likely did not in fact know the men's precise activities before arriving in Petah Tikva, denigrates the tax collector and his men on several levels within his narrative: they are incapable of watching the suffering they themselves inflicted on the peasants and thus lacking in masculinity; they are irreligious (in drinking alcohol); and they are reckless. The details work to suggest local knowledge: not only of the businesses and street layout of Petah Tikva but also of the land ownership and tax farming patterns outside Petah Tikva as well as Arab leisure-time practices in the surrounding area. These descriptions lay the groundwork for an apparently detailed though likely inaccurate narrative display of Shapira's heroism, masculinity, and restraint within an Ottoman Palestinian economic and social landscape.

Shapira heard the shot while sitting in the home of David Novick, a wagon driver whom he had assisted as a child and with whom he remained close. Shapira rushed outside "like a bullet from a rifle" and saw four riders fleeing the scene. He rushed to his house to get his sword and rifle—which his wife handed to him "without excessive conversation," the text stated, "in order that he be able to fulfill his obligation without delay."[159] As the tale of the chase begins, Rosenzweig the butcher effectively falls out of the story. He's neither a heroic casualty nor the victim of a pogrom. His blood doesn't "water the soil" of the Jewish homeland, and nothing about his death seems to support the national mission—except for the display of heroism that is compelled by it.

Instead, it becomes a story about Shapira, who paints the specific landscape he traverses on the chase: he galloped in pursuit, "north to the location of today's Kvutzat Rodges," then to Ras al-'Ayn, where he knew that Salim would go to free the peasant and his wife "whom he had forgotten and left tied to the trees since the previous afternoon." The reference to the religious Zionist youth settlement Kvutzat Rodges, founded in 1931 northeast of Petah Tikva, encourages the reader to imagine the narrative taking place on their contemporary Zionist cognitive map (in 1940, however, Kvutzat Rodges moved to its current site, now known as Kvutzat Yavne, farther south). Eventually Shapira outflanked the riders and called upon them to halt, at which point Shapira used the butt of his rifle to knock Salim's assistant off his horse and then to hit Salim "until the wood split from the metal" and Salim gave in. Shapira briefly discusses the involvement of state authorities, first the police who came to investigate and then the Ottoman court system, which brought the case to trial after pressure from the Rothschild administration. But the proceedings in Jerusalem do not really interest Shapira: rather, he notes that the transfer of the case to the Ottoman courts did not mark the end of the affair on a local level. On the contrary, he says, Bedouins came from the village of Jaramla to the north and stole four of Shapira's cows as vengeance for Salim's imprisonment; Shapira then chased them down.[160] Throughout the memoir, Shapira names the villages on his horseback itineraries. This form of meta-knowledge—knowing about someone else's knowledge of the land—allowed his readers to project the past onto their own present.

Shapira's ongoing adventures are reflected in a *chizbat*, or satirical anecdote, from the 1940s that presents him as a mythical man prone to physical confrontations who belonged to a period in which conflict was apparently simple and manageable. At one of the conventions of veteran guards, it goes, someone asked Shapira whether he had ever been injured. "'Gentlemen,' said the oldest of the guards [*zekan ha-shomrim*], 'the scars from blows and injuries that I have gotten in my life are many. In Hebron I got a stone right in the shoulder. In the swamps of Petah Tikva I got a blow from a *nabout* [club]. In the Galilee I was hit twice in the back, and in Wadi Milk [in the Carmel region near Haifa] they dropped curses of '*yil' an abuk*' (damn your father) at me. In Istanbul I got two slaps in the face, but those were justified.'"[161]

Shapira lays out a physical map of injuries, inscribed on his body, that corresponds to the geographic map on which he acted, a topography of swamps and wadis, hills and metropoles. The land he maps is both wild and open: there are still swamps in Petah Tikva. He has traditional weapons: sticks, stones, and the iconic club. He mentions no gunshot wounds, no shrapnel embedded in an arm or leg, none of the markers of later combat, only the superficial scarring from an apparently simpler Oriental frontier whose weapons were curses, honor, and intergenerational displays of masculinity ("damn your father") rather than instruments of modern war. The end of the *chizbat*, of course, is the punch line. While the setup implies heroic injury and pain incurred through justified fighting; the punch line presents Shapira as foolhardy, irresponsible with his body and words, but lovable for all that.

Moshava accounts of positive Jewish-Arab relations share a few features: these relations are hierarchical and begin and end with employment and other economic relations. The proximity created by employment, however, creates limited personal relationships that enable certain iconic locals, and those who remember them, to claim that they avoided or addressed conflict and could respond heroically to reassert dominance via these same relationships. To a mandate-era readership both discouraged by the increased conflict over Zionist settlement and increasingly less likely to have regular contact with Arab Palestinians, these historic encounters mixed the exotic with the nostalgic. As we will explore further in the next chapter, these stories operated within a wider framework of Yishuv-wide public commemoration, performance, and spectacle that was particularly targeted to Jewish immigrant youth.

(CHAPTER 3)

THE OLD GUARD ON DISPLAY

At the end of May 1940, a fourth-grade student in Tel Aviv named Yosef Aschheim took a field trip with his class to the nearby colony of Rishon LeZion, founded in 1882 as a Jewish agricultural colony. The highlight of the trip was to be a visit with the elderly Menashe Meirovitch (1860–1949), whose struggles and achievements as a rural settler Yosef had read about in school. He would subsequently write Meirovitch a letter, now preserved in the Central Zionist Archive, breathily recounting the experience. On the way from the city to the colony, he recalled, the bus passed a "very old" Assyrian inscription, a Russian monastery, and the Arab villages of Yazur and Bayt Dajan where, he recalled, "I saw Arabs sleeping on the sidewalk like dead people." But these layers of history and present, summarily glossed and dismissed, only briefly piqued Yosef's interest. He wondered the whole time, "When will we get to Rishon LeZion?" "Finally [*sof kol sof*]," he expressed impatiently, "we got to Rishon," where he saw "huge pools of wine" at the winery, Rishon LeZion's most important export business. He recounted the much-anticipated visit to Meirovitch's home with particular ardor: the schoolchildren had to leave their backpacks on the first floor of the house before going up to the second floor to meet the "gray-haired man with a young heart." They heard him recount that when he came to Palestine in 1882 there were "few Jews there" and the land was "an abandoned wasteland" that he and his Bilu organization comrades needed to build and make beautiful "so that all the Jews would want to come."[1] The experience of an encounter with a member of the settler old guard, known by the nickname "the Last of the Bilu members" (*Aharon ha-Biluim*), was a pedagogical highlight for hundreds of other Jewish school children in the 1930s and 1940s as well, who were also encouraged to write and mail Meirovitch their accounts of the visits.

Hundreds of thousands of new Jewish immigrants arrived in Palestine during the mandate period, their numbers increasing in the late 1920s and then climbing dramatically after Hitler's rise to power in 1933. Aschheim may have been one of these new German-speaking arrivals. The Jewish population of Palestine, which stood at only 15 thousand in 1878, according to the Ottoman census, grew to 61 thousand in 1920, 122 thousand in 1925, 175 thousand in 1931 and over 350 thousand by the end of 1935. By the end of the British Mandate, the Jewish community, known as the Yishuv, numbered 650 thousand, or 31% of the population of Mandate Palestine.[2] The majority of these immigrants, as before, arrived out of need or economic calculus, not burning ideology. Now, however, that "lack of ideology" became one of their distinguishing features in the eyes of veterans. While Tel Aviv has gotten the most attention as the destination of capitalistically and individualistically inclined immigrants with little ideological attachment to Zionism, many also moved to growing moshavot in the central and coastal regions of the country, including Hadera, Rishon LeZion, Rehovot, and Petah Tikva. Over two years in the 1920s, the number of Jewish workers in moshavot doubled and came to exceed all workers in collective labor settlements.[3] Petah Tikva gained the status of municipality in 1937, the second Jewish municipality after Tel Aviv. With employment opportunities in industries and businesses adjacent to the citrus and wine industries, prosperous moshavot offered jobs for packers, shippers, accountants, and equipment makers as well as entrepreneurial opportunities for those so inclined. When scholars, thinking of kibbutzim, treat agricultural settlements writ large as bastions of a more ideological socialist Zionism, the foil to Tel Aviv's urban capitalism and its "non-ideological" Jewish masses, they occlude the large moshavot, their traditional leadership, and the ways in which their narratives of a non-ideological Zionist past that was both agricultural *and* capitalist captivated audiences both locally and in Tel Aviv.[4]

Many of these Jewish immigrants, competing for employment

opportunities, gravitated toward Labor parties fighting against owners who hired "foreign" (i.e. Arab) labor. The Histadrut (General Federation of Labor), pushing for workers' candidates in the 1935 municipal elections in Hadera (est. 1891), noted that the community, now five thousand residents strong, remained under the control of forty-four landowning agriculturalist families who "got rich and live lives of excess" and "lack Zionist, settlement, or civic vision."[5] In the face of demands for representation from labor, the embattled moshava elites also barred non-landowners from voting and used tactics of intimidation toward municipal workers to keep them loyal to the status quo.[6] This struggle in Hadera over work and representation bled into a struggle over the past. "Every stone and house that are remnants of that [founding] time proclaim exceptional heroism and pioneering," the Histadrut pamphlet asserted, but the agricultural elites "aren't commemorating these heroes even though they are members of their own families."[7] Only workers' parties, it suggested, truly cared about both the settlement past and the settlement future.

But archival records show that as colony elites faced the activism of local laborers, they also responded to this pressure by turning with greater vigor to commemorating their fathers and grandfathers and presenting them as the foundations of private agriculture and the Jewish economy of Palestine. Geographically and economically central but symbolically peripheral, they recast themselves as ongoing exemplars of rural settlement for a new generation of immigrants and native-born Jews. In announcing "a week of propaganda [*hasbara*] and celebrations" in 1932, the Farmers' Federation conveyed to members that their audiences consisted of "not only the urban population, but also many of the younger generation in the moshavot [who] are far from knowing what their fathers did."[8]

In the 1930s and 1940s, moshava educators, boosters, and municipal leaders promoted educational curricula, student visits to founding figures, and countrywide radio broadcasts in order to promote narratives of national settler beginnings that they believed transcended partisanship. These efforts did not stem the tide of economically motivated criticism from local Jewish workers, but they did find a popular resonance. By this period, many in the Yishuv no longer identified the cultural types and figures associated with the moshavot solely as exemplars of "one side" of an ongoing debate over economies and labor. Instead, they increasingly viewed them as symbols of a generic, nonpartisan, Zionist heroism rooted in the not-so-distant past. This legacy provided an area of apparent consensus, a centrist space beyond the rancor of party politics, but one that concealed its own national and settler politics.

In the early-twentieth-century United States, Matthew Frye Jacobson has shown, immigrant children read schoolbooks that emphasized the European conquest of "an otherwise 'savage' continent" and communicated that to be American was "to have arrived on American shores on some kind of journey from Europe" on the basis of a "natural, God-given claim to North America." Pride in the "legacy of conquest," Jacobson writes, is "integral to American nationalism and national belonging."[9] Eastern European and Ottoman Jews, along with Italians, Irish, Poles, and other so-called white ethnics, had real, if tenuous, claims to membership in the (white) national collective, unlike Chinese arrivals, formerly enslaved African Americans, or Native Americans. White ethnics were often especially enthusiastic about the nationalist narrative and resisted having it questioned.[10] Jewish immigrants to Palestine may have arrived indifferent to late-nineteenth-century (or, for that matter, early-twentieth-century) histories, but found them particularly enchanting after they arrived because those stories offered them a path toward membership in the emerging settler collective, in contrast to both the Arabs of Palestine, who had no such path, and diaspora Jews, whose families had (foolishly, in the dominant view) not yet chosen it.

Local commemorations evoked both modern martyr figures and ancient heroes but, more than anything else, they celebrated living exemplars of the First Aliyah era: old men eager to perform the past, tell their stories, and serve as surrogate grandparents.[11] Writing about Menashe Meirovitch in 1936, the archeologist and Zionist activist Nahum Slouschz emphasized the value of such figures: "I always respected these pioneers . . . there is more heroism in living than in dying."[12] Meirovitch himself suggested the same in 1942: "[let's compare] a man who is killed and dies immediately with one who is injured and lies dying for a long time but continues to breathe. He suffers but he is alive. He continues the wick of life. He doesn't give in to death [*mar ha-mavet*]. That's how we were."[13] In 1945, when Meirovitch was eighty-five years old, the Rehovot settler and moshava chronicler Moshe Smilansky called him "the last of the firsts." This "lastness," attached to a variety of elderly moshava figures, reflected the cultural power of figures who had not died within an effort to preserve and promote a past that was losing its immediacy for descendants and newcomers both.[14]

While national societies love to commemorate dead heroes, figures who survive serve a public need to look optimistically toward a rosy national future.[15] Young people wear clothing styles that evoke the military uniforms they see on parade after wars[16] or, in the case of settler societies, the clothing or accoutrements—including weapons—associated with frontiersmen who successfully braved the hostile wilderness. The national symbolic, Lauren Berlant's term for the set of forces that define the national citizen in the American context, "is filled with fantasy images from the mythic frontier."[17] Zionist fantasy images from the moshava, a mythic frontier within a different, much more geographically circumscribed context, were conveyed to youth through school curriculum, personal visits to and by living elderly figures, and on the radio. The fact that the frontier site was typically just a quick drive from the city (or, in the case of Petah Tikva, was itself a city) made these exercises all the more accessible. Members of the agriculturalist old guard, including guardsmen on horseback, appeared in parades and in newspaper stories about memory and bravery. As we will see later in this chapter, some also had a place in an emerging discourse about training non-ideological urban youth in narratives of Jewish frontier bravery. This self- and collective presentation telegraphed a model of private initiative, both economic and interpersonal, and heroism ostensibly beyond politics.

Youth Education

As Jewish immigrants moved to the cities and the moshavot, schools ballooned in size. In 1936, the right-leaning *Do'ar ha-yom* (Daily Mail) noted that moshavot in the central part of the coastal plain (Judea and the Sharon) had seen their student numbers grow by 24.1% just in the previous year, a jump second only to that of Haifa, which had seen an increase of 27.6%.[18] In terms of raw numbers, those colonies, which included both "First Aliyah" colonies and private colonies established later, had absorbed 1,682 students, a number second only to that of Tel Aviv.[19] Immigrants to the moshavot and the cities, because they often came from families who immigrated for a mix of personal and economic motivations but not as declared Zionist activists, were prime audiences for up-close encounters with veteran First Ones.

Visits to elderly colony veterans complemented broader curricula in "knowledge of the land" (*yediʿ at ha-aretz*) and "love of the homeland" (*ahavat ha-moledet*). These subjects typically combined hiking and the identification of flora and fauna with the study of biblical geography. Children would be taken out of the classroom and onto the land in order to form a personal and national connection to Palestine's physical geography. Physical contact with and traversal of the land (as Lorenzo Veracini writes, discussing the American case) communicated ownership by inscribing sites as settler ones and conceptualizing the land beyond the cities and settlements as wild, presently ownerless, and in need of reclamation by the land's true natives, settlers able to cultivate it.[20] The idea of getting out into the field also drew from European principles of experiential education, which recommended leaving the toxic city environment for the countryside where children could breathe fresh air and bond as a group.[21]

The linkage between the ancient past and settler present figured prominently in Zionist field trips, as groups were asked to observe the topography of hills and valleys, streams and lakes and conjure up the memories of biblical and ancient heroes who had lived on the landscape millennia before. When people did happen to wander into the rural frame, the Jewish children on these outings were encouraged to see them as a non-evolving part of the biblical landscape or, as seems to have been the case with Yosef Aschheim, to note their ill-health and degeneracy.

Visits to sites mentioned in the Bible helped young visitors imagine an ethnonational bridge between ancient and contemporary times,[22] but biblical legend was not the only fodder for the nationalist imagination. Trips to modern sites, including moshavot, offered students from multiple communities and immigrant waves views of living people engaged in what was presented as a process of ongoing reclamation and cultivation. Local field visits also evoked the contemporaneous German practice of teaching *Heimatkunde*, the study of history on the level of the individual town, believed to link local knowledge to the greater national territory.[23] Kibbutz children, too, would visit different types of rural Jewish settlements to observe machinery, growing techniques, and young people at work on lands mentioned in the Bible.

The large moshavot at the core of our study, however, were many times larger than any individual kibbutz or workers' settlement and thus enabled a robust local and national identity rooted in individual First Ones. Smaller labor settlements during this period, in contrast, emphasized bringing children together across multiple settlements and affirming shared ideology.[24]

When settler elders spoke to school groups, they emphasized their own grit and persistence. While they might have alluded to those who died of malaria or violence, they defined "life" not as the opposite of death but as the opposite of submission to a hostile but masterable landscape and to forces that might have pressed them to leave Palestine (and in practice did cause most settlers to leave). This sort of elder testimony thus stands in stark contrast with the post-traumatic testimony of Holocaust survivors, who have been the object of most scholarly studies on Jews and historical testimony.[25] If the "diasporic" Jewish practice of personal testimony emphasized a lachrymose narrative of Jewish displacement and trauma, the emerging Zionist practice of testimony bequeathed a narrative of rootedness-despite-everything. In retrospect, this emphasis on staying put evokes the post-Nakba Palestinian inverse discourse of *sumud*: dedication to the land despite ongoing Zionist processes of displacement.

In a society where most biological grandparents were presumed to be diasporic antimodels, these elderly figures also presented themselves as the true collective grandparents. As one student wrote to Meirovitch, "all the children of the land are your grandchildren because you were the first Zionists, and all the fruits of the land are from the trunk of your tree."[26] This language evokes the construction of Lenin as "grandfather" in Soviet Russia, although that transformation occurred after the Bolshevik leader's death and in connection with visits to his mausoleum.[27] Moshava elders, in their relationship to schoolchildren, appeared as at once symbolic and literally, vitally tangible.

Maurice Halbwachs, in his formative work on collective memory, wrote that the older person is tasked with preserving traces of the past and indeed "to devote whatever spiritual energy he may still possess to the art of recollection." He is encouraged to remember the society "in which he no longer has an active memory, but in which he nevertheless continues to have an assigned role" and through this social process comes to imagine that "he has left there the best part of himself, which he tries to recapture."[28] By being brought on a narrative journey to this same past, younger listeners are encouraged to discover their own national selves.

Archives show that the educators, students, and the old hosts themselves all eagerly anticipated such visits. On March 17, 1931, the teachers David Yellin and Ben-Zion Dinaburg (Dinur) wrote to Menashe Meirovitch indicating that the third- and fourth-year students at the Jerusalem Teachers' College (a high school) would leave in two days for a trip to the moshavot of Judea (southeast of Tel Aviv and Jaffa) and the Sharon (north of Tel Aviv). Because the purpose of the visit, he wrote, was "to familiarize the students with these places, their history, and their problems," he asked Meirovitch to lecture to the students, thinking that this would have a "great educational-settlement [*hinukhi-yishuvi*] value."[29]

Some years later—on December 3, 1948, in the midst of the Arab-Israeli regional war—the Petah Tikva municipality received a letter from Shmaryahu Elenberg, principal of the Benzion Mossinsohn School in the moshava of Magdiel (est. 1924, part of the wave of second-generation colonies in the Sharon region). In it, he thanked the local leadership for arranging for his students to visit with the old guards Avraham Shapira and Yehuda Raab. The tour as a whole was informative, Elenberg said, and both "the meeting with the elderly Mr. Raab and the heartfelt conversation with Mr. Avraham Shapira and the reception in his house had a strong influence on our children and enabled them to recognize the First Ones of the Yishuv and the greatness of their project."[30] Elenberg doesn't indicate the date of the visit, but given Raab's death on May 27 of that year, this student group must have been one of the very last to visit him.

Baruch Oren (1915–2004), who worked as a teacher in the Moses Hess School in Petah Tikva in the 1940s before turning to commemoration and museum work after Israeli statehood, remembered in a later interview that he would bring his students to visit Avraham Shapira, particularly on Shapira's birthday. Oren speculates about why Shapira was so able to win the hearts of the young listeners. In addition to his being impressively tall, his style of speaking and his adventure stories captivated them: "his sentences were generally short and his style was simple and his Hebrew was mixed with Arabic words and here and there with Yiddish. Sometimes this made his listeners laugh, but he built trust and respect."[31] This mix of mockery and respect, Halbwachs indicates, is typical in intergenerational encounters, given the tendency for old people's devotion to memory-keeping "to become exaggerated."[32] While Hebrew marked authenticity in the emerging hegemonic culture, here Shapira's multilingualism marks the authentic settler who was the product of an encounter between Yiddish-speaking Eastern Europe—the archetype of the "exilic"—and Arabic-speaking "authentic" Palestine, encounters that had become rarer thanks to increasing Jewish residential and economic separation. This linguistic combination sounded funny to young people but was precisely what allowed Shapira to function effectively as both the marker of a historical break and an indication of historical continuity.

The archival file of student correspondence with Meirovitch contains more than three hundred pages of letters, notes, and drawings. Children praised him for reclaiming and transforming the wilderness; expressed awe at his stories; recalled the details of his suffering; and sent him crayon sketches of farmers, fields, and farm tools. An unsigned student letter attributed contemporary comforts to Meirovitch's sacrifices: "We learned a lot—for example that you had little water and now we don't need to drink dirty water. And we don't suffer at all—all thanks to you."[33] "When I heard how you lived in holes," another student wrote, "I was shocked and a shiver ran down my body. I thought, what if I lived like that, how would it be for me?"[34] Their sense that Meirovitch had sacrificed such that they could live in comfort renders him a Christlike figure worthy of their national devotion. This sort of sacrifice-for-salvation language also reflects the extent to which both they personally—and nationalist rhetoric more generally—had been steeped in Christian notions of vicarious substitution.[35]

Multiple visitors noted the awe they felt listening to Meirovitch, using terms that had entered the nationalist lexicon from the religious and biblical realm (all italics added): "We all sat in *reverent silence* in a half circle," wrote Haviva Friedman, "and listened as if to the voice of history, to the voice of one of the most important doers in Hebrew history. . . . We sat in *suspense* to hear about the travails of our brothers who prepared our place in the land . . . Planting a *garden of Eden* in the heart of the desert, turning nothing to something."[36] A teacher from the Kiryat Avodah neighborhood of Holon, south of Tel Aviv, wrote of his students after the visit: "They are still under

FIGURE 6. Cover of ha-⊠Olam ha-zeh, June 5, 1947, showing Menashe Meirovitch of Rishon LeZion with his grandson Dan. The text below the photo reads "the Last of the Biluim is not last" (courtesy of Yedioth Ahronoth).

the powerful impression of that *holy hour*. They listened as if to the sound of the flapping of the wings of history. They felt during that hour that you were the representative of the generation of the past. A generation of *glory and power* standing before them, the generation of the future."[37] The fifth-grade student Yitzhak Ahuvia from the cooperative labor settlement Kfar Malal announced, in more practical terms, that "I have decided to follow in your footsteps and to go into agriculture as part of building the land."[38]

These elderly remnants of the settler past and avatars of the settler present, in different ways, felt that their example could and should transcend partisan divisions. Meirovitch, by far the most prolific writer among the figures who became objects of popular adoration, chastened Jews in Palestine for "the division of hearts, partisanship that has led to civil war," and "quarrels over labor, education, and the desecration of Shabbat," all of which had been iconic sources of tension between owner and worker constituencies.[39] Meirovitch had sided with landowners on key debates over the years, but positioned himself as a man who could speak to a nonpartisan centrist unity. The more Meirovitch, Shapira, and others succeeded at presenting themselves as exemplars of a past beyond politics, however, the more they were echoing a discourse *about* politics associated historically with particular sets of Zionists: owners of private capital whose economic interests placed them outside the Labor movement.

Radio Waves

New media created further opportunities to project narratives of the First Ones. As we noted in chapter 1, Lord Arthur James Balfour's 1925 visits to several Jewish colonies were captured on film by the French filmmaker Camille Sauvage. A decade and a half later, in 1940, the noted film reel producer Nathan Axelrod was invited to produce a 300-meter (10-minute) film for Rehovot's fiftieth anniversary, to be paid for jointly by the Rehovot local council and the Jewish National Fund.[40] After the Palestine Broadcasting Service and its Hebrew section were inaugurated in 1936, stories of the moshava past could also travel over the airwaves. On November 27, 1940, as the Anniversary Committee of Hadera planned its fiftieth-anniversary celebration for the following year, they invited the new director of Hebrew radio programs in Jerusalem, Eliezer Lubrani, to participate in the event.

Shlomo Meirson, head of the colony committee (and married to a daughter of the colony founders Baruch and Leah Shmuelzon)[41] expressed hope that "the anniversary of Hadera [would] find an appropriate resonance [*hed*] on Radio Jerusalem." He suggested that lectures, memories of Hadera, readings, and speeches could all be appropriate genres for radio.[42]

Though printed media maintained its iconic force in binding nations together, radio in the interwar and World War II periods was "a force more immediate than the printed linguistic sign yet more abstract than the ritualized image."[43] A 1936 list of tips for radio presenters on the Hebrew section of the Palestine Broadcasting Service emphasized that "your style needs to maintain a conversational quality and refrain from the form of a lecture or article." It encouraged presenters "to mask the fact of your reading and create the impression that you are having a conversation."[44] This intimacy could have an emotionally powerful effect on listeners.

Instituting a Hebrew language service on Palestine Radio reflected the British commitment, expressed even before the Mandate for Palestine came into effect, to recognize Hebrew as the national language of the Jewish community in Palestine.[45] In an era of Hebrew print publications published by parties and thus ideologically aligned, the Hebrew radio service purported to speak for the entire Yishuv rather than for any one community or politically oriented subgroup. As a result, radio was unique in its ability to "offer its (unofficial) credentials as the voice of the Zionist movement" and "mold the collective consciousness" beyond partisanship.[46] Factions that felt they had a message of nonpartisan national significance also particularly gravitated to radio, the historian Andrea Stanton has shown.[47] When Lubrani came to Hadera looking for material for his program, then, he was helping a local committee promote its commemorative goals in a way that would also support the broader objectives of the radio service.

After learning of the planned program for the celebration, Lubrani emphasized that the anniversary of Hadera "especially touched his heart" and that he was ready to devote the entire day's Hebrew broadcast to it: the afternoon broadcast from 12:30 to 1:30 pm, the "Children's Corner" from 4:15 to 5:15 pm, and the evening Hebrew hour from 8:15 to 9:30 pm. He intended to personally attend and report from the opening event of the celebrations, a memorial gathering at the local cemetery. He envisioned that First Ones would pass before the radio microphone and "share memories from the first days of Hadera (3–4 minutes each)" and that for the children's program he would create a radio play for children. He also suggested that the broadcast include voices of British army commanders and "the Arab neighbors," who could attest to the achievements of the colony. The very presence of the radio microphone at the event directed its scheduling and shaping. The organizing committee had intended the event to be on December 31, 1940, but Lubrani informed them that they would have to delay the celebration if they wanted a full radio program. The committee agreed.[48] When the celebration eventually took place, following several delays (not all caused by the radio scheduling), in late February 1941, *ha-Boker* called it an "historic event."[49]

The Hadera broadcast fit into Lubrani's ongoing interest in bringing narratives of the First Aliyah to the radio. An extensive file in the Central Zionist Archive contains correspondence between Lubrani and Menashe Meirovitch over nearly a decade, starting in 1936. It gives a sense of the way the interests of the radio host and the living representative of the past converged to produce cultural texts intended for consumption by the masses.

Lubrani first invited Meirovitch to come to the Jerusalem studio in June 1936 to give a prepared lecture on "The First Biluim in the Land." Lubrani suggested a length of fifteen minutes, or "five average pages on a typewriter." If Meirovitch had trouble coming to Jerusalem, he would have the option of sending the text and having it read by someone else.[50] The initial date and time were set: July 9, 1936, from 8:40 to 8:55 pm. Meirovitch would be paid 1.750 Palestine pounds in addition to any travel costs.[51] In the end, Meirovitch was in fact not able to make it to Jerusalem but expressed his satisfaction at the "pleasant young woman" who read the text in his stead. The content, on the other hand, was not to his liking: he accused the editors of "erasing the important ideas" and "editing mercilessly."[52]

While we don't have access to the final version that was delivered, the original text exists in the archive. It is a narrative of commitment, not triumph. As rioting against Jews spread in the Russian Empire in 1882, Meirovitch says, young people asked, "How do we save those who have remained alive?" As contemporaries mulled engaging in local efforts where they lived and a small group called ʿAm Olam (Eternal People) looked into sending Jews to engage in agricultural work in North America, Meirovitch joined Bilu to promote settlement in Palestine. A group of fourteen arrived in Jaffa on 19 Tamuz (July 6), 1882, and later arrivals brought their numbers to fifty. Meirovitch accentuates the economic failures, sickness, cold, and hunger experienced by the Bilu group and recounts their repeated requests for help. But, he says, they distinguished themselves because "despite it all they plowed the first furrow and remained loyal to their objective until the last day."[53] As against conceptions of heroism oriented toward national death, he defines the persistence of a settler colonist as true heroism: "it's easy to die from the bullet of the enemy, but heroism is standing in the trenches year after year under raining bullets and explosions next to you, without light or air and sometimes without bread, and not to give in until victory." He admits that few of the Bilu group stayed—most left the country—but stresses that those who did remain became heroes.[54]

Meirovitch, a consummate self-promoter, feigns modesty when Lubrani thanks him for his insights: "As a veteran soldier it was hard for me to hear so much praise at my expense. I didn't devote all my days to this. I just did *what I was obligated to* and I hope to continue my modest work until my final day."[55] In fact, there was little that was modest about Meirovitch's extended engagement with Lubrani. Immediately upon replying to the first invitation, Meirovitch began to suggest additional and alternative topics for coverage on the radio, including from writings that his friends and admirers had compiled on the occasion of his seventy-sixth birthday that year.[56] (Those friends published that collection five years later.[57]) Then, in July, he mentioned that his own memoirs might interest the public and that he also had a series of other lectures he'd hoped to share, including, "My first trip to the Galilee 30 years ago," "My first visit to Gaza 40 years ago," and "Pages from my journals during the first years."[58]

When he submitted a text called "The First Seeds I Planted" (*ha-Zir'onim ha-rishonim she-zara'ti*) and didn't get an answer, he wrote impatiently for an update.[59] Meirovitch would not be disappointed this time. Not only was Lubrani planning to air the "First Seeds" program, he also expressed his satisfaction that the Department of Education had published the speech in pamphlets for scouts and youth.[60] The Meirovitch texts were widely disseminated in various forms, including to students who used them in the 1930s and 1940s to learn about the moshavot. As a schoolboy named

Yosef Tzumer wrote to Meirovitch in 1945, enchanted by his stories and eager to meet him, "We read your book *The First Seeds*. . . . We read about your worries about Reb Issachar [the donkey] and about getting water from Wadi Soreq and about the man who swallowed a leech with the dirty water. Now we are finishing reading. We have decided to have a party and invite you." Reading about Meirovitch's settler tribulations in the midst of a Jewish refugee crisis in Europe made a clear impression on Tzumer. "In your days the land was wasteland and only isolated settlements [*moshavim*] and now [there are] flowering settlements. I bless you that you merit seeing the Aliyah of many refugees to the Land of Israel."[61] Over radio waves, moving images, published material, and handwritten text, flowing through homes, schools, and community centers, Meirovitch, like Shapira, Raab, Smilansky, and others, cultivated a past that the youth were eager to consume.

Making the Popular Hero

In the emerging public narrative, taught to students and presented on the radio, the moshava First Ones had braved a forbidding landscape to lay the foundations of the Yishuv. Presented as apolitical and nonpartisan, their stories also resonated within the Yishuv's growing middle-class society. Along with Meirovitch, Avraham Shapira came into particular public view in the 1930s. Over the next several decades, until his death in 1965, he became the face of a folksy, throwback moshava heroism associated with Petah Tikva specifically and the First Aliyah colonies generally.

Shapira's self-presentation combines the three elements discussed in this book: first, the efforts of moshava elites to present themselves as servants of the nation outside partisan politics; second, nostalgia for an era of "hierarchical coexistence" and Jewish-Arab economic proximity that enabled local figures to resolve conflict outside state frameworks; and, third, the capacity of moshava First Ones to charm a less nationalistically engaged immigrant population both within and beyond the moshavot. This discourse emanated from a small class of elite agriculturalists and veteran moshava leaders but it gained the attention of several other non-Labor constituencies in the Yishuv—religious Zionists, Revisionists, and urban businessmen—as it enchanted wide swaths of an ideologically diverse immigrant population.

By the 1930s, Shapira had become known for solving crimes and resolving disputes through relationships he had cultivated with rural Arab leaders, villages, and communities since becoming head of the Petah Tikva guardsmen. He made the news again in 1931 when he and a group of fellow Petah Tikva landowners and guards, together with other moshava figures and organizations, successfully solved a cold case: the double murder of two young Jewish immigrant lovers, Solia Zohar and Yohanan Stahl. To observers from within a nexus of non-Labor forces, moshava icons had chalked up a nationalist victory for the Yishuv as a whole on the basis of Jewish heroism rooted in local knowledge, Arabic proficiency, and long-standing personal connections between Jewish owners and Arab employees. All of these things had become characteristic of commemorative narratives in the moshavot, but now they were finding a national stage as the centrist and right-wing periodical press claimed that these communities and individuals were uniquely serving the Yishuv in a way that Labor Zionists did not and could not, but that they were being systematically overlooked by Zionist institutions.

The juicy story was presented to the public in terms that they were increasingly recognizing from the Orientalist narratives starting to proliferate in Hebrew detective fiction. In them, an Ashkenazi Jew would use knowledge of Arab society to solve crimes. This detective fiction gained particular readership among non-ideological immigrants. Both the details of the real-life crime-solving and the high-stakes chases, salacious crimes, and heroic Jewish men of the fictional genre shaped the memoirs that Shapira published in 1939. We discussed one of these episodes, the murder of the Petah Tikva butcher, in chapter 2. David Tidhar, a private detective and supporter of private initiative generally, promoted both the emerging detective literature and Shapira's packaged story to an informal coalition of private interests eager to celebrate a trans-political national hero.

A Detective Education

In his 1931 introduction to the first story in the "Detective Library," the first collection of original Hebrew-language detective stories, the writer and publisher Avigdor Hameiri suggested that detective literature could serve an important pedagogical function for the Jewish youth—implicitly, the male youth—of Palestine. "Our wretched lives make clear to us," he said, "that we are living here in a primeval forest of murders and rapes of women and there's nothing like it in the whole world." In this situation of "utter lawlessness" (*hefker gamur*), the younger generation needed what he called a detective education (*hinukh balashi*) to help them help the police solve cases.[62]

Hameiri offers the Stahl/Zohar murders as a contemporary illustration of lay involvement helping to solve real-world crimes: the "secrets [of the case] were discovered by native-born citizens."[63] The young lovers Stahl and Zohar had traveled north from Tel Aviv soon after they arrived in Palestine and had disappeared somewhere near Herzliya, the Jewish agricultural colony founded in 1924 in the Sharon region north of Tel Aviv and initially populated in part by children of older colonies. After the British police in Tulkarm and Qalqilya dragged their feet and failed to solve the case, Avraham Shapira and Avraham Druyan from Petah Tikva, both moshava agriculturalists and figures on horseback who spoke Arabic, took on the case independently. Through the careful use of tracking, mapping, rewards, conversations with Arab Palestinians, and witness testimony, Druyan and Shapira finally solved the crime, which involved not only the double murder but also, it was later revealed, the horrific gang rape of Solia Zohar. To great, sensationalized acclaim in the local press, Shapira and Druyan revealed the location of the buried bodies and, four and a half months after they disappeared, the couple received formal Jewish burials.[64]

To Hameiri, the success of Avraham Shapira and his partners in their private detective initiative affirmed the power of detective literature for the younger generation. The Detective Library, with Hameiri's introduction, inaugurated a heyday for original Hebrew lowbrow, noncanonical literature in the Yishuv.[65] Historically, popular literature called *shund*, "trash," in Yiddish, often based on or translated from French melodramatic fiction, was intended for women and critiqued for its low moral values. Such texts were often imported to Palestine in serialized form and published in newspapers. The allure of these imports was so great that some original Hebrew works even masqueraded as translations.[66]

Lowbrow literature met with scorn from establishment literary figures, mostly associated with the Zionist left, but the emerging Zionist political right lauded heroic adventure plots in particular as a means of building the masculine self-determination of young Zionist men against the (implicitly feminine) contemplation and softness that they saw in the hegemonic

Labor-oriented Hebrew literary scene. In a 1919 essay, Vladimir Jabotinsky, soon to become the leader of the Zionist Revisionists, distinguished between "literature of action" and "speculative literature." Whereas the first was active and full of imagination, the second, which he associated with the left, was self-absorbed and navel-gazing. Strong leaders, not ideas, were the "flywheel of history." In 1920, therefore, he forwarded a proposal to publish popular fiction for children translated into Hebrew from European languages.[67] While he was imprisoned in the Acre Fortress in 1920, Jabotinsky translated Arthur Conan Doyle's Sherlock Holmes detective stories into Hebrew. These became some of the best-known tales in a wide field of popular literature—detective fiction, Westerns, and adventure stories in Hebrew and in translation—that would take the urban Yishuv by storm in the ensuing decades thanks to the writing, publishing, and translation efforts of people largely outside the Labor Zionist camp who were blocked from Labor-funded publication centers and reliant on revenue from sales.

The first series of detective stories overtly written in Hebrew for native audiences, however, was promoted by David Tidhar, who also gave his name to the stories' protagonist. Tidhar was the Yishuv's leading private detective and an opponent of Labor who affiliated himself with the centrist Citizens Circles that represented those engaged in private enterprise.[68] The stories themselves were written by Shlomo Gelfer, a police commander and reporter for the right-leaning *Do'ar ha-yom* who wrote under several pseudonyms, including Shlomo Ben-Yisrael and B. Havakuk. The first series, consisting of twenty-three stories, served as a kind of advertisement for Tidhar's detective business. His name, in turn, helped drive sales. The first pamphlet sold four hundred copies, the second one thousand, and the fourth four thousand.[69] Some came out in two editions. Tidhar later emphasized in his memoirs that they appealed to readers "specifically from circles that didn't typically read Hebrew books," in other words, non-intellectual, non-ideological, and newly arrived.[70] Tidhar stopped being involved in the series a year later and other protagonists followed. Over the course of the 1930s several competing series came out, moving increasingly from detective stories to adventure and Westerns, also with Orientalist plot lines.[71]

The society on display in these detective stories was cosmopolitan and consumerist. The detective often paired up with the British Mandate forces, together forming a bulwark against the wild east. While Jabotinsky hoped that translated European literature could instill universal values of heroism and bravery, detective stories written in Hebrew could emphasize local heroes. It was straightforward, therefore, for Hameiri to imagine that such protagonists had been modeled after—and could help shape—real-life Zionist heroes.[72] Hameiri thought it was time for the Hebrew language to take off its "priestly clothing [*bigdei ha-kehunah*]" and come down to the realm of the ordinary. Rather than focusing on "boring pseudo-psychological literary questions," Hebrew literature should offer interesting stories, "all of whose spirit is in the fabula, the plot, in the action that was."[73]

A Real-Life Murder

The 1931 case that put real-life examples of detective work on display was a saga full of suspense, intrigue, imprisoned and violated women, impotent men, and the strong men who, four and a half months after the disappearance of the young hikers, made the lurid discovery of decomposed bodies, a dagger, and details that suggested that the young woman had been gang-raped by five Arab men. In an interview with the Labor newspaper *Davar*, Avraham Shapira revealed the detective strategies that he had used. They would have been familiar to anyone who had been following Shapira's story since his Ottoman-era youth: he had leveraged his understanding of the land's geography, his contacts and past financial negotiations with residents of villages in the Jaffa region, and his relationships with local leaders.[74]

Shapira's continuing feats seemed to prove that his legend was based in fact. But he also inspired a next generation possessed of similar skills: his partner Avraham Druyan and the investigators Oved Ben-Ami and Gad Machnes were all born in Petah Tikva around the turn of the century (about thirty years after Shapira) and were leaders of Bnei Binyamin, the settlement organization founded in 1921 to represent moshava youth and counter what they considered to be the deleterious politics of the dominant Labor institutions (see chapter 1). The success of the detective story was the success of a non-Labor heroism that, in the narrative that was created, had existed since well before Labor Zionism was dominant and now continued to exist as an exemplary force within the Yishuv.

Coverage of the case was led by *Do'ar ha-yom*, founded in 1919 and edited by Itamar Ben-Avi. Ben-Avi, who had been born on the same day in 1882 that Rishon LeZion was founded and was an early leader of Bnei Binyamin, intended for the journal to be the conservative, anti-socialist mouthpiece for Palestine's Jewish "native born": both first- and second-generation Ashkenazi colony farmers and urban Sephardim. It saw the Zionist Executive as wrongly allied with workers' interests. In late 1928, following growing ties with the Revisionist movement around a shared opposition to "socialism," the paper was transferred to Jabotinsky's editorial control. It continued to reflect the voices of farmers and other private-sector interests.[75]

Do'ar ha-yom's front-page article, printed after the discovery of the bodies, emphasized that the critical lead in the case came specifically to *them* and that the police "greatly thanked Mr. Shapira and the representative of *Do'ar ha-yom* for their help in the case." Suggestively, the article ended its praise of Shapira and *Do'ar ha-yom* with the phrase "From the Valley of Akhor," an allusion to the biblical verse that contains the source for Petah Tikva's name: "I will give her . . . the Valley of Akhor as an opening of hope [*petah tikva*]. There she shall respond as in the days of her youth" (Hosea 2:17). The Valley of Akhor, a biblical location near Jericho where Petah Tikva's founders had initially attempted to purchase land, became a metaphor for the powerlessness of exile and the hope attached to Jewish settlement. In 1931, the extended metaphor was clear: from the frustration, outrage, and isolation of powerlessness in the face of the crime and the ineffective Palestine Police, a group of men from Petah Tikva, including the iconic Oldest Guard of that colony, provided the ray of hope that eventually cracked the case.[76]

If "from the Valley of Akhor to Petah Tikva" became the rallying cry for the founding settler generation, "from Petah Tikva to contemporary Jewish heroism" was its logical present corollary. The power of Petah Tikva as a symbol of founding and the transformation of despair to hope marked succeeding generations of farmers as well. In his eulogy for the young couple, Tel Aviv mayor Meir Dizengoff said that "the murderers and the bodies were found only thanks to Avraham Shapira and the youths from Bnei Binyamin—Machnes and Ben-Ami." He gloated that "*Do'ar ha-yom* preceded the police in solving this mysterious murder" and that "the bravery of Mr. Avraham Shapira went above and beyond [*le-ma'lah min ha-efshari*]."[77]

Voices from across the political spectrum lamented that the sort of individual initiative-taking that had defined the early days of rural settlement had declined. In July of 1931, the Labor newspaper *Davar* had expressed consternation that "The Jews of Palestine have nearly lost the vital instinct that had been expressed through guarding life and recognizing its worth."[78] But where *Davar* posited a general decline in the quality of the Yishuv, Shapira held up his and his partners' heroism as an example of First Aliyah-inspired vitality, daring, and successful activism that had been thwarted specifically by the Labor movement and the central Zionist institutions (the Jewish National Fund, the Palestine Foundation Fund, and the Jewish Agency for Palestine), all of which promoted national rather than private land ownership. Shapira had the editors of *Davar* append a note to the bottom of his statement indicating his strong sense that there was bias against him as a non-Laborite. He intimated that the Jewish National Council, the main representative body of the Yishuv, had pushed aside his requests for money for political reasons. Shapira claimed that he "couldn't hold back" and had a message delivered to council chair Yitzhak Ben-Zvi: "Of course, the National Council belongs to the workers, and the Jewish Agency belongs to the workers . . . but the fact that Avraham Shapira works on their behalf should also belong to [be the business of] the workers."[79] The man solving crimes for the Yishuv should have the respect of the Yishuv's institutions, he insisted.

The murder also became a cause célèbre for those who had been lobbying the British Mandate government for greater access to weapons. On November 18, 1931, Josiah Wedgwood, a supporter of Zionism in the British House of Commons, asked the Secretary of State for the Colonies whether, in light of the "murder of a young Jew and Jewess on the coast north of Tel Aviv" and the difficulty the police had had in making an arrest, "he is now prepared to allow the Jews the right to carry weapons for self-defense in the face of the dangers surrounding them."[80] Wedgwood repeated this request on December 7. R. Hamilton replied that the High Commissioner was looking into it and Wedgwood pressed:

> Has the hon. Gentleman had any information from Palestine about the murder of two Jewish hikers; and is he aware that there have been 22 separate cases of murder by Arabs in Palestine in the present month [and] that the

discovery of the murderers of the two Jewish hikers was only effected by the offer of a reward of £200?[81]

Both the failure of the British to intervene effectively in the case and the perceived heroism of armed Jewish individuals helped to concretize a perception that only grew over the course of the 1930s and toward 1948, that a kind of elemental armed Jewish frontier heroism conducted outside the formal bounds of national or political institutions (even if authorized or supported by them) would become the essence of national security.

Hameiri had these events in mind when, in late 1931, he penned his introduction to the first issue of the "Detective Library Series." Citizens inspired by high morals and individual initiative-taking had helped solve a crime. The details of the Stahl and Zohar murders were indeed lurid and the press only accentuated the horror and shock they inspired, eagerly describing the fact that all that investigators had discovered from Solia's body were "bone fragments, shreds of clothing, clumps of black hair, and a fully intact brain—the flesh had decomposed" and noting eerily that as the coffins were carried up Allenby Street on their way to the Trumpeldor Cemetery, "they didn't weigh heavily on their bearers, for they contained only skeletons."[82]

Descriptions like these had dominated the much-feared fictional *shund* literature, but Hameiri insisted that just as the Stahl/Zohar murder case had become a story of moral courage and strength, so, too, could detective literature serve a national purpose. Literature doesn't become *shund* only through a criminal plot, he insisted. It becomes *shund* when immorality, pornography, and terror become "an end and not a means." Instead, "erotica and allure" should serve as a means toward the goal of uncovering the guilty and the not guilty, a goal that requires a detective who has "a highly and completely ethical character."[83] If Arab sexual violence toward Solia Zohar had led to a nationally humiliating double murder, the eroticism of the Jewish male hero would redeem Jewish virtue.

David Tidhar, as the first Jewish private detective in Mandate Palestine, embodied these qualities, Hameiri thought. He founding it fitting, therefore, for "David Tidhar" to be chosen as the name of the fictional detective in this series, as it was a name that evoked "a characteristic Hebrew detective, with uncommon diligence . . . an ethical character with a long list of detective work attached to his name, about which any detective in the world would boast."[84] Tidhar would go on just a few years later to recreate the historical—but still living—figure of Avraham Shapira in a similarly heroic role. In doing so, he was simultaneously promoting himself, capitalizing on a growing public demand for gripping detective stories, and drawing attention to a particular historical settler figure who combined primacy, exemplarity, and national devotion, all in a package that could be particularly attractive to middle-class Jewish youth.

In 1932, Tidhar offered a rejoinder to a writer who called the new fictional detective stories "poison pills" that would give children nightmares and blunt their appreciation of good literature.[85] Why, he asked, should original detective fiction be so troubling when the daily newspaper is full of cases of murder, rape, "the heroism of police officers, and the excellence of detectives"? Zionist leaders, moreover, loved the series. Tidhar cited a range of figures who approved of the work: Chaim Weizmann, head of the World Zionist Organization; Moshe Glickson, editor of Haaretz; the citriculturalist Shmuel Tolkowsky; and the Revisionist leader Zeev Jabotinsky. Not only was Hebrew detective fiction not bad, Tidhar argued, it could fulfill the more elevated national goals shared by all of these leaders: "When the children are educated to be good Jews and healthy detectives, they will bring benefit to the land: some in the police, some in guarding, and some in ordinary labor. Through detective work, they learn self-defense for all eventualities, the theory of heroism [*torat ha-gevurah*], and orientation during days of confusion." The land needs more detectives, not fewer, he concluded: "Don't be afraid of the 'Detective Library'! It has come to help you!"[86]

In 1939, eight years after his detective series came out, Tidhar unveiled a new project to model heroism and bravery for the immigrant Jewish youth of Palestine. This time, it wasn't (explicitly) fictional: he published Shapira's memoirs. Granted, the text was not actually written by Shapira. In reality, Tidhar had dispatched the writer Yehuda Edelstein to conduct interviews with Shapira and rewrite them into a third-person narrative that reads more like a heroic biography. Edelstein was a Hungarian Jew who immigrated to Palestine in 1925. He worked for the Roman ha-za'ir publishing house translating Hungarian adventure novels, including stories by the pulp fiction writers Jenő Rejtő and Illés Kaczér, into Hebrew. Though the text about Shapira was marketed as a memoir, its third-person form means that it bears an ambiguous relation to Shapira's own reported memories (which had in turn, been shaped over the years by the narratives other people had made from them). Edelstein's rendition of Shapira is packed with high-stakes chases and careful investigations, one of which we related in chapter 2. Shapira's careful tracking, his besting of Ottoman and British authorities at their own game, and his ability to extract confessions all reflected narrative features common in detective stories at the time. All three "authors" of the text—Shapira, Edelstein, and Tidhar—thus participated in constructing a nominally historical cultural text dominated by a real-life hero who was compelling because he resembled the sort of fictional detective heroes that Tidhar and others had been promoting (a kind of reverse simulacrum).

A passage toward the beginning of the memoirs reflects the authors' awareness of the fluidity between history and fiction. It is in the section that describes Shapira's motivation for learning Arabic in Jerusalem and Jaffa soon after his family's 1880 arrival in Palestine:

> Because he learned to understand the [Arabs'] curses, which stirred up his emotions and gave him a strong sense of vitality [*tehushat hayim harifah*] (whose replacement children today have to get from movies or high-suspense detective stories), he had to learn how to respond to the Arabs.[87]

The national message in the text is clear: the Ashkenazi Shapira learned Arabic, overcame weakness, and became a man of the East. But while conveying the start of Shapira's heroic transformation into an Oriental native, the text also sends a contemporary cultural message about the convergence between nationalist action and fictional narrative. The parenthetical remark breaks the historical narrative to emphasize the distance between past and present. It is implicitly directed not only at children, but also at adults concerned that the children around them lacked opportunities to cultivate authentic bravery and had to resort to film and literature to stimulate these fundamental traits. But the aside also implicitly promotes film and literature, and specifically thrilling, non-canonical detective fiction, as a source of "vitality," indeed, the best available means to communicate a set of values to a younger generation. If Shapira's stories of encounters with adversaries could be constructed like fictional texts, perhaps they themselves could instill a similar sense of vitality.

Fiction-inspired biography converged with a fiction-like news story in a seventeen-page-long chapter in the memoirs about Shapira's role in cracking the Stahl/Zohar murder. The chapter not only highlights Shapira's skill and cunning as a detective, it also more explicitly presents Shapira as a delegate of the past—a specific First Aliyah moshava past—who brings his unique skills of "hierarchical coexistence" into the mandate-era present. The chapter begins by stating that circumstances had forced Shapira "to return to the kind of activities that he specialized in before the war—tracking down criminals, like in the good old days of the Ottoman Empire."[88] While Jews had tended to denigrate the Ottoman authorities as ineffective and corrupt, Shapira insisted that the Turkish police were better than the British because they knew village customs and were willing to use pressure tactics to gain information. The British, by contrast, seemed soft on crime and unwilling to deter attacks. When the Palestine Police initially offered a reward of only 20 Palestine pounds for leads, this seemed like an embarrassment. In the absence of British support, other Jews had instinctively turned to methods that Shapira regarded as essentially diasporic: seeing as Solia Zohar was from Poland and Yohanan Stahl from Germany, some had approached the Polish and German consuls for assistance. But the capitulations agreements of the Ottoman period, which gave consuls the authority to advocate for their citizens, had been abrogated. The appeals led nowhere.

Shapira and his agriculturalist partners from Bnei Binyamin, in contrast, channeled a different symbolic facet of the Ottoman period: their personal connections with tribe and village leaders, one-on-one negotiation, and payment of money rewards, all outside the purview of the Ottoman state or any other state or consular authorities. Shapira and his younger partner Avraham Druyan find that the money indeed works to persuade a population they had long assumed to be avaricious, and leads start flowing in. As they follow a series of reports of kidnapped women that turn out to be false leads, they gain access to an intimate, sexualized realm of local life: coffee shops, fortune-tellers, brides purchased and drugged, and finally a dancer from Damascus who, they discovered, had willingly left the city to marry a Palestinian villager.[89] The descriptions are titillating and exotic. They reflect a broader Orientalized scene of sexual depravity. Ultimately, though, the two Avrahams claim not to care about these lurid scenes: presented as rational, nationally motivated actors, they are laser-focused on their goal of finding the missing Jewish youngsters. These agriculturalists are as effective as they are, in the narratives promoted first by *Do'ar ha-yom* and eight years later by Tidhar, Edelstein, and Shapira, because they have hierarchical relationships with rural Palestinians, Arabic language skills, and access that they can leverage on behalf on the Yishuv.

The decisive tip in the investigation came through a network of moshava-connected knowledge. Avraham Shapira started to spread the word among Arab acquaintances that he would offer a prize for information leading to the resolution of the case. One man, who appears not to have known Shapira personally, heard of the reward and, in search of leads, paid a visit to a friend in Miska, a village ten kilometers northwest of Qalqilya. As the two Arab men socialized, a shepherd in the host's employ overheard the conversation between host and guest and visibly perked up. After the guest left, the host asked the shepherd, his employee, about his coy smile and the latter replied that he had leads in the crime and was willing to talk about it in exchange for the reward. Eventually, the shepherd revealed to his employer that a group of Bedouins from the al-Qur'an tribe in Sheikh Muwannis, just north of Tel Aviv, were reputed to have a prized dagger that had "eaten human flesh." His source, the shepherd explained, was Ahmad ibn 'Ayyad abu Hadib from the Malaha Bedouins in the nearby village of al-Muwaylih. Ahmad had been out in the field with his friend, Mustafa ibn Shaykh Rabi', when they saw three men from Sheikh Muwannis stabbing a man with a dagger and then gang-raping his female companion. Ahmad and Mustafa were later invited to participate in the gang rape so that they would be complicit and wouldn't report the crime. The group buried the bodies in the sandy soil.[90]

The landowning host in Miska, called an *effendi* in the text, recognized that this story was real, say the memoirs, thus amplifying the veracity of a tale that may not in fact have been entirely real. His initial steps to share the information confidentially reveal his own lingering connections with Jewish agriculturalists in the area. He first turned, Shapira recounts, to Alexander Sultz, a Petah Tikva native who settled in Herzliya after its founding in 1924 and who had been involved in Bnei Binyamin. But Sultz couldn't get money to pay off the *effendi* and get the information, so he dropped the matter. Next, the *effendi* turned to another Jewish acquaintance, Druyan, who had moved to the nearby moshava of Kfar Saba. Kfar Saba had begun as an outgrowth of Petah Tikva in 1898 and became an independent moshava in 1903. Druyan was a latter-day Shapira: a mounted guard and an organizer of horsemanship competitions in the region.[91] The *effendi* indicated that he was willing to turn over the names of the murderers and point out the location of the bodies, but insisted that "he wanted to speak first with Avraham Shapira and get an assurance of anonymity from him."[92] The *effendi*, it seems, was willing to approach the younger generation of agriculturalists in Kfar Saba and Herzliya, a group with which he seems to have had ongoing contact, but his preferred Jewish confidant remained the elder Avraham Shapira, who had offered the reward and who would, he knew, offer the desired discretion.

Druyan hurried to Petah Tikva and woke up Shapira, telling him that they needed to get money urgently: the informant had demanded 300 Palestine pounds. Their next two stops were further links in the chain of agriculturalist and General Zionist power brokers in the Yishuv. First, they approached Meir Dizengoff, the mayor of Tel Aviv, who was worried about giving them money after all the earlier false leads, but agreed when Shapira promised to return the money to him if the case wasn't solved.[93] They then turned to the political and media center of the agriculturalist class: the offices on Allenby Street that housed Bnei Binyamin, Hanotea (its offshoot citriculturalist organization, which had founded the moshava of Netanya in 1929), and the newspaper *Do'ar ha-yom*.[94] Oved Ben-Ami and Gad Machnes, leaders of Bnei Binyamin, ponied up further funds for the payoff. In 1929, Ben-Ami had founded and become the head of the colony committee of Netanya. (After statehood, he would continue as mayor of Netanya and help found the newspaper *Maariv* and the Israeli Chamber of Commerce.) As the agriculturalist class set its gears in motion, however, the central Zionist institutions in Jerusalem continued dragging their feet.[95]

All parties in the Yishuv agreed that the Palestine Police and the mandate government were derelict in their duties for not properly funding the investigation after the disappearance and for originally suggesting that the pair had probably just left the country. But they differed in assigning credit to the individuals who took on the investigation privately. While *Do'ar ha-yom* and its supporters lauded the Arabic-speaking Jewish agriculturalists and proudly connected their methods to those of the Ottoman Era, *Davar* barely mentioned them. The heroes in *Davar*'s story, published November 15, were relatives of the missing Solia Zohar: her brother, Zvi Zohar, a noted educator and member of the Marxist-Zionist ha-Shomer ha-Tza'ir, and her brother-in-law, Moshe Zeltser. The pair had scoped out the area between Tel Aviv and Herzliya, come to suspect the al-Qur'an Bedouins in Sheikh Muwannis simply because some Arabs had run away as they approached, and reported this suspicion to the Jaffa police chief (who did not follow up). Their efforts were unsuccessful.[96]

Taken as a story about the Yishuv as a whole, the Stahl/Zohar murder and investigation speaks to an overall souring of relations with the mandate government, in the wake of the 1930 Passfield White Paper, that would only increase over the course of the 1930s and 1940s. But when the story is interrogated through the lens of its chief protagonist and the geographically and politically specific communities that particularly lauded him, its symbolic ramifications shift. More than a story about British failure, it is a tale about localized pride in the persisting rhetorical and practical utility of some of the First Aliyah moshavot's defining features: independent initiative, agriculturalist networks, meaningful contacts between Jewish owners and Arab workers, and knowledge of Arabic among a small group of men labeled as heroic.

Selling the Moshava Hero

If Hebrew detective fiction, according to its promoters, could encourage nationalist sentiment, the prospect of a "real-life" detective story was the holy grail. Tidhar began to solicit money for the publication, which would include the above story, on August 15, 1938. "I didn't have any money," he wrote in a report following completion of the work, "so I turned to the public to get donations." Tidhar sent out hundreds of appeals across the political spectrum of the Yishuv and also to Jewish communities abroad on behalf of the "Committee of Friends of Publishing the Memoirs of Avraham Shapira, Hero of Petah Tikva." Because there were already rumors that war might soon break out in Europe, he tried to accelerate the publication process.[97]

Already skilled in the publication of popular literature and in self-promotion, as we have seen, Tidhar designed a product that he believed would have maximum appeal. Between the publication of the first and second volumes, a Tidhar appeal letter emphasized the point that while the first volume had had sixty-three photographs and forty-three stories, the second volume would surpass it, with over two hundred photos, and would focus on the fact (and this point was in boldface) that Shapira maintained "relations with the [Arab] neighbors on both sides of the Jordan." This was no mere chronicle, no standard history book, and no work of fiction, Tidhar seemed to be insisting: this was an action-packed story of real-life battles, conflict, and derring-do that would give youngsters the feeling of "the honor of a nation raising heroes in its own land."[98]

Young people were given their marching orders: activists would receive booklets from Tidhar containing slips to be sold for 10 mils (in other words 0.01 Palestine pound) each. Anyone who sold a full booklet of forty-five slips would receive three copies of the published book.[99] A variety of institutions and constituencies received similar letters. "During these crazy days," said one of them, "when circumstances have forced the Yishuv to defend its existence, life, property and honor in the face of malicious assassins and to revive Israelite bravery [*gevurah Yisre'elit*] in its homeland," this is the time to present Shapira as an example to the younger generation and to new immigrants. On another letter, Tidhar added a handwritten note in green pen that "new immigrants (may their number increase) didn't know Avraham (Shapira)" and therefore "if our native-born, veteran leaders in the Yishuv don't support this important project, who will support it?"[100] The Shapira promotion project was thus an attempt by veterans and elites, inspired by the merits of the moshava First Ones, to impose a particular nationalist commemorative scheme onto new immigrants who had no prior connection to it.

In reaching across social and political lines, Tidhar tried to assemble a coalition of groups each of which might, for its own reasons, be attracted to the moshavot as a model for national development in the present. All had reason not to accept the "Second Aliyah" and its associated Labor Zionists as the unquestioned founding generation.

Because Shapira combined national loyalty with religious devotion, Tidhar hoped that he could appeal to Orthodox Jews. In addition to their reputation as hirers of Arab labor, First Aliyah moshavot tended not only to have been more religious in the past but also, in the case of Petah Tikva, to have remained so. Even in less fervently religious moshavot, like Rehovot and Hadera, landowner populations were typically religiously traditional, established synagogues and ritual institutions, and had included provisions for religious life in their founding covenants.[101] Hadera protocols from its 1941 fiftieth-anniversary celebration specify that the synagogue cantor would recite an *azkarah* (remembrance) prayer for the fallen.[102] The colony synagogue, located in the Khan (the first dwelling place of the First Ones), also hosted a 9:30 am "celebratory prayer service."[103] Around the fiftieth anniversary of Rehovot, celebrated the same year, Meir Berlin (Bar-Ilan), the head of the religious Zionist organization Mizrachi, offered blessings to the colony: "May God be with the builders of Rehovot, which was a precious gem [*even segulah*] also in the religious and Torah sense." He hoped that the community would "renew its life in the spirit of the Torah and the tradition and be an example for its daughters and sisters."[104] The scholarly emphasis on the secularization of Jewish motifs by the Labor Zionist movement[105] has neglected a population whose conceptions of Jewish productivization through agriculture did not emerge from or require a secularized Judaism.

The Hadera commemoration in 1941 included a play called "Yom Kippur in the Khan: A Sketch from the Lives of the First Settlers in Hadera," which combined pioneering and sacrifice with numerous markers of piety and traditionalism. The play is set at the deathbed of one Rabbi Yossi, "one of the First Ones of Hadera," who is dying of malaria. This character may have been modeled on Yosef Dov HaCohen, the first rabbi of the colony. As the scene opens, Rabbi Yossi's wife Hannah recalls his commitment to supporting religious practice in the colony: "with what torment and hardship you brought the Torah scroll to Hadera and what labor and trouble you put in before you arranged a special room for the prayer quorum."[106] After Hannah announces that she's going to go to the synagogue and pray for him, Yossi proceeds to tell the story of his immigration, blurring the line between religious motivations and nationalist ones: "For many years I waited for the happy moment when I could ascend to the Land of Israel, to work its soil, and to perform the commandments connected to the land."[107] This framing of the obligation to come to Palestine, sometimes labeled "proto-Zionist," is also essential to the moshava self-image: the text here implies that this combination of piety and commitment to the land is what laid the foundations for the Yishuv as a whole.[108] Malaria, what kills Yossi, was one of the chief killers (along with yellow fever) in the early agricultural colonies and Hadera in particular, and a potent cultural marker of the suffering of the First Ones.

The urban religious audiences for Tidhar's fund-raising letter could appreciate the elision of nationalist and religious language connected to moshava commemoration. Yossi's death is not a classically heroic death, but nor does it fit into the scheme that Yaakov Zerubavel put forward in 1912 distinguishing martyrs, religious people "far from a life of labor" who "did not water the soil of their homeland with their blood," from heroes, who "fought and died."[109] Yossi was religious and died of illness, not confrontation with an enemy. But in this 1941 commemoration the distinction is collapsed: the heroic First Ones were both martyrs and heroes, both religious and nationalist in braving the harsh landscape and passing along their love for it to their children.

Zerach Barnett, one of the founders of Petah Tikva, emphasized in his memoirs the uniquely religious character of the colony and its connection to the religious Ashkenazi community of Jerusalem (the so-called "Old Yishuv"). In a note appended to Barnett's 1928 memoirs, an editor wrote that "Most writers are too focused on the 'Herzliyan moment' and on politics and not focused enough on devout Jews [*haredim*] and the long-standing Jewish connection to the land. Indeed, the first agricultural settlement in Palestine among Jews was religious Jews from Jerusalem who wanted to fulfill commandments connected to the land."[110]

Tidhar's appeal to the Orthodox community emphasized Shapira's Torah observance. Shapira, the appeal said, would not travel on Shabbat without permission from the rabbi (which he would seek in cases where breaking the Sabbath was necessary to save a life). He would insist on Jewish dietary restrictions when dining with Arab companions, and even insisted that the Baron Rothschild have kosher food at his table. Moreover, he would not leave for a journey "without tefillin [ritual phylacteries] in his pack." The religious community, Tidhar's letter concluded, "had a special obligation" to contribute to "this important project, both nationally and religiously."[111]

The community did not fail to respond. On May 25, 1939, Shapira received an admiring letter from Pinhas Grayevsky, who had just read the published memoirs. Grayevsky was born into the same circles of Orthodox Ashkenazi institution builders in Jerusalem as the founders of Petah Tikva, but remained in Jerusalem and went on to become a leader of the Mizrachi (religious Zionist) party and a chronicler of the history of Jews in Jerusalem. The book, he wrote to Shapira, described "days when men of particular spirituality [*she' ar ruah*] worked in secret, fulfilled their roles in life with modesty, each man in his corner or his profession." Every chapter of the book "symbolizes faith and hope and true heroism."[112]

Tidhar also published glowing blurbs of the project from nonpartisan and General Zionist figures. Uri Kesari, writing for *Tesha' ba-'erev*, wrote that the market had never before seen "such an interesting plot-driven novel [*sefer 'alilah*]. . . . It is as compelling and captivating as a real novel." He thought that the nonfiction memoir, precisely because of its literary appeal, could furnish young people the "detective education" that Avigdor Hameiri had felt was so lacking. (Kesari himself had written detective fiction: in 1932 he had published *The Mysterious Wardrobe at the 1929 Exhibition* in Tidhar's Detective Library series.) "The book is more than a biography," gushed Shalom Schwartz, a founder of the General Zionists, in *ha-Boker*, that movement's newspaper: "It is a kind of history of the whole Yishuv."

But the books' appeal to Revisionists was especially striking. A letter written on behalf of Zeev Jabotinsky noted that the Revisionist leader "congratulated the Friends' Committee which took this task upon itself, the publication of the memoirs of Avraham Shapira, the distinguished man who has so many memories, in order to cultivate heroism [*gevurah*] among the Jewish people."[113] A more overtly political reading of the Shapira volumes came from Alexander Ikar, an early leader of the Revisionist youth organization, Beitar, whose blurb suggested that the book would provide young people a "treasury" full of sources to serve their "literary and poetic visions." These partisan messages were joined by a statement of the non-idological and apolitical character of the work: an anonymous review emphasized that "Avraham Shapira is neither a scholar nor a party man. He is a man of action and his actions can serve as a model and an example to many through his ways of guarding, his daring and even his relations with the Arab neighbors: he can be a teacher to many."[114]

Ikar's full book review, published in the April 7, 1939, issue of the Revisionist newspaper *ha-Mashkif*, situated the publication in the context of the ongoing Arab revolt, an event that had sharpened divisions within the Labor movement and between Labor and Revisionist Zionists over the approach to force, the interpretation of Arab nationalism, and the meaning of Jewish heroism. The Zionist political right was particularly critical of the Labor Zionist policy of restraint (*havlagah*), arguing instead for loosening restrictive moral restraints and embracing Jewish power. It was such restraints, they argued, that had led Arabs to see Jews as cowardly and weak and the British to put forward a partition plan for Palestine, which Revisionists fervently opposed.[115] Leaders of both Beitar and the Irgun militia (formed out of Beitar in 1931), including Ikar himself, also elevated other historical figures that embodied unapologetic Jewish pride and strength, particularly ancient heroes, Joseph Trumpeldor, and the members of the Nili espionage organization founded by colonists in Zichron Yaʿaqov.[116] Shapira, though a bit player in the epic drama of Zionism, could serve a similar rhetorical purpose. "The fact rings in our ears like a paradox," wrote Ikar, not exactly truthfully, "that in all the days of Avraham Shapira's guarding and defense, not so much as a hair fell from the members of his tribe." He contrasted that achievement with the situation at the time of his writing: now, when a Jew disappeared, it was hard to imagine finding him alive. Even when people chased after murderers, they couldn't always be sure that they would be able to capture and punish them. This decline, Ikar made clear, could be explained by the fact that "many of the founders of [Labor Zionist] ha-Shomer" sat at the helm of political leadership.

In this situation of Zionist weakness, Ikar continued, Shapira could be a source of "instruction for the future." The contrasts he drew between Shapira and the present Labor leadership reflected contrasts in the present between right-wing and left-wing Zionists. While the former represented an authentic and original national spirit, the latter, he believed, had come onto the scene later, and had proven inauthentic and ineffective. At age 13, Shapira owned a *nabout*, an Arab club, Ikar reminded the reader, and never passed up an opportunity to engage in a battle between "the men of the colony" and the "men of the desert." In contrast, he charged, the Labor-led Employment Bureau (*Lishkat ha-ʿavodah*) was treating defense as a matter of employment rather than heroism. No wonder, then, that "every investigation ends without results." Ikar's recommendation for the present was explicit: "Why don't we adopt the same method as Avraham Shapira for returning stolen goods and catching lawbreakers? Our 'Arab politics' is wrapped up in all of these questions."[117]

Sadly for Tidhar, in spite of the positive reviews, most of the people he contacted did not contribute at first: the governing councils of the moshavot "were slow to give their contributions" and even Petah Tikva, which "made big promises" early on, came through with only a small contribution in the end (3 Palestine pounds). Tidhar expressed frustration that "institutional clerks, who receive reasonable salaries and could have donated money, demanded books for free on the basis of their institutions' donations." Moreover, instead of giving themselves, individuals eagerly suggested the names of others they felt should donate instead.[118] But the lack of willingness to donate money did not reflect a lack of interest in the project, as people wrote to Tidhar to order copies of the book even if they hadn't donated. More promisingly, a representative from Rishon LeZion wrote to tell him that he had only been able to sell two copies, not because of a lack of interest but because "every house that [the sellers] entered had already purchased a copy."[119]

In the end, more than three hundred individuals, institutions, and municipalities donated to the Shapira biography project. In the tradition of the European and European Jewish *prenumeranten*, or lists of individuals that had "subscribed" to, and thus funded, a project before its publication, Tidhar lists all of their names and the amounts of their contributions in a published report.[120] We can presume that all of them donated because they believed in the value of elevating Shapira's story: whether out of nostalgia or enthusiasm for Shapira's heroic legacy, religiosity, settler Firstness, support for private enterprise, or respect for the First Aliyah moshavot as a group or for Tidhar himself. Taken as a whole, the list reveals the emergence of a coalition of memory—though not yet a coalition in practical or political terms—between private agriculturalists, urban capitalists, Sephardim, religious leaders, and Revisionists who each had their reasons to celebrate a figure who represented social features that they felt had been overshadowed by the Labor movement's commemorative project.[121]

Shapira, unlike Joseph Trumpeldor or the ancient Bar Kokhba, never became a classic national myth or a center point of Yishuv cultural memory.[122] Nonetheless, Shapira could serve as an exemplar in a particular cultural space that included "non-ideological" consumers of titillating news, capitalist farmers, businessmen and their associated organizations, and a growing political right wing. Shapira's appealing story, on the boundary of the apolitical and the explicitly partisan, calls into question the typical distinction between (implicitly apolitical) bourgeois popular culture and the growth of political factionalism during the 1930s. The potency of these texts lies in their appeal to readers via popular media. They do not demand, and they exist outside of, explicit statements of party allegiance. Simultaneously, however, they work to promote messages that right-leaning political actors were particularly eager to claim as their own.

The Past on Parade

As local visits drew students from the cities and newer agricultural settlements to the moshavot and news stories and quasi-fictional biographical texts brought stories of the moshavot to the masses, entertainment venues and large public events continued to draw Jews from the colonies to the big city, Tel Aviv. In a joke published by the Tel Aviv municipality's Purim activities committee in 1935, a new Jewish immigrant asks his friend: "How do you feel in the moshava?" "Thanks, excellent," the friend replied, "you have no idea how nice and good it is to live on one's own land [*nahalat sadeh*] in the moshava. I've never been bored." "And what do you do in the evenings?" the friend asked? "In the evenings," he replied. "I go to Tel Aviv."[123] The joke, which captures the economic and social position of many central moshavot relative to Tel Aviv in the later mandate period, prefigures similar jokes today about certain former moshavot, both First Aliyah moshavot and later-established ones, that are now seen as unremarkable and boring. During the mandate period, in contrast, they offered detachment from the noise and commotion of Tel Aviv while allowing their residents to participate in the cultural life of the city.

This presentation of the moshavot as uniformly rural and boring, Anat Helman argues, belies the fact that "Petah Tikva turned into a special focal point and urban center" for other moshavot and kibbutzim in the area. Moreover, in the 1920s and 1930s, multiple "Tel Aviv-like" features made their way in: public transit, noise, electricity, road improvements, a public library, movie theaters, and a full range of commerce.[124] But even as Petah Tikva gained more and more of the trappings of urban life, as well as actual municipal status in 1937, it retained the historical mystique and rural imaginary that smaller and more geographically peripheral moshavot like Gedera, Rosh Pinna, and Zichron Yaʿaqov maintained and amplified. Unlike the rural kibbutz, which remained the synchronic epitome of rural Jewish connection to land and geographic and ideological foil to city, the larger moshava's rural idyll was increasingly rooted in the past.

This past idyll was regularly and ritually put on display in Tel Aviv each year during its Purim parade. The yearly spectacle attracted thousands who came in from all over the country thanks to the British railway system that connected many of the central moshavot with Tel Aviv.[125] Once they arrived at the parade route, visitors would see a colorful range of political floats and costumes, Yemenite marchers symbolizing their historical presence as workers in the colonies, and delegations of Zionist and mandate officials. But the crowds especially anticipated the honorary procession of horses at the start of the parade, led by Avraham Shapira and younger riders from several moshavot. In the 1931 parade, Shapira and Mayor Dizengoff were followed by "groups of riders from Hadera, Raanana, Kfar Saba, and Rishon LeZion," all moshavot based on the principle of private ownership and all but Raanana (est. 1922) associated with the First Aliyah. The Labor newspaper *Davar*, noting the abundance of moshava figures in the parade, griped that most of the riders were "children of farmers and [only] a minority were the children of [other] residents in the moshavot or workers."[126]

The display of bourgeois farmers rather than Jewish workers, whose numbers in the moshavot grew throughout the 1930s, became a topic of contention in 1935 when Shapira and his riders from Petah Tikva were almost prevented from riding in their ceremonial role because of Petah Tikva's opposition to the Hebrew Labor movement. The "non-political" parade suddenly became political when it was revealed that the neutral "non-politics" it represented were not in fact shared by all. As several newspapers later reported, the well-known actress Hannah Rovina approached Shapira the morning of the parade telling him that "Those who excommunicate Hebrew Labor will not participate in the public celebration." Others yelled, "Shame!" Shapira, in his own account of the incident in a letter, recalled that Rovina yelled "Go to Hell [*lekh le-ʿazazel*]!" But Shapira recalls himself saying, "Avraham Shapira never retreats and here, too, he will not retreat."[127] *Doʾar ha-yom*, which published the letter, was eager to paint those who opposed Shapira as a leftist political fringe who, according to the headline, "wanted to shut down [*lehashvit*] the happiness of the holiday." The newspaper emphasized that even as an organized group of Labor protesters yelled insults at Shapira and his riders and tried to prevent them from participating, the masses of crowds cheered them on and considered them "one of the most pleasant and interesting parts of the parade thanks to the skilled riding and excellent music."[128] The head of the Farmers' Federation, Hayim Ariav, subsequently wrote a letter to the Tel Aviv municipality complaining about the "harmful and humiliating treatment that our friends, the riders from Petah Tikva led by Mr. Avraham Shapira, faced publicly."[129]

The riders from Petah Tikva led by Shapira, it is clear, represented a politically divisive site. By the 1930s, Petah Tikva was closely associated with the labor practices of the citrus sector, which politically active Labor Zionists condemned but which the Farmers' Federation saw as its professional duty to defend. But the public, it seems, came to the parade route—as to detective stories, heroic memoirs, school trips, or radio broadcasts—not out of interest in the synchronic moshava—the moshava of the 1930s or 1940s that occupied a real place in the contemporary labor and political relations of the Yishuv—but in the diachronic moshava, the moshava whose significance lay in its continuous past. Many, whatever their class, were apparently unconcerned with the contemporary political splits and were happy to see Shapira and the parade. The moshava of legendary guards, of horsemanship, of Jewish rural productivity could be a source of political unity whose distinctive power came from its apparent separation from the sphere of "politics."

(CHAPTER 4)

THE COLONY AND THE VILLAGE
Constructions of Coexistence after the Nakba

> The [Arabic] name *Duran* [the site of Rehovot] stayed etched in our memory for a long time. In order to remove the old name from our memory we used a "simple" method: every one of us would take a needle, ready to lightly stab anyone who uttered the name *Duran* ... Little by little the name *Rehovot* became rooted in everyone's hearts.
> —Eliyahu Zeev Levin-Epstein, 1932[1]

On January 6, 1964, when he was ninety-three years old, the former Petah Tikva guardsman Avraham Shapira received a letter from the Israeli Ministry of the Interior informing him that his weapons permit had expired. Pertinent to the Firearms Law of 1949, he was obligated to turn in his guns to the nearest police station within ten days.[2] Perhaps he bristled at the suggestion that he needed his weapons permitted by a state—British or Jewish—at all. Those guns—along with his horse, Bedouin sword, and walking stick—had long symbolized his status as representative of a bygone but still active frontier. But even as the state consolidated control over pre-state militias and presented its army and police as the sole legitimate users of force, the narrative of extra-legal, locally mediated, Jewish-dominated Jewish-Arab hierarchical coexistence persisted in moshava commemorations and, indeed, beyond.

In the first two decades of Israeli statehood, the moshava heritage elites and their local commemorations continued to evoke the early settlers' good relations with rural Arabs. Now, however, the thousands of Arab peasants who had sold their labor to the colonies were mostly gone and the physical landscape of hierarchical coexistence was upended. Upwards of 700,000 citizens of British Mandate Palestine had been displaced to beyond the 1949 ceasefire lines and the approximately 150,000 Palestinians who remained, some as internally displaced peoples within Israel, had received citizenship but lived under a restrictive military government that would last until 1966.[3] Israel and pre-state Zionist militias, seeing an emerging opportunity to remake the demographics of the country in their favor, depopulated villages through impromptu wartime decision-making and, in certain cases, explicit expulsion orders. They also had done little to halt the Palestinian flight that occurred amidst or in anticipation of fighting. Following the war, Israel prevented the return of most refugees (deeming them security threats), bulldozed village structures, and repurposed the land for forests, recreation areas, or housing for new Jewish immigrants.[4] Many of those new residents were Mizrahim, Jews of Middle Eastern and North African origin, either already poor in their countries of origin or stripped of their assets upon their departure, who then took up usually subordinate positions within new ethnic labor hierarchies in Israel.[5]

Within the Zionist national narrative writ large, the ongoing expansion of Jewish residential areas in the homeland symbolized a "steady movement away from the influence of Europe," as Frederick Jackson Turner famously wrote regarding U.S. western expansion. The European diaspora lay in literal ruins after the devastation of the Holocaust, and ongoing settlement efforts symbolized a decisive break and a pathway toward a reborn national Jew.[6] As the Petah Tikva landowner Efraim Gissin put it during the colony's seventieth-anniversary celebration in November 1948, as the war for Palestine/Israel was still ongoing, conquests of land in the present, like purchases of land in the past, would provide national rights: "Every bit of land—security! Every furrow—rights! Every tree—a source of life! Every roof, a roof for refugees!"[7]

The spaces into which cities and moshavot expanded and where new settlements were built had contained cultivated agricultural land and built-up village centers with homes, fences, and mosques, some of whose stone remnants remained even as their occupants were dispersed and agricultural lands built over.[8] Both the wreckage of Palestinian space and the demands of Mizrahi Jewish immigrants for rights and recognition from within that space kept the village lands at the center of local politics even as the state moved to redevelop them. The political demands of the Jewish residents from Yemen, Iraq, and Morocco who moved into the village of Qubeyba near Rehovot, Shlomit Binyamin shows, make the site a "ground zero" that reveals a "connection between the Arab space and the Arab Jewish residents" that is obscured by the Zionist national narrative.[9] Colony veterans, for their part, now experienced Palestinian village sites as demographically transformed spaces of new Arab absence and not-yet-assimilated Jewish immigrant presence.

How did communities that had built parts of their commemorative identity on narratives of Arab proximity shift their thinking to accommodate a new reality of living in mostly Jewish, though increasingly ethnically diverse, surroundings? They did so, on the one hand, with the same apologetics other Zionists used: (some) villages had to be destroyed because of rising Arab hostility, for which Jewish settlers bore no responsibility. Gil Eyal documents wartime attempts by moshava farmers to intervene in the process of displacing Palestinian Arabs: not to stop this displacement writ large, but to articulate, on the basis of their own personal contacts, a rationale for displacing some villagers while allowing others to remain. These interventions, Eyal argues, "should be understood as claims for expertise, claims that their knowledge and advice were relevant to the conduct of the expulsions and should be taken into account."[10] The narrative of coexistence, deployed since the mandate period, now became a bid for expertise within Israel's military intelligence apparatus.

First Aliyah colonies, with their mandate- and Ottoman-era hierarchical labor economies, also doubled down with nostalgia about the intimate hierarchical relations that had been lost, justified the destruction of the villages that were gone, and then spoke to the ongoing relationships of hierarchical coexistence that they believed should be possible with the newly minoritized Palestinian population—even as they commemorated their histories on the ruins, sometimes the literal ruins, of villages. The commemoration and adulation of First Aliyah figures in this era worked not only to instill pride in origins; these practices also assuaged the cognitive dissonance produced by the destruction and transformation of the very landscape in which their own commemorative processes had developed.

Narrating Security

Mandate-era constructions of "hierarchical coexistence" in the Jewish colonies, we can recall from chapters 2 and 3, combined stories of functional employer-employee relationships with figures of heroic men who were said to have established positive relations with rural sheikhs and peasant populations through a combination of economic power and physical and moral strength. While Labor Zionists constructed the "security situation" in the early colonies as an antimodel from which they had rescued the Yishuv through labor separation and Jewish militias, moshava commemorators, many of them children of the founding generation, offered narratives of heroism and relative serenity within a multiethnic but hierarchical space.

Competing narratives about "First Aliyah" security and violence appear in oral histories collected as part of a multivolume project to tell the history of the Haganah, the Labor Zionist militia in which many colony residents also served.[11] The transcripts of these testimonies are now held in the Haganah Archive in Tel Aviv. In some testimonies, the security situation in early First Aliyah colonies is remembered as particularly dire: "it was total lawlessness: marauders, murderers, and terrorists," said Shmuel Alman from Yavniel (a private colony founded in 1901 in the Lower Galilee), until the Labor Zionist ha-Shomer guards took over.[12] Hayim Margalit Kalvarisky, who brokered purchases of several plots of land for Galilean colonies, said that the security situation in the Rothschild colonies, firmly associated with the "First Aliyah," was "damaged and lacking." If Jews were to "acquire for themselves a homeland among foreigners (i.e. Arabs)," he thought, they could not "rely on guarding from foreigners or neighbors."[13] Nahum Horovitz, a former member of ha-Shomer, recalled the tendency in the pre–World War I Rothschild colonies to hire "strongmen" as guards from among the local Arab families. We, he said of his comrades, "rejected this approach, considering it a damaging, losing proposition."[14] Yisrael Shochat, also a ha-Shomer leader, noted that "we didn't have faith in the words of the veteran Jewish residents" and so we "relied on our powers alone."[15]

According to the resulting publication, *History of the Haganah*, whose volume on the "First Aliyah" period appeared in 1954, the early moshavot had weak security against local threats during the "years of lawlessness and savagery" because of their reliance on non-Jewish guards. Following a period of occasional local Jewish heroism that nonetheless required the regular intervention of European consular officials, it claimed, the moshavot deteriorated into relationships of dependency and weakness. "A change needed to come, and it came with the Second Aliyah."[16] A collection of ha-Shomer testimonies published in 1957 praised exemplary figures, like Avraham Shapira, who had won the respect of rural Arabs despite the unrespectable state of their community at large: "The Arabs respected these individuals for their bravery [*gevurah*], but in general denigrated the Jews in the land, both in the city and in the village, because they thought of them as weak and cowardly."[17] *The Palmach* (1954), a history of the Haganah's elite fighting force, calls these men "sparks" of pioneer heroism.[18] Drawing from such materials, the Israeli historian Yaakov Goldstein describes a brief "heroic period" of the First Aliyah before the involvement of the Rothschild administration, associated with Jews who "showed unusual bravery" and "became folkloric characters" in the "sagas of the First Aliyah colonies."[19] But these heroes' time in the sun ended there, according to this narrative. The gradual institution of more formalized Jewish self-defense organizations—ha-Shomer, the pre-state Haganah, and then the Israeli Defense Forces—gave the Yishuv and then the State of Israel security. The fact that this process of ever-increasing Jewish militarization covered a period of increasing interethnic conflict and Jewish casualties—that is, less lived security—seems only to highlight the necessity, from the beginning of settlement, for organized Jewish-only security efforts.

Moshava farmers who offered oral histories to the Haganah project also celebrated icons like Shapira but offered a broader defense of the moshavot rooted in a different selective reading of the past. Though they did not deny that their security situation was imperfect, they associated the early colonies with a period before violence. In his 1882 efforts to assure diasporic readers that prospects for colonization in Palestine were good, the Jerusalemite supporter of Petah Tikva Yehiel Michael Pines had written that "on the west side of the Judean hills [the coastal plain], there are no marauders [*shodedim*] and no oppressors [*homsim*] and even in the hills there is tranquility and security. Theft is present to the same extent as in all enlightened countries, but excellent guarding overcomes it."[20]

The narrative of the early colonies as places of relative calm persisted in memory discourses in subsequent decades. Hayim Keller (1892–1979) of Rosh Pinna emphasized the relative tranquility created in his Galilean colony through Jewish strength: "We didn't fear the Arabs. There was therefore no reason to prepare a young man for self-defense, because he saw himself as a brother and friend to the Arab neighbors and more than that, as stronger than the Arab both physically and spiritually." Moreover, said Keller, the son of one of the founders of Rosh Pinna's predecessor colony, Gei Oni, "they feared us." In other words, the transformation toward Jewish security and muscular strength that the Second Aliyah claimed to have engineered had in Keller's narrative already been achieved in Rosh Pinna.[21] When interviewed for the Haganah history project, Avner Davidson (1910–1994) of Rishon LeZion evoked the narrative of the New Jew transformed from diasporic weakness to national strength, saying that Arabs "respected Jews, saying that they are smart, successful, know how to work and do wonderful things."[22]

Keller attributed this sense of peace to a Jewish capacity for both violence and persuasion. He spoke of Menahem Grabovsky (1866–1917), who came from the southern Pale of Settlement to settle in Rosh Pinna and was said to have regularly gathered with Arab sheikhs from the surrounding villages. "Thanks to him and his influence, nearly all the stolen goods were returned. His name became known in the whole area and all the way to the Bedouin tribes in the Damascus and Beirut areas." Keller attributed to Grabovsky a legendary mien rooted in a conflation of the Arab Bedouin and the Russian peasant: tall and broad-shouldered, similar in his appearance to a "Russian farmer," excellent at riding and able to compete with sheikhs at horsemanship competitions (*fantaziyot*). Arabs would try to attack him in the fields at night, Keller said, but once they learned of his heroism they would identify themselves and tell him that they were just testing him.[23]

Baruch Ben-Ezer's interview for the History of the Haganah project situates his Petah Tikva father, Yehuda Raab, in a similarly heroic role. There was no guard position in the moshava, he said, "there were just North Africans [*Mughrabim*] who guarded. [My father] was just the coordinator." He cited Avraham Shapira's reported comment about Raab, "This was the first Jew I had seen with a gun and a rifle in his hand." Like Keller, Ben-Ezer (1887–1960) narrates a story from before his own birth that he knew because "I heard this from my parents." "In those days, there was still no professionalism in guarding, just as there was none in other professions. But that's not to say that we felt any special hatred from the Arabs." Ben-Ezer describes low-level threats from peasants but instead of concluding that the colonists were ill-equipped to deal with them, he tells a story of Jewish fortitude.

Ben-Ezer emphasizes, as David Tidhar did in his mandate-era appeals (chapter 3), that those who deployed force and put their bodies on the line in defense of the colony remained religious Jews:

> And one Shabbat, one of [the Arab peasants], came with oxen onto a plot of land planted with watermelons, plowed it, and wanted to sow on the contested land ['*krav*']. The rabbi went up to the pulpit and announced that everyone should go out to the field, and indeed, men left their prayer and went out to expel the Arabs of al-Yahudiyya. There were women with them, too, and among them my mother, and they lay down over the furrow in front of the animals and said, "Let them plow over our backs." The men of the colony beat the Arabs and expelled them.[24]

In placing the heroic call in the mouth of the rabbi speaking in the synagogue on Shabbat, the story marks the moshavot as distinctly able to combine traditional observance with muscular defense (on the part of men) and passive resistance (on the part of women). In other settings, moshava accounts cite the synagogue or its steps as the location of sacrifice and heroism, even when historical sources clearly suggest that the events did not occur that way: Yaakov Abramovich, for example, was killed on a weekday near the Rishon LeZion synagogue in 1902, but some retrospective accounts place him on the steps, on Sabbath eve.[25] If the classic Labor Zionist held a hoe in one hand and a rifle in the other (an image taken from Nehemiah 4:11), the classic First Aliyah colonist used the first hand to hold a prayer book.

Ben-Ezer asserts that Jews, through such bravery, overcame Arab ridiculers (*mitlotzetzim*) from the nearby villages of al-Yahudiyya and Kafr 'Ana who "would make fun of them, saying that they were not heroes" but rather "children of death." "We are consequently exposed afresh to contempt," Theodor Herzl had written in his 1896 manifesto, *Der Judenstaat*, but insisted that "The creation of a new State is neither ridiculous [*lächerliches*] nor impossible."[26] Ben-Ezer's own sensitivity to ridicule, too, informs his assertion that the Jews of the first colonies had indeed been transformed and that the

First Aliyah colonies (and not later Zionist immigrants) were the original site of Jewish historical and national transformation.

In this view, iconic figures like Shapira were not aberrations but reflections of their place and time. In his 1955 biography of Avraham Shapira, the collector, writer, and First Aliyah aficionado Getzel Kressel asserted that Shapira, the famous hero,

> was a natural outgrowth of Petah Tikva and of the new reality that was created in the first Hebrew colony and, in its wake, other colonies established in all corners of the country. We shouldn't forget this fact, for without it we are ripping a spectacular phenomenon out of its historical context and making it seem like it came down to us out of nowhere.[27]

When interviewed later as part of a Rishon LeZion local Haganah oral history project, Zerubavel Haviv, too, asserted the heroic bona fides of the early colony as a whole. The interviewer, Yoske Fein, had suggested that Zerubavel (1894–1987) should divide his narrative into three periods: "guarding in the vineyards," i.e. early disorganized efforts; the period of ha-Shomer (founded 1909); and the period distinguished by the growth of the Haganah organization (founded 1920). Haviv, however, bristled at this periodization: "I'm sorry to say that the division you present is not complete and doesn't include the first pioneering period that was realized by the founders of Rishon LeZion and their friends." Where Fein wanted to consign the founders to a prehistory of disorganized local guarding, Haviv wanted this period reclassified as the point of definitive break: "the appearance of the New Jew in the country, in opposition to the people of Jerusalem, people of the *halukah* [charitable donations] who lived off of the support of the diaspora, those who were waiting for the messiah to come." Speaking again not from personal experience but on the basis of testimony by his parents and their friends, he affirmed that "the men of the First Aliyah had a completely different idea around security and national pride than the men of Jerusalem." You could also include, he quickly admitted, the men of Petah Tikva, like Sender Hadad, Menachem Mendel Kaufman, and Avraham Shapira, "you could say that they were earlier than the Haganah, along with the people of Rishon [LeZion] and Rehovot."[28] Haviv was engaging in a Zionist variant of what Jean O'Brien calls "firsting."[29] When the interviewer suggested that his settler cohort belonged to what I've called the "pre-first," those outside the temporality of heroic national revival, Haviv redrew the constructed division line between First Aliyah and pre-Zionist community ("Old Yishuv") so as to reassert his group's firstness within the Zionist settler paradigm.

Haviv was speaking, he told Fein, "not only with criticism but with a bit of anger at the fact that the writers of history start history from "the day the Bar-Giyora [the 1907 predecessor to ha-Shomer] appeared in the world." With all due respect to the casualties in Sejera [i.e. of ha-Shomer], "this removes from history the wonderful chapter of the pioneers of Rishon LeZion and those who came after them." He accused proponents of ha-Shomer of blurring and obscuring history, but, he assured Fein, "It won't help. I revealed [those parts of history] and I will continue to reveal them as long as I live." He urged Fein not to let the "curtain fall over what came before. You have to be loyal to the historical truth."[30] Haviv, recounting a story within a hegemonic project of national commemoration, nonetheless sees himself as the champion of a forgotten narrative and the critic of a system that appears to be sidelining him, his community, and the First Aliyah as a symbol.

The Simple Hero

In practice, those who sought to publicize the "forgotten" narrative produced increasingly flattened, inaccurate accounts. Avraham Shapira remained an icon up to and beyond his death in December 1965, as narratives about him obscured and misrepresented the concrete details of his life. In his 1965 obituary for Shapira, the journalist Mordecai Barkai discusses the Petah Tikva defender's role in apprehending those who killed Petah Tikva's butcher (discussed in chapter 2). Barkai gets basic facts wrong: the date, the name of the victim, the sequence of events.[31] But the story, marked in the headline as an "*alilah*," or narrative tale, doesn't rely on facts or documentation; it relies on selective tropes of nativeness and bravery.

A similar process of flattening and exaggeration occurs in the post-1948 narrative about Sender Hadad (1859–1899), who had participated in the defense of Petah Tikva during an 1886 grazing conflict with the nearby village of al-Yahudiyya.[32] The *History of the Haganah*, which published the volume containing this section in 1954, played up the dramatic dimensions of the attack that injured six and led to the subsequent death of one of them,

Hadad's mother, Rachel Kriniker. Like the Ben-Ezer testimony from the same era, it also inserted women into the story as protectors of settler land and bodies: women "grabbed whatever they could in order to defend their honor," presumably against a perceived Arab propensity to sexual transgression related to their perceived territorial transgression.[33] David Tidhar's 1952 biographical entry on Hadad specifically constructs him as a muscular defender who rode out alone into battle "on a beautiful Arab horse": "he was a strong man [*gibor hayil*] who brought down his heavy hand on all," and "with his handsome and tall stature he proved to the marauders and robbers that they should take care not to fall under his hand."[34] All of these features—the Eastern mien, the horseback riding, and the imposing figure who has access to violence and deploys it effectively—were an extention of a broader gendered typology of First Aliyah bravery, corralled in the service of a state that was both boastful and doubtful of its capacity to neutralize pervasive Arab opposition and win respect.[35]

Local narratives about Hadad in this statehood period took the form of explicitly didactic texts. Baruch Oren (1915–2004), head of the *Yad la-banim* (local memorial site) in Petah Tikva from 1953 to 1980, helped concretize the Hadad myth and others by compiling mythological stories from the early days of the colony, including in a book called *'Alilot rishonim* (Adventures of the First Ones), published in 1964. His story about Sender Hadad, "Sender Hadad's Stick," is seemingly based on a story he heard from the family and contains a dialogue between Hadad's daughter Rivka and his great-granddaughter Liora that brings together several tropes of heroic masculinity. Liora has just injured herself on Hadad's sharp stick after finding it in her grandfather's bureau drawer. After being comforted by her grandmother, she asks to hear the story of this object. Rivka begins with the sorry state of the colony at the time:

> At that time the First Ones suffered greatly from attacks by the neighbors, who saw them as wretched "*walad il-mut*" [corrupted Arabic, sons of death], incapable of defending themselves and their property. Therefore it was necessary to rein in the "*shabab*" [Arabic, young men] from the neighboring villages, to teach them a lesson, and with that to accustom the Jewish settlers to respond with violence [*lehashiv milhamah*] in the hour of need. Your great-grandfather appeared in the colony like an angel of salvation.[36]

Hadad is not just a strong man in this story; he is the agent of redemption for the whole colony, which had been seen as emasculated and under attack by implicitly virulent Arab male youth (the story repeats the "children of death" trope that we saw in Ben-Ezer's testimony). After proving his bravery in the Russian army, the story explains, Hadad came to Palestine, mastered Arabic, and achieved respectability among rural Arabs. Locals would bring their horses to be shod and would call him "Khawaja Skander" (Mr. Skander, using the Arabic version of his first name). Nonetheless, he would come out fighting, "purifying [*metaher*] the landscape of thieves and robbers" without the use of guns.[37] The language of expulsion (in Ben-Ezer's testimony) and purification (in Baruch Oren's) is used to describe limited, local settler victories over peasants committing theft or grazing their animals, but continuing to coexist alongside the colonies. Yet in a post-1948 context where "purification" and "expulsion" had been used to describe the displacement of whole villages, these late-nineteenth-century incidents of Jewish triumph take on a different resonance and message: the implied obligation and heroism of more permanently removing threats to the Zionist settlement project.

The Sulha at Kafr Qasim

Figures like Hadad and Shapira, their lives stripped of specifics but elevated as exemplars of "hierarchical coexistence" in both its economic and military senses, offered models and symbols for the new Israeli state as it attempted to control and influence a displaced Palestinian population within and beyond the borders of the state. Unlike Hadad, who had died half a century before Israeli statehood, Shapira, who lived until 1965, was able to participate in forging this next stage of Zionist collective memory. On November 20, 1957, more than four hundred Israeli Jews and Palestinians gathered for a ceremony in Kafr Qasim, one of a small number of Arab villages within the central part of the new state to have survived the 1948 war. Israeli forces had assumed that its region would become part of Trans-Jordan, but in the final 1949 armistice agreements with Jordan (renamed after its conquest of the West Bank), Israel gained the territory in a land-swap agreement. The area, at the edge of a region known during the mandate as "The Triangle," came to be known as "The Little Triangle" or "The Southern Triangle." Kafr Qasim became part of a chain of Palestinian villages lying to the east of a dense area of Jewish settlements that had previously been flanked by villages on multiple sides.

The Israeli Jews in the crowd, some of them official representatives of the state, had come to Kafr Qasim to communicate a desire for coexistence—what we would view as hierarchical coexistence—following what the Mapai government eventually admitted had been an excessive use of force. A year earlier, the Israeli border police had killed forty-eight Palestinian citizens of Israel, including one pregnant woman, after residents of the village unknowingly disobeyed a curfew imposed by the Israeli military government in the context of the Suez Crisis. These were only some of the between twenty-seven hundred and five thousand Palestinians killed by either the Israel Defense Forces (IDF) or Israeli border police between 1949 and 1956, but these casualties were unique in that the dead had been Israeli citizens, whose communities could use the incident to demand civil rights within Israel. Leaders of the Israeli Communist Party, in which Palestinian citizens were active, led this charge.[38] After attempting but failing to cover up the massacre and then jockeying to determine how damages would be assessed, the Mapai-led Israeli government arranged a reconciliation ceremony, a sulha, to settle claims.[39] They chose Avraham Shapira, the iconic rural settler "peacemaker," to lead the sulha committee. At the time, mainstream Zionist outlets celebrated the ceremony, and the payment of damages at the core of the proceedings, as a definitive conclusion to the affair, but Palestinians as well as left-wing Jewish Israelis criticized it as a farce. In the years that followed, the state attempted to prevent the commemoration of the event while Palestinians sought forms of grassroots memorialization that became a model for protests against civil inequality.[40]

In choosing a sulha, a long-standing method of restorative justice and conflict resolution in rural Palestine and one that Jewish settlers had participated in before 1948, Israel claimed to be resolving the affair on the Arabs' "own terms." The historian Shira Robinson argues that "by presenting the sulha in Kafr Qasim as a reconciliation between two warring parties, the government would situate the massacre within a narrated history of symmetrical violence between Arabs and Jews."[41] Shapira himself emphasized this framing when he said that "violence between the Jews and Arabs of this country did not start at Kafr Qasim and violence breeds violence."[42] Moreover,

THE COLONY AND THE VILLAGE 163

FIGURE 7. Avraham Shapira presides over the Israeli-orchestrated sulha ceremony at Kafr Qasim, November 20, 1957. Members of the sulha committee sit to his sides (courtesy of the Historical Archive of Petah Tikva).

Robinson argues, "the choice of the term 'sulha' revealed and reproduced an Orientalist image of Palestinians as ancient tribesmen who either rejected or did not understand modern judicial procedures."[43]

But the choice of a sulha not only reproduced an essentialized image of Palestinians, though it certainly did that; it also revived and advertised an essentialized image of early Zionists and, via the choice of Shapira, specifically First Aliyah colonists. Shapira personally reminded the gathered crowd that he had participated in "dozens of sulhas." As the historian Alex Winder has written of the sulha, "mediation requires status, status is gained by mediation. It also allows emergent and recently empowered actors to cement their legitimacy through mediation, thereby reinscribing new power arrangements as 'traditional.'"[44] Shapira had gained his purported status through decades of mediation, and the state was tapping it now.

Shapira represented a rugged rural frontier population that lived near and employed Arabs and, as a consequence, claimed to have the personal relationships necessary to meet Arabs on their own terms and resolve conflict outside the formal judicial mechanisms of the modern state. Mark Rifkin, in his work on Native American literature, has argued that the frontier is not a geographic space but a "structure of feeling" that offers a way of envisioning "a place paradoxically within the state yet beyond it," free of legal strictures and outside any jurisdiction. In other words, Shapira and the sulha conjured a place and time intrinsically outside politics: populated only by non-political Jewish settlers and by Arabs lacking nationalist sentiment or political awareness. Israel entered this conceptual space of frontier possibility both by employing a native custom and by evoking a historical moment when Jewish settlers had purportedly done so "authentically."[45] This despite the self-evident fact that this was a state-run event orchestrated in response to a state-perpetrated massacre.

In staging the Kafr Qasim sulha and arranging it under the oversight of a Petah Tikva old guard, indeed the iconic "Oldest of the Guards," Israel was also trying to legitimize its own new power arrangement. The sulha committee did not in fact wish to tell a narrative of symmetrical violence. They wanted to craft a narrative of reasonable Zionists able to deploy force and establish their dominance but also able, through real personal contacts and expert knowledge, to restore order and preside over a situation of calm. This message was not only about violence and its use, however; it was also about labor relations. Kafr Qasim exemplified what the anthropologist Abner Cohen calls the "border situation": the village was cut off from nearby villages by a border and "in intense interaction with the Jews in Israel with whom they [had] great economic interests."[46] In his remarks at the event, the Petah Tikva mayor Pinhas Rashish (Mapai) noted that "many residents of Kafr Qasim make a living from working in Petah Tikva, so I saw it as my obligation to intervene for their benefit and set matters straight." Hierarchical labor relations, now between Israeli Jews and Palestinian citizens of Israel living under a military regime, produced the proximity and familiarity that, Rashish claimed, both compelled and enabled coexistence.[47]

Some of the older people present at the sulha would have heard of some of the "dozens of sulhas" that Shapira had been involved in over the preceding generations. In the late Ottoman period itself, some Jewish settlers and settlement organizations expressed discomfort with the sulha mechanism (known in Arabic and Ottoman Turkish as *sulh*), rejecting what they considered "blood money" payments and preferring instead to take cases to the relatively new Ottoman criminal court system. Ex post facto narrators of this early period, however, would see participation in the sulha as evidence that Jewish settlers were familiar with and could prevail within local systems of justice and that those who opposed it were reflecting their "diasporic" lack of familiarity with Palestine.[48] In 1950, the Rehovot settler and First Aliyah chronicler Moshe Smilansky (1874–1953) lauded the "native" expertise that led to the resolution of an 1891 incident. Arab peasants from Zarnuqa (also called Zarnuga) had grazed their flocks on lands that Jews had recently purchased and developed as the colony of Rehovot. Though aware that Ottoman authorities permitted grazing on uncultivated land, the colonists barred their neighbors from doing so. A conflict broke out when Jewish settlers stole the peasants' animals and the peasants came to steal them back. No one was killed in this particular incident, but the colonists faced a judicial choice: to hold a sulha with Zarnuqa or to take the case to the Ottoman state courts. Smilansky's account, published in a volume produced for Rehovot's sixtieth anniversary, suggests a difference of opinion between "foreign" Jews, who demanded a trial, and nativized Jewish settlers, who understood the utility of the sulha. "Those [Jews] expert in local affairs [*beki' im be-' inyane ha-aretz*]," he wrote, "advised the colony to make an agreement," while the people of the colony whose "hearts were hot" were swayed by the Russian consul who "incited" them to request a trial. Ultimately, they did seek a trial, but it dragged on for years at great cost and in the end, two years later, the colony entered into a sulha with the village anyway.[49]

Amihud Nahmani (1899–1985), writing for a local Rehovot publication in 1966, recalled further clashes with Zarnuqa residents in 1913 (when he was 14).[50] After difficulties finding someone to mediate a sulha, they got Avraham Shapira who, Nahmani recalls, arrived not in his usual Oriental attire but in Western clothing and was warmly greeted by a sheikh who had also been invited from Hebron for the occasion. Shapira, said Nahmani, "became the interior minister and foreign minister" of the Yishuv, someone who could "speak to villagers in their language, to the tent-dwellers in their melody, to children in Hebrew, and Jewish elders in Yiddish."[51] Shapira was thus, in local memory, the government before the government, the savvy settler located betwixt and between populations, languages, and eras. He served and ultimately symbolized the entire nation and represented a liminal period, an embryonic Jewish state, and a raw pioneer ethos that transcended "stateness" altogether.

During the mandate period, Hebrew-language journalistic accounts normalized the sulha and emphasized the respect afforded to Avraham Shapira. One particular sulha loomed large: the sulha of 1921. In the midst of the general anti-British, anti-Zionist riots of 1921, a group from Abu Kishk, to the west of Petah Tikva, attacked Petah Tikva on May 5. Led by Shapira, the much-commemorated story goes, Petah Tikva put up a defense and lost only four men while the village lost forty-six.[52] The head of the Abu Kishk clan, Shaker Abu Kishk, refused to conduct a sulha at that time and was imprisoned by the British, but Shapira managed to successfully negotiate for Abu Kishk's release from prison and broker a subsequent sulha. As the story goes and as Shapira himself recounted in his testimony to the Shaw Commission in 1930, this sulha remained intact until 1948, despite an arson incident in 1929 that threatened to abrogate it.[53]

In January 1947, the *Davar* reporter Yitzhak Yaakovi reported on a sulha ceremony conducted in Kibbutz Gvar'am, near Gaza, following an incident where Jewish guards had murdered an Arab man from the nearby village of Simsim. The kibbutz had prepared a delegation, including its *mukhtar* (head of external relations) and the guard Yosef Teitelboym, the *mukhtar* at Kibbutz Givat Brenner, adjacent to Rehovot. Teitelboym was born in the First Aliyah Galilean colony of Yesud HaMa'ala (est. 1883) and, since migrating southward, was known locally to have maintained "close connections and affairs among southern and Negev Arabs," as his obituary put it. (He was killed in December 1947 in the midst of Palestine's Civil War, along with the Arab guard accompanying him, and was buried in Yesud HaMa'ala.[54]) When he arrived for the sulha, Teitelboym came dressed in brown boots, riding pants, and a keffiyeh and agal headdress, in the Orientalist style adopted by Ashkenazi Jewish guardsmen since the late nineteenth century. Four kilometers from the kibbutz, the delegation met Avraham Shapira, who was coming by car with two Bedouin sheikhs from the Petah Tikva area. The reporter described at length the ornate decorations and refreshments, including coffee specially "sweetened in honor of the 'Muskovim,'" that is, the Russian Jewish guests. The matter of financial negotiations began. It was clear to the Jewish reporter that Shapira and Teitelboym were "respected and accepted by the sheikhs."[55]

Over the course of the mandate period, the presence of the British had transformed the sulha. It was not simply an arrangement between two local parties, nor a petrified traditional remnant, as Alex Winder has shown; it had become a matter of government interest and evolved as a result of that interest.[56] A British officer from the Gaza district was present at the Gvarʿam proceedings, the reporter noted, and the hosts made sure to feed him well. A verbal agreement was also no longer sufficient—a protocol needed to be entered in the Gaza district registering the agreement reached and the sum of money paid. Things had changed in other ways, too, the reporter noted. "It is necessary to point out that in this ceremony they dispensed with some of the accepted customs from the beginning," adding, "this time they were more practical and the display of the sulha lost some of its value." "I asked to make use of my camera and memorialize this exotic occasion," the reporter recalled, but one of the sheikhs who had accompanied Shapira said something that made the reporter understand that photography would not be appropriate given the Arab customs. These "customs," however, may have been distinctly modern and "connected to *'bolitikah'* [politics]." The reporter agreed to deposit his camera for safekeeping for the remainder of the event.[57]

Over the years immediately following Israeli statehood, the Hebrew press reported on several Jewish-Arab sulhas. One in 1949 occurred in Jaffa after a quarrel between the Arab café owner Abu Shundi from the Ajami neighborhood and the Jewish Lucian Fisher, owner of his own café in the adjacent Jabalya (later, Givʿat Aliyah) neighborhood. Jabalya had recently been emptied of its Palestinian residents, confiscated, and inhabited by Jews, many of them recent immigrants. After Abu Shundi stabbed Fisher, Jews had come out from the Café Gan Tamar to capture him, but he escaped. Some Jews then went to Ajami, and street riots broke out.[58] This sulha, it was reported, occurred on the initiative of Yehuda Prag, assistant chief of police for the Tel Aviv district. It happened "without the customary lamb and rice"[59] and included just "eggs, cucumbers, hummus, and beer," because of the austerity measures recently put into place.[60] In 1951, the Arab village Naʿura and the Jewish workers' settlement Tamra in the Lower Galilee arranged a sulha, "according to all the accepted customs and rules," after a Jewish resident, Zeev Friedman, was killed by local shepherds. The ceremony ended with "speeches for peace and friendship" and a song of praise for Jewish-Arab peace sung by a choir.[61]

Turning to the sulha mechanism after the 1956 Kafr Qasim massacre, therefore, seemed to be in keeping with a tradition that dated back to late Ottoman times, continued with British involvement under the mandate, and had been episodically employed in cases involving Jewish victims or perpetrators in the new Israeli state. But whereas the aforementioned sulhas addressed murders by civilians, the Kafr Qasim massacre was perpetrated by agents of the state, members of the Israeli border police. It pitted not individuals, neighborhoods, or local communities against one another, but rather the state itself, and its military and police apparatus, against a civilian community reeling from the losses of 1948 and fearing for its future. The Mapai government employed the sulha not only to quiet the conflict or prevent local acts of revenge. Rather, it wanted to communicate the more existential message that Israel had and continued to have essentially peaceful intentions. In recruiting Shapira as the head of the sulha committee, it was projecting this narrative into the settler past. But in hitching itself symbolically to a First Aliyah defender, Israel laid bare the fact that the sort of coexistence it had in mind for its Palestinian population was hierarchical, involving Arabs living alongside Jews and working for them within a situation of Jewish economic and political control.

It was clear from the outset that the sulha wouldn't work out the way earlier ones had. The Israeli state had imprisoned the members of the Israeli border police who had perpetrated the massacre, including the brigade commander Colonel Issachar Shadmi, and unlike the British in 1921, was unwilling to release prisoners to participate in the sulha. Rather than there being a payment from one family to another to acknowledge personal responsibility, the Israeli government paid the damages to the affected families, while Shadmi himself was acquitted and asked to pay only a nominal fine. Initially, Shapira refused to participate in the ceremony, saying that the sulha could only be held in the presence of the two sides, but he eventually agreed: "in the end he was convinced because on such an important matter, one can't nitpick."[62]

Ultimately, the sulha lacked legitimacy across the Palestinian community of Israel, which saw the incident as a symbol as they advocated for their rights as citizens.[63] But multiple sectors of Israeli Jewish society lauded Shapira's leadership role in the sulha. Five years later, in 1962, the State of Israel paved a road connecting several Arab villages, including Kafr Qasim, within the Triangle region. The minister of labor, Yigal Allon, gave the honor of cutting the ribbon to Shapira, aged nearly ninety-two at the time. Allon said of Shapira in a speech, "This man isn't just a symbol of heroism but he has also long become a symbol of true friendship between Jews and Arabs." As a *Maariv* article subsequently added, "Shapira fulfilled a large and crucial role in the general reconciliation between the Jewish Yishuv and the residents of Kafr Qasim after the great tragedy in which 49 residents of the village were killed in 1956 at the start of the Sinai Campaign."[64]

Petah Tikva was particularly eager to celebrate him. At a press conference at Shapira's house during his ninetieth-birthday celebration in 1960, Shapira's son Yehoshua said, "I want to present my father to you, my Avraham Shapira, to tell you what he symbolized in his time and to correct distortions that were said or written about him." "The Arabs respected him so much," Yehoshua said, "that they preferred to be judged by him even after the establishment of the state." He cited an incident between the Arab villages of Sandala and Muqeibila (located in the Marj ibn 'Amir/Jezreel Valley). When the secretary of police and military governors intervened, "the Arabs said: Sheikh Ibrahim Mikha [Shapira] should come and we'll accept his judgement, and indeed so it was and within two hours Avraham Shapira resolved the conflict." The younger Shapira seamlessly connected this mandate-era incident with his father's invitation to participate in the sulha at Kafr Qasim: "he was also the one who concluded the Kafr Qasim affair without getting thanks from the authorities." Just as "he was considered a Jewish leader during the Turkish period," he added, so too did he defend Petah Tikva in 1921 and thus prevented a further attack until 1948. Therefore he was equipped to manage Israel's Arab relations after statehood.[65]

Baruch Oren, active in a range of commemorative activities through the Petah Tikva Museum and local memorial site, shared a similarly rosy recollection of Shapira's role:

> When he was already very old, the state imposed on him one of the hardest and final tasks of his action-packed life. I mean the tragedy that occurred near Kafr Qasim on October 29, 1956. After what happened happened [*mah she-karah karah*], the Oldest of the Guards was given the mission of order-

ing [*hasdarah*] relations with the injured village. Avraham was appointed as the chairman of the "sulha committee" and over many long months worked to achieve peace and reconciliation. To our great happiness there are still members of the sulha committee living among us and they can testify to the dedication and wisdom that the Oldest of the Guards brought to deal with the problems that were swirling around it. Through unceasing intelligence and patience, he did what was imposed on him and didn't give up on it until he merited ... to sign the sulha agreement.[66]

Calling the Kafr Qasim sulha one of the last in a series of escapades in an "action-packed life," rather than a highly unusual and novel arrangement imposed by a sovereign state on a vanquished minority population, Oren positions it within a natural lineage of heroism that went all the way back to the late Ottoman period. This lineage, he suggested, had not been interrupted by the establishment of the Israeli state or the events of the 1948 war. This was a narrative that could be and was adopted by the Labor government that arranged the sulha: the convener of the sulha committee, Pinhas Rashish, and all of the committee's members aside from Shapira were Mapai members. Oren keeps the substance of the incident ("what happened") vague, noting only that Shapira's task was as it had always been: "reordering" relations, in other words, returning the situation to an apparently conflict-free status quo ante. In the world symbolized by Shapira, there were no collective grievances, no historically weighted wrongs, no national conflict, only a series of unfortunate incidents committed in the heat of passion or out of greed or vengeance that could be canceled out through Jewish bravery, personal relations, and a ritual process of reconciliation. Once the sulha was achieved, Oren implies, the conflict was over.

The conflict wasn't over, of course. But the historically and commemoratively laden symbolism that Avraham Shapira brought to Kafr Qasim—the image of hierarchical coexistence—would persist. Israel had taken an economic structure that was previously iconic of (if not limited to) the First Aliyah moshavot—mainly Ashkenazi Jews hiring a mixed Arab-Jewish work force—and applied it within the state. Israel acknowledged that Palestinian citizens (officially called Arab Israelis) had the right to work in Jewish-owned enterprises, relegated them in practice to more menial positions, and cited their economic and now civic inclusion as evidence of Israel's contribution to their standard of living.

Rationalizing Destruction

Kafr Qasim, a symbol of the relations between Israel and its Palestinian minority, sat within a short drive of a half-dozen other villages that had been destroyed. How did moshava hierarchical coexistence narratives evolve to accommodate these spaces? In the decades after the war, Israeli Jews widely believed that Palestinians had willingly fled, having been encouraged by inimical Arab states. This explanation for the sudden, massive demographic shifts that they saw assuaged the cognitive dissonance of having participated in that displacement (in the case of soldiers) and of seeing the country's demography suddenly changed.[67] For Jews who had personal memories of hierarchical contact, however, a narrative of nostalgia coexisted with the perception of enmity that created a retroactive justification for the destruction of the villages.

Palestinians rarely physically attacked Jewish colonists (or vice versa) during the "First Aliyah" period. During the mandate period, as we saw in chapter 2, colonists tended to reference such incidents as there had been not to suggest an inherent enmity but to insist on the exceptional nature of such violence, the absence of political ideology on the part of *either* the Arab attackers or the Jewish colonists, and the capacity of the colonists to restore peace through hierarchical coexistence. During and after 1948, in contrast, several Zionist writers cited and re-narrated incidents from the early colonial history to suggest an ongoing enmity and to link past offenses to present destruction. Even so, their narratives included components of nostalgic hierarchical coexistence discourse that recall the mandate-era colonies. We can observe these paradigms in two articles published in the Hebrew press, both in 1948, about two villages: al-Maghar near Gedera, and al-Yahudiyya (al-Abbasiyya) near Petah Tikva.

The first article, "Maghar: Village of Murderers," is about the murder of Fishel Ferber on March 21, 1900, at the age of 34, on the road to Jaffa. The suspected culprit was a resident of the nearby village of al-Maghar, to the north of the colony. Amnon Horvitz (1887–1966), a son of the Gedera founder Zvi Horvitz and one of the central heritage elites there, now recalled it in the context of an ongoing civil war for Palestine.[68]

Ferber's murder was grisly. The initial messengers sent to find him came back with no news. He had been seen last, they said, near Mikveh Israel, the agricultural school just southeast of Jaffa, on a donkey outfitted with purchases from a trip to that city. As a second delegation went out from the colony, spirits sank. Horvitz, thirteen years old at the time, remembers that a group of children "also decided to go out in a group, quietly and secretly, to help out the grownups," but before they did, a rider came back: Ferber had been found. It took a while for all the information to come out but eventually they learned that the search party had found a trail of blood near al-Maghar that led to Ferber's body. His hands and feet had been tied to the legs of the donkey and he had received axe blows to the back of his head such that "his eyes were bulging out of their sockets." His friends tried to revive him, but they failed. The murder appeared to have taken place in the context of a highway robbery. Colonists guarded the body until police arrived from Gaza, and only then did they give Ferber a Jewish burial. The investigations were "long and tiring" and in any case, Horvitz thought, the trial was useless: though the murderer was imprisoned, the colonists heard a rumor that he had gained his freedom by offering several hundred Turkish lira, along with a horse, to the judge.[69]

Taken at face value, the article about the murder argues that al-Maghar had always been a "village of murderers," per the article's title, and that the Jews, now finally strong, were justified in any attacks on it in the context of the 1948 war. After Ferber's murder, Horvitz says, "a separating partition and a border of blood was placed from then on between Gedera and Maghar."[70] In May 1948, immediately after Israel's declaration of statehood and only three weeks after Horvitz published his article about Ferber's murder, the IDF's Givati Brigade destroyed al-Maghar, along with other villages north of Gaza, as part of Operation Barak. Horvitz, writing on the cusp of al-Maghar's destruction, is simultaneously writing about a still extant place with a long history of relationship to Gedera, and a place that has become set off by a "separating partition" and "border of blood." If al-Maghar is destroyed, he suggests—when it is destroyed, we know in retrospect—he will not mourn it, but he will also not forget it.

Remembering Ferber's murder, however, also conjured up a more intimate set of domestic memories from the past that presented a story of tranquility. Ferber had been renting a beautiful house belonging to Horvitz's father: "the house in which I spent the first seven years of my life." Ferber, born in the Russian Empire, was the colony's first shoemaker. Where the colonists had previously had to go to Jaffa for their shoe repairs, now they could be done locally at "the low shoemaker's table, crammed full of lots of things: a shoemaker's knife; a small bowl made of half a coconut shell full of yellow glue, whose smell was sour-sweet and spicy; laces with pig bristles on their ends that served as needles; and the can of small nails of all types, steel and copper, with and without heads, and wood nails." These were traditional Jews, Horvitz emphasized, using Yiddish terms to recall another colony member's "velvet hat on top of his skullcap [*yarmulke*] and a silk overcoat [*zhupakha*], and curly side locks [*peyes*] that peeked out from beneath the edges of the skullcap."

This scene of pig bristles, glue, and religious colonists, Horvitz remembered, was also the site of settler encounters with Arab peasants. Horvitz recalled that Ferber "was known in the whole area, including the villages." Arabs would go to visit him and "get laces from him to fix their shoes [*mashayya*, Arabic] or get an extra piece of leather." They would stay to have a conversation. Ferber was able to do these things, Horvitz stressed, "because his Arabic was fluent, something that wasn't widespread among farmers in those days." His murder only seemed to highlight to Horvitz the extent of the good relations. Horvitz was certain, moreover, that the residents of al-Maghar had no personal vendetta against Ferber since he "didn't have any enemies among the Arabs. On the contrary, they all loved and respected him."[71] The fact of Ferber's murder, then, though used in 1948 as evidence of Arab enmity against Jews, also provides Horvitz an occasion to narrate the moshava as a site, Ferber as a person, and the First Aliyah as an era that were all outside conflict. This narrative thread pushes against the title and main claim of the article.

Petah Tikva's relationship with one of its village neighbors, al-Yahudiyya, also took on a new cast in the context of the 1948 war, during which Zionist and then Israeli troops captured it. Al-Yahudiyya was five kilometers from Petah Tikva. It was near the site where Michael Shapira, Avraham's older brother, had purchased a plot of land and built a house in 1883. It was also the origin of the first major attack on the colony, in 1886, when local shepherds sought to defend their grazing rights and Hadad participated in the colony's defense. Al-Yahudiyya thus played a role in creating Petah Tikva's—and the Yishuv's—retrospective heroic narratives and frameworks.[72]

In 1932, the village changed its name to al-Abbasiyya to remove the Jewish-sounding name, a reference to the biblical Judah whose purported tomb was located there. "*Yahud*," the word for Jews, no longer solely evoked an ethnoreligious group, one that had lived in a workable equilibrium with Muslims and Christians for centuries in the Ottoman Empire; it now connoted a group with ethnonational political ambitions over the territory.[73] In 1947, sixty-two years after the conflict over grazing rights, al-Abbasiyya found itself at the heart of a battle. In December of that year, Irgun troops infiltrated the village, located in a strategic spot near Tel Aviv and the Lydda airport (today the site of Ben-Gurion Airport). Twenty-four attackers firebombed several houses and threw grenades, killing seven Arab residents and wounding seven more. On May 4, 1948, as hostilities continued, Irgun troops captured the village and held it for five weeks before losing control of it to the Trans-Jordanian Arab Legion. Then, in the midst of Operation Danny in July, better known for the expulsion of residents from nearby Lydda and al-Ramla, troops from the newly constituted Israel Defense Forces decisively conquered al-Abbasiyya.[74]

Two weeks after Irgun's first conquest of the village in early May and five days after the British departure from Palestine and the Israeli declaration of statehood, the Revisionist Zionist newspaper *ha-Mashkif* published an article entitled "The Descendants of the '*Wilad al-Mayit*' [Children of Death] are the conquerors of al-Yahudiyya."[75] Part a history of relations between al-Yahudiyya and the nearby Petah Tikva, part a justification for the recent Irgun assault, the article by Y. Svorai reveals the role of the past in the creation of narratives about coexistence, weakness, and masculine transformation in the new Israeli state.

The article frames its historical arc using narratives of Arab assault and Jewish bravery: the 1886 attack on the one hand, and the 1948 conquest on the other. In the middle, however, it describes a period of good relations achieved through Jewish goodwill and then scuttled by Arab nationalism and hubris. The 1886 attack "came suddenly, like a storm [*ba'ah pit'om ke-sho'ah*] on 24 Adar," Svorai writes (getting the date wrong: it happened on 22 Adar II [March 29]), calling it "the first attack of the Arabs of al-Yahudiyya on Petah Tikva."[76] He includes no information about the causes of the attack (the denial of grazing rights), Ottoman involvement, or the ambiguous land laws at the heart of the issue—all issues recognized by Jewish settler onlookers at the time.[77] In this 1948 framing, local opposition was sudden, unwarranted, and cruel and the Jewish response was strong and courageous. The phrase "*ba'ah pit'om ke-sho'ah*," from the book of Jeremiah, had been used to describe this incident decades before, including in the 1929 Petah Tikva anniversary volume.[78] But a new resonance for the biblical word *shoah* was emerging in 1948, three years after the end of the Nazi Holocaust, as Svorai must have known.

Svorai pits the European Jewish helplessness in the face of the Nazi Shoah—seemingly emblematic of the already-dead quality of diaspora Jews—against the heroic reaction of the Yishuv. While Arabs had referred to Jews as "children of death," Svorai notes after his first use of the term in the article, "the [Arab] shepherds quickly realized their errors: the youths of the moshava, and at their head the guards Sender Hadad and Yehuda Raab . . . chased away the attackers and caused them casualties." If Jews were expected to be weak "children of death," a Jewish reversal had left Arabs dead instead.[79]

This show of Jewish strength, Svorai implies, enabled a period of peace to follow: a sulha after the 1886 attack and the second sulha in 1921 (mentioned above) after the residents of al-Yahudiyya joined an attack by the Arabs of Abu Kishk who he claims, hyberbolically, "wanted to completely destroy Hebrew settlement in the country." He contrasts Arab annihilationist tendencies—another echo of *shoah*—with a claim of Jewish willingness to come to a peace agreement brokered by Avraham Shapira. Hierarchical coexistence followed. Arabs continued to labor in the Petah Tikva orchards.[80]

But, Svorai intoned dramatically, 1936 marked the beginning of the end: "the poison of [Arab] nationalism penetrated and spread through all the Arab villages" and the Arabs attacked again, but this time hit an "iron wall."[81] The "iron wall" reference invoked the Revisionist theory of Zionist militarism, forwarded by Vladimir (Zeev) Jabotinsky in 1923, in which peace would prevail only after Arabs encountered an iron wall of Zionist strength and realized that their opposition, though a legitimate response to Zionist colonization, was ultimately futile.[82]

Arabs would continue to doubt the force of the iron wall, the story continues, to their own detriment. When the first sappers of Irgun took control of the village, the *shabab* [young men, Arabic] of al-Yahudiyya mocked them: "You were heroes in Haifa, where the English showed you the way, but try to come to al-Yahudiyya and we'll show you the force of our hands!" The *shabab* had been a stock part of descriptions of Arab villagers, as in the Sender Hadad story that Baruch Oren published: they were cocky young men bested by the newly masculinized Zionist fighters. In this case, their bold claims and ostensible preparation could not keep out Irgun's attack: "When the Hebrew soldiers got to the mosque, where words of peace had been spoken [after the 1921 sulha], there was not a living soul in the village, except for abandoned cats and dogs, and many casualties." The year 1886 had returned, this time in full military gear: the descendants of the "children of death" had been inspired by that first generation of transformed Jews as they undertook what Svorai calls "the war of liberation and conquest [*milhemet ha-shihrur veha-kibush*]".[83]

Al-Yahudiyya was completely destroyed, with the exception of its mosque, which survives today in the Jewish town of Yehud (established in 1948 and populated by Turkish, Yemenite, and Polish Jews). A plaque on the building indicates nothing of its history as a mosque, however, stating only that the minaret, which it calls a "tower," served as a lookout point for Irgun forces. It also mentions that on June 11, 1948, while the Irgun controlled the village before finally conquering it, two female Jewish soldiers—Ruth Moritz and Miriam Aharoni—were killed on that spot.[84] Jewish fighters, the 1948 article proclaimed, had fully trounced not only the message of "the children of death" but also the (supposed) speakers of this accusation. Nonetheless, the village's former residents would still be episodically remembered and evoked as proof of the good relations in colonies past.

Just over a decade later, when students in Rehovot wrote essays in honor of the city's seventieth anniversary, they combined the dissonant tropes of Arab absence, past coexistence, and native menace that could allow memories of coexistence to exist with rationalizations of destruction. An essay by

Esther Lipka, a primary school student, imagines a tree whispering to her about Rehovot founders who cleared the thorns to build in the midst of "the great wasteland" while the women "went to the neighboring Arab village where they bought a bit of wheat, ground it, and returned to their homes." The tree also tells her that "Bedouins attacked the [settlers] and wanted to steal all their food, and they only barely managed to escape, with the Bedouins chasing after them. As a result, the parents had to stand guard all night."[85] Absence, economic dependency, and shadowy threat are all wrapped into this same short text, which exemplifies Kevin Bruyneel's characterization of settler memory as "a habitual mnemonic process that leads [settlers] to, at once, see and not see Indigenous people and settler colonial practices."[86] Another essay, framed as an elderly resident's dream, recalls an attack on Rehovot by the Arabs of al-Satariyya with whom "we never had good relations," and the bold defense by the colony that followed. At the end of the dream the old man is awakened by his 10-year-old granddaughter (the writer of the essay), who tells him about her school assignment and demands, "Tell me what to write." He tells her that she should write about "how we overcame the Arabs of Satariyya."[87] Ultimately, the replacement of Arab spaces with Jewish spaces seemed simply natural. In the words of another school essay, "The small moshava expanded, the Arab villages that were nearby and would plot murder, theft, and hatred are now settled with Jews from the whole diaspora."[88] These villages were menacing, it suggests, and now they are simply and rightfully gone. These schoolchildren, like new immigrants of all ages in central Israel, had relatively few Palestinian neighbors with whom to be in contact. The Arab villagers of days past had become both a figment of history and an ongoing prism through which Israelis would understand the unfolding regional hostility against Israel.

Shapira Forest, Talmei Menashe, and the Absent Village

In the aftermath of their displacement, Palestinians newly resident in Jordan, Lebanon, and elsewhere produced village memory books that recounted local histories from a position of displacement and dispossession. Moshava and other Zionist local memory books, in contrast, offered local histories of still-inhabited places. The anthropologist Rochelle Davis writes that this latter genre of memory document maps "a geography of possession—a geography that may describe longing for long-gone ways of life while still being present in the place."⁸⁹

To newly arrived Jews, the village sites seemed stunningly empty. Some described their aspirations to conquer the wasteland they saw. Residents of Barkai, built in 1949 on the ruins of Wadi ʿAra, proclaimed, "There was nothing there! . . . in this desolation, upon the *effendi's* house, between the flags of the nation and the class—our motto: 'Through building and creating we will make the wasteland fertile.'" Residents of Kibbutz Erez, founded in 1949–1950 in the northern Negev (Arabic Naqab), on lands that had been part of the village of Dimra, wrote in verse: 'By the sands and the desolate hills near the border / Erez rose and shaded by abandoned fruit trees / tents were pitched."⁹⁰ These tropes of the conquest of wasteland resemble those used a half-century earlier by those coming to purchase lands for the first colonies. But while the newcomer Jews from Romania, Poland, or Yemen were encountering the land for the first time, the veteran Jewish settlers knew that their towns and cities had not always been Jewish islands in an uninhabited landscape. In many "First Aliyah" moshavot, residents of these villages had served as workers or wagon drivers, guards or vegetable sellers, friendly neighbors or occasional attackers. This knowledge, however, did not prevent veteran farmers from celebrating their own origins and apotheosizing heroes. The two figures we have repeatedly discussed—Menashe Meirovitch and Avraham Shapira—were both honored through the creation of new Jewish sites named for them, both on confiscated Palestinian village lands.

Menashe Meirovitch died in 1949. A year later, in May 1950, the Jewish National Fund announced that it would issue a stamp in his honor.⁹¹ In December 1950, Rishon LeZion handed out the first Menashe Meirovitch prize for the best essay on "Bilu and the Rebirth of Israel [*tekumat Yisraʾel*]." The 25-lira prize funded by his son Zeev (who later changed his last name to Ha-Bilui, the Bilu Member) went to three students in the city.⁹² The contest seems to have gone on at least through the 1960s.⁹³ By 1965, the prize was 500 liras, and Zeev was thinking about increasing it to 1,500 liras and opening the competition up beyond Rishon LeZion to the whole country. That year, Zeev also donated a collection of Menashe's papers and belongings to the Central Zionist Archive in Jerusalem with the intention of creating a "Bilu Room."⁹⁴

On May 7, 1953, the General Zionist party, still the main political representative of private agricultural interests, founded a new *moshav* (a cooperative settlement of individual farms or residential plots on state land, not to be confused with "moshava"). They called it Talmei Menashe (Menashe's Furrows), after Menashe Meirovitch. It was located on land confiscated from the Arab village Abu al-Fadl near the eastern outskirts of Rishon LeZion, where Meirovitch had lived most of his life. Talmei Menashe was part of the "City to Village" movement spearheaded by David Ben-Gurion to encourage already settled Israelis, who often preferred city living, to resettle in rural communities. The State of Israel Government Yearbook for 1953 lists "Talmei Menashe (Abu Fadl)" as a cooperative settlement affiliated with the Farmers' Federation and "established for middle-class settlers" from Eastern Europe.[95] It would eventually be absorbed into the territory of the town of Be'er Yaakov, established in 1907 on privately owned lands between Rishon LeZion and Rehovot.

Abu al-Fadl, only four kilometers from the city of al-Ramla (Ramle), was located on the Rafah-Haifa railway line and had been home to settled Bedouins who worked in agriculture. Its population, which was over fifteen hundred in 1931, had declined to around five hundred by the mid-1940s. Benny Morris indicates that the villagers dispersed on May 9, 1948 in the course of Operation Barak (the same operation that depopulated al-Maghar), as the Givati Brigade cleared the coastal area west of al-Ramla and Lydda. Some villagers, however, appear to have remained until July, when the village was captured during Operation Danny, the largest operation to take place during the ten days of fighting between two summer truces. The village was occupied at the same time as al-Yahudiyya/al-Abbasiyya, discussed above. In 1949, Abu al-Fadl was replaced by the Jewish community of Sitria and later, Talmei Menashe was also established on its land. When Walid Khalidi investigated remnants of destroyed Palestinian villages in 1992, he found remains of "no more than five" original village houses, all in a state of collapse, one of them "located in the middle of a citrus grove."[96]

The site, also known as al-Satariyya after the name of the Bedouin tribe that settled there ('Arab al-Satariyya), was well-known to the early Jewish colonists, particularly those in nearby Rehovot. One of the student essays from 1961 that we cited above mentioned it. Incoming letters to the colony committee in

1891–1892, among others, include correspondence and agreements regarding Arabs from al-Satariyya grazing their animals on Jewish-owned vineyards and fields.[97] In 1948, Yitzhak Ziv-Av, president of the Farmers' Federation, recalled the residents of al-Satariyya as people "who would sell things during the day and ambush passersby at night," again speaking to a split image of intertwined, hierarchical economic relations and duplicitous enmity.[98] Moshe Smilansky recalled in 1950 that "various Bedouins had been living on the land" that would become Rehovot, including the Satariyya tribe. He recalled that young men would play along the roads at night throwing stones at the *"Yahud"* (Jews, Arabic) traveling between the colonies of Ekron (Mazkeret Batya) and Rishon LeZion. "Among these [Jewish] passersby," Smilansky said, were some of the men who would come up with the idea of creating a Hebrew settlement there. Members of the Satariyya tribe, then, had been present at the very inception of the colony—the colony had been founded despite them, relied on them for decades, and eventually displaced them.[99]

Smilansky had also written a fictional story, "Sheikh ʿAbd al-Qadir," about the Arabs of Satariyya. It was part of his "Children of Arabia" (*Bnei ʿArav*) collection (1911), which was characterized by paternalistic sentiments about Arabs and admiration for rural Semitic authenticity. In "Sheikh ʿAbd al-Qadir," the members of a fictional Bedouin tribe debate whether or not to protest Jewish settlement.[100] One character, Abu Khatab, argues for protesting, saying that the fact that Jewish settlers had been transferred title (*kushan*) to the land should not outweigh the fact that the tribe had worked the land for more than forty years. "I will not rest!" this fictional character says, "I will make sure the foreigners do not get the land!" Abu Daʿi, however, speaks in favor of accommodating the Jews: "it is not good to get into a quarrel with the Jews" (314–15). Moreover, he argues that the existing colonies pay Arab workers well. Those taking his side in the debate cite their amazement at the Jews' technological abilities and the benefit they would derive from well-paying jobs. A fight breaks out among the two factions, but the sale goes through and the community breaks in two. Quickly, the younger men in the tribe become fascinated with the Jewish settlers, "amazed at the equipment for surveying, the thing on three legs and the metal chain" and also "the white bread, the fruits" (318). When Bedouin boys go to work for those erecting "buildings sprouting up from dust," with their plastered sides and red roofs, tall doors and wide windows, they receive "coins of silver, real silver" (320). Ultimately those who had opposed the settlement, Abu Khatab's faction, are scattered.[101] The fictional story ventriloquizes a rationale for hierarchical coexistence through the mouths of Arab characters who, Yochai Oppenheimer notes, are present and even speak, but have their own memory stolen.[102] It also suggests that those who cannot recognize the benefits of this arrangement might as well disappear.

In 1948, not only half but all of the residents of al-Satariyya, now Abu al-Fadl, did "disappear," from the perspective of many in Rehovot. Like other lands and property confiscated from Palestinian owners who left during the war and were prohibited from returning, the lands came under the guardianship of the Custodian of Absentee Property, which transferred lands to a state-run development authority that authorized the formation of new Jewish settlements.[103] Talmei Menashe was founded on some of those lands in May 1953, by representatives of the Farmers' Federation and General Zionists. The new settlers agreed at that time that the Custodian, which now controlled and farmed large amounts of abandoned agricultural land, would complete the upcoming orange harvest, after which the orchards would be transferred to the ownership of Talmei Menashe. But when the new residents of Talmei Menashe arrived, around the start of 1954, they found that Custodian employees had already begun fertilizing the orchards in preparation for the following year, which had not been agreed to. *Ha-Boker* reported in late December 1953 that "the sons of the village," by which it meant the new Jewish residents, protested by barricading the entrances to the orchards. When the Custodian of Absentee Property sent tractors to break down the barricades, fistfights broke out.[104] As far as these new Jewish inhabitants were concerned, they were the "sons of the village" and they were being deprived of their cultivation rights by a hostile state authority. From their actions, it seems that they viewed the Custodian of Absentee Property in 1953 the way that the First Aliyah colonists viewed the Ottoman authorities in the late nineteenth century: state-level administrators unjustly putting up barriers in front of returning native sons. The fact the lands had been confiscated not even five years earlier from other long-standing owners and local residents—ones who may well have worked for Meirovitch, their new settlement's namesake—was clearly irrelevant to them.

The Shapira Forest

A few years later, in July 1960, the Petah Tikva municipality celebrated the eightieth anniversary of Avraham Shapira's arrival in Ottoman Palestine. Mayor Rashish, flanked by city officials, Knesset members, and the "last of the founders of the Mother of the Colonies," announced his intention to plant a forest in honor of Shapira. The history of Shapira's life, Rashish said, was a source "for the history of the Yishuv in the last eighty years."[105] Shapira still had some grievances against the colony: when he was imprisoned by the Ottomans for a period during World War I, the colony committee had refused for a time to pay him his wages as head guard. Planting the forest in his honor would be one way to mend relations. Vice Mayor David Tabachnik noted that, after all, Shapira had created good relations with "all strata of the nation."[106]

The land chosen for the forest had been confiscated near Qula, a village of 50 dunams and approximately a thousand residents east of Petah Tikva, on the site of the medieval Cola fortress and close to the road that linked al-Ramla and Tulkarm. Part of the land of that village had (in 1950) already become the settlement of Giv'at Koah, named for the twenty-eight (rendered *K-H* in Hebrew) fighters of the Alexandroni Brigade who had perished there while conquering the village.[107] This kind of "ancestor veneration" through naming, the historian Jean O'Brien says, is typical of "firsting": it works to establish the settler population as the first on the land. In the Israeli case, too, the perceived incursion of savagery into the civilized space was regularly commemorated by the consecration of more settlement space named after casualties.[108] Giv'at Koah was populated mainly by Jewish immigrants from Yemen who had previously been housed in a transit camp on the site.

The Shapira Forest became part of a larger Jewish National Fund forest on Qula lands called the Qula Forest (or, after the fighters who conquered the area, the Koah Forest). Qula was thus one of 149 villages whose lands, in whole or in part, had been converted into 46 Jewish National Fund forests, 41 national parks, and 25 nature reserves.[109] In this, Israel resembled other settler societies that created protected park, recreation, or wilderness areas on lands of displaced native populations assumed to lack a meaningful claim to the territory. Parks simultaneously prevented the return of the displaced,

FIGURE 8. Avraham Shapira in the Jewish National Fund "Avraham Shapira Forest," 1961 (courtesy of the Historical Archive of Petah Tikva).

converted land perceived as neglected or desolate into verdant territory amenable to plant and animal life, and offered ongoing recreation opportunities for those who had settled in nearby cities or towns.[110]

The first trees were planted in the Shapira Forest a little more than a year later, on September 14, 1961, on the occasion of Shapira's ninety-first birthday. (At this point it became generally and mistakenly assumed that the initial occasion for planning the planting had been Shapira's ninetieth birthday a year earlier, not the eightieth anniversary of his arrival.) The goal was to plant ten thousand new trees at first, with a total, eventually, of twenty thousand trees.[111] The tree-planting ceremony included remarks by Avraham Kamini, director of the Jewish National Fund; Rashish, the mayor of Petah Tikva; and Yosef Weitz, of the Israel Lands Authority (which had been formed in 1960 and now oversaw the Custodian of Absentee Property). Weitz shared memories of meeting Shapira years before, and Rashish promised to host a yearly celebration of Shapira in the forest bearing his name. Emmanuel Zamir, born in Petah Tikva in 1925, read a poem he had written for the occasion. Shapira stood up and thanked the assembled crowd, adding blessings for "world peace and the security of Israel."[112] The following Tu Bishvat, the festival of trees, groups of students from twenty-three schools came back to the site to plant even more saplings.[113]

Planting a forest in honor of a notable defender seemed wholly appropriate, as fitting as the naming of a residential community for Meirovitch. It mattered little that the forest would be built on the ruins of Qula. During the mandate period, the village's mostly Muslim population had a village center with a mosque, shops, a school for between between one and two hundred students, and around 4,000 dunams (~100 acres) of citrus orchards. Starting in July 1948, the village passed back and forth between Israeli army and Arab Legion control several times before it was eventually captured by the Alexandroni Brigade, which, as we noted, sustained twenty-eight casualties. David Ben-Gurion marked the village for destruction on September 13 of that year. "A forest covers much of the village site," Walid Khalidi wrote in 1992, noting that "the rubble of crumbled houses and terraces lies among the trees, and cactuses and fig, mulberry, and eucalyptus trees grow there as well." Remains of the school survive on the west side of the site.[114]

Notably, First Aliyah-specific claims to have predated conflict or been part of intimate personal connections played no role in the tree-planting ceremony, nor did those who planted trees in memory of Shapira mention the Palestinian history of the sites. Rather, this history was obscured through two mechanisms. First, the site is described as "the desolate hills of Qula," which evoked the language used to describe the sites of original colonies and implied the need for Zionists to resurrect them. Second, the significance of the site lay in its Jewish casualties, the victims of faceless Arab masses: "these hills were filled with the blood of dozens of young men, who stood heroically during the War of Independence as few against the hundreds and thousands" and who through their deaths blocked the advance of the enemy to Petah Tikva."[115] Rashish noted that, eighty-three years earlier, "the first furrow was plowed," and that "those same First Ones laid the foundation for the State of Israel."[116] Moreover, "without those who fought here as the successors of the First Ones, we wouldn't be able to live in Petah Tikva."[117] Stories of individual relationships between Jewish colonists and individual Arab workers or neighbors, posited against a trend of separation, are replaced here with a generic Zionist vision of Arab enmity, anonymity, and the necessity of defense against hordes of attackers, what Nurith Gertz calls the Zionist commemorative trope of "the few against the many."[118]

"When I arrived eighty-two years ago," Shapira noted, "the whole area was destroyed and now I've seen the state created. Long live the land of Israel!" Shapira was drawing a clear distinction between the narrative of Zionist creation and a narrative of degradation at the hands of Arabs and Ottomans. Around the same time, he gave an interview in which he recalled impressing upon Lord Balfour, during the British dignitary's visit to Petah Tikva in 1925, the stark divide between civilization and wasteland. "Balfour went up to a high point, stood and looked left and right, right and left. I said to him, 'Lord Balfour, every place that you see trees, that's a Jewish settlement, and every place where you see wasteland [*shemamah*], that's Arab.' He said to me 'Is it really so?' and I said 'As you hear it Lord Balfour.'"[119] If during the mandate period, the tradition of creation ex nihilo was accompanied by stories of moshava First Ones who forged personal, individual relationships with Arab neighbors against the Labor Zionist push for communal separation and who used these relationships to resolve conflicts, now the founders emphasized a more generic—though by no means new—settler narrative of Jews reclaiming neglected land and fighting Arabs bringing destruction.

But people commemorating Shapira continued to reference his interpersonal connections in Palestinian villages even as they planted trees in his honor on the ruins of one of them. One year after his death, at the end of 1966, the *Yad la-banim* memorial site in Petah Tikva hosted an exhibition in his memory. "The name of Avraham Mikhal traveled far," proclaimed a plaque in large letters, using a version of Shapira's nickname. "All of the Gaza Strip praised him. His feats were known up to the Jordan Valley. His name was great in the Galilee and his praises were sung in Judea, Jaffa, Jerusalem, Ramla, Lod [Lydda], Hebron, Nablus, Beirut, and Damascus." Shapira, coverage of the exhibition proclaimed, taught the lesson of cultivating good relations with "the neighbors." In this, his story reflected "the history of Petah Tikva from its first days." The exhibition was full of portraits of Shapira with leaders and dignitaries, including Shaker Abu Kishk, with whom he had coordinated the sulha agreement in 1921, and photographs of the sulha ceremony thirty-six years later at Kafr Qasim. But an article about the exhibition in *ha-Tzofeh*, with these details of past coexistence, also contained a picture of Shapira in the forest bearing his name. It described the forest's location using only Israeli reference points: "between Midgal Tzedek and Nahshonim, not far from Petah Tikva."[120] If anything, this form of commemoration intended to offer compensation for a perceived *Jewish* destruction, the forgetting of First Aliyah settlement on the part of later-arriving Zionists. This slight by other Zionists, perceived since the early twentieth century, obscured the violence of the more recent destruction of Palestinian villages.

In May 1968, a fire broke out in and around the Shapira Forest and consumed thousands of acres. After battling the blaze from mid-afternoon until three in the morning, firefighters from Petah Tikva were able to extinguish the flames.[121] Five years earlier, A. B. Yehoshua had published his story "Facing the Forests." Its protagonist is a firewatcher at a remote post who cannot, in the end, prevent the incineration of the Jewish National Fund forest he is hired to protect. In the charred remains of the forest a destroyed village and a voiceless Palestinian, both previously hidden by the forest, become visible.[122] The Shapira Forest, however, didn't just cover a Palestinian past; it also celebrated a particular local Zionist narrative of hierarchical coexistence that both referenced the Palestinian past and, like the forest, participated in obscuring it. When I wrote to the Jewish National Fund offices to learn about the current status of the Shapira Forest, a representative confirmed that the sign marking the Shapira Forest is no longer in place in the Qula Forest.[123] She explained that, in recent years, Jewish National Fund policy has been to remove signage that has been damaged by weather or vandalism—she did not specify which had been true in this case.[124] The Shapira Forest sign is now located in a commemorative site at the Jewish National Fund offices in Beit Nehemia, an Israeli town established in 1950, by Iranian Jewish immigrants, on the lands of the village of Bayt Nabala.

On the occasion of Shapira's ninetieth birthday in 1960, a team of reporters from *Davar* published an article about "The Oldest of the Guards" entitled "The Past Is Still Here." While Shapira "belongs to history," as do others about whom "many myths have been woven," "Shapira is also reality," they wrote. Reporters arranged a visit to Petah Tikva to visit him but couldn't find him. A neighbor said that nearly every night he was out of the house attending a party, an anniversary, or a wedding as a guest of honor. He was a myth in high demand.

When the reporters finally found Shapira the following morning, reading the newspaper at home, they asked him not only to remember the past but to foretell the future, specifically the future of regional relations between Israel and the Arab states: "Do you think that there will be another war between us and our Arab neighbors?" Shapira responded that he had been asked that very same question while on a visit to New York four years earlier. "I replied," he said, "that I'm a private person, not a politician and not a diplomat, but I'll allow myself to say: if all our friends and enemies (I mean, the big countries of France, England, Russia, and the United States) would just leave us alone, there would already be peace and we would have figured things out [*mistadrim*] with our neighbors. And that's what I always say."[125]

By the last decade of his life, Shapira was associated in Israel with the resolution of Jewish-Arab conflict in connection with a nostalgic past that provided Israelis, not only in Petah Tikva or the "First Aliyah" moshavot but also in a range of residential and political settings, with an escapist commemorative experience and narrative about their own good intentions. Israel was enmeshed in a regional conflict that had been playing out in the IDF's cross-border raids into Jordan, a boycott of Israel by the Arab League, and fighting in the Suez Canal area and the Sinai after the Free Officers' coup in Egypt. Though Shapira had no experience in government or formal military service, nor expertise in political science, reporters treated him as a resident expert on regional affairs. When they asked him to prognosticate, however, he responded by separating himself from geopolitics. He knew nothing about these matters, he seemed to protest, but he did know something about Jewish-Arab relations: peace could be obtained only by removing all geopolitical and regional interests in it.

Shapira's wish, of course, was counterfactual. Jews, including his own family, had settled and were continuing to settle in Palestine/Israel within larger geopolitical and economic contexts that facilitated, enabled, or compelled Jewish settlement. Likewise, Palestinians' protests against Zionism and evolving relationships with emerging Arab states reflected the politics of imperial and neo-imperial interactions and economic change. There had never been a Jewish settler encounter with Arabs or with older urban Jewish communities, nor with Palestine itself, that was detached from imperial, regional, local, transnational, or global political concerns, not during the "First Aliyah" period and not after. Yet in Shapira's mind all that mattered were individual relations and goodwill beyond politics. Therein lay his charm and mystique, a mystique that Petah Tikva, his home, and the First Aliyah colonies in general had been long working to claim for themselves.

⟮ CHAPTER 5 ⟯

JEWISH IMMIGRANTS AND THE POLITICS OF SETTLER "FIRST ONES"

In 1957, less than a decade after Israel's founding, the Rishon LeZion municipality circulated a pamphlet, "The Celebration of Your City's Anniversary: When and How?" With a population consisting overwhelmingly of immigrant Jews lacking familiarity with the city's pre-state history, let alone its founding as a Jewish agricultural colony in 1882, the municipality emphasized that the upcoming event was intended for all residents, new and old. "Citizen!" it exhorted its readers, "On your holiday, forget everything, be happy and joyful because it's your day."[1] Mayor Hannah Levin, the first female mayor in Israel, urged residents "to adopt this wondrous project called Rishon LeZion, make every tree and flowering bush dear in your eyes as though it were yours. Consider every public building as though you yourselves had built it and cultivated its appearance."[2] Vice Mayor Eitan Belkind invited all residents to embrace Rishon LeZion's inclusive, nonpartisan ethos. The founders, he said, were "not representatives of political parties" but simply "pathbreakers [*nahshonim*] who answered the call of the people."[3]

Levin and Belkind's "apolitical" rhetoric belied a stark class divide. Levin, who had immigrated to Palestine in 1923, had married Michael Levin, a son of the "First Aliyah" settler Asher Levin. Asher Levin had become a leading figure within several organizations serving private farmers: the Farmers' Federation; the Farmers' Bank, a low-interest-loan-granting arm of the Federation established in 1934; and the Amir agricultural marketing and investment company (est. 1942).⁴ Belkind was the son of Shimshon Belkind, a prominent local landowner and head of the colony council before statehood. The offer of symbolic private ownership ("as though it were yours; as though you yourselves had built it") was thus being presented by representatives of the city's true owner class to a population that relied on state services and had no access to private property.

Anxieties about educating new immigrants had animated mandate-era commemorations, as we have seen. Now, rapid demographic change and growing material, spatial, and economic pressures on the moshavot following statehood created a new urgency in the minds of local leaders, planners, and heritage elites. By 1952, the State of Israel had doubled its Jewish population through a policy, codified in 1950 with the Law of Return, of admitting nearly all Jews who wished to immigrate. These new arrivals, especially children, were prime educational audiences. In 1962, a member of an anniversary planning committee in Zichron Ya'aqov, founded the same year as Rishon LeZion, remarked, "We'll do well to continue to tell of these acts of heroism to our brothers the new immigrants, to encourage them and to prove to them that effort and persistence has a reward."⁵

Through local celebrations, commemorations, and curricula, as well as museum exhibits, parades, and song, local educators pushed for a moshava-specific narrative of the past that could augment the broader Zionist one. They combined nostalgia with a mission to carve out a space for a Zionism they presented as prior to politics and supportive of the common good. An agricultural project based (in part) on individual capital and private initiative, sustained by settler virtues not restricted to the owning class and unmoored from partisan loyalties, they said, had brought the Yishuv to statehood and would assure the new country's viability into the future. Yet in the context of Israeli statehood, firstness was a prize that multiple Zionist constituencies wished to claim, including within the framework of commemorations tied to the "First Aliyah."

As Israel attempted to absorb the first massive waves of Jewish immigrants, many of them indigent, from both post-Holocaust Europe and the Islamic world, it established Jewish Agency-funded immigrant camps (*mahanot 'olim*) and then transit camps (*ma'abarot*), many of them on confiscated Palestinian lands in central areas of the country. As one Israeli geographer writes with no apparent sense of irony, it was possible to build more quickly on these lands than within the municipalities because "there was no need for a long and tiresome process of buying up small lots."[6] Unlike the often isolated and resource-poor development towns and rural *moshavim* (cooperative settlements) that the state later created, these transit camps were often close to centrally located moshavot that—at least in theory—offered jobs and services to support a growing population.[7] Of the first 129 transit camps, 98 were located next to or within the boundaries of existing towns, many of them moshavot established on the basis of private ownership, which eventually saw their populations tripled, quadrupled, or even quintupled as a result.[8] The Amishav camp near Petah Tikva, originally slated for 500 newcomers, received twice as many within two months in early 1951.[9] As of early 1952, 48% of the 240,000 people in transit camps were within the municipal boundaries of moshavot (including moshavot founded later, during the mandate period), and 50% of those seeking work in moshavot came from the transit camps.[10]

Eventually, multiple areas that had formerly been part of Palestinian rather than Zionist space were annexed into the municipalities, though often only following clashes with municipal bodies.[11] In 1952, Petah Tikva also annexed Sha'ariya, a Yemenite neighborhood that had been established in the 1930s and whose residents had worked within the colony alongside Palestinian Arabs. Other nearby areas became majority-Mizrahi cities and towns. Rosh HaAyin, the site of a former British military camp and the Palestinian village of Ras al-'Ayn, to Petah Tikva's east, became home to several thousand Yemenite Jews soon after Israel's declaration of statehood. Al-Yahudiyya (al-Abbasiyya) to its north became Yehud (as we saw earlier), where a community of Ladino speakers from Turkey settled, along with Yemenite Jews and Polish Holocaust survivors. The villages of Saqiya and Kafr 'Ana, south of Petah Tikva, became the site of several transit camps for Iraqi Jewish immigrants who arrived in 1950–1951. In 1955, the Saqiya site became the core of Or Yehuda, now the location of a museum of Iraqi Jewish immigration to Israel. Though Israel soon made it policy to settle new Mizrahi immigrants on the geographic periphery near borders, in practice it failed to completely prevent an ongoing outmigration to the center of the country by those looking to exercise individual choice and unwilling to be pioneers. Migrants also gravitated away from work officially provided by the Jewish Agency to better-paying informal labor arrangements in central cities and moshavot.[12]

Residents of transit camps in the 1950s, and to a lesser extent those who were transferred to public housing in or near moshavot, found themselves in low-quality habitations with incomplete infrastructure, physically isolated from moshava town centers by areas of privately owned land that was not available for public housing.[13] Those who could move to more established neighborhoods eventually did, leaving a poorer and majority-Mizrahi population on the periphery—that is, in the cases of the largest moshavot, the periphery of the country's center.[14] A spatial pattern emerged in which a middle-class Ashkenazi core, sometimes itself called "the moshava," was surrounded by a spatial periphery that was also a social and political periphery. "This kind of distinction between inner and outer urban areas," Amiram Gonen writes, "was particularly marked in the towns that grew out of the moshavot."[15] Such immigrants were naturally more concerned with making a living and securing basic rights than with participating in the historical commemoration of towns that seemed to be neglecting them and whose elites sought to preserve their influence, including through undemocratic means.

A November 9, 1948, editorial in the General Zionist newspaper *ha-Boker* had emphasized the functional capitalist relations in seventy-year-old Petah Tikva, which provided a "model for other villages and colonies" in its "working hard on behalf of private initiative in cultivating fair, just relations between the employer and the employee."[16] But this was an assertion made to defend against accusations to the contrary. Despite their economic and local political power, the moshava elites felt squeezed by immigrant arrivals. The General Zionists had maintained control in the municipalities in the later mandate period thanks in part to the British Municipal Corporations Ordinance of 1934 which gave the vote only to men over 25 who paid 500 mils (1/2 pound) per year in property taxes and 1 lira per year in municipal taxes. It thus excluded laborers and low-wage earners, who were more inclined to support Mapai, the strongest workers' party, though one that in effect tried to minimize class struggle. With municipal elections democratized in the statehood era, the traditional elites, previously reliant on patronage relationships with the British, feared the electoral influence of immigrant Jewish

FIGURE 9. A Jewish immigrant in rainy conditions at Zarnuga Transit Camp, near Rehovot, on the site of the Palestinian village of Zarnuqa, January 1951 (David Rubinger, courtesy of the KKL-JNF Photo Archive).

workers.[17] The veteran working classes, meanwhile, feared that newcomers would flood the labor market and compete with them for jobs. The General Zionists, representing the interests of owners and other more established residents, won a plurality of votes, 24.5% overall, in the local municipal elections of November 1950 after having won only 5.8% (seven mandates) in the national Knesset elections a year earlier.[18] In the 1951 Knesset elections, they went on to triple their representation nationally, becoming the second-largest party for the next four years, before again declining. Highlighting corruption in and coercion from the Mapai establishment, they appealed to wide swaths of the middle class concerned that their freedoms were being suppressed by the highly centralized Mapai bureaucracy. Four of the General Zionists' twenty Knesset members in this period—Ezra Ichilov, Hayim Ariav, Israel Rokach, and Joseph Sapir—had family connections to private agriculture.[19]

Sapir, the General Zionist mayor of Petah Tikva until he entered the Knesset in 1951, did not approve of transit camp construction nearby, but his successor as mayor, the Mapai member Pinhas Rashish, agreed to it after succeeding him, likely compelled by promises of additional government funding.[20] Immigrant demonstrations within or on the boundaries of moshavot—Hadera, Petah Tikva, Zichron Yaʿaqov, Ness Ziona, Raanana, Herzliya, Binyamina—further unsettled veteran elites already concerned about the ongoing costs of absorbing immigrants with enough means to settle within the municipalities rather than rely on state-provided housing.[21] For some old-timers, like veteran Zionists in other communities, the sacrifices asked of new citizens evoked the ascetic lifestyles they or their families had taken on as rural settlers decades before, and they considered the immigrants' complaints unreasonable.[22] Thus, the process of persuasion played out on a spatial level as well as a cultural one: as the moshava elites saw immigrant populations settling in transit camps on their geographic periphery (and ultimately felt pressure to annex many of these areas), they also considered how to extend the gravitational field of their symbolic discourse to draw them in.

Municipalities knew that new immigrants lacked an intuitive connection to the founding figures: "The old-timers' memories of their experiences are different than the impressions of new immigrants," said the 1957 anniversary pamphlet from Rishon LeZion. This observation prompted a writer named Avraham Levy to conduct interviews and then juxtapose a longtime resident, Zippora Yudilovitz, with a newcomer from Egypt, Vita Azulay. Upon meeting Yudilovitz, the 85-year-old daughter of one of the city's "First Ones" (Mordechai Freiman) and wife of another one (David Yudilovitz), Levy was surprised by her vitality. Yudilovitz didn't even have a cane, and she eagerly shared her story in "slangy Hebrew whose Yiddish melody played within it," a marker of both her seniority and her symbolic liminal status between the Ashkenazi diaspora and the Israeli State (despite her length of residence). Yudilovitz recalled the deprivation she had experienced upon her family's arrival at the Jaffa port and the pioneering fortitude required for their move to an unfinished house. She described hauling water on the backs of donkeys, seeking a schoolteacher to be sent from Jerusalem, and riding on the backs of wagons. Levy summarized Yudilovitz's nostalgic narrative of sacrifice and achievement as "many forms of happiness alongside suffering," and noted that as she looked back on "this first period [*tekufah rishonit zo*]" her eyes lit up.[23]

Levy contrasts Yudilovitz's experience with that of Azulay, a 60-year-old from Egypt whose family was struggling. Azulay lived in the Ezra u-Vitzaron neighborhood on the city's west side, where many new immigrants were settled by the state in the early years of statehood. Levy traveled to the neighborhood on a "crowded bus" that he described as a "moving Tower of Babel": "Dark, curly-haired children speaking Arabic with their mothers sit alongside light-haired and light-eyed girls speaking the hard-to-pronounce Hungarian language." This attention to linguistic pluralism reflected a widespread anxiety among veteran Zionists that a diasporic multilingualism repressed by Zionism had reemerged.[24] To these immigrants, Levy noted disappointedly, "the name Rishon LeZion means nothing."[25]

Azulay had been in the country for only two months at the time of the interview. He was a Zionist, he told Levy, and he had fallen in love with Israel "at first sight" despite having been warned in Egypt that it was a desert full of hungry people. Nonetheless, his family's current situation was not bearing out his optimistic hopes. His 30-year-old daughter Rachel revealed that, although she had worked in a professional role in the Jewish hospital in Cairo, her lack of Hebrew had prevented her from finding work in Israel. Other daughters revealed that they were also unemployed: "There's no work! No classes! Nothing!" The youngest daughter, Loretta, had found work in the Gamish rubber factory but found it unsatisfying. Gamish, founded in Tel Aviv in 1930 and relocated to Rishon LeZion in 1935, made news during the mandate period for its management's distinctively reactionary labor practices. One pro-Labor piece from 1945, following the signing of its first union contract, compared it to a "factory from the Middle Ages" that prevented unionization, compelled workers to work unpaid overtime, and recruited its workforce from "the street" in heavily Sephardic neighborhoods of World War II refugees, likely from Salonika, Greece, rather than from the Histadrut

(General Labor Union). The factory owners denied these claims and defended themselves with reference to acts of violence and sabotage carried out by the workers.[26] Despite the past unionization, Gamish continued to resist cooperation with the Histadrut after 1948. Labor struggles and strikes recurred at Gamish throughout the 1950s.[27] Loretta's "unsatisfying" experience reflected a new intra-Jewish ethnonational labor hierarchy in which Mizrahi immigrants would continue to serve in the lower rungs.

Though the interviewees clearly conveyed their frustration, Levy nonetheless spun his impressions into a story of national growth: he praised the neighborhood where children slept "peacefully, without fear" in "new houses" outfitted with "electric lights that drove out the foreignness and the darkness." These new immigrants, Levy concluded, were "the Biluim of 1957" who were waiting "in anticipation of the moment when they would turn into good and loyal citizens of the state in their city of Rishon LeZion."[28] Projecting the settler past onto the settler present both justified the ongoing Israeli settlement expansion by attaching the mantle of firstness to new arrivals and communicated a set of expectations for newcomers: they must come to understand and embody their neo-firstness, as it were, and act accordingly as citizens. The very statement, however, indicates the suspicion of disloyalty and insufficient commitment that motivated the city's outreach efforts in the first place.

The Local Politics of Commemoration

Immigrant workers were suspicious of the undemocratically inclined General Zionist elite that was supposedly welcoming them into their historical narrative. Mapai encouraged this suspicion as it recruited their support, sometimes citing these landowners' long-standing practices of overlooking the needs of the Jewish working class. As one piece of Mapai propaganda during the 1961 election summarized the settlement past: the farmers "fought against the Jewish workers so that they could hire Hauranim [migrant Arab workers from Syria] on their farms for a pittance. They were aided by the British police in arresting Jewish laborers who demanded their right to employment in the homeland."[29] As farmers promoted an apolitical narrative of the past, as they had done for several generations already, their commemorative events reflected the ongoing partisan stakes of collective memory. Petah Tikva, which had come under the control of a Labor Zionist mayor (Pinhas Rashish) in 1955 while Rishon LeZion and other First Aliyah colonies retained their General Zionist leadership, found its eightieth-anniversary events in 1958 beset by partisan squabbles.

With Labor interests newly elevated locally, the Petah Tikva municipal anniversary celebration had emphasized the historical role of workers in the colony. The Agricultural Union (*ha-Histadrut ha-hakla'it*), representing the private farming old guard, wrote to *ha-Boker* on October 15, 1958, to complain that the city's general celebration "hadn't emphasized the founding of Petah Tikva or agriculture in the moshava."[30] In response, descendants of the founders got together to plan a separate celebration "for the remnants of the agriculturalists, the builders of Petah Tikva." It is desired, said Efraim Gissin, chair of the Agricultural Union, "that the remnants of the founders meet for a party along with those continuing their work, to sit together and elevate the memory of the past. We still haven't clearly determined what form the celebration will take."[31] The planning committee was entirely constituted of agriculturalist families, many of whom had arrived in the colony's early days. We have already encountered some of their family names in our stories thus far: Gissin, Machnes, Raab, Sapir, and Ichilov. Nehemiah Ichilov, a citrus magnate and the founder of a citrus packing company, wanted to go all out with a "big public celebration" to be named the "Celebration of the Eightieth Anniversary of the First Hebrew Furrow." Mordechai Shalom Simkin, who had purchased an orchard in Petah Tikva in 1906, approved of the idea. He now presided over the successful Maadan ice and refrigerator company while also continuing in citrus sales.[32]

Last-minute efforts got underway in mid-October to plan an event for the founding date of 9 Heshvan (November 3), from 3–5 pm. The committee reached out to potential speakers and recruited couriers to personally deliver invitations to each head of household.[33] Efraim Gissin, also a citrus magnate, contacted Yehezkel Dagan, general manager of the Rishon LeZion-based Nesher beer company, and asked him to make available 750 bottles of beer ("600 of white beer and 150 of the newer malt beer") "as your contribution to the success of this celebration."[34] He wrote to the Maccabi Avshalom sports club, historically affiliated with the General Zionists and capitalist interests in the moshavot, requesting "sixty young Maccabees in full dress to help us carry out the event."³⁵ He wrote to David Novick, also of a veteran Petah Tikva family, about filming the event.³⁶ The police band was selected to perform, and the committee planned to lay wreaths to remember "sons and founders."³⁷ Finally, they had notices prepared for newspapers and Israel Radio.³⁸ Gissin expressed regret that space constraints limited the event only to "the remnants of the founders of the Mother of the Colonies, representatives of the agricultural settlement points [*nekudot*] that were founded in the country before World War I, representatives of the Farmers' Federation, and the agriculturalists of Petah Tikva."³⁹

Things seemed to be going well at first: Gissin felt buoyed by telephone calls from all over the country expressing congratulations. But conflict was about to erupt. On October 19, 1958, just a couple weeks before the farmers' event, the organizers got word that the interior minister Yisrael Bar-Yehuda (of the Mapai coalition partner Ahdut ha-ʿavodah), one of the invited guests, had just delivered a controversial speech at a separate event organized by the Petah Tikva Workers' Council to celebrate the opening of an exhibition on "The First of the Hebrew Workers in the Land." The founders, he had said, were motivated by the desire "to turn from merchants to *effendis*," that is, Arab-style landowners believed to be motivated only by profit. "Their penetration into the land," he said "came only from a desire for *effendism*, as was accepted then in the country."⁴⁰ In other words, *Yedioth Ahronoth* reported, the founders were exploitative landowners, they had come to the country to open business ventures, and they quickly accommodated themselves to the retrograde practices of existing Arab landowners.⁴¹ Another article, entitled "Defaming the Founders," reported that this characterization shocked even leftists in attendance, enough so that even the former head of the Petah Tikva Workers' Council stepped in to point out that one could find "failures and defects among the Second Aliyah" as well.⁴²

Agriculturalists mounted a protest against Bar-Yehuda. After reading an account of the speech in the right-wing Herut party newspaper, Gissin wrote to him: "I was astounded to read your insulting words in *Herut* which rudely humiliate and attack the honor of the founders." Gissin reported that members of the public had been writing, visiting, and telephoning him all morning to express outrage: Bar-Yehuda needed to write something to calm them if he expected to speak at the upcoming event.⁴³ One such letter had come from a man named Moshe, who had read the report in *Herut* and found himself "amazed that a minister would say these words of defamation about our forefathers." Identifying himself as a "farmer from birth, whose grandfather and father were farmers," he insisted that "we remained farmers despite the malaria and we are farmers and vegetable growers until today." He encouraged Gissin to reach out to the minister and denounce his words.[44]

It's helpful to think of this squabble as a national-level partisan contest playing out at the local level over the meaning of a local past. The papers reporting critically on Bar-Yehuda's remarks included the General Zionist *ha-Boker*, the Herut-affiliated *Herut*, and the nonpartisan *Yedioth Ahronoth*. *Yedioth Ahronoth* was founded by Gershom Komarov, son of a First Aliyah agriculturalist who had worked in Ness Ziona, Rishon LeZion, and Kfar Tavor (founded 1901 in the Galilee). Labor-aligned papers, on the other hand, accused those newspapers of trying to besmirch the image of a Labor leader. *La-merhav*, the newspaper of Bar-Yehuda's party Ahdut ha-ʿavodah (which had broken from the further-left Mapam in 1954), claimed that "People from Herut, for whom the whole topic of the exhibition [on the Hebrew worker] was insufferable, took a part of his speech and through an acrobatic distortion 'cooked up' a libel against him with a strong 'before the elections' smell to it." As evidence, *La-merhav* offered the full text of Bar-Yehuda's remarks: the First Ones of Petah Tikva, he had said, had undertaken "one of the biggest revolutions in their lives and the history of the Jewish people" by moving from the urban religious communities dependent on diasporic Jewish philanthropy (*halukah*) to land settlement. But they didn't finish the revolution: they simply followed the typical practices of the time, without realizing that "Israel is a people without comparison whose special problems demand special solutions." The Second Aliyah, in this account, provided those solutions.[45]

Bar-Yehuda replied to Gissin on October 22. Like *La-merhav*, the newspaper that represented his party, he claimed to be "astounded by the insulting content and style of your telegram." He accused Gissin of "join[ing] the libel of Herut with closed eyes," despite not having been at the gathering and not having heard the speech. In reality, Bar-Yehuda stressed, he had praised the first settlers of Petah Tikva in his speech and emphasized their revolutionary quality and importance.[46]

Bar-Yehuda was in fact deploying a classic "Second Aliyah"-style supersessionist discourse in damning the Petah Tikva founders with faint praise. His remarks could easily either be taken to imply that the entire founding group were *effendis* out for financial gain or refitted into the smooth continuous narrative of one Aliyah leading to another in a teleological progression toward statehood. When confronted, Bar-Yehuda stressed that he had not meant to offend the founders of Petah Tikva. Nonetheless, the outcry tells us that despite the outward show of unity around commemoration, ongoing fractures revealed themselves precisely because those divides were rooted in the very history being commemorated, its decades-long commemoration, and the electoral politics and class struggles of a young country. The local actors who took offense were not isolated individuals but rather a particular class of landowning agriculturalists, many of them children or grandchildren of founders, who were invested both in their own economic success and in the national importance of their past.

Ridicule of Founder Figures

As new immigrants chafed at the undemocratically inclined leadership of the moshavot and protested their subpar living conditions, Labor Zionist leaders tried to exploit this resentment for electoral gain. Meanwhile, the farming elites also found themselves criticized from a different direction. Young Ashkenazi "sabra" Jews, born in Israel, found new ways to mock the old guard.[47] Their skepticism added a new national suspicion about Zionist heroes in general to a long-standing and ongoing Labor Zionist distaste for moshava farmers. "Who was this wondrous hero after all?" asked Aharon Megged's protagonist in his 1965 novel *Living on the Dead*, after learning that the hero he was supposed to write a biography about was just an ordinary man. "Here for almost forty years we've been standing at attention in his memory, singing the anthem, waving the flag, sending the kids home at eleven and letting the teachers lie down to rest . . . What do we need heroes for in this country?"[48] If even classic Zionist heroes were losing their luster at this time, the ambivalent First Aliyah figures stood to be ridiculed not only as representatives of a specific economic sector and class but as generic icons of the settlement old guard.

Avraham Shapira became a figurehead for this ambivalence. Ehud

Ben-Ezer, grandson of the Petah Tikva settler Yehuda Raab and a First Aliyah history buff who published a biography of Shapira in 1993, remembered that Shapira would come speak to school groups about his heroic past roles, including leading the Petah Tikva guardsmen in defense of the colony during the Nebi Musa riots of 1921, which resulted in the death of four Jewish guardsmen.[49] When Shapira spoke of that incident, Ben-Ezer recounts, he would fill his speech with grammatical errors and borrowings from Arabic and Yiddish that made the students laugh.[50] The poet and songwriter Yossi Gamzu (1938–2020) placed Avraham Shapira at the center of his broader poetic skepticism about heroic narratives of the past. His first collection of poetry, published in 1958, took its title, *You, Are You Youth?!* (Atem no'ar atem?!) from a *chizbat*, the genre of satirical anecdote associated with the pre-statehood youth culture of the Labor Zionist Haganah's elite Palmach force. The *chizbat* genre gained wider circulation with the publication of the 1956 collection *Yalkut ha-kezavim* (Pack of chizbats/pack of lies) by Dan Ben-Amotz and Hayim Hefer.[51] (Hefer and Ben-Amotz also organized the musical production "Little Tel Aviv" (*Tel Aviv ha-ketanah*) for the fiftieth anniversary of Tel Aviv in 1959.) The pair have been considered exemplars of a certain kind of nostalgia for the early Zionist settlement period that combined parody with poignant emotion and helped develop the genre of "Songs of the Land of Israel" (*shirei Eretz Yisra'el*).[52]

When Avraham Shapira was invited to speak to a youth convention in Petah Tikva, went the *chizbat* that inspired Gamzu's poem, he glanced over the crowd and exclaimed, "You! Are you youth? You are shit [*hara*]!" And got off the stage.[53] One reviewer of the poetry volume remarked that the "Avraham Shapiras" of Israel were constantly lobbing such accusations against the younger generation. Here, the Petah Tikva figure marks a broader generational rather than specifically partisan or ideological gap.[54] Another reviewer praised Gamzu for offering a "partial defense of the younger [native-born] generation," in the face of "the claims against them" by an older generation who doubted their nationalist commitment.[55] The cover of the book featured a caricature of Shapira with his iconic pipe, large mustache, and walking stick, pointing an accusing finger at a group of startled children.

The Shapira *chizbat* evoked intergenerational strife that had been going on for decades. The archeologist and Zionist activist Nahum Slouschz had written in 1936 that Menashe Meirovitch, who, as we have learned, arrived in Palestine in 1882 as a member of the Bilu organization and settled in Rishon LeZion, sometimes got frustrated with the youth and, "getting resentful of their pettiness, would turn to those latecomers [*aharonim*] and demand that they apologize to the First Ones [*rishonim*]: 'You, what are you?' Those were the days and they are over. Heroes—not you!"[56] Scholars of Hebrew literature and culture have noted the widespread sense among the "State Generation" of being castigated by their fathers for being coddled or nonheroic.[57] The intentional irony of choosing Shapira as the icon of the "older generation," however, was that he represented not the hegemonic political elite but an old guard (in both senses) that Labor Zionist leaders had mocked and derided since the early twentieth century even as they welcomed his role as a living symbol of settler authenticity. In ridiculing this First Aliyah figure, Gamzu added yet another layer to a history of people employing iconic images of the moshavot, alternately nostalgic and derisive, as the emblems of a deep but ambivalent Zionist past.

Gamzu's opening poem imagines Shapira's speech at the youth convention that is described in the *chizbat*. While parodying Shapira's denunciation of the youth, however, it also conveys nostalgia about early Petah Tikva, the nostalgia Shapira had been conveying to school groups and visiting dignitaries for years:

> Thus spoke Avraham Shapira
> a man of gray hair and heroic acts and rank.
> Thus said Avraham Shapira
> at one of the youth conventions.
>
> At one of these youth conventions
> on some holiday or *Shabbes*
> it's possible even now to hear
> the echo of its glory in Melabes.
>
> "Gentlemen," he said, "I won't go on
> about things without "brakes" or "switches."
> Because a man like Avraham Shapira won't
> stand here

and stick you with "speeches."

But as long as the *marantses* tree grows
its oranges, and Wadi Musrara stinks
and as long as, over a half watermelon,
we share memories of the *shatara*

I won't stop asking and rebuking:
You, are *you* youth?
You are . . . shit."

. . . and it's said that suddenly many young faces
turned white
When Mr. Avrum Shapiro
said the things you've just heard.

Since then, children, in our country
there's no flaw or insult or description
(we're blameless, whether it's a spiritual crisis or the corruption of values and innocence)
that the grown-ups among us
won't throw around the necks of the youth.[58]

The message of the poem is a youthful protest against attacks from "grown-ups" who blame the younger generation for spiritual deficiencies rooted in their lack of connection to the founding past. But Gamzu also constructs a portrait of ironic nostalgia for Petah Tikva. Through his speech and allusions, Shapira embodies foreignness to Hebrew culture, familiarity with the Palestinian landscape, frontier adventure, the blending of religion and nationalism, and the sweet smells of the private citrus economy. The rhyme of "Shabbes" (the Ashkenazi/Yiddish pronunciation of Sabbath) and "Melabes" (the Arabic name for the site of Petah Tikva, also rendered Umbeles) makes the name of the early settlement sound like a Yiddish term while aligning the Yiddish word with the Arabic. Other Yiddish and Arabic terms are peppered throughout: the Yiddish pronunciation of Shapira's name (*Avrum Shapiro*), the citrus trees named in Yiddish (*marantses*), the Arabic *shatara* (high jinks), and the stink of the Wadi Musrara (renamed Nahal Ayalon in Hebrew by the Israeli Government Names Committee in July 1952).[59]

Another poem, in the 1966 second edition of the volume, reflecting on Shapira's recent death, refers to his "clumsy Hebrew-Arabic-Yiddish."[60] Shapira is from "here," indeed from the most established part of "here," Gamzu's poem suggests, but he brings along with him the aura and ambivalence of both the Ashkenazi and Palestinian past. Gamzu speaks as a member of a generation that understands itself as native and expresses ambivalence about the foreign-born generation that achieved their status precisely because they came from abroad and established agricultural colonies in a hostile landscape—in other words, because they came as settlers.

The moshava, here the stereotypically and enduringly religious Petah Tikva, is a site of ambiguity in the midst of a seemingly ideologically engaged society. It symbolizes incomplete transformation and uncertainty even from its economically and demographically central position within Israel. Shapira speaks from (and to) a society that hasn't "overcome" or moved beyond the inconsistencies and failures of the First Ones and continues to dwell in the disjunctures and contradictions of their time. These tensions are also reflected in Israeli commemorations of the First Aliyah in the 1950s and 1960s, which wavered between an earnest and politicized discourse about the nature of the First Ones in Zionist society and a parodic, if loving, caricature available to be marched through the streets on horseback as an apolitical nationalist statement of origins.

Commemoration for the Next Generation

Moshava commemoration—and commemoration of the historical moshava—thus occurred against the backdrop of immigrant-led demographic shifts, partisan strife, and generational change among native-born Jews. Some planned full slates of events every five years for their uneasily mixed populations of established veterans and newcomers struggling to find employment. On its seventieth anniversary in 1952, Rishon LeZion arranged an agricultural exhibition to show children that "there wasn't always a tractor and combine harvester: in the beginning they were truly working with their fingernails [*mamash ba-tzipornayim*]." Children were invited to celebrate both the colony's humble origins and its industrial present. The Gavish glass company and Ben-Gal radio manufacturer, as well as the Gamish rubber company where Loretta Azulay would later work, displayed their wares alongside the winery's famous vintages.[61]

Five years later, in 1957, the seventy-fifth-anniversary festivities began with a documentary exhibition in the newly renovated community center on Levontin Street, named for the colony founder and banker Zalman David Levontin (1856–1940). Designed by Hiram Ben-Ami, son of Zippora and David Yudilovitz (mentioned above), the exhibition showed the colony's development since its founding. According to plans for the celebration, a famous cantor would lead Sabbath prayer services in the Great Synagogue and there would be "celebrations in all the synagogues," an indication that synagogues remained, as they had been during the mandate period, an important locus of collective identification and commemoration. Over the next several days, the city would present a variety of speeches by children of First Ones and by local and national officials. Two immigrant artists would perform: the singer Shoshana Damari (who had arrived in 1925 from Yemen) and the ballerina Hannah Ringold (who had arrived in 1933 from Poland).[62]

Mayor Levin put forth an agenda of municipal priorities for the anniversary year which she said "would be presented as a gift to all the citizens of Rishon LeZion, an anniversary gift." These priorities included absorbing two thousand Jewish immigrant families, which would grow the city's population 40% from seven thousand to more than ten thousand residents; building a road connecting Rishon LeZion to the sea; and establishing leisure facilities that would "be a source of work and livelihood for many citizens." Levin, moreover, promised to build public housing to the west on the "sands, which [still] stand desolate ['*omdim be-shimemonam*]" and also to enhance employment opportunities, educational institutions, and municipal services. All this, she emphasized, would be the continuation of an ongoing tradition of the fathers of the city "cultivating . . . an enchanting dream [*halom kesem*] of developing the city to the west."[63] Her phrasing linked a program of future expansion with a history of the past on a landscape imagined to be (and always to have been) desolate.

A few years later, in 1961, the Rehovot municipality encouraged its schoolchildren to write essays in honor of its seventieth anniversary. We encountered several of them in the previous chapter. These essays stress the ongoing nature of Zionist settlement, the moshava as a force for capitalist growth, and nostalgia for the founding past. The student Rachel Lipkin's eighth-grade essay expressed her complex nostalgia through the perspective of a house that "had once known happiness" as "a center, a meeting place for farmers." Though it had lived through so many events, celebrations, visits of dignitaries, and fights against local Arabs, now "no one paid attention to it." Modern buses "rushed loudly by," as did the "thousands of people, new immigrants, settled in the town." "A new house will be built in its place, and not a trace of it will remain; the last remnant of days past will be destroyed."[64] In recounting all the things that house "had seen," Rachel narrated the curated history that she had learned while simultaneously celebrating the growth and expansion that had destroyed these remnants.

Other students expressed wonder at the "fact" that their modern city had been founded on a desolate site. Yael Bern told of visiting her grandfather Michael along with other children from her school and being told of the "desolate land, only thorns" that had made up the colony, and the First Ones' dedication to "working from morning to night and then, despite their tiredness, gathering to dance until midnight." "You lived an easy life and didn't suffer," the grandfather told his grandchildren, telling them that because of his labors "we became a free people on its own land."[65] Yael Hochberg, in sixth grade at the time, imagined an untamed Ottoman frontier wilderness on the site where now she saw contemporary bustling roads and architect-designed houses. "Could it be," she asked, "that there was once wilderness here" populated only by "drowsy Bedouins"? Was it here, in the city that had become a "city of science," that men would wake up in the nighttime to build a house that the Turks would turn around and destroy?[66] Making children imagine themselves as settlers who are uprooted and go to another place might lead them to question the rootedness that had been self-evident to them up till then, Tamar Katriel writes in her study of kibbutz museums. But revisiting the moment of settlement is essential to the Zionist construction of belonging.[67] The children's rhetorical skepticism about the desolation that preceded the colony in fact reinforces the "fact" of that desolation and obviates any need for true skepticism about whether the specific lands they lived on and the broader country they called home had *in fact* been empty.

Other essays explicitly praised Rehovot's capitalist achievements in citriculture, presenting its founding legacy as one of economic growth. Schools in the moshavot became arenas for the teaching of capitalist values. In 1948, half of all Jewish pupils were in General Trend schools, which described themselves, much like the General Zionist party, as apolitical. By 1953, when the General Trend and Labor trend were united into one secular stream, that proportion had declined to 27%.[68] However, these schools were concentrated in the veteran moshavot, as Labor and Religious schools came to dominate in immigrant towns.[69] Seeing their educational market share, as it were, diminishing, those same veteran moshavot continued to use commemorative moments to get schoolchildren to revere their city's past and to insert it within a narrative of progress and economic development.

Tzila Dorfman's essay for the Rehovot anniversary imagined oranges calling out to be picked, packed, and shipped out "to be sold abroad, where the demand is great, because they are tasty and good for health." Through these sales, "the country buys important things for its citizens." There is no economic branch in the country more important for its economic value, she boasted; and it "paves the way for other agricultural products."[70] Avital Weinstock's essay, meanwhile, took the perspective of an orange and offered a lengthy paean to the fertile agricultural landscape and its glistening citrus. Anthropomorphized oranges celebrated their role in Rehovot's booming produce economy and quarreled over who would be sent first. Finally, a giant orange intervened with the reassuring "right" answer: "You are crazy. We will all be sent . . . Because we are all nice-looking and hearty, sweet as honey, and there are none like the Rehovot oranges known for their praise, beauty, and taste . . . We will all be sent overseas, to faraway lands, where there are no oranges because it is very cold there and it's always snowing." The agricultural economy of Rehovot was vindicated. It boomed and blossomed against the eternal winter of the Jewish diaspora.

The overseas market, Weinstock's essay emphasized, was Rehovot's proving ground. One orange named Ketina ("Little One," "after all, all oranges have names") feared being shipped overseas, but was reassured by a bird who promised that not only would she "see lovely and wonderful things" abroad, she would help Israel achieve one of its main goals: "bringing *olim* [Jewish immigrants] to the country." After all, "when people overseas taste us, they will desire to come to our country, to see how we grow, our ways of life, and to tour the land." And indeed, the story continued, the demand for citrus was fierce. An orange called Admoni ("Redhead"), placed on display in England, caught the attention of a wrinkled old lady, who exclaimed, "My grandson Johnny is sick and the doctors can't find a cure, unless he eats the orange that grows in Israel. And he wants the nicest orange." Sensing the woman's anxious demand, "the storeowner demanded a very high price: 4 shillings, which is like 120 agorot." When the 12-year-old grandson ate Admoni, he immediately gained color in his face and stopped sweating. Of course, as he was eating, the grandmother told him stories "about the land intended for the children of Israel . . . about the people of Israel who revived their youth and returned to their homeland to settle it and make it fruitful." And just as the bird in Rehovot had promised, Johnny then felt a strong desire to see the land. "Thanks to the oranges," the story concluded, "the number of *olim* is increasing." Weinstock ended with a sort of capitalist prayer, "that our country will not have many competitors so that the oranges will be sold at a good profit to all the nations of the world and will bring us many *olim*."[71] Weinstock, instructed by her seventh-grade teacher, her family, and the ethos of the colony, had constructed a clever infomercial celebrating Rehovot's profit-making capacity, a capacity historically built in part with Arab labor and now increasingly built on the informal labor of Mizrahi Jews.[72]

As they showed off their planning for the future and encouraged schoolchildren to imagine and narrate the settler past, the moshavot literally displayed their few remaining founder figures. At its 1952 seventieth-anniversary celebration, Zichron Ya'aqov featured Alter Albert, aged 80. He "stood as upright as a veteran soldier, the skin of his face wrinkled as though by a plow." But Albert hadn't really been among the very first First Ones, as the journalist D. Dyoknai (David Lazar) admitted in *Maariv*: Albert was 15 when he arrived in Palestine from Poland in 1887, five years after the colony's founding. Nevertheless, Lazar creatively turns Albert into a conduit for the founders by presenting a litany of things that Albert *doesn't* remember: he "doesn't remember the Aliyah of the First Ones to the land of Zamarin." He knows of the journeys of the first Romanian settlers "only through rumor." He "heard only from elders" about how the immigrants got to Haifa and managed to purchase the land in the Samarian hills. He "doesn't remember" how the British vice consul communicated to London that the settlers were hungry and in need of help. Nonetheless, he shared in the suffering characteristic of First Ones. Though he arrived a few years after the colony's founding, he underwent "all the hardships and suffering [*tela'ot vi-yisurim*]" of the moshava: the conflicts with the Rothschild administration, the bouts of "every color of fever," and the suffering at the hands of the Ottoman authorities. "He, the last remnant of the first generation, even if he wasn't among the firsts—is a living symbol of all that passed over Zichron in those three generations, for good or ill [*la-hesed ula-shevet*]." It didn't matter that Albert wasn't a "first": he could still be a "last," the best and most authentic transmitter of memory, if only second-hand. He was tapped to say the traditional *Shehecheyanu* prayer to mark the colony's having reached that auspicious anniversary.[73]

Albert was able to play this role because, despite his later arrival, he nonetheless had preceded the leaders of the Labor Zionist government. Many years after Albert's arrival, the reporter recounted, the veteran colonist met the future prime minister, David Ben-Gurion, at a conference. The future prime minister asked him, "Don't you remember me? You were my employer in Zichron Ya'aqov. I worked with you during the grape harvest." Albert was unmoved. Though he could have lied, allowing himself to bask in his connection to this now powerful former employee, he denied knowing him. "I don't remember a worker by the name of Ben-Gurion who worked for me, but if he remembers me, I'm sure he's right. It could be." Albert, with a hint of a jest, made his point clear: David Ben-Gurion was just one of many Jewish workers who had come through his vineyard, just a Johnny-come-lately, not a true First.[74]

Avraham Shapira, too, continued to display himself and be displayed in the Tel Aviv Purim parade as a site of memory. The festivities had been suspended during World War II and the period of the 1948 War. By the time Purim 1950 rolled around, those who remembered the pre-state celebrations pined for them. "People remember the Adeleyada [Purim parade] from those days," an article in *Maariv* intoned: the singing and dancing until dawn, "[Mayor] Dizengoff at the head of the parade, riding a white horse, with magnificence and splendor, and to his right Avraham Shapira, the oldest of the guards in our land."[75] The memory of Shapira and the settler phenomenon he represented, in other words, now also incorporated the memory of the *later*, mandate-era commemorations of that past. Come 1950, Shapira rode alongside Mayor Yitzhak Rokach and other city figures. A Dizengoff puppet rode along with him to recreate the comradeship between the old guard and the former General Zionist mayor, as the real Dizengoff had died in 1936.[76]

First Aliyah figures and related images lent the parade its aura of charm and nostalgia. One part of the 1955 parade, according to the planning materials for the gala, included actors playing the late-nineteenth-century supporters of Jewish colonization Avraham Moyal, from Jerusalem's Sephardi community, and Yehiel Michal Pines, from its Ashkenazi community. The former was played by Yoram Hankin, son of the Bilu member Mordechai, wearing Moyal's distinctive Ottoman tarbush. The latter was played by the Revisionist leader Zeev (Wolfgang) von Weisl, wearing Pines's top hat. After this ostensibly serious segment, linking rural settlement to the historical urban communities of Palestine, "would come the main satirical portion of the parade."[77]

But Shapira was the main attraction for a crowd that *Maariv* described as otherwise "apathetic," because he "aroused sentimental feelings among older viewers." Sentimental feelings, that is, for commemorative practices they associated with their youth. "To loud cheers, they got to see the first of the guards, the elderly Avraham Shapira, riding a noble white horse, with a group of guards from those times: mustachioed and wearing wide-brimmed hats." The younger guards were in costume, reenacting the history "from those times," but Shapira, the article emphasized, was the living instantiation of the past, much like the "(real!) Bedouins with their colorful, saddled camels."[78] The emphasis on the "reality" of both Shapira and the Bedouins places them both outside the overall satirical and representational thrust of the parade. Indeed, a move that transparently orientalized Bedouins as representatives of a static, authentic past also essentialized Shapira and his generation as part of a mythic past—still living in the present—that also appeared to exist outside the political sphere.

A further report in the Mapam (left opposition) newspaper 'Al ha-Mishmar (On Guard), emphasized the importance of the 1955 event for the people, the ordinary ('amkha) Jews who longed for "anything with the hint of life or independent expression" after the long wartime hiatus from the celebration. But the writer was not happy with the parade's association with the political center and right, calling its style characteristic of the "General Zionists/Herut." Most of the acts in the parade "got blurred together in a sea of advertisements and general futility." Where was the "creative spirit" that could come from the kibbutzim? he wondered. But one act stood out: "the appearance of Avraham Shapira, the veteran guardsman from Petah Tikva, whom the crowds saw as a living symbol of the revival of Israel [tekumat Yisra'el]." Even though Shapira and other moshava figures had been displayed for decades precisely to bolster the image of the same Zionist pro-capitalist center right that this writer was now denouncing, Shapira seemed to stand above, prior to, and outside these contemporary politics.[79]

A *Maariv* writer corroborated Shapira's trans-political effect. The crowd's overall apathy could be attributed to their confusion: many of the floats and cars were unlabeled and their meaning unclear. Moreover, though they were full of "pure Zionism," they didn't have even "a hint of carnivalesque joy." "Only Avraham Shapira had a big personal victory. He was received with true enthusiasm and cheers that went up all the way to the sky." Shapira, the writer suggests, uniquely managed to be both transparent in his meaning and "carnivalesque." The crowd knew who he was and what he stood for: the Zionist settlement past, heroic masculinity, familiarity with the local landscape and Arab culture. He alone transcended the more heavy-handed "pure Zionism" of political production and provided escapism through mythic heroism.[80]

Shapira was still getting cheers in 1959, at age 88. *Davar* reported that year that "the Adeleyada was opened by a cowboy riding on a pony, escorted by police cars. With great cheers, the oldest of the guards, Mr. Avraham Shapira, was greeted by the crowds as he rode a white horse while surrounded by mounted guards."[81] The cowboy figure and Shapira the guard were juxtaposed opposites. The cowboy was the comic figure, the Purim-adapted mockery of that figure of the colonial past that Herzl, during his visit to Rehovot in 1898, had both revered and mocked: "they cried and dashed away cross-country on their little Arab horses."[82] But if the cowboy on his little pony was the self-critical comedy act, Shapira was the formal parade marshal.

According to a report about the 1960 parade, the 89-year-old Shapira participated again, in a further act of historical reenactment: "Shapira passed by riding on his white horse, with his chest decorated with rows of medals, waving his staff left and right."[83] Aside from his horse and his pipe, Shapira's staff had become his most iconic object. The public may not all have known that "waving a staff left and right" was at the heart of a local legend. As a young man, probably in the 1880s, Shapira had reportedly gone out into a crowd of Bedouin attackers and continued waving his stick left and right, acting in a kind of fugue state even after other Jewish defenders retreated and the attackers dispersed.[84] But if they lacked the specific commemorative reference, the crowd certainly knew that the stick was the marker of the early defender, the kind of masculine figure with the honor and the knowledge of local custom and weaponry. They also had likely become familiar with Shapira and expected him to act "in character."

Shapira played along, putting on the anachronistic act for the edification of the crowds. In a 1960 newspaper interview, he pointed to an image of himself riding and said, "Here I'm on a horse again, but I haven't had horses for a long time already. Only for the Adeleyada, they bring me a police horse and I ride."[85] Shapira, of course, wasn't only the subject of a myth about the past, he was a person capable of reenacting the myth in cooperation with the municipality, aware of his own role as a "cynical performer," to use Erving Goffman's term for one who deludes audiences "for [the audience's] own good, or the good of the community." The carnivalesque reenactment suggested that he had emerged straight out of the past while, in the process, participating in the social construction of that past. Goffman notes of the performer that "we may even expect to find typical careers of faith, with the individual starting out with one kind of involvement in the performance he is required to give, then moving back and forth several times between sincerity and cynicism before completing all the phases and turning-points of self-belief for a person of his station." By age 90, Shapira was well aware of his evolving, constructed role.[86]

The Built Commemorative Environment

As their elders were ritually displayed and moshava stories anchored the broader commemorations of the Zionist First Ones, municipalities also began, in the 1950s and 1960s, to build sites of remembrance in their historic cores. That way, year-round educational content could be added to the affective experiences of once-a-year or episodic events. When Rishon LeZion celebrated its seventieth anniversary in 1952, veterans "made sure that documents, pictures, and mementos of the first days would not get lost" and organized an impromptu public "museum" featuring some of these documents.[87] In 1954, members of the Aaronsohn family in Zichron Yaʿaqov, who had been working to preserve the memory of the family and their espionage activities since the mandate period, decided to open a museum in a part of the home formerly owned by Aaron Aaronsohn, the area where he had kept his plant collection. The museum opened in 1956.[88] In 1962, *ha-Boker* reported that the first school in Gedera would be turned into a historical museum to commemorate the Bilu settlers.[89] In early 1963, a committee gathered in Petah Tikva to plan "The First Ones Wing" (*Agaf rishonim*) at the soon-to-open Petah Tikva Museum. Leading that project was Baruch Oren, head of the Petah Tikva memorial site (*Yad la-banim*) that had been established in 1953, the first such institution in Israel to formally commemorate local Zionist war casualties. It had become clear, *Maariv* reported in 1965, that despite the farmers' real fears that the Labor Zionist mayor Rashish would "rewrite history," in practice "not only was the role of the founders not diminished, but there isn't a single local or governmental ceremony that does not put the deeds of the First Ones at its center."[90]

The Petah Tikva municipality invited several architectural firms to submit proposals for the permanent exhibition of the wing, which would cover 170 square meters (~1,830 sq. ft.) over two floors.[91] Yitzhak Ziv-Av of the Farmers' Federation emphasized that the Petah Tikva Museum needed to provide a transparent historical narrative for visitors: "Youth and simple Jews will come and they won't understand symbolism. We have to give them simple things and as few symbols as possible."[92] The municipality eventually granted the contract, in December 1963, to the Tel Aviv architectural firm of S. Amiran and D. Gutstein.[93] Amiran and Gutstein had already been recruited to plan several other exhibitions, including Petah Tikva's city exhibition in 1955.[94] They also designed the International Exhibition for Children's and Youth Literature in Petah Tikva in 1961,[95] as well as exhibition spaces to show off the innovations of private companies like Kargal, which made boxes for citrus, and the Nesher cement company in Haifa.[96]

The exhibition would be divided into two parts, over two floors. On the ground floor, visitors would see large images of eucalyptus trees and a low pool with water plants, a symbol of the swamps that the first European settlers remembered finding in Umlebes. The first floor, one level up, would contain dioramas depicting the building of Petah Tikva through the transformation of the swampland. A wall covered with kurkar, a local sandstone, would lead to the memorial site. The transition from the story of the pioneer builders to the localized national narrative of loss would "unify and connect the sons who died defending and reinforcing the values that the First Ones initiated."[97]

Baruch Oren's personal papers contain a more detailed outline of the exhibit displays. The "introduction" section he outlines narrates "landless Jerusalem Jews" looking for land to purchase against the opposition of the Ottoman authorities, finding 5,000 dunams for sale, and acquiring the parcel despite the warning of a doctor who took the absence of birds as a sign that the area would cause sickness. In the sections on "The Building of Petah Tikva" and "First Agriculture," visitors would see the progression from tents to cabins and learn about the efforts to dig the first well, view display cases showing tools and images of workers and animals, and read about the reconstitution of the settlement after a period of abandonment. Section Five of Oren's handwritten notes is dedicated to topics related to Arabs. It includes "pictures of people . . . diary excerpt . . . weapons . . . a photo of a *fantaziya* [horsemanship competition]." A printed set of planned captions, representing a later stage in the planning process, sharpens the narrative: "The Jews of Petah Tikva fight against Arabs. The Jew is no longer a 'child of death.' A small set of first guards teaches the Arab marauders a lesson. The shadow of the Arab's threats hovers over the heads of the moshava. Theft and murder—their daily allotment."[98] Visitors, he suggests, would see a combination of agricultural progress and settlers fighting off Arab attackers. The structure of the exhibition resembles that of settler colonial museums in the United States and Canada, which consist of "eclectic displays of artifacts and themes" including cooking and farming implements used by early settlers, images of exemplary guardsmen, and a limited and reductive discussion of the broader political and economic contexts and processes of erasure that enabled the settlers to arrive, survive, and eventually prosper.[99]

The exhibition in Petah Tikva opened to the public as the Remembrance of the First Ones (*Zekher rishonim*) wing on Sunday, May 2, 1965, at 6:30 pm.[100] The reporter Miriam Shir came by a year later and reacted just as the planners had hoped: "I saw a connection between this gallery and the [galleries devoted to commemorating casualties]: because the first settlers in the country were also the first to defend it." She was pleased to hear from Oren that Petah Tikva was building a dormitory so that students from elsewhere in the country could come to Petah Tikva to learn about "issues connected with security consciousness [*toda'ah bit'honit*], the history of defense, and the War of Independence." This was needed, Shir thought, because the local youth, many of them recent immigrants, knew only about Jewish weakness and the devastation of the Holocaust. Reminding students about bravery in ancient times, for example through trips to the Masada fortress, would not suffice, for there were "manifestations of Masada in every generation," including in early Petah Tikva.[101]

In addition to the city museum, some also saw Avraham Shapira's house in Petah Tikva as a potential educational site. In his nineties, Shapira told Oren that he intended to make his own house into an alternative museum. "I intend to bequeath this house and everything in it to the city," Oren recalls him saying, reporting that Mayor Rashish had promised him that the city would take care of the house "just like the Aaronsohn house in Zichron Ya'aqov." "Everything, my dear," Shapira directed, "will stay in its place: the souvenirs, the pictures, the old weapons, the letters, the newspapers, the furniture." Oren remembered thinking that Shapira was right, "this house and its contents would become a loyal monument [*yad ne'eman*] to Shapira's life's work."[102] In 1957, Shapira formally gave the house to the Petah Tikva municipality, with the understanding that they would use it for community purposes after his death.[103]

An extensive documentary survey of the house, prepared for the Petah Tikva municipality in 2016, conveys how not only the personal effects but also the architectural space itself would have invoked the Ottoman-era past for visitors. Built in 1901, the one-story, plaster-covered sandstone structure had a tiled roof and arched windows. Its wooden walls were decorated with Islamicate geometric patterns and plant motifs. A horse stable, recalling the owner's escapades and work as a guardsman, stood to its southeast.[104] After functioning as a municipal library from 1957 to Shapira's death in December 1965, the house's long-term status remained unclear because Shapira's deaf son Mendel continued to live in part of it, receive ongoing support from the city, and oppose any attempts to take it over completely.[105] The city was chagrined, noting that Shapira had been "one of the living monuments to an important chapter and difficult and glowing days in the beginning of the settlement [*hitnahalut*] of the land."[106] In 1967, with the house falling into disrepair, the Petah Tikva city council unanimously declared it a "public asset [*nekhes tziburi*]" and promised to renovate it as a museum to Shapira's life.[107] Only after Mendel's death in 1978, however, was the house fully turned over to the public.[108] It underwent renovations to make it into a communal space and museum that now contains photographs of Shapira with foreign dignitaries and a display case of Shapira's weapons, moving backward (right to left, in the logic of Hebrew readers) from military-style rifles on one end to Shapira's prized Bedouin sword on the other.

As Baruch Oren and the Petah Tikva municipality made efforts to dedicate a wing of the museum to the First Aliyah and acquire the Shapira house for a local community space, however, the journalist Uri Kesari questioned the canonization of Shapira and his story. Kesari was involved in the larger orbit of moshava-affiliated projects and institutions: he contributed to *Do'ar ha-yom*, had assisted the Aaronsohn family in publishing memoirs related to the Nili organization's World War I–era espionage work, and had even written detective novels in the 1930s. In 1939, we saw in chapter 3, he praised the Shapira memoir volumes. But when Shapira's son Yehoshua claimed in 1960 that his father was a uniquely distinguished representative of the Jewish community in Ottoman times, Kesari suggested that this was an overstatement: "It's not the truth. If Mr. Avraham Shapira was a leader in that period, what were Arthur Ruppin, Aaron Aaronsohn, Meir Dizengoff, and Siegfried Hoofien?" These figures, active during the same period, took part in national rather than strictly local achievements. Of them, Aaron Aaronsohn was most linked with the First Aliyah as a denizen of Zichron Ya'aqov, which continued to memorialize him. Ruppin worked for the Palestine Office of the Zionist Organization, hatching larger national settlement plans, and Dizengoff had become the mayor of Tel Aviv. Siegfried (Eliezer) Hoofian was the director general of the Anglo-Palestine Bank. The photographs of Shapira with visiting dignitaries were misleading, and the highly individualized historical commemoration that Shapira had garnered beyond Petah Tikva was misplaced, Kesari suggested. The "true" representatives of the past were political figures, international figures, those who had made national history and not only settler history. Ultimately, he concluded, Shapira was connected to the men of history, but he himself was part of "small history."

To explain what he meant by "small history," Kesari used the example of Napoleon. Small history "is the packet of spices, the pepper and the mustard, the honey, the roses, and the thorns during the life of Napoleon. But the history of Napoleon is something else, it is the blood, sweat, the muscles and the nerves, the soul and the flags." By the time of Kesari's article, the Annales School of history in Paris had begun to suggest that history was not only about great leaders and their escapades, and that a new social history could encompass previously unacknowledged actors, the social context of major events, and the mentalities of common people.[109] But Kesari was uneasy about ceding the big history to the small history. Only one who has contributed something to big history, he said, also has a small history worth writing about. Who, then, was this ambiguous figure from Petah Tikva? Kesari doubted that Avraham Shapira

FIGURE 10. (Opposite page) Avraham Shapira in an undated photo, with sword and gun (courtesy of the Historical Archive of Petah Tikva). (Above) Contemporary display case of weapons belonging to Avraham Shapira, Shapira House Petah Tikva (courtesy of the author).

could enter through "the front door of big history" and proposed that he might remain, instead, merely a character in the small history of other, greater men.

But even while acknowledging that Shapira wasn't as important as his son and his museum had suggested, Kesari nonetheless hoped that critiques wouldn't undermine the image of the old guardsman too much. It's very likely, he reflected, that "over the decades teachers will bequeath to their students the story of the guard from Petah Tikva," so long as "someone doesn't come to overturn it and protest against it." In fact, he was concerned that Yehoshua's insistence on uncorroborated specifics of Shapira's life would make "doubt . . . arise in everyone's hearts." Sure, he admitted, the books about Shapira, including Edelstein's memoir that he had previously praised, "were terrible and distorted the truth," but even those problematic texts served a wider social function: the books "taught

the youth, and not only the youth, to recognize and value the oldest of the Petah Tikva guardsmen."[110]

Kesari may not have been conscious of it, but he was making an important point about Zionist settler memory as opposed to Zionist ethnonationalist memory. Shapira, he recognized, was not a significant player in Zionist ethnonationalist memory, insofar as he never played a leading role (or, often, any role at all) in the cultural institutions, ideological movements, governing bodies, political parties, or military campaigns that produced Zionist cultural revival or Israeli political independence. But he played a significant role, alongside others, in Zionist settler memory: the memory of the frontier that lay outside of—but also framed and legitimized—more formal institutions. The memory of the First Aliyah itself, created during the mandate period and early statehood period and disseminated to the masses, had its social effect and, ultimately, political power because of its embedded distortions, not despite them. Because of its distance from "politics" and "culture," institutionally defined, not despite it.

The Year of the First Ones

Indeed, the "First Aliyah" didn't belong to the First Aliyah colonies alone. In national commemorations, it became a signifier and a site of memory that multiple parties used to claim "firstness." The Year of the First Ones celebration in 1962–1963, the eightieth anniversary of the First Aliyah, provided lawmakers with opportunities to reframe the past and define "firstness" well beyond its "First Aliyah" private agriculturalist instantiation. On July 22, 1962, Yitzhak Ziv-Av, head of the Farmers' Federation at the time, wrote to Prime Minister David Ben-Gurion with a suggestion: declare the upcoming Hebrew year, 1962–1963, "The Year of Farmers" (*Shenat ikarim*). Ziv-Av thanked Ben-Gurion for his opening greetings at a commemorative Bilu night held a few days earlier, where the Mapai leader commented that the Bilu group, whose 1882 arrival had come to mark the start of the "First Aliyah," had "brought about a historical turning point in the vision of the national revival [*hazon ha-tekumah*]." Ziv-Av imagined that a commemorative year would be marked in schools, youth groups, and immigrant absorption centers.

Eighty years before, he said, the year 1882 had been "the year of a change of values [*shinui ʿarakhin*] in the national revival," and this moment deserved to be commemorated.[111] Ben-Gurion agreed, saying that such a recognition would "give glory to the state." The Knesset ultimately approved a planned year of events and publications, many taking place in the former colonies themselves, but decided on the broader term "Year of the First Ones (*rishonim*)."[112]

In placing the First Aliyah on the symbolic national agenda, Ziv-Av hoped for the revision of a historical narrative that he believed had systematically excluded the achievements of the founders that mattered. In an interview with Yosef (Tommy) Lapid for *Maariv* in December 1962, Ziv-Av called the moshavot the exemplar of trans-historical Jewish settlement: "the moshavot have been the red thread in Jewish history since ancient times . . . and through today." Ziv-Av was performing a sleight of hand in his conversation with Lapid (who would go on to head Israel's liberal centrist Shinui [Change] Party at the turn of the twenty-first century): the moshavot were "first," but they were also markers of continuity in their own right: older historic Jewish farming communities, Ziv-Av insisted, were also, in retrospect, "moshavot."[113]

Unfortunately, Ziv-Av thought, the mainstream Israeli narration of settlement history focused on the socialist-oriented immigrants, rather than those who had preceded them in the late nineteenth century and who also deserved to be recognized: "The First Ones, long may they live, would have had to wait another eighty years before their merits were praised and recognized [*ʿad she-yeʿalu ʿal nes et zekhuyotehem*] if an energetic Jew [Ziv-Av himself] hadn't decided that it was time to honorably remove the yellow stain of Boaz."[114] The "stain of Boaz" stuck to those farmers involved in twentieth-century labor disputes with Jewish workers who protested their employment of Arab laborers. The term came from a comment by Ahad Ha-ʿAm (Asher Ginzburg), who in 1912 compared private farmers to Boaz in the biblical book of Ruth, who hired and oversaw laborers but did not work. Ahad Ha-ʿAm used the term ambivalently at the time, criticizing the private farmers' approach but praising them as "close to the land" and "very different in [their] inclinations from the urban Jew." Soon, however, it became a wholly derogatory Labor Zionist epithet for the First Aliyah farmers and their communities.[115]

Why, with so much commemoration of illegal Jewish immigration under the British during World War II, Ziv-Av lamented, do people not remember that "the First Ones of Zichron Ya'aqov were the first illegal immigrants?" "Why do residents of Tel Aviv not know that the colony of Ness Ziona had a workers' neighborhood called Tel Aviv? Why don't people know, as they sing the national anthem, "Hatikva," that it began as a workers' song in Rehovot?" The later commemorations so enshrined in the statehood narrative of Zionism were misplaced.[116]

In practice, the Year of the First Ones was not specifically a celebration of the "First Aliyah" but rather a broad commemoration of Zionist settlement that could be claimed by multiple parties. The Israel Coins and Medals Corporation put out a commemorative medal for the occasion that depicted a Jewish man planting in a swamp, coupled with the text of Leviticus 26:45: "I will remember the covenant of their ancestors [lit.: first ones, *brit rishonim*]."[117] The coin connected a modern rhetoric, which rooted Israeli statehood in modern settler First Ones, with an ancient narrative that rooted Israelite conquests in the Land of Canaan in the merits of the patriarchal First Ones of Genesis. The image, moreover, evokes the sense of the land's emptiness: aside from the swamp, the pioneer, his planting, and his water tower are the only active forces in an otherwise dead space. The English-language version of the pamphlet advertising the medals printed the text "First Settlers Year" in a woodblock-style font that evoked the Old West and strongly alluded to the mystique and heroism of the American frontier, likely in an appeal to American Jewish buyers.

After approving the commemoration, Ben-Gurion used the occasion to pen a long introductory essay to that year's *Government Yearbook*, entitled "First Ones" [*Rishonim*]. In it, he undermined First Aliyah claims to primacy both by situating them in a longer history of aliyah and by reconfiguring the nature of "firstness" itself so as to elevate later arrivals over earlier ones. This was a long-standing Labor Zionist strategy: their ambivalent view of the moshava farmers and desire to claim primacy had led them to construct the idea of the "First Aliyah" in the first place. The

FIGURE 11. Marketing brochure for the "Year of the First Ones" Medal, 1963 (courtesy of the Israel Coins and Medals Corporation).

Labor leader Berl Katznelson had said in 1944, "Firstness is not related to chronology; nor is it the merit [zekhut] of the one who had the luck to come first to make aliyah." Firstness, Katznelson wrote, is proven through exemplary personal characteristics.[118] Without the Second Aliyah, Ben-Gurion wrote in 1955, we would have remained "exilic and atrophied, subjugated to foreigners and dependent on the goodwill of the Arab majority, like the Yishuv that was established in the twenty-five years before the Second Aliyah."[119] In his *Government Yearbook* essay, Ben-Gurion admitted that "the turn to settling the land out of independent pioneering initiative" marked a significant break and that "the crown of being the first founders of agriculture" indeed goes to the founders of Petah Tikva, Rishon LeZion, Zichron Ya'aqov, Rosh Pinna, and Gedera. But he emphasized that the label "First Ones" should belong to those who brought pioneering innovation."

Any number of generations in Jewish history, Ben-Gurion felt, could claim innovation. Moving backwards from 1962, he noted that while

1948 marked the founding of the state, it was preceded by "decades of action and pioneering creativity." In 1897, Jews had organized to create a secure refuge, but before them came the Lovers of Zion movement. But these modern thinkers were only expressing an age-old desire for redemption voiced by Jeremiah and by Jews over the generations. "The terms common among us now for the First, Second, and Third Aliyah, are incorrect and misleading." They obscure the Yemenite, Sephardic, and Ashkenazi aliyot that built the "Old Yishuv" and the fact that members of the "Old Yishuv" first founded Petah Tikva and Rosh Pinna and that Yemenite Jews also became farmers.[120] Ben-Gurion was ostensibly acknowledging the erasure accomplished by the paradigm of numbered aliyot: it obscured Jewish immigrants who arrived in Palestine before 1882. But his comments about "innovation" suggested that pre-Zionist Jewish claims to firstness on the basis of historical continuity were provisional. Earlier waves of Jewish immigration rooted modern settler claims in a long authentic history, but until those populations could be inculcated with the appropriate Zionist settler ethos, or at least political support for it, they functioned as pre-firsts, outside the articulation of the modern historical break that Israel was in the process of celebrating. Palestinian Muslim and Christian populations, meanwhile, had no claims to firstness whatsoever.

In practice, the particular referent of the commemoration became largely obscured in the countrywide programs connected to it. In the summer of 1963, more than twenty-five thousand children of all ages participated in summer camp activities in Tel Aviv linked to the celebrations. A representative of the Agricultural Laborers' Union, affiliated with the Labor Zionists, commended "the educational aspect of this project for the second generation."[121] Each morning, children would sing "*Anu nihyeh ha-rishonim*" (We will be the First Ones) despite the fact, newspapers reported, that educators had warned the culture department of the Education Ministry that they didn't want to impose Zionism in such a heavy-handed way in the summer camps. As it turned out, "The children were actually very interested in this 'antiquated' [*meyushan*] topic" and found that the popular songs [*shlagerim*] from the early days of Rishon LeZion, Rosh Pinna, and the Second Aliyah worked well in a "competition" with more contemporary songs. The programming encompassed multiple periods in the history of the Yishuv, with every group taking on different topics.

Hillel Barzel, head of Tel Aviv's culture department, reported that children from multiple socioeconomic and ethnic backgrounds, including Palestinian citizens of the state (*'Aravim*), had enthusiastically taken on the activities, likely, in the latter case, out of a need to establish themselves as loyal citizens within a state that still kept them under the restrictions of a military government.[122] In a revealing quote, the reporter Aryeh Kinarti noted that "the topic of the First Ones excited the kids in the summer camps no less than that of the Indians [*Indianim*], Negroes [*Kushim*], Eskimos [*Eskimosim*], the heroes of Anderson and Grimm, and other 'traditional' summer camp topics."[123] American summer camp activities during the interwar period, on which these games and racialized typologies appear to have been modeled, often involved white children exoticizing and appropriating the identities of nonwhite others as a means of escape from the present.[124] American campers would also reenact iconic elements of America's settler colonial narrative, for example Columbus's "discovery" of America.[125] Zionist camps, too, seem to have engaged in the exoticization of both iconic foreign "others" and representatives of the broad Zionist pre-state settler past.

The year concluded with a nighttime IDF parade in Petah Tikva on September 4, 1963. The parade route was lined with advanced lighting, barricades, and watchtowers. Prime Minister Levi Eshkol (Mapai), Army Chief of Staff Zvi Tzur, and Commander of the Central Command Yaakov Geva were in attendance. A few minutes before 8 pm, a convoy of twenty-eight elders representing the first fourteen settlements in the country took their places alongside the stage. When the prime minister gave the sign, the elders were led forward by escorts to receive a blessing from him. The elders were then handed the flags of the first settlements, which were planted in the middle of the road as the IDF band played songs associated with the First Ones. A large model of a tree was lit up, symbolizing the "bush of pioneering" that burns and is not consumed "from the days of the First Ones until our days." At the end, the elders returned to their seats and the Oldest of the Guards, Avraham Shapira, then 92, said the *Shehecheyanu* prayer.[126] In this militarized commemorative event, moshavot became army battalions and First Ones became their (literal) standard-bearers.

But what standard, exactly, were they bearing? What values or ideologies were encoded in those flags? Ziv-Av would have had no doubt: they stood for the First Aliyah colonies. But the framework of "firstness" was malleable enough that representatives of various parties could interpret those flags according to their own self-image.

Postures of Firstness

On December 4, 1962, the Knesset hosted a special celebratory session for the Year of the First Ones. After Kaddish Luz, the speaker of the Knesset, opened the session, members were given the opportunity to praise and offer reflections on the First Ones. Each of them, as we will see, interpreted the notion of firstness differently and inserted their own political logic into their framing of the past.[127] The combination of religious, economic, cultural, and chronological features of the "First Aliyah" construct meant that a variety of ideological groups beyond the core constituency of farmers could find in it a story that reflected their contemporary values. The fact that the First Aliyah could be so readily and flexibly appropriated speaks to its malleability as a historical cipher for Zionist authenticity, for firstness, for roots in the land.

The Zionist right was reflected in the Herut party, which had evolved from the Revisionist Zionist movement and become the chief opposition to Labor. For decades, it had echoed and promoted aspects of the private farmers' narratives of pragmatism, pro-capitalism, and devotion to national interests rather than "political" ones, ethnoreligious solidarity rather than class-based politics or anything with the whiff of "socialism." Finding certain of their religious and economic values reflected in the settlers who had preceded both themselves and the Labor Zionists, they suggested that Israeli society make a turn to the right not only to reject Labor politics and forge a new path, but to return the Zionist settlement project to its true roots.

Abba Ahimeir, a disciple of Vladimir Jabotinsky, had already taken to defending the moshavot in the 1950s and attacking Labor for denying them their due. The distortion of the history of the early private colonists mattered to Ahimeir not because they were Revisionists—they generally were not—but because in retrospect they seemed to embody an economically liberal ethos that had become, alongside militarism, the central calling card of the Revisionist movement. In a series of articles in his party's newspaper, *Herut*, Ahimeir revived the idea, voiced in the early twentieth century, that Second Aliyah laborers had been essentially lazy: they "preferred to come to Palestine rather than immigrate to America, a place where it would have been necessary to really work and not chatter and write about work." The Zionist left, he claimed, had imported a detrimental "politics" and "hatred" into the internal dynamics of the Yishuv, "something that was almost unknown until then." The workers' "hatred" was directed against "those who gave them a living, the farmers in the moshavot and the businessmen in Jaffa." The leftists were effectively antinationalist, he claimed, saying that "they did not believe in the Jewish state" and respected socialist ideologues more than they did Herzl.

Instead, he believed, the private colonies in all of their stages deserved to be lauded. They had established the trade in wine and citrus, which became the largest branch of the economy. They employed hundreds of Jews (in addition to Arabs, whom he did not mention). Not only did the Zionist left "not lift a finger to do any of those things, they related to [the moshavot] negatively." They had had no role in making the moshavot self-sufficient or in founding Tel Aviv. "That which the Zionist left got involved with remained weak" and the institutions they established wasted more money than the Rothschild administration ever had. Historically, Revisionists had supported hiring only Jewish labor in Jewish-run enterprises out of ethnonational solidarity, but opposed the class-based rhetoric of Labor Zionists. In an article several years later, Ahimeir accused ideological Labor Zionists of directing their hatred at "the [Jewish] son of the First Aliyah who disliked [Friedrich] Engels's Erfurt Program and [wasn't] ready to delve into the theories of [Socialist Zionist thinker Ber] Borochov" instead of decrying "the Arab thief who killed his guard friend in the middle of the night." Because the Arab was the ultimate foe, Ahimeir thought, Labor Zionist attempts at organizing

Arab workers were foolish. Even though the First Aliyah, in Labor Zionist memory, was defined by its use of Arab labor, Ahimeir used its history as a cudgel against the Zionist Labor movement.[128] Denigrating Labor had been the Revisionist modus operandi since the founding of the party in 1925, but this text is notable for its explicit evocation of the past, and specifically the First Aliyah past. As Labor Zionists celebrated the fiftieth anniversary of the Second Aliyah in 1954, Ahimeir suggested that the occasion should be cause for reflection: "How and why did Zionist and settlement history get so distorted?"[129]

Ahimeir's reflections on the 1949 death of Menashe Meirovitch also revealed the selective ways that Herut found utility in First Aliyah history. Meirovitch, as we have seen, had been a member of Bilu, the tiny and largely unsuccessful settler cohort that Labor Zionists later seized on as the only honorable, respectable part of the "First Aliyah." He participated in the popularization of the Bilu story within Labor Zionist circles even as he maintained the economic interests and "apolitical" discourse of his fellow farmers. For Ahimeir, however, that Bilu firstness story was uncompelling. The group had misrepresented their origins and achievements and were not in fact "first," having been preceded by earlier waves of Ashkenazi and Sephardi religious immigrants: "There were First Ones to the First Ones." In fact, the one colony established by Bilu members, Gedera, remained small and less prosperous when compared to other "First Aliyah" colonies. Ahimeir wished to elevate precisely those aspects of the "First Aliyah" that Labor Zionists had criticized: authentic Jewishness and the will to private initiative. "Until today," he concluded, Gedera symbolizes weakness, as opposed to "the many people in Petah Tikva, Rishon [LeZion], and Rehovot, and the flourishing village of Zichron Yaʿaqov, because the settlers in Petah Tikva and Zichron were simply Jews and dreamt of private [economic] arrangements." These settlers, he suggested, made aliyah "without making a scene [*le-lo hakhamot*] and didn't seek approval from the bigwigs promoting the usual false theories." Simplicity, non-intellectualism, fierce dedication to Jewishness above all, and private initiative. This was the First Aliyah to him.[130]

At the 1962 special Knesset session, in contrast, the Herut Knesset member (MK) Esther Raziel-Naor never mentioned the "First Aliyah" specifically. Instead, she suggested a progression from a failed "Conquest of Labor" paradigm to a Revisionist paradigm of outright conquest after World War I. The firsts worthy of recognition, she nonetheless implied, in echo of Ahimeir before her, were purely committed to settlement and land acquisition, without the distraction of leftist Labor ideology. "The First Ones were pathbreakers," she said, not in the sense of an abstract "innovation" but because they deliberately acquired land through the "force of the liberator" [*koah ha-meshahrer*]. "The lands to which the force of the liberator didn't come are not in our control today, fifteen years after the founding of the state." Speaking five years before Israel's conquests in 1967, Raziel-Naor supported the broad Zionist consensus around "Judaizing" the Negev and Galilee. A few settlements had been founded in the Galilee during the "days of the First Ones," she noted, but the region as a whole was "still waiting, standing mostly desolate, waiting for the Jewish Man to come to it." Indeed, she implied, military strength, not Labor ideology or symbolic pioneering, would ensure the Zionist future: "Because days came where the wonderful Conquest of Labor was not sufficient, and it wasn't even enough [simply] to conquer land and own it," it was necessary to embrace the "reverse commandment: 'to beat plowshares into swords'" and to adopt a right-wing platform: "political and military pioneering." Only in the sense of their commitment to territorial expansion and self-defense were the First Ones "pathbreakers [*nahshonim*] who rebelled against the inheritance of exile, and rose up to change the course of the history of the People of Israel."[131]

Religious parties, in contrast, emphasized the distinctive religiosity of the First Aliyah colonists who—in contrast to the Labor Zionist activists who denigrated them—retained their traditional observances and continued to center prayer and liturgy in local commemorations of settlement. Yitzhak Refael, representing the National Religious Party (Mafdal), which had joined Mapai in the governing coalition, emphasized the roots of the so-called "New Yishuv" in the religious communities that immigrated to Palestine in the eighteenth and early nineteenth centuries. These included religious thinkers like Zvi Hirsch Kalischer, whose nineteenth-century texts were later considered harbingers of Zionism, and Yoel Moshe Solomon, who built the first Jewish neighborhood outside the Old City of Jerusalem before founding Petah Tikva. All of these developments, in urban as well as rural Jewish settlement, were brought about "by the hand of God, an awakening and directing hand."[132] Refael expressed his admiration in the words of the Babylonian Talmud, Tractate Shabbat 112b: "If the First Ones were the children of angels, we are the children of men. And if the First Ones were the children of men, we are like donkeys." This phrase encapsulates the talmudic concept of *yeridat ha-dorot*, the belief that divine prophesy diminishes over time and that earlier texts hold greater interpretive authority than later ones. Just as in the Jewish legal principle, so too in the realm of Zionist commemoration. Echoing Rabbi Abraham Isaac Kook's philosophy that divine redemption could be achieved through earthly means, Refael asserted that those who "paved the way and prepared the path . . . were spiritual pioneers" who laid the foundation for "full redemption."[133]

What united these First Ones, urban and rural alike, Refael emphasized, was their unwavering religiosity, a point that David Tidhar had also stressed while raising funds in 1939 for the Shapira biography (see chapter 3). Neither Israeli citizens nor observers from abroad should assume that the transformative effect of Zionism came through a process of secularization. Quite the contrary: "The First Ones were full and complete Jews, full in their aspirations, and complete in their faith. Everywhere they came, wherever they put down stakes, they also established a tent for the Torah of God, which always accompanied them on their obstacle-ridden journey, and strengthened them on their dangerous mission" (361). Citing the Talmud in connection with the recent foundation of a religious kibbutz in the Beit She'an (Beisan) valley, Mitzpe Gilboa (now Ma'ale Gilboa), he asked, "What is the difference between the earlier generation, for whom miracles occurred and us, for whom miracles do not occur? . . . The previous generations were wholly dedicated to the sanctification of God's name [while we are not as dedicated]." Any settlement activity not undertaken by God-fearing Jews would be compromised. A decade later, a similar set of sentiments would animate Gush Emunim, the religious movement that undertook rural settlement in the West Bank and beyond with a similar combination of pioneering sentiment and religious imperative (361).

Non-Zionist religious parties, too, could find affinities with the religious settlers of the First Aliyah. Menachem Parush, from the non-Zionist party Agudat Yisrael, initially appeared to disparage the very framework of the event, asserting (like Ben-Gurion) that "aliyah to the Land of Israel never stopped." Asking rhetorically, "Who are the First Ones?" he answered with the names of medieval and early modern Jews including Nahmanides (Moses ben Nahman, 13th c.) and the Vilna Gaon (Elijah ben Solomon Zalman, 18th c.), people who supported Jewish migration to the Land of Israel but long preceded the Zionist movement. Nonetheless, he too could find special meaning in the anniversary date being celebrated—1882—and in the First Aliyah specifically. The Rosh Pinna colony's initial regulations that year, he said, obligated all residents to observe land-based Jewish law related to planting and harvesting and, he added, "the vast majority of the first colonies had regulations like this," built synagogues and ritual baths, and opened houses of Jewish learning. To him the first moshavot were signs not of a radically new political movement, the first step of a transformation, but the inheritors of a spiritual Zionism, a longing for Zion that had nothing to do with statehood or sovereignty. This combination of denying the First Aliyah colonies' "firstness" claims and nonetheless emphasizing their admirable religiosity had characterized the so-called Old Yishuv's engagement with the colonies from their beginnings, as the historian Yehoshua Kaniel has shown.[134]

Similarly, Yaakov Katz from Poʻalei Agudat Yisraʾel, a splinter group of Agudat Yisrael that represented the interests of ultra-Orthodox workers, stated that the project of Jewish life in Israel could continue effectively only if the next generation based its efforts on a "pure and refined nationalism [*leʾumiyut*], unmixed and not taken from a non-Jewish way of life. We need to strive to make sure our country is built on the basis of pure Judaism, without the intermixing of a foreign spirit" (365–66). Nationalism is defined here in a religious sense, "apolitical" in its own way in ostensibly preceding and transcending modern politics.

While Herut saw militarism and land conquest as the distinctive legacy of the first rural settlers and the religious parties emphasized the piety and traditionalism of those Jews, the Liberal Party saw this celebration as uniquely its own. The Liberal Party had been founded in 1961 through a merger between the urban professionals of the Progressive Party and the General Zionists, which had attracted owners of capital and private farmers since the times of the British Mandate. In its campaign materials, Orit Rozin has shown, the General Zionist Party of the 1950s claimed it was championing a capitalist ideology that was more egalitarian than socialism because of its commitment to individual freedom. Though the party's electoral gains were short-lived, the constituency of industrialists, business owners, and moshava agriculturalists influenced a longer-term turn in Israeli society toward individualism and, later, economic liberalization.[135] The General Zionists, which remained a part of the World Zionist Organization even after they ceased to be a stand-alone Knesset party, had consistently claimed that they transcended political schism. The General Zionists, wrote Itzhak Carmin in a 1951 survey, "took pride in standing above the Zionist party battles, in working for the general interests of the Jewish national home," and in offering "a balancing factor" that could wield a "wholesome influence" amidst the "extremes of partisanship."[136] In a keynote address delivered at the World Union of General Zionists in Tel Aviv in 1964, the American president of the organization, Emanuel Neumann, expressed remorse that "the Zionist movement had suffered in the past the consequences of schisms and the fragmentation of large groupings into splinter groups." The goal of achieving "maximum unity," he said, rested on the shoulders of the General Zionists.[137] While the General Zionists historically contained some less conservative factions more favorable to coalitions with Mapai, including urban professionals and some business interests that formed the Progressive Party, the founding of the Liberal Party, which entered the Knesset as an opposition party, represented its right-leaning flank. In 1964, the Liberal Party would join with Herut to form Gahal and, in 1973, the Likud party, an amalgam of traditional capitalist interests and right-wing ethnonationalism. Indeed, the General Zionists' legacy went a long way in giving legitimacy to

Herut, known for its historical lack of moderation. "There could be no question," writes political scientist Jonathan Mendilow, "of its efficacy in conferring legitimacy on Herut, seeing that it was a long-established, moderate, centrist party."[138]

In his comments to the Knesset in 1962, the Liberal Party MK Joseph Sapir, the prominent citrus owner and former mayor of Petah Tikva, praised First Aliyah First Ones explicitly for their "noble modesty which is hard to find these days," a reference to the "non-ideological" self-image that farmers had been promoting—and which had been pejoratively attributed to them—since the early part of the century (359). Alluding to Ben-Gurion's effort to sideline those who had "simply" arrived "first," Sapir also insisted that the firstness of the First Aliyah was not simply chronological; rather, the founders and communities associated with it embodied essential national characteristics.

First, he said, the First Aliyah had laid the foundations for self-rule and "independent statist institutions." He clarified what he meant by independent: "not in a communal framework, but through nuclei for building an independent, sovereign, and democratic state." These terms—independent, democratic—evoked the rhetoric of the General Zionist party in the 1950s, which held that support of the [Jewish] individual was the true meaning of democracy. Moreover, Sapir stressed, land settlement was important not, as Labor ideologues would have suggested, primarily as a method for Jewish cultural revitalization but rather as "the foundation of a national economy" (360).

Second, the moshavot set the borders of the country—indeed, the pattern of Jewish land settlement that the colonies had initiated eventually shaped the 1947 United Nations partition plan. Echoing the comments of the Herut MK, he lamented, "if only there had been more First Ones and if only the Hebrew plow had been extended out over the remaining parts of the land," then the shock of Hebrew weaponry, when the time came, could have burst through new areas and walls [*lifrotz tehumim ve-homot*]" (360). When, five years later, during the Six-Day War, Israel captured the West Bank, Gaza, East Jerusalem, the Sinai, and the Golan Heights, this counterfactual wish would become a reality. The realization that settlement would define future borders, whether de facto or de jure, motivated much of the subsequent settler movement, not only for the religious Zionists but also for those who saw territorial spread as the recipe for both individual flourishing and collective security.

Finally, the moshavot seemed to embody an ethos of security. Their "deep political [and] security sense," he said, made them realize the necessity of having "Hebrew weaponry to defend their territorial conquests." Through a selective reading of the moshavot, Sapir created an image of a society defined by its individual initiative, territorial conquest through land purchase, and ethos of security, one that reflected some of the perspectives of Herut but with a claim to moderation and capitalist pragmatism.

The Farmers' Federation, in which Sapir had been active, would continue to set itself apart from more "ideological" actors. In a pamphlet published in 1967, the organization asserted that private agriculture "predated by dozens of years the new ideas of binding and total cooperation" that define the kibbutz. Moreover, unlike on the kibbutz, membership in a moshava does not require a specific ideology: the moshava member is "sole owner of his farm with no limitations." He can market his produce however he wants and join professional organizations without being forced to do so. The critique is clear: the kibbutzim—like those who would elevate them in collective memory—are selective, coercive, and overly ideological. In the moshavot, in contrast, "we certainly are not planning to turn ourselves into an ideological laboratory to satisfy the curiosity of the modern world." Rather, their goal, implicitly apolitical, neither left nor right, is to "support families."[139]

"Recognition of the past is influenced by the present," wrote the *Davar* writer (and future sociology professor) Dan Horowitz in his coverage of the special Knesset session to mark the Year of the First Ones. "The residue of eighty years' worth of arguments and disagreements, ideological disputes, and differences in values showed themselves in the Knesset yesterday." This eighty-year history, not only its vaunted origins, "was reflected in the mirror of the Knesset via its many faces." As such, he noted, the proceedings could offer great material for a historian: "Not a historian of the 'First Ones,' the people of the First Aliyah per se, but maybe first and foremost a historian of the history of the Yishuv that also continues today."[140] Horovitz was articulating the argument that has been at the center of this book. Those gathered in the Knesset, like those in and beyond the moshavot who had been commemorating, reflecting on, and alluding to the First Aliyah for decades, were not telling the story of the First Aliyah. Rather, they were telling the evolving story of their own political evolution, contemporary anxieties, and future hopes through the malleable substance of the Zionist settler past. But the internal contention that reveals texture and multiplicity within the history of Zionism, which shows us that not all Zionists built the image of the past in the same way or toward the same ends, also confines all claims to firstness to within the national conversation. Zionist firsting, the insistent and ongoing attention to First Ones and First Things, directs attention to the Zionist settler past per se. In so doing, it mutes and overwrites competing claims to space and place even as it selectively integrates them, especially in the case of the Zionist capitalist political center, into narratives of hierarchical coexistence. These, too, are the stories we uncover when we look carefully and critically at the documentary evidence of local Zionist memory.

CONCLUSION
Thinking about the First Aliyah after 1967

Mention Petah Tikva to an Israeli and, after they share a joke about the central Israeli city's now iconic banality, they might start humming "The Ballad of Yoel Moshe Solomon." Written by Yoram Taharlev, arranged by Shalom Hanoch, and first performed by Arik Einstein in 1970, the ballad valorized four Jewish settlers and a Greek doctor who set out from Jaffa "on a humid morning in the year 1878" to scope out the site for a new colony near "Umlebes, in the heart of swamps and thickets." The doctor warned the group that the absence of birds in the area was a bad omen for settlement, but Solomon decided to forge ahead alone with the founding of the Jewish colony. The ballad then shifts to magic realism as Solomon sprouts wings in the middle of the night. Come morning, the "cursed valley" is filled with birds, who continue to sing of the settler Yoel Moshe Solomon.[1]

The ballad song genre, argues the literary scholar Shlomo Yaniv, was intended not "to surprise listeners" but to offer a "recognizable and authorized" narrative of the past that "express[ed] their world." Ballad songs came into Hebrew via Yiddish and Russian traditions at the start of the twentieth century and became popular in the Yishuv around the time of World War II, particularly as performed by the Palmach Chizbatron, a satirical musical group that mythologized contemporary and historical figures and events.[2] Through metric consistency, rhyme, and accessible spoken language, it was a perfect medium for expressing a piece of the imagined past before politics that had become a site of both nostalgia and political negotiation. Most listeners did not know that the place of Yoel Moshe Solomon in the story of Petah Tikva had been (and because of the song would again become) a bone of contention in a local dispute between families. They may not have been familiar with the intricacies of the labor politics that had made the "First Aliyah" into an object of both disdain and commemorative discourse.[3] A society of immigrants, politically fractured and still enmeshed in regional conflict, looked to its multiple pasts for soothing figures. They found them in a pleasant, packaged narrative of frontier settlement.

At the same time that the ballad was catching on, however, built environments associated with the "First Aliyah" were experiencing neglect. Israel was investing in settling immigrants in new development towns on the country's periphery, rather than in historical preservation. A 1973 article in *Maariv* lamented that the last original cabin in Gedera, built in 1884 by members of the Bilu settlement organization, was collapsing. The owners, Hana and Yigal Sverdlov, descendants of the house's first owner, said that they habitually ignored the groups of schoolchildren who rang the old metal bell wanting to be let in because they were embarrassed by the structure's condition. Soon, the Sverdlovs donated the house to the municipality in the hope of getting it restored, but the antiquities department told the city that the house wasn't an antiquity because it was of too recent a vintage. The prime minister's office and the planning department added that they had no budget for restoration, and the interior and tourism ministries also passed on the project.[4] Though it was marked as a museum in 1978, the house was not restored until 2007–2008. The First Aliyah had fallen between the commemorative cracks: not an antiquity but no longer a symbol of progress, it remained an aging icon to be selectively elevated or disregarded.

Another piece of the Bilu legacy, this one in Jaffa, also appeared to be imperiled. People who passed through this city of "mashed sandstone blocks, fragments of buildings, and rotten rafters," Avraham Rotem reported for *Maariv* in 1979, didn't realize that one of those structures was the building the Bilu members first lived in after the group's arrival in Palestine on July 6, 1882. Recently, Rotem alerted readers, a tractor had started dismantling the structure while passersby looted roof tiles and other building materials. "No one cared about the house except for history buffs." This neglect troubled

Rotem, who felt it could have been "the ideal place for commemorating the history of the Biluim," a place where "we would breathe history."[5] The house survived, but only barely, alongside the Ayalon highway that had threatened to displace it and which would eventually connect four major cities formed through private settlement initiative: Rishon LeZion (1882), Tel Aviv (1909), Herzliya (1924), and Holon (1935, from several neighborhoods established by Jewish industrialists). But Rotem chose not to mention another piece of the building's history: the Jaffa citriculturalist Anton Ayub owned the building when the Bilu members stayed there in 1882, and it remained in Arab hands until 1948, when the state expropriated it along with several other exemplary well houses (*biyarat*) that had been used to irrigate citrus orchards.[6] Ayub's loss of property didn't bother Rotem, nor did the smashed remnants of other Arab houses he had passed by in Jaffa. He was concerned that the house would be lost as a potential monument to the Jewish settlers of nearly a hundred years earlier.

Rosh Pinna, founded in 1882 and located on the country's geographic periphery in the Upper Galilee, seemed slated for a similar loss. In 1962, the reporter Zvi Lavi had complained in *Maariv* that Rosh Pinna was "not on the map."[7] In 1969, Aviezer Golan reported for *Yedioth Ahronoth* that "people pass by without notice, casting a sanctimonious smile in its direction and pressing hard on the gas pedal" as they speed on to Kiryat Shemona, the development town established in 1949. Golan juxtaposed this slow process of neglect with the actual destruction of the Palestinian village of al-Ja'una, where the very first residents of Rosh Pinna (originally called Gei Oni, after the Arabic name) had purchased their land. Al-Ja'una had been mostly depopulated in the spring of 1948; the IDF forcibly relocated its remaining residents within Israel in June 1949. "The Arab Ja'una was destroyed by bulldozers," Golan wrote, "but Rosh Pinna doesn't need bulldozers. Its own residents have neglected it" as they move away from the original colony center on the top of the mountain and into newer buildings. "The antique ['*atikah*] Rosh Pinna," he said, using language that projected the late nineteenth century back to the dawn of Jewish history, that "in any other country in the world would have been turned into a historical preserve, cultivated, and made into a destination for pilgrimages, is crumbling." Here, even without bulldozers, "it will become ruins ['*iyei horavot*] in just a few years."[8] These anxieties about decay and loss reflected the perennial perilousness of a settler project even in an active period of expansion.

Settlers Past, Settlers Present

The Zionist project of land settlement and development never ceased. Before the conquests of the Six-Day War in 1967, the Israeli government pegged the Negev in the south and the Galilee in the north as sites of Jewish population dispersion (a process they called "Judaization"—*Yihud*) and funded development towns and other Jewish settlements, while viewing agricultural settlements specifically "as a political instrument for absorption of immigrants, for dispersion of population, and for defense purposes, all as integral parts of state policy."[9] After Israel's land conquests during the 1967 Six-Day War, development and displacement continued in the Negev and Galilee while new civilian settlements began to take root in East Jerusalem (which Israel had quickly expanded and annexed), the Golan Heights (which it annexed in 1981), and the West Bank, Gaza, and northern Sinai. The drive for settlement both before and after 1967 came in part from immigrant demand for housing, but its particular urgency and geographic distribution in peripheral and border areas reflected concerns about ongoing regional threats, militant groups made up of Palestinian refugees who now resided in Jordan, Lebanon, or Gaza, and, within Israel, protest from Palestinian citizens (Arab Israelis) who began to unite across political divides around the threat and practice of land confiscations.[10] Many Israeli Jews perceived attacks, as well as anti-Zionist rhetoric and civil rights organizing, to different extents, as extensions of the anti-Zionist rhetoric and violent resistance that Jewish settlers had faced from within Palestine before 1948. Such incidents continually reminded the state and its Jewish citizens of the precarity of Zionist political control over space, despite Israel's military strength. "Settlement is on-going," Kevin Bruyneel writes, on the topic of American settler colonialism, "because politically the matter of claims to space are not settled. They are contested. Settlement is thus a practice, a status, and a site of conflict."[11]

Labor-led governments from 1967 to 1977, though they spoke of captured lands as bargaining chips for eventual peace treaties, also saw strategic and security rationales for settlement and initiated construction and infrastructure planning in East Jerusalem, the Golan Heights, the Jordan Valley, and northern Sinai.[12] Settlement throughout the Occupied Territories accelerated—through both state investment and retroactively recognized settler initiative—after the Likud party, a blend of right-wing ethnonational and center-right capitalist interests, took power in 1977. Settlement after 1977, moreover, occurred within a broader context of renewed political support for private enterprise and religious Zionism, skepticism about Labor Zionist history and claims, and support for a movement that saw itself as continuing the story of settler bravery on the new frontier. As the international community called upon Israel to return conquered lands in the context of peace negotiations and reiterated its position that civilian settlements in the Occupied Territories constituted a violation of international law, the principle that had animated Ottoman-era settlement now pertained again. In the absence of international approval—even, in the case of unauthorized settlement, of Israeli state approval—Israel and its settlers established communities on the premise that facts on the ground would ensure Jewish security and primacy, with or without a formal extension of borders, and would shape any borders to be drawn in the future.

By the 1970s, the sociologist Baruch Kimmerling has written, "the dormant codes of the immigrant-settler political culture" had been reawakened.[13] As the settler movement grew, its supporters connected themselves to the historical legacy of Zionist settlement and appealed to a broader, ongoing belief across the Zionist spectrum that settlers and settlement were the bedrock of the Zionist project. On February 8, 1982, the Knesset convened a special session to mark one hundred years of settlement in the Land of Israel, again choosing the conventional 1882 start date of the First Aliyah as its reference point. The Knesset chairman, Menahem Savidor (Likud), praised Yitzhak Ziv-Av, the head of the Farmers' Federation who had chaired the public committee for the celebration and had also promoted the Year of the First Ones in 1962–1963 (see chapter 5). Ziv-Av, he said, had "not allowed history to pass over the mute heroes of the revival. He extracted them from the abyss of forgetting."[14]

Knesset members had a more proximate wave of settlers on their minds, however: those in the Occupied Territories. Israel was on the verge of withdrawing around twenty-five hundred settlers from the Yamit corridor in the northern Sinai in the context of the Israel-Egypt peace treaty of 1979 as it continued to expand settlements in the West Bank and Gaza Strip.[15] Geula Cohen, who had founded and now represented the ultranationalist, pro-settlement Tehiya party, used the opportunity to make a statement. Cohen, a fighter in the mandate-era Revisionist Etzel and Lehi militias and a Likud Knesset member until 1979, suggested that the gathering instead take place "in the only place where the principal fight for preserving Jewish settlement in the Land of Israel is happening: the Yamit corridor." Cohen knew the suggestion would be rejected, but she was using it to grandstand: "If the Knesset doesn't accept this proposal we will be witnesses here to a cynical display by the Knesset, which is using its voice to elevate settlement while taking up an axe in its hand to uproot it." The commemoration of the hundredth anniversary of the First Aliyah was not going to pass in isolation from the debate about contemporary settlement and settlement withdrawal in Israel. And yet the ensuing session did not feature disagreement about settlement (*hityashvut*) writ large. It confirmed not only that right-wing supporters of settlement in the Occupied Territories saw the settlers of eras past as models, but that all Zionist Knesset members who spoke wished to elevate the settler origins and settler ideology of their ongoing project as an uncontroversial and praiseworthy feature of Zionism, despite their different strategies regarding contemporary settlement and regional foreign policy.[16]

Likud MKs, in particular, connected nineteenth-century settlement to twentieth-century settlement in the Occupied Territories. Savidor noted wistfully that "if the founder of Rishon LeZion, [Zalman David] Levontin, had indeed realized his plans near Gaza, or if Yoel [Moshe] Solomon had realized his intentions to strike root near Jericho, as he intended, and not in Umlebes [Petah Tikva], how much blood, how many casualties, and how many debates about the borders of Israel could the following generations have been spared?" But a celebration of "First Aliyah" founders was also a celebration of all Jewish settlers, "all workers and builders of the land, from all settlement streams" who "turned a wasteland into a flowering Garden of Eden" (6).

The minister of agriculture, Simha Erlich (General Zionists and then Likud), echoed Savidor: "Let this day celebrate not only the First Ones, but everyone working and building the land now." After all, "settlement [*hityashvut*] hasn't ceased over 33 years of statehood." On the contrary, the establishment of settlements [*yishuvim*], which had previously been done "under the watchful eye of a foreign occupier [*kovesh*]" now occurs "publicly and without shame [*be-resh galei*]" (16). Settlements established hastily in Judea, Samaria, the Golan, and Gaza, the former Ness Ziona farmer noted with approval, "are now becoming more established through increased budgets and a broadening of their human population base" (17). Overall, the agricultural sector was producing a billion dollars of export goods through the use of advanced technology, including electronic irrigation computers that crunch numbers. "This is the agriculture of today."[17]

The Labor Zionist Alignment (Maarakh) party, in the opposition at the time, supported evacuating Yamit but also favored ongoing settlement in other areas of the Occupied Territories that they believed would confer security. MK Shimon Peres, speaking for the party, shared in the full-throated praise of the Zionist settlement project coming from the Likud party and did not explicitly distinguish in his rhetoric between the settlement then unfolding within the Green Line, which had marked the limit of Israel's territory until the land conquests of the 1967 War, and that taking place in the Occupied Territories. He boasted of "861 new settlements," including "300 kibbutzim and 400 cooperative settlements and 4.5 million dunams cultivated, considered the best agriculture in the world, with the ability to produce an output of 20 billion shekels a year," in commodities ranging "from oranges to flowers." He noted that Jews in America might be wealthier, but "if there are new settlements there, it wasn't Jews who built them." Only in Israel, he said, could Jews undertake the process of Jewish settlement.[18]

Peres's seamless description of the trans-historical Jewish settlement process blends the settlers of yesteryear with newer ones. His framing also obscures the political turning point of 1948:

> The land that waited for them was arid and exposed. They lived in caves, thickets, tents, cabins, metal and fabric shacks, in camps [*mahanot*] and transit camps [*ma'abarot*] and abandoned houses and temporary apartments, small apartments. They worked in swamps, sands, rocks, feverish valleys, and unknown hills. They fought against murderers, gangs, foreign powers, and the Arab armies. Always few in number, without strategic reserves and lacking manpower, weapons, and resources, they paid a heavy and cruel price. Until

the day that they could turn back and see behind them a flowering and verdant land, whose reputation had traveled as far as that of the best agricultural producers, the strongest armies, the most advanced societies.[19]

The story that Peres, Savidor, and Erlich were celebrating that day, across their political differences, did not begin with ideas or political organizing. It began with acts of settlement and continued with acts of settlement. Amidst the blistering and ongoing partisan fights over the specific contours of settlement, the rival Zionist parties expressed agreement about its centrality to Zionist memory and ongoing practice. The speakers at the 1982 commemorative session recalled a barren and hostile landscape that was waiting to be settled and modernized. The distinction between private and public land-ownership, that had been so salient for those commemorating or criticizing the "First Aliyah" during the mandate period, was no longer as significant. Now both categories of pre-state land ownership, along with the lands confiscated from Palestinians and those taken over from the British in 1948, had become Israeli territory. In 1985, Yitzhak Ziv-Av authored an educational curriculum for the Israeli Department of Education and the Jewish National Fund that sought to jointly celebrate the plowing of the "First Furrow" in Petah Tikva (1878), the establishment of Rosh Pinna (1882), and the founding of the Jewish National Fund (1901), all of which occurred around Hanukkah time and which Ziv-Av suggested should be marked together on a new holiday called "The Celebration of the First Furrow."

His pamphlet consisted of a script to be read aloud by teachers and students. "Let us elevate the memory of the first of the First Ones [*rishonim*]," it began. "They, who established a long chain of colonies within the desolation of the land." The process of settlement to be celebrated was ongoing: "we will elevate the memory of First Ones in every generation . . . Standing erect, we unite as ones continuing on the path of the First Ones by remembering them." After reciting the names of the first First Aliyah colonies—Petah Tikva, Rishon LeZion, Rosh Pinna, Yesud HaMa'ala, and Mazkeret Batya—teachers and students were to declare that those communities had "created the foundation from which emerged many other settlements [*yishuvim*], and an infrastructure for settlement [*hityashvut*] throughout the country and for the *State of the Jews*." This last phrase is bolded in the original, accompanied by stage directions that prescribe reading it "slowly and with emphasis." The ceremonial curriculum then reviews a history of settlement in a landscape "almost empty of people" but full of corruption, thievery, and gangs.[20]

The Evolution of Hierarchical Coexistence

Ziv-Av had offered a First Aliyah narrative entirely consistent with Zionist collective memory across partisan lines, one that obscured the more distinctive features of earlier First Aliyah commemoration: the rhetoric of hierarchical coexistence with hired labor and what I've called the "politics of apoliticism," a nationalism rooted in private initiative that sees itself as explicitly moderate and located outside spheres of deleterious "politics." Yet those who took up the government-supported project of settlement began, perhaps unknowingly, to echo some of those distinctive threads as they encountered, and hired, Palestinians. Though Israeli Jews, "settlers" and "nonsettlers" alike, evoked the frontier hero on a barren landscape at moments of commemoration, they also discussed their ongoing, more quotidian experiences of interethnic contact using what we can identify as a rhetoric of hierarchical coexistence.

Following 1967, a new split labor market arose as West Bank and Gaza Palestinians became Israel's reserve army of unskilled labor, to be tapped and untapped as needed. Though their overall share in the Israeli labor market was below 10%, Palestinians from the Occupied Territories filled a substantially higher share of positions in agriculture and construction.[21] Salim Tamari has argued that the integration of Palestinian workers after 1967 "entailed the demise of Hebrew Labor." Instead, "normalcy was redefined as a strategy of coexistence between a largely disenfranchised Palestinian population and a colonizing Jewish society."[22] Meron Benvenisti, the former deputy mayor of Jerusalem, warned in a 1984 report on West Bank settlement that a "hierarchy of superiors and inferiors, a 'horse and rider' coexistence, will prevail throughout Greater Israel, but nowhere more so than in the settlement enclaves in the Occupied Territories."[23] As he explained to a reporter that year, "Nobody [among Jews] will challenge the reality of a society of horse and rider. We'll take good care of our horse. It will get excellent food. But we'll be the rider."[24] This arrangement, in addition to preserving Israeli

Jewish superiority, seemed also to promise a measure of security. As Shlomo Gazit, the first coordinator of civilian affairs in the Occupied Territories, put it, the ongoing provision of labor to Palestinians "could certainly head off mounting tensions and would bolster internal [i.e. Israeli] security by insuring that every Arab had something to lose if he or she should act improperly or if the peace should be disrupted."[25] The anthropologist Ethan Morton-Jerome argues that allowing Palestinians into the Israeli labor market "was and remains an important strategy of the military to control and pacify the population."[26] Palestinians have continued to work within Israel through the present, albeit in smaller proportions as a result of Israel's authorization of foreign workers from abroad following the First Intifada in the late 1980s. Palestinians who enter Israel for work remain subject to a complex and capricious permit regime put into place in 1968 and modified several times, most notably during the period of the Oslo Accords in the 1990s.[27]

When Jewish employers on both sides of the Green Line hire Palestinian noncitizens, they interact with them on a daily basis, albeit in the limited ways typical of an employer-employee or customer-server relationship. As would certainly have been the case in the 1880s and 1890s had Arab workers on Jewish farms sat for ethnographic interviews, contemporary Palestinian employees have described wage theft, abuse, and mistreatment from employers. Though Israeli law obligates Israeli employers to pay Palestinians, like Israelis, the Israeli minimum wage, this provision is rarely enforced. Morton-Jerome's Palestinian interviewees attest to the fact that they also face mistreatment and wage theft on the part of Palestinian employers, who, in addition, pay a lower wage than Israeli employers. But the tendency of Israeli employers to cite that fact in defense of the status quo arrangements only further amplifies the historical resonance with the "First Aliyah" colony farmers of the past, who also argued that they were providing the best employment available in a context where Arab elites also cared little for protecting the rights of peasant laborers.[28] Nonetheless, Israelis simultaneously idealize their coexistence with Palestinian workers in the past and allude to ongoing, even if more limited, sites of contact in the present.

Sara Yael Hirschhorn's interviews with American Jewish West Bank settlers, most of whom came from liberal American backgrounds and settled into center-right or right-wing Israeli politics, are replete with such reminiscences. Carole Rosenblatt, who lived in the northern Sinai settlement of Yamit in the late 1970s before it was evacuated, recalled that she had hired Palestinians from Rafah in the Gaza Strip to work at her beachfront kiosk down the coast.[29] "We had peace, even more than that," recalled the Tekoa founder Eli Birnbaum, noting that he would bring his children to visit a Palestinian neighbor's home, "where they would drink coffee and chat in Arabic." Palestinians also "worked in settlement industries, including home construction."[30] Bobby Brown described coexistence in Tekoa using paternalistic language reminiscent of the Rosh Pinna colonist Yitzhak Epstein's comments in 1907: "They learned about sheep vaccination from us," Brown said, and "they gathered open-mouthed in front of our drip irrigation systems—and adopted them."[31]

When the outbreak of the First Intifada made it clear that hierarchical coexistence alone would not bring Palestinian complacency, some settlers reacted with shock. "I thought we're making peace with the Arabs by living with them. They work with me, I visit, they visit. I thought we were moving in the right direction, but the intifada threw me for a loop."[32] "You want to talk coexistence?" Sharon Katz, an Efrat resident, asked in an interview. "That was coexistence. It was only when they decided they're going to have Oslo that we weren't allowed to talk to each other anymore." Internationally brokered peace negotiations and promises of Palestinian autonomy, Katz feared, would mean the end of coexistence: "The left is always talking about coexistence, but they don't mean coexistence, they mean separation. The right—and the majority of the people who live in Judea and Samaria are right wing—we are living in coexistence."[33]

Settler discourses that emphasize hierarchical coexistence and personal relationships, and that blame violence or tension on outside "political" actors, whether Israeli or Palestinian, persist despite increasingly layered and complex mechanisms of ethnic population separation within the West Bank.[34] In October 2016, the mayor of Efrat, Oded Revivi, invited more than a hundred local Palestinians, both blue-collar workers and community leaders, to share fruit and brownies with Israeli settlers, IDF officers, and local officials during the festival of Sukkot. Ahmad Mousa from nearby Wadi al-Nis was quoted speaking admiringly of his village's relationship with the settlement:

"Seventy percent of our village works in Efrat. They treat us very well and we are very good to them, too." Riad Abu Ahmad shared that "we make a living in Israel, and so we have to protect the plate we eat from."[35] As reported in many Israeli and Western news outlets, the encounter was a local vision of peace cruelly undermined by the Palestinian Authority, which subsequently arrested some of the Palestinians who had attended the settler gathering. Some heaped additional scorn on "leftists" for failing to recognize this market-driven coexistence.[36] On the basis of fieldwork conducted at a Jewish supermarket in Maale Adumim near Jerusalem, the anthropologist Jeremy Siegman observed that "not only did settler corporations exploit cheap, vulnerable laborers but settler consumers also often enjoyed the everyday, albeit limited, experience of interacting with Palestinians in ways that left their power apparently uncontested." Jewish settler interviewees, he wrote, "readily offered up smiling, wistful references to individual Palestinians who had worked or still worked for them, often mixed in with broader anti-Palestinian sentiments."[37]

This rhetoric of hierarchical coexistence came into public view internationally in 2015 when activists called for a boycott of SodaStream, the soda machine company whose factory, staffed by Palestinian workers, was located in the Mishor Adumim industrial area next to Maale Adumim. The CEO, Daniel Birnbaum, and those who came to his defense claimed that Palestinians who worked for the company benefited from their access to employment and would suffer if the factory relocated. In this form of pro-Israeli rhetoric, which was used to try to counter the larger BDS (Boycott, Divestment, Sanctions) campaign first launched by Palestinian civil society organizations in 2005, "the workplace becomes the key arena in which peaceful relations grow and develop."[38]

Echoing these claims, *Bloomberg Businessweek* noted that Birnbaum's concern for his West Bank Palestinian workers had been "parental—verging on paternalistic." When he discovered that some of his employees had never been to the ocean (a result of Israeli policies limiting the movement of West Bank Palestinians to the coast), he got government permission to take some of them for a swim in the Mediterranean Sea, just 25 miles away. He then joked that they went into the sea in their clothes and "they can't swim to begin with." This disdain, *Bloomberg Businessweek* reported sympathetically, was nonetheless accompanied by "bighearted deeds," like having a swimming pool later constructed in the West Bank village of Jabʻa where many of his employees lived, "supporting his claim . . . that he truly cares and doesn't just see Palestinians as another corporate asset."[39] After relocating his Mishor Adumim plant to the Negev town of Rahat, within the Green Line, Birnbaum also prided himself on employing Bedouin citizens of Israel. He claimed that he was doing so not merely for pragmatic reasons (their availability to work unskilled jobs) but as part of a vision of coexistence. When, in late 2018, Birnbaum announced at the Globes Business Conference in Jerusalem that SodaStream would open a factory in the Gaza Strip, he proclaimed: "At SodaStream we manufacture peace every day, and along the way we also make soda." The factory would offer Palestinians there "jobs, real jobs," reported the *Jerusalem Post*, because "where there is prosperity there is peace."[40]

Generations earlier, one might have heard a Hadera or Petah Tikva citrus farmer making a similar argument about relations with Palestinian employees that had been, in their view, scuttled by the intrusion of "politics" from either the Zionist labor movement or Palestinian elites, depending on precisely who they were framing the argument to. Contemporary proponents of such perspectives, the anthropologist Callie Maidhof writes, describing so-called non-ideological settlers, including those in Efrat or Maale Adumim, "juxtapose a sane, rational middle class with an ideologically driven movement that places a theological mandate before the comfort and safety of its adherents—as well as that of the nation at large."[41] Conceptually, many Israelis consider themselves distinct from what they see as an overly zealous right wing and a dangerously ideological left and look favorably on the idea of achieving peaceful relations through the mechanisms of the capitalist market, whether they live in a West Bank settlement or a coastal Israeli city or town. Violence, in this worldview, seems to break an otherwise workable arrangement in which Jews hire Palestinians and everyone benefits.

Palestinians from Jabʻa who were fired when the SodaStream factory in Mishor Adumim closed sometimes ended up finding employment at other Israeli factories in the same industrial area. But their experiences make clear that the discourse of hierarchical coexistence flows only in one direction. As Maidhof notes, "'coexistence' as a model hinges on the normalization of radical inequalities."⁴² Working-class Palestinians, Ethan Morton-Jerome remarks, "are forced to work for the very economic system that exploits them and within a political structure that does not provide them labor rights or rights as citizens." They have faced difficult decisions about where and for whom to work since the beginning of the Occupation.⁴³ Jeremy Siegman has argued that "economic peace discourse . . . aid[s] in the further entrenchment of a de facto, non-democratic one-state reality in Israel/Palestine."⁴⁴ What settlers, past and present, perceive as hierarchical coexistence is intrinsically unequal, unstable, and always subject to resistance in the context of movements for economic and political justice.

Avraham Shapira's 135th Birthday

The Petah Tikva Museum, which established its "First Ones Wing" in 1963 (as we discussed in chapter 5), began to expand its archival holdings in the 1980s. As David Goldenberg, head of the Petah Tikva Archive, described it in 1991, "we met with many of the great-grandchildren, grandchildren, and the last of the sons of the founders. We prepared a card for each of the First Ones who had a plot of agricultural land and for each of their children born before 1900 and between 1900–1914" to create a catalogue of "600 heads of families." Goldenberg found all the books he could—two hundred twenty of them—on the topic of Petah Tikva's history and "read, researched, recorded, transcribed, copied, and duplicated all the material on the topic."⁴⁵ Landownership and early arrival became the local markers of "firstness," not only rhetorically but also within the archival record and built environment of the First Aliyah moshavot.⁴⁶

Municipalities, local councils, and museums continued to commemorate the First Aliyah settler past; they host many of the archives that I consulted to write this book. On December 18, 2005, the Petah Tikva municipality held an event in conjunction with the city museum to mark one hundred thirty-five years since Avraham Shapira's birth and forty years since his death. The ceremony took place in the Shapira house, which by then had become a community space. The museum director and chief curator, Drorit Gur-Aryeh, welcomed the assembled guests, reminded them of the city's efforts to preserve the past, and invited them to contribute archival materials of their own.⁴⁷

Shapira's grand-nephew Reuven Rivlin, speaker of the Knesset from the Likud party, took the podium next. Shapira had gained the status of myth,

Rivlin said, both through his life mission ("defense for Jews in their land") and his personal appearance ("a tall man with blue eyes, riding his horse, with a straw hat on his head and a pipe in his mouth"). This quintessential Ashkenazi settler-farmer-defender had become known for "the relations he created with his Arab neighbors," Rivlin stressed, adding that "he learned the Arabs, their language, their way of life, and their customs. He also became a fierce fighter who didn't compromise and therefore he earned the respect of the Arabs in the area." As a result, Rivlin recalled nostalgically, "before Petah Tikva was a city" there would be a "big *hafle* [party, Arabic]. There would be a *fantaziya* [horsemanship competition] every time my uncle would come. The last *fantaziya* I remember was the *fantaziya* for his ninetieth birthday, there wasn't another like it, and the elders of Petah Tikva still talk about its greatness today."[48]

In 2014, Rivlin became the president of Israel. He has systematically opposed the partition of the land and the creation of a separate Palestinian state (endorsed historically by Labor Zionists) while also opposing ongoing efforts by the Israeli far right to further concretize the legal separation of the Palestinian Arab citizens of Israel. His remarks have garnered occasional praise from leftists who see him as a rare voice for Jewish-Arab coexistence within the Israeli right-wing establishment. The year he became president, Rivlin visited Kafr Qasim, where his uncle Avraham Shapira had overseen the state-run sulha fifty-seven years earlier (see chapter 4). Dahlia Scheindlin, writing for *+972 Magazine*, praised Rivlin's apology for "the terrible crime that was done here." Scheindlin called it a "sign of brotherhood" and "bold moral leadership," in recognizing that Arabs were "indigenous citizens and equals."[49]

Rivlin comes to his thinking, however, not from the left but from the right. His vision, at odds with that of the most overtly militaristic and racist strands of his party, holds that Jews can and must be benevolent toward and provisionally inclusive of a large population of Palestinian citizens and noncitizens who work for the most part on the lower rungs of the economic ladder and have varying degrees of unequal rights, while being aggressive against any violent resistance and uncompromising about Jews' right to live in the land of Israel. This complex of views, however, also has a deeper set of historical lineages. The Hebrew writer S. Yizhar (Yizhar Smilansky), nephew of the Farmers' Federation president and Rehovot citriculturalist Moshe Smilansky, noted in 1993 that his uncle had "employed Jewish and Arab workers in his orchard according to the principle that two peoples would always live here and both should have equal opportunity for work and an equal basis for coexistence. He spoke Arabic, intermingled with them, and wrote stories and romances under the [Arabic] pseudonym 'Khawaja Musa'. . . . In short, he was a complete 'leftist' according to our contemporary categories."[50]

Smilansky was demonstrably not a leftist, but his and his fellow farmers' historical rhetoric, sharpened and articulated around historical claims to "firstness," could appeal across partisan divides precisely because it could appear inclusive, pragmatic, and apolitical, even as it normalized structures of historical erasure and economic and ethnic inequality. We could continue to trace variants of this thinking through the industrial capitalists and then high-tech entrepreneurs who came to define the Israeli bourgeoisie and drove Israel's turn to neoliberalism in the later twentieth and into the twenty-first century. Future researchers might probe those lineages, and their associated self-justifications and cultures of memory, in light of the suggestion by the scholar of politics Jonathan Dean that the apparently apolitical, capitalocentric present "comes into being by way of contrast with an imagined radical past of possibility and politicization."[51] This imagined past, however, obscures a different past, whose proponents emphasized their remove from the political and the ideological.

The First Aliyah colonies—which were unsuccessful in their early years but gained an enduring, if always ambivalent, symbolic form in the twentieth century—generated, promoted, and represented a fundamental and increasingly accepted Zionist logic. Their exemplars—settlers, farmers, and their descendants—created their past through memoirs, biographical literature, and articles in the periodical press and via school curricula, radio programs, and public events, first in the Yishuv and then in the State of Israel. The ex post facto twentieth-century conception of the "First Aliyah," far more than its historical reality, provided rhetorical ammunition and a sense of collective purpose for diverse elements within the Yishuv and Israel, including those who defined themselves against it. That many of its proponents considered themselves fundamentally apolitical, even as they stressed their contribution to the Zionist political project, helps explain both their decades-long exclusion from the historical scholarship and the reach and power of aspects of their worldview into the present day.

NOTES

Introduction

1. "Brandy bottle, Friedman-Tnuva Winery, with stickers showing picture of Avraham Shapira on horseback." Oded Yarkoni Archives of the History of Petah Tikva (henceforth PTA) 003.136/4, undated, probably 1964–1972. Friedman, like Shapira, was an entrepreneur and a participant in Palestine's private sector. Born in the traditional Jewish community of Tiberias, he had founded his winery in Haifa in 1889 but had moved it in 1912 to Petah Tikva.

2. "Be-hatzagat ha-bekhorah ha-hagigit shel ha-seret 'Adamah zot sheli hi' ha-mutzag be-kolnoa 'Yaron'" [At the festive opening night of "This land is mine" at the Yaron Cinema], *Maariv*, February 29, 1960, 4.

3. Yizrael, "Le-vikoret ha-historiyografyah shel shenotehah ha-rishonot shel Petah Tikva"; Lang, "Hityashvut ha-Yarkonim: nisayon she-hikhziv." Shapira's father, Yitzhak Zvi, initially settled in Jerusalem in 1880 while investigating options, including the already faltering Petah Tikva, for land settlement. Around 1883, he moved to Jaffa and purchased 120 dunams there, but continued to live in Jaffa. Around this same time, his older son Michael joined a group of settlers from Bialystok who were resettling Petah Tikva at a nearby site, closer to the village of al-Yahudiyya. Michael's wife and children initially stayed behind in Jaffa. Michael summoned Avraham to help him with driving wagons, and Avraham commuted to this work from Jaffa for a time before fully settling in Petah Tikva. Edelstein, *Avraham Shapira*, 1:37.

4. Contracts from 1900 to 1916 record several of Shapira's land purchases from several different Jews. PTA 003.002/3.

5. The figure for December 31, 1962, was 58,700. "Israel: Statistical Survey," 265.

6. The Fajja neighborhood (later Naveh Kibush and then Kiryat Alon) was estab-

lished as a workers' neighborhood in 1951 on Fajja village lands. The Amishav transit camp, also the site of the village of Fajja, was annexed to Petah Tikva in 1955, with a population of 8,500 at the time. Yeshayahu Aviam, "ha-Kol mitragshim seviv 'Amishav: anshei ha-ma'abarah 'atzmam adishim" [Everyone is getting worked up about Amishav: the residents of the transit camp themselves are apathetic], *Maariv*, July 5, 1955, 2.

7. The term *moshava* also remained the conventional Hebrew translation for "colonies" in the sense of French or British overseas colonies. In the Palestine/Israel context, *moshava* (pl. *moshavot*) refers exclusively to those communities that were acquired using private funds and that remained under private rather than Zionist national management (though there was some fluidity of terminology in the early twentieth century). The easily confused term *moshav* (pl., *moshavim*), from the same Hebrew root, refers to cooperative settlements of individual farmers on nationally owned land. Several different types of moshavim were established over the years; the first was Nahalal, founded in 1921. Kibbutzim, or agricultural communes, also were premised on national land ownership but engaged in more radical experiments in communal living and community property. Degania (est. 1910) is typically considered the first kibbutz, though it was preceded by several years by experimental communes known as *kvutzot* (sing, *kvutza*) at Kinneret and Sejera, the latter of which was founded as a moshava.

8. Pierre Nora claims that a public focus on memory emerges at "a turning point where consciousness of a break with the past is bound up with the sense that memory has been torn—but torn in such a way as to pose the problem of the embodiment of memory in certain sites where a sense of historical continuity persists." The "First Aliyah" colonies were such a site of perceived, if contested, historical continuity. "Between Memory and History: Les Lieux de Mémoire," 7.

9. Kabha and Karlinsky, "ha-Pardes ha-ne'elam: ha-pardesanut ha-'Arvit-ha-Falastinit 'ad shenat 1948"; Karlinsky, *California Dreaming*; Seikaly, *Men of Capital*.

10. Moshe Lissak, *ha-Elitot shel ha-yishuv ha-Yehudi be-Eretz-Yisra'el bi-tekufat ha-Mandat*, 83–92; Ben-Porat, *Hekhan hem ha-burganim ha-hem?*, 49; Karlinsky, *California Dreaming*, 219.

11. Ross, *May '68 and Its Afterlives*, 1.

12. Matsuda, *The Memory of the Modern*, 15.

13. Yerushalmi, *Zakhor*, 11.

14. Lepore, *The Whites of Their Eyes*, 7.

15. Ben-Artzi, "ha-Hityashvut ha-Yehudit be-Eretz Yisra'el 1900–1917," 348.

16. Zahra, *The Great Departure*; Alroey, *An Unpromising Land*; Alroey, *Bread to Eat and Clothes to Wear*; Alroey, "Two historiographies"; Alroey, "The Jewish Emigration from Palestine in the Early Twentieth Century."

17. Pappé, *A History of Modern Palestine*, 32; Ben-Artzi, *Early Jewish Settlement Patterns in Palestine, 1882–1914*.

18. Shilo, *Etgar ha-migdar*; Shilo, Kark, and Hasan-Rokem, *ha-Ivriyot ha-*

hadashot; Ben-Artzi, "Have Gender Studies Changed Our Attitude?"; Green, "Defuse hekerut ve-shidukhim ba-moshavot bi-tekufat ha-ʿAliyot ha-Rishonah veha-Sheniyah"; Green, "Meʿoravut vaʿade ha-moshavot u-vne ha-moshavot be-ʿinyane ha-perat ba-ʿAliyot ha-Rishonah veha-Sheniyah"; Berlovitz, *Le-hamtzi eretz le-hamtzi ʿam*.

19. Bartal, "Petah Tikva." Urban Arab intellectuals, in particular, took up thinking connected to the Nahda, or Arab Awakening, with the extension of press freedoms after 1908. See Seikaly, "Christian Contributions to the Nahda in Palestine Prior to World War I."

20. Ben-Arieh, *ʿIr bi-reʾi tekufah*.

21. Yehoshua Kaniel has described the range of factors that led members of the so-called "Old Yishuv" to question the viability of land settlement, factors that included security fears, concerns about non-adherence to Torah law, and doubts about economic viability. Kaniel, "Ha-vikuah ben Petah Tikva le-Rishon LeZion."

22. Bartal, "ʿAl ha-rishoniyut"; Bartal and Ben-Arieh, *Shelhe ha-tekufah ha-ʿOthmanit*; Kaniel, *Hemshekh u-temurah*.

23. Kaniel, "ha-Vikuah ben Petah Tikva le-Rishon LeZion"; Eliav, "Hevle bereshit shel Petah Tikva"; Yizrael, "Le-vikoret ha-historiyografyah shel shenotehah ha-rishonot shel Petah Tikva"; Eliav, *Eretz Yisraʾel vi-Yishuvah be-meʾah ha-19, 1777–1917*, Part 2; Bartal, *Galut ba-aretz*.

24. Nineteenth-century Jewish purchases were part of a larger de jure process of land privatization generated by the Tanzimat. Solomonovich and Kark, "Land Privatization in Nineteenth-Century Ottoman Palestine."

25. Shafir, *Land, Labor and the Origins of the Israeli-Palestinian Conflict 1882–1914*, 31–36; Gurevich, *ha-ʿAliyah, ha-Yishuv veha-tenuʿah ha-tivʿit shel ha-ukhlusiyah be-Eretz Yisraʾel*, 18–19.

26. Ben-Arieh, "ha-Nof ha-yishuvi shel Eretz-Yisraʾel ʿerev ha-hityashvut ha-Tziyonit."

27. Raab, *ha-Telem ha-rishon*, 67.

28. Jonathan Gribetz considers discussions about Jews, religion, and race in *al-Hilal*, *al-Manar*, and *al-Muqtataf*, journals of the Arab Awakening (Nahda) published outside of Palestine but sometimes with Palestine-based contributors. He identifies this trend in particular following the Young Turk Revolution in 1908, after which Palestinian intellectuals also published in new local Arabic publications. Gribetz, *Defining Neighbors*.

29. Judea and Samaria are now used exclusively in reference to the southern and northern halves, respectively, of the West Bank, and are not associated with the coastal plain. This transformation of terminology occurred only after Israel's 1967 conquest of the West Bank. For a discussion of the importance of settlement blocs for the creation of roads, administration, joint security, and relations with local Arab villages, see Ben-Bassat, "Proto-Zionist–Arab Encounters in Late Nineteenth-Century Palestine, 50–52."

30. Aaronsohn, *ha-Baron veha-moshavot*; Aaronsohn, *Rothschild and Early Jewish Colonization in Palestine*; Schama, *Two Rothschilds and the Land of Israel*; Penslar, *Zionism and Technocracy*, 13–25.

31. Gvati, *Me'ah shenot hityashvut*, 1:346.

32. Giladi, "Rishon LeZion be-hasut ha-Baron Rothschild (1882–1900)"

33. Ben-Artzi, *Early Jewish Settlement Patterns in Palestine, 1882–1914*, 31–32.

34. Giladi, "ha-Moshavot she-lo be-hasut ha-Baron bi-shenot ha-90."

35. Ben-Artzi, "ha-Hityashvut ha-Yehudit be-Eretz Yisra'el 1900–1917," 349.

36. Cited in Giladi, "ha-Moshavot she-lo be-hasut ha-Baron bi-shenot ha-90," 534.

37. Shafir, *Land, Labor and the Origins of the Israeli-Palestinian Conflict 1882–1914*, 55.

38. Roi, "Yahase Yehudim-'Arvim be-moshvot ha-'Aliyah ha-Rishonah"; Ben-Bassat, "Proto-Zionist–Arab Encounters in Late Nineteenth-Century Palestine; Ben-Bassat, *Petitioning the Sultan*.

39. Tzahor, "ha-Mifgash ben ha-ikarim le-fo'ale ha-'Aliyah ha-Sheniyah be-Petah Tikva"; Azmon, *Historiyah basar va-dam*.

40. Ben-Bassat, "The Challenges Facing the First Aliyah Sephardic Ottoman Colonists"; Klorman, "Hityashvut po'alim temanin ve-Ashkenazim"; Klorman, *Traditional Society in Transition*; Klorman, "ha-Yahas el ha-'aher' be-tarbut ha-politit shel ha-moshava."

41. Glass and Kark, *Sephardi Entrepreneurs in Jerusalem*, 277.

42. Halperin, "Trading Secrets."

43. Ben-Zeev, "Foundations of Inequality."

44. See for example in Ben-Bassat, "Proto-Zionist–Arab Encounters in Late Nineteenth-Century Palestine."

45. Matthias Lehmann discusses Hirsch as an exemplar of a new modern Jewish figure, the "banker as philanthropist," who was interested more in questions of Jewish productivization than in questions of Jewish nationalism or religious continuity strictly speaking. Lehmann, "Baron Hirsch, the Jewish Colonization Association and the Future of the Jews."

46. Karlinsky, *California Dreaming*, 52.

47. Goldstein and Stern, "PICA: irgunah u-matarotah."

48. Ben-Artzi, "ha-Hityashvut ha-Yehudit be-Eretz Yisra'el 1900–1917," 345.

49. The legacy of the colony of Sejera, founded by the JCA between 1900 and 1902, lies firmly in its status as a site of Labor Zionist organizing among workers; David Ben-Gurion was one of the organizers who saw the Galilee as a more conducive region for Jewish labor organizing. In 1907, a Jewish guard organization called Bar-Giyora, the precursor to ha-Shomer, began efforts to take control over guarding in Sejera. In 1908, Jewish Labor activists established an Agricultural Collective that became a center of Labor Zionist organizing. Kfar Tavor, founded in 1901 by settlers from earlier "First

Aliyah" colonies, also become a center for Labor Zionist organizing. Yair Seltenreich has written extensively on education, Jewish-Arab contacts, gender issues, and labor politics in the JCA colonies in the Galilee. See Seltenreich, *ha-Anashim mi-kan*; Seltenreich, "Gavriyut, kavod, ve-guf"; Seltenreich, "Jewish or Arab Hired Workers?"; Seltenreich, "Mifgashe tarbuyot?"

50. Karlinsky, *California Dreaming*, 52.

51. Eliav, "Yihudah shel ha- Aliyah ha-Rishonah," ix. Landowning farmers and their Labor Zionist critics had written non-scholarly histories and reminiscences about the private colonies as early as the turn of the twentieth century, during a period of European nationalist memory-making that the historian Jay Winter has called the "first memory boom." Professional historians of the Yishuv, however, didn't take up this task until the period in the 1970s and 1980s that Winter, calling attention to Pierre Nora's work at that time on sites of memory (*les lieux de mémoire*) in modern France, associates with a transnational "second memory boom." Winter, "War, Memory, and Mourning in the Twentieth Century," 97.

52. For example Hakohen, *Immigrants in Turmoil*; Graiczer, "Spatial Patterns and Residential Densities in Israeli 'Moshavot' in Process of Urbanization"; Gonen, " Iyur ha-moshavot ba-mishor ha-hof be-Yisra'el"; Gonen, *Between City and Suburb*; Seltenreich, "Jewish or Arab Hired Workers?"; Shapira, *ha-Ma'avak ha-nikhzav*.

53. Aryeh-Sapir, "'Sefer Gedera' le-Amnon Horvitz"; Yosef Lang, "Sefarim ve-yovlot"; Helman, "Place-Image and Memorial Day in 1920s and 1930s Petah Tivkah"; Melman, "Motah shel sokhenet."

54. Karlinsky, *California Dreaming*, 6; 217. See also Ronen Shamir's 2000 call to recenter the stories of Palestine's urban Jewish capitalists and their close relationship with British colonial rulers, in Shamir, "Burganut Yehudit be-Palestinah ha-koloniyalit."

55. For Washington, the first president of the United States, this verse represented individual serenity, security of personal property, and freedom from oppressive government. He would include this phrase in his famous letter to the Hebrew Congregation of Newport, Rhode Island, in 1790. Dreisbach, "The 'Vine and Fig Tree' in George Washington's Letters," 314.

56. Karlinsky, *California Dreaming*, 6.

57. Katz, *The "Business" of Settlement*, 34.

58. The principle enshrined in the founding documents of the Jewish National Fund was that nationally owned land was in effect the property of the Jewish people and therefore could not be sold, but only leased long-term. With the reform of the Israel Lands Administration in 2009 and the formation of the Israel Lands Authority in 2013, Israel has sought to allow land privatization in some cases in order to encourage economic development. See Katz, *The Land Shall Not Be Sold in Perpetuity*.

59. Piterberg, *The Returns of Zionism*, 65; Bhandar, *Colonial Lives of Property*, 129; Wolfe, "Purchase by Other Means," 154.

60. Shumsky, *Beyond the Nation-State*, 10.

61. Zeev Smilansky to Arthur Ruppin, June 1924. from CZA L18/228/2. Cited in Karlinsky, *California Dreaming*, 68.

62. Jaffa, connected to the grid in 1921, is an important exception. Shamir, *Current Flow*, 140–41; Meiton, *Electrical Palestine*, 112–13.

63. More Palestinian villages survived in Galilee, the Negev/Naqab, and a strip of land known as "The Triangle" within Israel that runs along the edge of the West Bank.

64. Gonen, "ʻIyur ha-moshavot ba-mishor ha-hof be-Yisraʼel," 31–44.

65. Shoham, "Meha-ʻAliyah ha-Shelishit la-ʻAliyah ha-Sheniyah uva-hazarah," 199.

66. Shoham, "Meha-ʻAliyah ha-Shelishit la-ʻAliyah ha-Sheniyah uva-hazarah," 205.

67. Descendants of the Fifth Aliyah published a commemorative volume in 1994, *ha-ʻAliyah ha-Hamishit: 60 shanah la-ʻaliyah mi-merkaz Eropah*.

68. Kaniel, "Ha-vikuah ben Petah Tikva le-Rishon LeZion"; Lang, "Sefarim ve-yovlot: Petah Tikva mitmodedet ʻim ʻavarah."

69. Bartal, "ʻAl ha-rishoniyut: zeman u-makom ba-ʻAliyah ha-Rishonah," 16

70. Derek Penslar is less interested in the "First Aliyah" colonists and colonies as local symbols and cultural objects than in the French model of productivization that influenced the Alliance Israélite Universelle and then Baron Rothschild to invest in agricultural development and colonization.

71. Levontin, "ha-Hityashvut be-Eretz Yisraʼel: emtzaʻeha ve-shitoteha."

72. Yavneʼeli, *Sefer ha-Tziyonut*, 1:46, 1:52.

73. Dowty, *Israel/Palestine*, 36.

74. Shapira, *Israel: A History*, 46; Shapira, *Herev ha-yonah*, 88.

75. Sternhell, *The Founding Myths of Israel*, 77.

76. Penslar, *Zionism and Technocracy*, 20–22, 67; Penslar, *Shylock's Children*, 243.

77. Zerubavel, *Desert in the Promised Land*, 29; Almog, *The Sabra*, 2.

78. Ben-Porat, *Hekhan hem ha-burganim ha-hem?*, 39–41.

79. Ben-Uzi, "Tenu lihyot ba-aretz ha-zot," 146–49; Shiloah, *Merkaz holekh ve-neʼelam*, 307.

80. Rozin, *The Rise of the Individual in 1950s Israel*, 103.

81. Kaplan, *The Jewish Radical Right*, xv.

82. Shavit, *Jabotinsky and the Revisionist Movement, 1925–1948*; Kaplan, *The Jewish Radical Right*; Heller, *Jabotinsky's Children*.

83. Kaye, *The Invention of Jewish Theocracy*; Mirsky, *Rav Kook*.

84. Gribetz, *Defining Neighbors*; Jacobson and Naor, *Oriental Neighbors*.

85. Myers, *Between Jew & Arab*; Pianko, *Zionism and the Roads Not Taken*; Fish, "Bi-Nationalist Visions for the Construction and Dissolution of the State of Israel."

86. Shapira, *ha-Maʼavak ha-nikhzav*, 102–3.

87. Zerubavel, *Recovered Roots*, 8–10.
88. Brown, *Undoing the Demos*, 211; Breuilly, *Nationalism and the State*, 399–401.
89. Seikaly, *Men of Capital*, 26.
90. Breuilly, *Nationalism and the State*, 401.
91. Gonen, "ha-'Ir Petah Tikva hi ha-yetzu'anit mispar 1 be-Yisra'el."
92. Israel Central Bureau of Statistics, "ha-Kibutzim ve-okhlusiyatam."
93. Maidhof, "A House, a Yard, and a Security Fence: Israel's Secular Settlers in the West Bank," 21.
94. Turner, *The Ritual Process*, 167.
95. Kaniel, *Hemshekh u-temurah*, 211–27.
96. Shafir, "Zionism and Colonialism."
97. Trofe, *Reshit*, 36–45.
98. Trofe, *Reshit*, xix.
99. Eidson, "German Local History as Metaphor and Sanction," 135, 143.
100. Wolfe, *Settler Colonialism and the Transformation of Anthropology*, 165.
101. Katz and Gans, *The First Shall Be the Last*, 14.
102. Katz and Gans, *The First Shall Be the Last*, 14.

103. However, as scholars of early Judaism have shown, even the claim to "monotheism" in Judaism is far from straightforward, as key biblical and extracanonical texts acknowledge the existence of other, if inferior, gods (henotheism) or the worship of one god among several (monolatry). Moreover, scholars have identified myriad ritual practices, incantations, angel worship, and demonology that appear to disprove strict monotheism. McNutt, *Reconstructing the Society of Ancient Israel*, 175–79.

104. On the ancient Jewish construction of divisions through tropes of loyalty and idolatry, see Schwartz, *The Curse of Cain*, 30. On the foreclosing of multiethnic possibility in late Ottoman Palestine, see Campos, *Ottoman Brothers*, 224–44. On the use of metaphors of "idolatry" in Zionist discourse, see Saposnik, *Becoming Hebrew*, 219.

105. Cameron, "Indigenous Spectrality and the Politics of Postcolonial Ghost Stories"; O'Brien, *Firsting and Lasting*, 55–57, 146.

106. Schwartz, *The Curse of Cain*, 20.

107. Moshe Smilansky, "Rishon LeZion," *Bustenai* 4:18 (special issue on the anniversary of Rishon LeZion), 15 Av /August 17 1932, 3–5.

108. Bruyneel, "Creolizing Collective Memory," 38.

109. Healy, *Forgetting Aborigines*, 10.

110. Shumsky, *Beyond the Nation-State*; Penslar, *Israel in History*; Saposnik, *Becoming Hebrew*; Halperin, *Babel in Zion*.

111. Spurgeon, *Exploding the Western*, 10.

112. Shanes, *Diaspora Nationalism and Jewish Identity in Habsburg Galicia*; Heller, *Jabotinsky's Children*; Moss, *Jewish Renaissance in the Russian Revolution*.

113. Slotkin, *The Fatal Environment*, 435.

114. Slotkin, *The Fatal Environment*, 35.
115. O'Brien, *Firsting and Lasting*, 4.
116. Zerubavel, *Desert in the Promised Land*.
117. Zerubavel, *Recovered Roots*, 93–95, 123.
118. Scholarship on French settler memory has been focused on the period following the Algerian war and the way settler memory functioned in French politics after decolonization. See Hubbell, *Remembering French Algeria*.
119. Shafir, "Zionism and Colonialism."
120. Zahra, "Zionism, Emigration, and East European Colonialism"; Lehmann, "Baron Hirsch, the Jewish Colonization Association and the Future of the Jews"; Rovner, *In the Shadow of Zion*.
121. Robson, *States of Separation*, 104.
122. O'Brien, *Firsting and Lasting*, 19.
123. Degani, "The Decline and Fall of the Israeli Military Government, 1948–1966"; Robinson, *Citizen Strangers*; Dallasheh, "Troubled Waters."
124. See for example the maps in Shapira, *Israel*, 31, and James L. Gelvin, *The Israel-Palestine Conflict*, 61.
125. Fredrik Meiton argues that the 1947 United Nations Partition Plan (resolution 181) followed the lines of the mandate-era Palestine electric grid, whose contours were driven, first and foremost, by the demands of energy-intensive industry in Jaffa, Tel Aviv, and Haifa, as well as by private agriculture (especially citriculture) on the Mediterranean coastal plain. Meiton, *Electrical Palestine*, 163, 212.
126. Trouillot, *Silencing the Past*, 16.
127. Gordon, *Making Public Pasts*, 49.
128. Confino, *The Nation as a Local Metaphor*, 35, 50; see also Applegate, *A Nation of Provincials*, 107.
129. Philco Refrigerator Five-Year Guarantee Certificate for refrigerator installed on December 31, 1948. PTA 003.002/9.
130. Furniss, "Timeline History and the Anzac Myth," 284.
131. Katriel, "Marking Time," 720.
132. Goffman, *The Presentation of Self*, 18.
133. Nelles, *The Art of Nation-Building*, 171.
134. "Zichron Ya'akov bat shemonim: hirhurim" [Zichron Ya'aqov at 80: reflections], Zichron Ya'akov Historical Archive, ZY-00175-1, folder: Yovel 80.
135. Trouillot, *Silencing the Past*, 26.
136. Yerushalmi, *Zakhor*, 8.
137. O'Brien, *Firsting and Lasting*, xvii.

Chapter 1

1. Amichal Yeivin, *'En-Ganim*; Shafir, *Land, Labor and the Origins of the Israeli-*

Palestinian Conflict 1882–1914; Habas and Shochat, *ha-ʿAliyah ha-Sheniyah*; Tzahor, "ha-Mifgash ben ha-ikarim le-foʿale ha-ʿAliyah ha-Sheniyah be-Petah Tikva"; Bein, *Toldot ha-hityashvut ha-Tziyonit mi-tekufat Herzl ve-ʿad yamenu.*

2. Sternhell, *The Founding Myths of Israel*, 7, 94.

3. O'Brien, *Firsting and Lasting*, xxiii.

4. Ahad ha-ʿAm, "Emet mi-Eretz Yisraʾel," 27–28.

5. Ber Borochov, "The National Question and the Class Struggle" [1905], in Hertzberg, *The Zionist Idea*, 358; Aaron David Gordon, "People and Labor" [1911], in Hertzberg, *The Zionist Idea*, 372. Both were influenced by their milieux of socialist and nationalist thought. See Frankel, *Prophecy and Politics*, 133–70.

6. Shafir, *Land, Labor and the Origins of the Israeli-Palestinian Conflict 1882–1914*, 60–63.

7. Council Secretary, "Yediʿot meha-moʿatzah ha-Palestinit: ʿad ha-shevitah ba-yekev Rishon LeZion" ["Report from the Palestine Council: regarding the strike at the Rishon LeZion winery], *ha-Poʿel ha-tzaʿir* no. 2, August 24, 1907, 6–7.

8. Tzahor, "ha-Mifgash ben ha-ikarim le-foʿale ha-ʿAliyah ha-Sheniyah be-Petah Tikva," 142–43; Shafir, *Land, Labor and the Origins of the Israeli-Palestinian Conflict 1882–1914*, 63.

9. Shafir, *Land, Labor and the Origins of the Israeli-Palestinian Conflict 1882–1914*, 16.

10. Shafir, *Land, Labor and the Origins of the Israeli-Palestinian Conflict 1882–1914*, 66, 191–94.

11. Tzahor, "ha-Mifgash ben ha-ikarim le-foʿale ha-ʿAliyah ha-Sheniyah be-Petah Tikva."

12. Shmuel Eisenstadt, "ha-Arkhiyon veha-muzeʾon shel tenuʿat ha-ʿavodah" [The Labor Movement Archive and Museum], draft of an article that appeared in Asufot #6 1959. PL IV-216-987.

13. Yaakov Tzidkuni, "Hug ha-meʾasfim" [Collectors' Circle], in Collection no. 6, *Arkhiyon veha-muzeʾon shel tenuʿat ha-ʿavodah*, Tel Aviv, December 1959. PL IV-216-987.

14. Eisenstadt to Histadrut Executive Committee, 29 Sivan 1934. PL IV-216-787.

15. Piterberg, *The Returns of Zionism*; Raz-Krakotzkin, "A National Colonial Theology."

16. Joseph Klausner, cited in Helman, "Place-Image and Memorial Day in 1920s and 1930s Petah Tikvah," 76.

17. Amichal Yeivin, *ʿEn-Ganim: sipuro shel moshav ha-poʿalim ha-rishon be-Eretz Yisraʾel*, 10.

18. Zemach, *Sipur hayai*, 44.

19. Ben-Gurion, "ʿAl he-ʿavar ve-ʿal he-ʿatid," 268.

20. Reicher, *60 shanah le-hakhrazat ha-herem al poalei Petah Tikva: Hanukkah 1906/6–Hanukkah 1965/6*, 2.

21. Ruppin. *Zionistische Kolonisationspolitik*, 4, cited in Karlinsky, *California Dreaming*, 31.

22. Karlinsky, *California Dreaming*, 31.

23. Giladi, "'Emdat ha-ikarim be-she'elat 'ha-'avodah ha-'Ivrit' be-moshvot ha-'Aliyah ha-Sheniyah (1904–1914)."

24. See Anita Shapira's discussion of similar "Second Aliyah" sources about arrival in the colonies in Shapira, *Herev ha-yonah*, 98–100.

25. Karlinsky, *California Dreaming*, 41, 45.

26. Laskov, *ha-Biluim*, xi, 347.

27. Shafir, *Land, Labor and the Origins of the Israeli-Palestinian Conflict 1882–1914*, 78–79.

28. Drori, "Hishtakfutam shel ha-'Aliyah ha-Sheniyah veha-ma'avak le-'avodah ''Ivrit' ba-'itonut ha-eretzyisre'elit ha-kelalit," 71–72.

29. Ben-Yehuda, *ha-Lohem ha-me'ushar*, 56–58.

30. Drori, "Hishtakfutam shel ha-'Aliyah ha-Sheniyah veha-ma'avak le-'avodah ''Ivrit' ba-'itonut ha-eretzyisre'elit ha-kelalit," 79.

31. "Le-matzav tze'ire ha-moshavot" [On the situation of the moshava youth], *Do'ar ha-yom*, December 7, 1920, 2.

32. Ikar Tza'ir, "Berur devarim" [Clarification], *ha-Zvi*, 12 Heshvan / November 6, 1908, 3.

33. Veracini, "Suburbia, Settler Colonialism and the World Turned Inside Out," 350.

34. Mordechai ben Hillel Hacohen, "ha-Po'alim ha-betelim" [The idle workers], *ha-Zvi*, 4 Heshvan / October 29, 1908, 1–2.

35. Tzahor, "ha-Mifgash ben ha-ikarim le-fo'ale ha-'Aliyah ha-Sheniyah be-Petah Tikva," 144.

36. Zeev Smilansky Archive, PL IV-104–95, File 14, cited in Alroey, *An Unpromising Land*, 178–79.

37. Mordechai ben Hillel Hacohen, "ha-Po'alim ha-betelim."

38. The root h.r.ph is used in 2 Kings 19:16 and 20:4 when the king of Assyria sends a messenger to "blaspheme" God and when the Israelites first catch sight of Goliath the Philistine and suspect that he has come "to defy Israel" (1 Samuel 17:25).

39. Typically, *aharonim*, those commentators who arose after the sixteenth century, are not allowed to dispute the rulings of *rishonim*, or earlier Tannaitic or Amoraic commentators, unless they can find support from other rabbis of that earlier generation. Mi-zikne ha-Yishuv [Menashe Meirovitch], "Katavah mi-Rishon-LeZion" [Letter from Rishon LeZion], *ha-Or*, 19 Tevet / January 9, 1912 [(letter dated 14 Tevet / January 4], 2–3.

40. Menashe Meirovitch, *ha-Herut*, Letter A, 26 Nisan / April 22, 1914, 2.

41. Letter from Zvi Horvitz to the people of Gedera, 26 Kislev / December 3, 1934–35, Gedera and Biluim Museum Historical Archive, Folder 20a (Yael Tzukerman).

42. Article by Nahum Slouschz, "Mishnato shel Menashe Ben-Zvi Meirovitch" [Menashe Ben-Zvi Meirovitch's doctrine], November 1936. RLZ A5/6/1 Folder 15.

43. Smilansky, *Im bnei artzi ve-'iri*, 217–18.

44. Interview with Gideon Makoff, Rehovot, June 15, 2016.

45. This statement is widely cited, for example in Jackson, *Crabgrass Frontier*, 231, but the actual original source is unclear.

46. Drori, *Ben yamin li-smol*, 162–63.

47. Yaakov Groman, "'Ir ha-'ovdim he-harutzim" [City of diligent workers], Netanya Municipal Archive, Netanya 25th Anniversary pamphlet, 1954, 134.

48. "Takanot le-histadrut ha-hakla'im ha-tze'irim Bnei Binyamin be-Eretz Yisra'el" [Regulations of Bnei Binyamin, the organization of young farmers in the Land of Israel] [1921]. Netanya Municipal Archive 06.03–162 (1361). See also Drori, *Ben yamin li-smol*, 162.

49. Drori, *Ben yamin li-smol*, 169.

50. Penslar, "Declarations of (In)dependence."

51. Drori, *Ben yamin li-smol*, 177.

52. Samsonov, *Zichron Ya'aqov*, 193, 450.

53. "Haya Rachel Leah Gissin," in Tidhar, *Entziklopedyah le-halutze ha-Yishuv u-vonav* (vol. 2, p. 778).

54. Yud-'Ayin [writer signed with initials only], "Hagigat Bnei Binyamin be-Herzliya" [Bnei Binyamin celebration in Herzliya], *Do'ar ha-yom*, July 16, 1925, 6.

55. Yud-'Ayin, "Hagigat Bnei Binyamin be-Herzliya," 6.

56. "Hagigat yesod Kfar-Aharon" [Founding celebration for Kfar Aharon], *Do'ar ha-yom*, July 7, 1926, 3.

57. Meiton, *Electrical Palestine*, 37–38.

58. Sydney Moody (British Colonial Office) to Sir John Shuckburgh (British Colonial Office), April 1923. In Cohen, *Britain's Moment in Palestine*, 156.

59. In Cohen, *Britain's Moment in Palestine*, 156.

60. Norris, *Land of Progress*, 112.

61. Sauvage, "ha-Lord Balfour be-Petah Tikva, 1925."

62. "Balfour be-Shomron uva-Galil" [Balfour in Samaria and the Galilee], *Do'ar ha-yom*, April 6, 1925, 3.

63. Mordechai ben Hillel Hacohen, "Eretz Yisra'el tahat shilton ha-tzava ha-Briti," *ha-Shiloah* 41 (1923–24): 46.

64. Helman, "Place-Image and Memorial Day in 1920s and 1930s Petah Tikvah," 83.

65. Gad Yagol, "ha-Etmol 'odenu kan" [Yesterday is still here], *Davar*, October 7, 1960, 20.

66. These interventions did not, however, prevent Shapira from being arrested and deported to Damascus and then Istanbul in October 1917 after the Nili organization's pro-British espionage activities were uncovered. Edelstein, *Avraham Shapira*, 275–80.

67. Rubin, "Falastin bi-shenot ha-milhamah be-ʿenei shenei nosʿim Othmanim," 25.

68. "Bikur ha-Lord Plumer be-Rishon LeZion" [Lord Plumer's visit to Rishon LeZion], *Doʾar ha-yom*, November 27, 1925, 1, 8.

69. "Speech by Mr. Meerovitch, M.B.E., during his Excellency the High Commissioner's visit to Richon LeZion" [spelling per original document] [1925?], RLZ A5/6/4, Folder 19.

70. "Fī mustaʿamarat ʿUyun Qāra" [In the ʿUyun Qara Colony], *Filastin*, July 30, 1931, 2.

71. "Mustaʿmirat Rishun," *Mirat al-sharq*, August 20, 1932, 3.

72. Ben-Gurion, "Be-hag hatzi ha-yovel," 15, 16.

73. Joseph Sapir, "Le-kinus ha-ʿAliyah ha-Sheniyah" [On the Second Aliyah convention], *Bustenai* 1:5, May 8, 1929, 4–5.

74. Sapir, "Le-kinus ha-ʿAliyah ha-Sheniyah," 4–5.

75. Letter from H. Ariav, Mazkir kelali, Farmers Federation Headquarters, Tel Aviv, August 9, 1932 to various recipients. CZA A32/90. Emphasis added.

76. Zvi Butkovsky, "Mah natnu ha-Biluim le-artzenu?" [What did the Biluim contribute to our land?], *Bustenai* 21, 6 Elul / September 7, 1932. RLZ, Menashe Meirovitch Collection, A5/11/2 Folder 26.

77. Butkovsky, "Mah natnu ha-Biluim le-artzenu?"

78. Ruppin, *Three Decades of Palestine*, 40, cited in Katz, *The "Business" of Settlement*, 69.

79. Frenkel, Shenhav, and Herzog, "The Ideological Wellspring of Zionist Capitalism," 56.

80. Meir Dizengoff, Chair of the council of the municipality of Tel Aviv to the local council, Rehovot, April 14, 1931. Rehovot Historical Archives (RHA) 1–3–8–4-16 1b-6 (40th anniversary).

81. Letter from Rehavia Kantorovitz to the members of the local council, Rehovot, 29 Nisan / April 16, 1931. RHA 1–3–8–4-16–18 1b-6 (40th anniversary).

82. Letter from Yehudit Levin-Epstein, Detroit, to the Rehovot Local Council, May 22, 1940. RHA 1–3–8–4-66–15 3a-4 (50th anniversary).

83. "New American Economic Committee for Palestine Formed."

84. Segev, "Between Jerusalem and Tel Aviv," 41.

85. Smilansky, "Irgun," *Bustenai*, June 1, 1938. Cited in Shiloah, *Merkaz holekh ve-neʿelam*, 286.

86. Shiloah, *Merkaz holekh ve-neʿelam*, 285–88, 307–8.

87. "Bnei ha-moshavot tovʿim et zekhutam ba-Yishuv: ba-veʿidat tzeʿire ha-

moshavot she niftehah emesh be-Tel Aviv" [Sons of the moshavot demand their rights in the Yishuv: at the conference of moshava youths that opened last night in Tel Aviv], *ha-Boker*, May 27, 1940, 6.

88. "Hitahdut Bnei ha-Yishuv pirsemah kol kore el bnei ha-Yishuv" [The Union of the Sons of the Yishuv publishes an appeal to the members of the Yishuv], *Ha-Mashkif*, March 26, 1940, 3.

89. "Hitahdut Bnei ha-Yishuv matria' be-ve'idatah 'al het haznahat Hevron, Tzfat, vi-Yerushalayim ha-'atikah" [Union of Sons of the Yishuv warns in its conference of the sin of neglecting Hebron, Safed, and the Old City of Jerusalem], *ha-Mashkif*, May 26, 1942, 4.

90. "Hitahdut Bnei ha-Yishuv" [Union of Sons of the Yishuv], *ha-Boker*, January 12, 1940, 9.

91. Dror, *The History of Kibbutz Education*, 28.

92. Hakohen, *Immigrants in Turmoil*, 164–65.

93. "Hitahdut Bnei ha-Yishuv be-Hadera lema'an hinukh ahid" [Union of Sons of the Yishuv in Hadera for the sake of unified education], *ha-Boker*, May 15, 1940, 6.

Chapter 2

1. Gene Currivan, "Two Worlds Meet in Tense Palestine," *New York Times Magazine*, November 18, 1945, 43.

2. n.n. Titled in Hebrew "Ne'um ba-mesibat yovel le-A. Shapira" [Speech at the A. Shapira birthday party], text in Arabic, November 12, 1940. CZA S25/1231.

3. "Tokhnit ha-hagigah" [Celebration program] [1945], CZA S25/1231.

4. Letter from Ali Mustakim, Jaffa, to Joseph Saphir [spellings as in the letter], Petah Tikva, November 30, 1940. CZA S25–1231 [English].

5. Ever Hadani, *Me'ah shenot shemirah be-Yisra'el*, 108.

6. Anderson, "State Formation from Below and the Great Revolt in Palestine."

7. Cohen, *Army of Shadows*.

8. Ari, "Orientalism Repeated," 338.

9. Zerubavel, *Desert in the Promised Land*, 42–51; Zerubavel, "Memory, the Rebirth of the Native, and the 'Hebrew Bedouin' Identity"; Almog, *The Sabra*, 185–93.

10. "Ibrahim Shabira: ihtafala al-Yahud wal-'Arab wal-inkliz bi-bulughihi al-sab'in" [Avraham Shapira: Jews, Arabs, and British celebrate his 70th birthday], *Haqiqat al-Amr*, November 19, 1940, 3.

11. Palestinian histories typically narrate the beginnings of the conflict with the Zionist movement as dating to the Balfour Declaration.

12. Beeri, *Reshit ha-sikhsukh Yisra'el 'Arav, 1882–1911*, 20–21.

13. Only limited efforts have been made to recover the farmers' perspective in these debates, most notably by Gur Alroey, Yair Seltenreich, and Nahum Karlinsky. Selten-

reich, "Jewish or Arab Hired Workers?; Gur Alroey, "Mesharte ha-moshava o rodanim gase ruah?"; Karlinsky, *California Dreaming*, 21–46.

14. Shafir, *Land, Labor and the Origins of the Israeli-Palestinian Conflict*, 17.

15. Veracini, "The Imagined Geographies of Settler Colonialism," 185.

16. Low, *Eclipse of Empire*, 230.

17. Edmonds, "The Intimate, Urbanising Frontier," 130.

18. Roi, "Yahase Rehovot 'im shekheneha ha-'Arvim (1890–1914); Ahad ha-'Am, "ha-Yishuv ve-apitroposav," cited in Shapira, *Herev ha-yonah*, 90.

19. A petition by four members of the Bedouin group Abu Hataba from Mazra'at Duran to the Grand Vizier Against the Establishment of the Colony of Rehovot, in Ben-Bassat, *Petitioning the Sultan*, 196.

20. The formation of the Muslim Christian Association in 1918, the Arab Higher Committee in 1936, and political parties from the communists (1923) to the liberal Istiqlal (1932), the Palestine Arab Party associated with the Husayni family (1935), and the National Defense Party associated with the Nashashibi clan in 1934 indicated a growing level of political organizing, albeit within a relatively constrained population of urban intellectuals. The 1936–1939 Arab revolt, in contrast, was distinguished not only by acts of violence but by its grassroots organizing and leadership. Lesch, *Arab Politics in Palestine, 1917–1939*.

21. Smilansky, "Meratzhim" [Murderers], cited in Kabha and Karlinsky, "ha-Pardes ha-ne'elam: ha-pardesanut ha-'Arvit-ha-Falastinit 'ad shenat 1948," 100.

22. Shapira, *ha-Ma'avak ha-nikhzav*.

23. Zachary Lockman first suggested the need for a "relational paradigm" of "mutually formative interactions," noting that Jewish-Arab contacts occurred between workers in private businesses, including the industrial Dead Sea Potash Works, the Nesher Cement Company, and the moshavot. Deborah Bernstein explores such contacts in the Nur match factory and the Mosaica tile factory, both in Haifa. Abigail Jacobson and Moshe Naor considered Sephardi and Oriental Jews and their attempts at joint economic cooperation with—rather than separation from—Arab businessmen while Nahum Karlinsky and Mustafa Kabha consider elite Jewish-Arab connections in the citrus industry. Nimrod Ben-Zeev, meanwhile, considers labor hierarchies in the field of construction. Lockman, *Comrades and Enemies*; Bernstein, "Challenges to Separatism"; Bernstein, *Constructing Boundaries*; Jacobson and Naor, *Oriental Neighbors*; Kabha and Karlinsky, "ha-Pardes ha-ne'elam"; Ben-Zeev, "Foundations of Inequality."

24. Shafir, *Land, Labor and the Origins of the Israeli-Palestinian Conflict 1882–1914*, 40–41.

25. Klorman, "Hityashvut po'alim Temanim ve-Ashkenazim," 91; Shafir, *Land, Labor and the Origins of the Israeli-Palestinian Conflict 1882–1914*, 104.

26. Klorman describes the difficult process for the Yemenites, having not been able to become owners in Rishon LeZion, of attempting just prior to World War I to get

permission to settle plots of nationally owned land in the adjacent Nahalat Yehuda. This process involved opposition and years of delays from Ashkenazim who saw Yemenite Jews as "others" who did not belong. Klorman, "Hityashvut po'alim temanim ve-Ashkenazim," 101.

27. "Rehovot," ha-Po'el ha-tza'ir, January 10, 1913, 14.

28. Shafir, *Land, Labor and the Origins of the Israeli-Palestinian Conflict 1882–1914*, 104.

29. Ahad ha-'Am, "Emet mi-Eretz Yisra'el," 29.

30. Shafir, *Land, Labor and the Origins of the Israeli-Palestinian Conflict 1882–1914*, 72.

31. "Mikhtav mi-Petah Tikva" [Letter from Petah Tikva], ha-Po'el ha-tza'ir, August 12, 1910, 18–19. The non-Arab Afghani guard was one of several categories of non-Arab guards hired by colonies. Druze and Circassians, the latter of which had been absorbed into the Ottoman Empire from the Russian Caucasus, served as colony guards primarily in the Galilee. Shafir, "Revolutionary Pioneer," 72–73.

32. Shochat-Vilbushevitz, "ha-Shemirah ba-aretz."

33. Edelstein, *Avraham Shapira*, 219. See also Gulst, "Avraham Shapira: ben mizrah le-ma'arav be-Milhemet ha-'Olam ha-Rishonah," 112.

34. Roi, "Yahase Yehudim-'Arvim be-moshvot ha-'Aliyah ha-Rishonah," 262–63.

35. Letter from J Grazowki (Rishon LeZion) to J Eisenstadt (Odessa), December 18, 1889, in Druyanow, *Ketavim le-toldot Hibat Tzion ve-yishuv Eretz Yisra'el*, 66–67.

36. Roi, "Yahase Yehudim-'Arvim be-moshvot ha-'Aliyah ha-Rishonah," 250–61.

37. Seltenreich, "Jewish or Arab Hired Workers?" 234–35.

38. "Section XV: Labor Conditions in Palestine, 1932," "Palestine Blue Book," 169.

39. Histadrut, *Hadera le-an?*, 19, 37.

40. Nadan, *The Palestinian Peasant Economy Under the Mandate*, 6.

41. Kabha and Karlinsky, "ha-Pardes ha-ne'elam," 100. The Arab press had regular reports on the Jewish colonies, e.g. an article from 1934 about the relocation of a French beer company to the Rishon LeZion winery: "Ma'mal bira jedid fi 'Uyun Qāra," *Mirat al-sharq*, November 4, 1934, 4; a report from the same year on a Jaffa notable's journey to Europe to promote the Arab citrus sector: "Edmond Bek Rock yusafir li-Uroba li-ijad aswak li-burtuqal wa-l-da'aya lil-watan," *Filastin*, October 31, 1934, 4.

42. Dowty, "A Question that Outweighs All Others."

43. Myers, *Between Jew & Arab*, 100.

44. Gorny, ha-She'elah ha-'Arvit veha-be'ayah ha-Yehudit, 48–51.

45. Epstein, "She'elah ne'elmah," 195.

46. Epstein, "She'elah ne'elmah," 195.

47. Khalidi, *Palestinian Identity*, 100.

48. Moshe Smilansky, "'Im zerem ha-melitzah" [With the flow of platitudes], ha-Herut, 8 Elul / September 1, 1913, 2–3; 9 Elul / September 11, 1913, 2–3.

49. Mi-Zikne ha-Yishuv [pen name of Menashe Meirovitch], Letter C, *ha-Herut*, 5 Sivan / May 29, 1914, 2–3.

50. ha-Tziyoni, "Melabes," *ha-Zvi*, 26:11, 27 Tishrei / Oct 12, 1909, 2.

51. Dover Emet, "Petah Tikva," *ha-Herut* [Jerusalem], November 1, 1909, 2–3.

52. Karlinsky, *California Dreaming*, 61–62.

53. He uses a term for settlers, *mitnahalim*, that was then becoming standard in the West Bank, Gaza, and northern Sinai. Belkind, *Rishon LeZion*, 49.

54. Testimony by Abraham Shapiro [sic], in Great Britain, *Palestine Commission on the Disturbances of August 1929*, 768–69.

55. Testimony by Abraham Shapiro [sic], in Great Britain, *Palestine Commission on the Disturbances of August 1929*, 769–71.

56. Testimony by the [former] Mayor of Nablus [Hajj Tawfiq Hammad] in Great Britain, *Report of the Commission on the Palestine Disturbances of August, 1929*, 113.

57. Ben-Gurion, *Mi-maʿamad la-ʿam*, 296. Cited in Karlinsky, *California Dreaming*, 40–41.

58. Shiloah, *Merkaz holekh ve-neʿelam*, 348.

59. Smilansky, "Tzeviʿut" [Hypocrisy], *Bustenai*, July 31, 1935. Cited in Shiloah, *Merkaz holekh ve-neʿelam*, 351.

60. Robson, *States of Separation*, 112–18.

61. Shafir, "Capitalist Binationalism in Mandatory Palestine," 621.

62. Shafir, "Capitalist Binationalism in Mandatory Palestine," 628.

63. Shiloah, *Merkaz holekh ve-neʿelam*, 378.

64. Schweitzer, "Making Equals," 350, 346. Emphasis in the original.

65. Nadasen, *Household Workers Unite*, 88.

66. Morris, "Why Do the Oscars Keep Falling for Racial Reconciliation Fantasies?"

67. Nadasen, *Household Workers Unite*, 88.

68. "Yaakov Bendel," in Tidhar, *Entziklopedyah le-halutze ha-Yishuv u-vonav*, 3:1141.

69. Yaakov Bendel, "'Shutafi Abu Hamdan" [My partner Abu Hamdan], *ha-Boker*, October 24, 1938, 4.

70. Captain the Hon. W. Ormsby-Gore, "Aaron Aaronsohn: A Tribute," Extract from *The Zionist Review*, July 1919. Beit Aaronsohn Archive, "Aaron" Division-0010–1.a.5.

71. Extract from *The Times* of May 20, 1919, "Eminent Zionist Killed, Dr. Aaronson in Aeroplane accident." Beit Aaronsohn Archive, "Aaron" Division-0010–1.a.14.

72. [Alexander Aaronsohn?] "Aaron Aaronsohn," [1919?], Beit Aaronsohn Archive, Alexander Aaronsohn Papers 2–9-6.

73. "ha-Abir mi-Zichron Yaʿaqov" [The Knight from Zichron Yaʿaqov], *ha-Tzofeh*, May 15, 1939, 3.

74. Herzl Hayutman, "Nasser Ghanem Abu Farid," *ha-Boker*, October 23, 1940, 3–4, 6.

75. Hayutman, "Nasser Ghanem Abu Farid," 3–4, 6.

76. Cohen, *Army of Shadows*, 36.

77. Union of Sons of the Yishuv, national executive committee, Tel Aviv, "Hatzharat Hitahdut Bnei ha-Yishuv ba-nogea' li-kevi'at hodesh mai le-zichro shel Aaron Aaronsohn" [Declaration of the Union of Sons of the Yishuv regarding establishing the month of May in memory of Aaron Aaronsohn], April 9, 1944. Beit Aaronsohn Archive, Alexander Aaronsohn Papers 2–3-9.

78. Letter from David Tidhar to Dr. [Eliyahu] Rosenbaum, Tel Aviv, March 31, 1944. Beit Aaronsohn Archive, Alexander Aaronsohn Papers 58–2-6.

79. "Hahlatot be-kesher le-hodesh mai le-zekher aharon" [Decisions related to the month of May in memory of Aaron], Zichron Ya'aqov, March 16, 1944. Beit Aaronsohn Archive, Alexander Aaronsohn Papers 43–8-40; Letter from the central office of the Union of Sons of the Yishuv to Tel-Tzur Colony Committee, Sharon region, April 11, 1944. Beit Aaronsohn Archive, Alexander Aaronsohn Papers 58–2-4.

80. Letter from Yaakov [last name unclear], Cooperative Association of Vinegrowers of Rishon LeZion and Zichron Ya'aqov, to David Tidhar, Tel Aviv, April 6, 1944, Beit Aaronsohn Archive, Alexander Aaronsohn Papers 58–2-22.

81. Yehoash, *Fun Nyu-York biz Rehovot un tsurik*, 158.

82. David Yudelovitz, cited in Roi, "Yahase Yehudim-'Arvim be-moshvot ha-'Aliyah ha-Rishonah," 252.

83. Shapira, *Herev ha-yonah*, 99.

84. Halperin, *Babel in Zion*, 252–62; Beinin, "Knowing Your Enemy, Knowing Your Ally."

85. These efforts during the mandate period laid the foundation for some of the IDF intelligence operations after 1948. See Eyal, *The Disenchantment of the Orient*.

86. Memo from Miriam Glickson to Moshe Shertok, re: conference of Arabic teachers in the communities (which took place on August 25–26, 1942), September 3, 1942, CZA, J17/322. The conference included the heads of the Department of Education as well as candidates for teaching in the communities.

87. 'Ivri, "Hashash."

88. O'Brien, *Firsting and Lasting*, 91–93.

89. These anecdotes involve tall tales and practical jokes, told to an in-group audience, about Labor Zionist symbols such as the kibbutz, the Hebrew language, as well as more politically weighty topics such as the British mandate authorities, conflict with Arabs, or attempts at conducting illegal immigration to Palestine during World War II. Oring, *Israeli Humor*, 31, 36.

90. Ben-Amotz and Hefer, *Yalkut ha-kezavim*, 37.

91. Epstein, "She'elah ne'elmah," 205.

92. Zerubavel Haviv, "ha-'Arvit be-vet ha-sefer ha-'amami" [Arabic in the Primary School], *ha-Boker*, July 2, 1946, 2.

93. Michelle Campos writes about the late Ottoman prehistory of the story that Jacobson and Naor tell. In that period, figures such as Avraham Moyal and Nisim Malul founded an organization called Magen (the Shield) to share in the local Arabic press their vision of Zionism as a struggle for a shared Ottoman homeland. Campos, *Ottoman Brothers*, 163–64.

94. Avraham Elmaleh, Oral History Project Interview, February 23, 1964, in Campos, "Between 'Beloved Ottomania' and 'The Land of Israel,'" 479.

95. Jacobson and Naor, *Oriental Neighbors*, 33–34.

96. Jacobson and Naor, *Oriental Neighbors*, 47.

97. E. H. H. Green, *Ideologies of Conservatism*, 2–3, 283.

98. Avraham Elmaleh, "Tazkir la-va'adah ha-malkhutit" [Memo to the Royal Commission], Jerusalem Municipal Archive 6322/1271. Cited in Jacobson and Naor, *Oriental Neighbors*, 38.

99. Gribetz, *Defining Neighbors*, 127.

100. Gribetz, *Defining Neighbors*, 128; Jacobson and Naor, *Oriental Neighbors*, 163, 171.

101. Alroey, *An Unpromising Land*, 25.

102. "Hitahdut Bnei ha-Yishuv masbirah matarotehah" [the Union of Sons of the Yishuv explains its goals], *ha-Boker*, March 25, 1942, 3.

103. Klein, *Lives in Common*, 45.

104. Klein, *Lives in Common*, 42–43.

105. Raab, *ha-Telem ha-rishon*, 68–69; for a fuller discussion of Raab's self-narration see Halperin, "Trading Secrets."

106. Edelstein, *Avraham Shapira*, 1:34, 32.

107. Kark, *Jaffa*, 56, 188.

108. Edelstein, *Avraham Shapira*, 1:37.

109. The foundation myth of Tel Aviv as a city built on the sands—and by extension, the modern Yishuv as a civilization emerging from a wasteland—emerged over time as it was "told, written, photographed, retold, rewritten, and reinterpreted in the city's homes, streets, newspapers, pamphlets, public events, and cafes." Shoham, "Tel-Aviv's Foundation Myth," 36.

110. LeVine, *Overthrowing Geography*, 53, 57.

111. Bartal, "Hanukkah Cossack Style."

112. Edelstein, *Avraham Shapira*, 1:37, 41.

113. On Shapira's forays into Trans-Jordan, see Alon, *The Shaykh of Shaykhs*, 119–20.

114. David Yellin, "Menashe Meirovitch veha-yishuv" [Menashe Meirovitch and the Yishuv], Jerusalem Shevat [January-February] 1931 (manuscript), RLZ A5/6/1 Folder 15.

115. Hazkani and Dolbee contend that the 'Isa-Meirovitch cooperation must be read as more than simply "collaboration" (in the negative sense) because it spoke to

short-lived linkages across confessional lines. Dolbee and Hazkani, "'Impossible Is Not Ottoman.'"

116. "Speech by Mr. Meerovitch, M.B.E., during his Excellency the High Commissioner's visit to Richon LeZion" [spelling per original document] [1925?], RLZ A5/6/4, Folder 19.

117. Yaakov Bendel, *Bustenai*, December 16, 1931, in Niv, *Rosh Pinah bat me'ah*, 93–94.

118. Livak, *The Jewish Persona in the European Imagination*, 321.

119. Pinsker, *Auto-Emancipation*, 6.

120. Herzl, *Complete Diaries*, 742.

121. See Philips, *Fairground Attractions*, 224.

122. Shoham, *Carnival in Tel Aviv*, 121.

123. Almog, *The Sabra*, 191.

124. Greene, *Horses at Work*, 26.

125. Mikhail, *The Animal in Ottoman Egypt*, 156; Halperin, "Trading Secrets," 11–12.

126. Postman, *The Disappearance of Childhood*, 144.

127. Gamzu, *Nahum Gutman*, 52.

128. Shimoni, "Yovel ha-eglonim," 353.

129. Hayim Nahman Bialik, "Le-susati" [To my mare], in *Shirim be-Yiddish*, 314.

130. Dizengoff, "Le-susati."

131. Greene, *Horses at Work*, 74.

132. Edelstein, *Avraham Shapira*, 1:75.

133. Turner, "The Significance of the Frontier in American History (1893)," 53.

134. Kasson, *Buffalo Bill's Wild West*, 15.

135. Koltun-Fromm, *Imagining Jewish Authenticity*, 43.

136. Y. Svorai, "R[eb] Yehuda Raab z"l" [Mr. Yehuda Raab of blessed memory], *ha-Mashkif*, June 3, 1948, 3; Binyamin Landau and Shmuel Steiner, "Sipurim 'al Avraham Shapira" [Stories about Avraham Shapira], *Ba-Mahaneh*, January 4, 1966, 26–27. On the trope of the disappearing Indian see O'Brien's discussion of "lasting" in *Firsting and Lasting*, 105–43.

137. Tzur, *Le-lo ketonet pasim*; Alroey, "Halutzim ovdei derekh?"

138. [Yaakov] Zerubavel, "Yizkor," *ha-Ahdut* 3:11–12 (12 Tevet / January 2, 1912), 31–32. Zerubavel differentiated "passive" elements of the Jewish people who died as holy people (*kedoshim*) from heroes (*giborim*). Whereas the former "did not water the soil of their homeland with their blood," the later revealed via their deaths "how strong their life force was."

139. "Yehezkel Nisanov [Obituary]," *ha-Ahdut*, 26 Shevat / February 24, 1911, 1. In Saposnik, "Exorcising the 'Angel of National Death,'" 568.

140. Foster, Nettelbeck, and Hosking, *Fatal Collisions*, 2.

141. O'Brien, *Firsting and Lasting*, 15.

142. Adam J. Barker, "Deathscapes of Settler Colonialism," 4–5.
143. Vadasaria, "Necronationalism," 119.
144. Zerubavel, *Recovered Roots*, 42, 93, 123, 227.
145. Moshe Smilansky, "Rishon LeZion," in "Le-Yovel Rishon Le-Zion" [On the Anniversary of Rishon Le-Zion], Special issue of *Bustenai*, 4:18, 15 Av / August 17, 1932, 3–5.
146. Trofe, *Reshit*, 19.
147. Menashe Meirovitch, "Al kivrot ahim Biluim" [On my Bilu brothers' graves], *Haaretz*, July 3, 1942, CZA A32/15.
148. Foster, Nettelbeck, and Hosking, *Fatal Collisions*, 2.
149. Smilansky, *Perakim be-toldot ha-yishuv*, 1:80–81.
150. Rabin, "Alfei kevarim: shelanu ve-shelahem."
151. Smilansky, *Perakim be-toldot ha-yishuv*, 1:80–81.
152. Moshe Levanon, "Lifne heyot Ness Ziona: perek zikhronot" [Before it was Ness Ziona: a chapter of memories], Written 11 Heshvan / October 19, 1926. Beit Rishonim Ness Ziona: Historical Archive, Avraham Yalovsky Binder.
153. "ha-Korban ha-rishon 'al admat Ness Ziona" [The first victim on the land of Ness Ziona], copied from "Dapei Ness Ziona" (April 1958), itself translated from Israel Belkind's text "Erste shrit fun eretz Yisroel" [First steps in the Land of Israel], Beit Rishonim Ness Ziona: Historical Archive, Avraham Yalovsky Binder.
154. Yellin, *Yerushalayim shel temol*, 36.
155. Yellin, *Yerushalayim shel temol*, 11.
156. Such assumptions would make sense, given the widespread European consular comments about the corruption of Ottoman officials and the Ottoman court system; however, as Avi Rubin shows, these comments do not comport with the court's actual performance. Rubin, "British Perceptions of Ottoman Judicial Reform." I consider perceptions of corruption in one particular case in Halperin, "A Murder in the Grove," 432–33.
157. Rifkin, "The Frontier as (Movable) Space of Exception," 176.
158. Edelstein, *Avraham Shapira*, 1:62.
159. Edelstein, *Avraham Shapira*, 1:63.
160. Edelstein, *Avraham Shapira*, 1:64–67.
161. Ben-Amotz and Hefer, *Yalkut ha-kezavim*, 30.

Chapter 3

1. Letter from Yosef Aschheim to Menashe Meirovitch, Tel Aviv, 27 Iyar / June 4, 1940 [based on May 30, 1940 visit], CZA A32/14.
2. Beenstock, Metzer, and Ziv, *Immigration and the Jewish Economy*, 7–8.
3. Sternhell, *The Founding Myths of Israel*, 221.

4. Helman, *Young Tel Aviv*; Deborah Bernstein, *Nashim ba-shulayim*. See also Halperin, *Babel in Zion*; Azaryahu, *Tel Aviv*, 36–38; Helman, *Or ve-yam hekifuhah*, 16.

5. Histadrut, *Hadera le-an?*, 6, 16, 22–23.

6. Shiloah, *Merkaz holekh ve-ne'elam*, 364.

7. Histadrut, *Hadera le-an?*, 16.

8. Letter from H. Ariav, General Secretary, Farmers' Federation Headquarters, Tel Aviv, August 9, 1932 to several recipients, CZA A32/90.

9. Jacobson, *Whiteness of a Different Color*, 214.

10. Zimmerman, *Whose America?*, 14–15.

11. Like other modern nationalisms, Zionist ideology urged young adherents to eschew their real diasporic parents and replace them with symbolic national parents, both the heroic father figure and the land as mother. Neumann, *Land and Desire in Early Zionism*, 33–35, 43–44.

12. Article by Nahum Slouschz, "Mishnato shel Menashe Ben-Zvi Meirovitch" [Doctrine of Menashe Ben-Zvi Meirovitch], November 1936 Tel Aviv, review of "miha-shvil el ha-derekh (manuscript), RLZ A5/6/1 Folder 15.

13. Menashe Meirovitch, "Agadat Bilu" [The Bilu Legend], n.d., RLZ A5/4 Folder 12.

14. Moshe Smilansky, "R' Menashe Meirovitch," *Haaretz*, June 14, 1945, 2.

15. Ahlbäck, *Manhood and the Making of the Military*, 104.

16. Moss, *The Media and Models of Masculinity*, 128.

17. Berlant, *The Anatomy of National Fantasy*, 22–24; Spurgeon, *Exploding the Western*, 10–11.

18. This region came in the 1930s to be known as "the center of the country" (*merkaz ha-aretz*), a term that, after Israeli statehood, came to refer to a discrete administrative region outside and around Tel Aviv. Gonen, "Ketzad kam 'merkaz ha-aretz' be-Eretz Yisra'el," 443–45.

19. "Ma'arekhet ha-hinukh bi-shenat 5696 (sekirah statistit)" [The Educational system in 1935–1936: statistical survey], *Do'ar ha-yom*, March 18, 1936, 2.

20. Veracini, "Settler Colonial Expeditions," 58.

21. Kesler and Goldstein, "Hiking as an Educational Tool," 44–48.

22. Stein, "Travelling Zion."

23. Tadmor-Shimony, "Shaping Landscape Identity in Jewish State Education."

24. Dror, *The History of Kibbutz Education*, 129, 208.

25. In these settings, both the trauma of the recounted experience and its incommunicability become the basis for student reactions, and for the theorizing of the process of witnessing. See Matthäus, *Approaching an Auschwitz Survivor*, 98–99.

26. Letter from Tamar Groiza to Menashe Meirovitch, n.d., CZA A32/14.

27. Borneman, *Death of the Father*, 213.

28. Halbwachs, *On Collective Memory*, 48–49.

29. Letter from David Yellin and B. Dinaburg to Menashe Meirovitch, March 17, 1931 / 28 Adar 5691. RLZ A5/2-9.

30. Letter from Sh. Alenberg, Principal of Benzion Mossinson School, Magdiel to the Petah Tikva municipality, December 3, 1948. PTA 003.002/4.

31. Baruch Oren, handwritten notes, "Pegishati 'im Avraham Shapira z"l" [My meeting with Avraham Shapira of blessed memory], undated. PTA, 003.043.007/588, Baruch Oren manuscripts, 1947–1991, 3–4, 7.

32. Halbwachs, *On Collective Memory*, 48.

33. Letter from [no name] to Menashe Meirovitch, 24 Shvat 1945, CZA A32/14.

34. Letter from [no name] (Yagur) to Menashe Meirovitch, 1946, CZA A32/14.

35. Kramer, *Nationalism in Europe and America*, 81–101.

36. Letter from Haviva (Shlomit) Friedman, 7th Grade, Kiryat Avodah School, December 17, 1943, CZA A32/14.

37. Letter from Z. Meitas to Menashe Meirovitch, Kiryat Avodah, 20 Kislev / December 17, 1943, CZA A32/14

38. Letter from Yitzhak Ahuvia to Menashe Meirovitch, Kfar Melel, n.d., CZA A32/14.

39. Meirovitch, *Minhat 'erev*, vi.

40. Letter from G. Rozhanski, Secretary of the Rehovot Local Council, to Nathan Axelrod, Carmel Film, Tel Aviv, March 11, 1940. RHA 1–3-8-4-66–15 3a-4 Yovel 50.

41. Tidhar, *Entziklopedyah le-halutze ha-Yishuv u-vonav*, 2:975.

42. Protocol No. 4, Session of the Anniversary Committee, November 27, 1940, KMHH 103, Document 4–1483, Plans for 50th-Anniversary Celebration.

43. Penslar, "Radio and the Shaping of Modern Israel," 61. See also Katriel, *Dialogic Moments*, 235–36.

44. "Li-tsumet libkhem shel ha-martzim ba-radio" [For the attention of radio lecturers], dated July 28, 1936, CZA A32/42.

45. An analysis of the broadcasts from 5:30 to 10 am for the three days from January 1 to January 3, 1937, shows that there were 238 minutes of Arabic talk program, 144 of Hebrew talk program, 164 of English talk, 120 minutes of Arab music, 85 minutes of Hebrew music, and 135 minutes of classical or other European music. Palestine Broadcasting Service, Jerusalem, Schedule for the week of January 1, 1937, *Palestine Review*, January 1, 1937, 754.

46. Liebes, "Acoustic Space, 71.

47. Stanton, *This Is Jerusalem Calling*, 169–70.

48. Protocol No. 4, Session of the Anniversary Committee, November 27, 1940, KMHH 103, Document 4–1483, Plans for 50th-Anniversary Celebration.

49. Y. Bergman, "Hadran le-hagigat Hadera" [Encore to the Hadera celebration], *ha-Boker*, February 21, 1941, 5.

50. Letter from Eliezer Lubrani to Menashe Meirovitch, Rishon LeZion, June 18,

1936, on letterhead of Sherut ha-hafatzah be-alhut shel Palestina [Palestine wireless transmission service], CZA A32/42.

51. Contract, June 22, 1936 between Mr. George Clive Kenworthy, Jerusalem and Mr. M. Meirovitch Rishon LeZion, for participation in radio, CZA A32/42.

52. Letter from Menashe Meirovitch to E. Lubrani, July 10, 1936, CZA A32/42.

53. Menashe Meirovitch, "ha-Biluim: ha-mityashvim ha-rishonim ba-aretz" [The Biluim: the first settlers in the Land] (Alternative/original title: "Reshitam shel ha-Biluim ba-aretz" [Early days of the Biluim in the land], CZA A32/42, 4.

54. Meirovitch, "ha-Biluim: ha-mityashvim ha-rishonim ba-aretz," CZA A32/42, 5.

55. Letter from Menashe Meirovitch to E. Lubrani, July 14, 1936, CZA A32/42. Emphasis in the original.

56. Letter from Menashe Meirovitch to Mr. E. Lubrani, June 21, 1936, CZA A32/42.

57. Meirovitch, *Minhat Erev*.

58. Letter from Menashe Meirovitch to Eliezer Lubrani, July 5, 1936, CZA A32/42.

59. Letter from Menashe Meirovitch to E. Lubrani, Jerusalem, August 5, 1936, CZA A32/42.

60. Letter from E. Lubrani to Menashe Meirovitch, August 7, 1936, on letterhead of sherut ha-hafatzah be-alhut shel Palestina, CZA A32/42.

61. Yosef Tzumer, Letter to Menashe Meirovitch, 24 Shevat [February 7], 1945. CZA A32/14.

62. Hameiri, "Mikhtav bimkom hakdamah," 5–6.

63. Hameiri, "Mikhtav bimkom hakdamah," 5–6.

64. "Gilui ha-lot me-'al pene ha-retzah ha-mistori: gufot ha-me'unim Yohanan Stahl u-Solia Zohar nimtze'u" [Unveiling the mysterious murder: Yohanan Stahl and Solia Zohar's tortured bodies found], *Do'ar ha-yom*, November 13, 1931, 3; "Eikh gilinu et ha-rotzhim: mi-pi Avraham Shapira be-Petah Tikva" [How we found the murderers: the account of Avraham Shapira in Petah Tikva], *Davar*, November 16, 1931, 3.

65. Already before World War I, Hebrew writers in Eastern Europe debated what types of works should enter a modern Hebrew canon that would bear the task of constructing a national subject. This debate continued in Palestine. See Hever, *Producing the Modern Hebrew Canon*.

66. Leket-Mor, "Israpulp," 5–11.

67. Shavit and Shavit, "Le-toldot 'sipur ha-pesha' ha-'Ivri be-Eretz Yisra'el," 32.

68. Leket-Mor, "Israpulp," 12–13.

69. Shavit and Shavit, "Le-toldot 'sipur ha-pesha' ha-'Ivri be-Eretz Yisra'el," 35–36.

70. Tidhar, *Be-sherut ha-moledet (1912–1960)*, 237.

71. Shavit and Shavit, "Le-toldot 'sipur ha-pesha'' ha-'Ivri be-Eretz Yisra'el," 35–36.

72. Shavit and Shavit, "Le-toldot 'sipur ha-pesha' ha-'Ivri be-Eretz Yisra'el," 37, 38.

73. Hameiri, "Mikhtav bimkom hakdamah," 5–6.

74. "Hakhanot la-mishpat retzah Stahl u-zohar: ne'esru od 3 ne'eshamim" [Preparations for the Stahl/Zohar murder trial: 3 more people arrested], *Davar*, November 16, 1931, 1.

75. Drori, "'Emdotav shel 'Do'ar ha-yom me-hivasdo ve-'ad sof 1924"; Aviv, "Ma'avak 'al hashpa'ah be-'itonut miflagtit."

76. "ha-Ma'arakhah ha-akhronah shel ha-ma'agam ha-mahrid: Yohanan Stahl u-Solia Zohar huv'u li-kevarot Yisrael" [The last battle of the shocking tragedy: Yohanan Stahl and Solia Zohar given a Jewish burial], *Do'ar ha-yom*, November 15, 1931, 1.

77. "ha-Ma'arakhah ha-akhronah shel ha-ma'agam ha-mahrid," *Do'ar ha-yom*, November 15, 1931, 1.

78. M. Zeltzer, "Devar ha-yom: Solia Zohar ve-Yohanan Stahl" [News of the day: Solia Zohar and Yohanan Stahl], *Davar*, July 24, 1931, 1

79. "Eikh gilinu et ha-rotzhim: mi-pi Avraham Shapira be-Petah Tikva" [How we found the murderers: the account of Avraham Shapira in Petah Tikva], *Davar*, November 16, 1931, 3.

80. HC Deb November 18, 1931 vol 259, c833, British parliamentary debates, Hansard, https://api.parliament.uk/historic-hansard/commons/1931/nov/18/palestine-jews, Last accessed September 2, 2020.

81. HC Deb December 7, 1931, vol 260, cc1513–4, British parliamentary debates, Hansard, https://api.parliament.uk/historic-hansard/commons/1931/dec/07/jews-arms, Last accessed September 2, 2020.

82. "ha-Ma'arakhah ha-akhronah shel ha-ma'agam ha-mahrid [The last battle of the shocking tragedy], *Do'ar ha-yom*, November 15, 1931, 1.

83. Hameiri, "Mikhtav bimkom hakdamah," 5–6.

84. Hameiri, "Mikhtav bimkom hakdamah," 5–6.

85. Y. Yeshurun, "Kadurei rigul" [Spy pills], *Davar*, May 19, 1932, 5.

86. Tidhar, *Be-sherut ha-moledet (1912–1960)*, 238–40.

87. Edelstein, *Avraham Shapira*, 1:37.

88. Edelstein, *Avraham Shapira*, 2:464.

89. Edelstein, *Avraham Shapira*, 2:470–71.

90. Edelstein, *Avraham Shapira*, 2:473.

91. Tidhar, *Entziklopedyah le-halutze ha-Yishuv u-vonav*, 6:2590.

92. Edelstein, *Avraham Shapira*, 2:474.

93. Edelstein, *Avraham Shapira*, 2:474.

94. "Mosdot ve-irgunim tziburiyim be-Tel Aviv" [Public institutions and organiza-

tions in Tel Aviv], *Yedi'ot Tel Aviv*, June 16, 1935, 141. Newspaper articles at the time also mention these shared offices.

95. Edelstein, *Avraham Shapira*, 2:474–75.

96. "Nigletah ha-ta'amulah: sheneihem nirtzehu bi-yede Bedu'im" [The news has been publicized: both were murdered by Bedouins], *Davar*, November 15, 1931, 1.

97. Tidhar, *Din ve-heshbon 'al hotza'at zikhronot Avraham Shapira bi-shenei kerakhim*, 3–4.

98. Friends Committee for Publishing Avraham Shapira's Memoirs in Two Volumes [Vaad ha-yedidim le-hotza'at zikhronot "Avraham Shapira," "Zikhronot 'Avraham Shapira'-bi-shenei kerakhim"], PTA 003.002/12. [PDF 11].

99. Friends Committee for Publishing Avraham Shapira's Memoirs, n.d. [probably 1939], PTA 003.002/12 Item Number 8404.

100. Friends Committee for Publishing Avraham Shapira's Memoirs, letter to Judah Magnes, head of the Hebrew University, January 6, 1939, PTA 003.002/12.

101. Troen, *Imagining Zion*, 10–12.

102. Protocol No. 4, November 27, 1940, KMHH folder 103 document 4–1483, Protocol of the 1940–1941 Anniversary Committee, Emmanuel Kokhavi Estate; Protocol No. 8, Session of the Anniversary Committee, December 12, 1940, KMHH 103, Document 4–1483, Plans for 50th-Anniversary Celebration.

103. Protocol No. 8, Session of the Anniversary Committee, December 12, 1940, KMHH 103, Document 4–1483, Plans for 50th-Anniversary Celebration.

104. Letter from Meir Berlin to M. Gorodisky, chair of the Rehovot Council, March 29, 1940, RHA 1–3-8-4-66–15 3a-4 Yovel 50.

105. Shapira, "Religious Motifs of the Labor Movement"; Kolatt, "Religion, Society, and State."

106. "Yom ha-Kipurim ba-'Khan': temunah me-haye ha-mityashvim ha-rishonim be-Hadera" [Yom Kippur in the 'Khan': a scene from the lives of the first settlers in Hadera], KMHH 13–1-1.

107. "Yom ha-Kipurim ba-'Khan'," KMHH 13–1-1. The narrative of leaving home in the Pale of Settlement and making one's way to Palestine evokes many travel narratives of the First Aliyah, as Margalit Shilo has explored: Shilo, *Etgar ha-migdar*, 13–35.

108. This framing was already put forward by Judah Alkalai and Zvi Hirsch Kalischer in the 1860s. It later influenced the growth of religious Zionism.

109. Y[aakov] Zerubavel, "Yizkor," *ha-Ahdut*, 3.11–12, 12 Tevet 1911–1912.

110. Barnett, *Zikhronot Zerach Barnet*, 1.

111. Va'ad ha-yedidim le-hotza'at zikhronot shel Avraham Shapira, form letter to religious community institutions, February 13, 1939, PTA 003.002/12 [PDF 8].

112. Letter from Pinhas Grayevsky to Avraham Shapira, May 25, 1939. PTA 003.002/12 [PDF 35].

113. "From a Letter," back cover, Tidhar, *Din ve-heshbon 'al hotza'at zikhronot Avraham Shapira bi-shenei kerakhim.*

114. Back cover, Tidhar, *Din ve-heshbon 'al hotza'at zikhronot Avraham Shapira bi-shenei kerakhim.*

115. Shapira, *Land and Power*, 244.

116. "I saw Jabotinsky as similar to Bar Kokhba," Ikar wrote in his diary in 1930. "I saw him leading the youth to action . . . materializing within themselves the attributes of the conquerors of Canaan and the fighters of Masada." Alexander Ikar, "Dapim mi-yomani" [Pages from my diary], *ha-Mashkif*, May 7, 1939, 4; Shapira, *Land and Power*, 242.

117. Alexander Ikar, "ha-'Aliyah ha-Rishonah ve-rosh ha-shomrim shelah" [The First Aliyah and its head guard], *ha-Mashkif*, April 7, 1939, 5.

118. Tidhar, *Din ve-heshbon 'al hotza'at zikhronot Avraham Shapira bi-shenei kerakhim*, 3–4.

119. Letter from Mordechai Abramovich, Zerubavel Haviv, and [not clear] to David Tidhar, July 4, 1939. PTA 003.002/12.

120. The University of Haifa Prenumeranten Project is a digital humanities project established in 2019 to collect more than 1,500 of these pre-subscriber lists from the eighteenth through the twentieth centuries, which provide a wealth of information about naming practices, institutions, professional affiliations, city and location data, and more. See Fischer, "The Prenumeranten Project." Thanks to Nahum Karlinsky for the insight.

121. Tidhar, *Din ve-heshbon 'al hotza'at zikhronot Avraham Shapira bi-shenei kerakhim*, 5. Tidhar offered a special thank you to the three individuals who had chaired the Friends Committee: Chief Rabbi Ben-Zion Meir Hai Uziel, Shlomo Stampfer (the mayor of Petah Tikva and the son of one of Petah Tikva's founders, Yehoshua Stampfer), and Yosef Rivlin, the chair of the Teachers Union (Merkaz ha-morim) and Shapira's nephew.

122. Yael Zerubavel writes about how the 1921 story of Tel Hai and Joseph Trumpeldor, its heroic casualty, could be adapted by both Socialist Zionist and Revisionists as it "fulfilled the classic role of a new national myth of a young nation in the process of defining its historical mission." Zerubavel, *Recovered Roots*, 1995, 148.

123. Tel Aviv Purim activities committee, "Min ha-humor ha-Yisre'eli: kovetz le-Purim 1935" [Israeli humor: a collection for Purim 1935], Tel Aviv 1935, 48. Cited in Helman, "Pardesim ve-hanuyot, 375.

124. Helman, "Pardesim ve-hanuyot," 373.

125. "Purim 694 [1934] be-Tel Aviv," *Do'ar ha-yom*, February 28, 1934.

126. "Tel Aviv: Purim," *Davar*, March 5, 1931, 4.

127. Avraham Shapira, "ha-Intzident ba-tahalukhat ha-'Adelayada'" [The incident at the Adeleyada parade], *Do'ar ha-yom*, April 1, 1935, 2.

128. "ha-Semol ratzah lehashvit et simhat ha-hag, ve-lo 'altah be-yado" [The left wanted to shut down the holiday happiness but it didn't manage], *Do'ar ha-yom*, March 21, 1935, 1.

129. Letter from H. Ariav, Jewish Farmers' Federation of Palestine, April 10, 1935, Tel Aviv Municipal Archive 04–3322A (Purim celebrations, 'Adeleyada, 1935–1950).

Chapter 4

1. Levin-Epstein, *Zikhronotai*, 149–50.

2. Letter from the State of Israel, Department of the Interior, Regional Command Petah Tikva, to Avraham Shapira. January 6, 1964. PTA 003.002/4.

3. See Robinson, *Citizen Strangers*; Dallasheh, "Troubled Waters"; Degani, "The Decline and Fall of the Israeli Military Government."

4. These assertions reflect research since the 1980s that, using previously sealed Israeli government and military archives, has complicated and at times overturned collective Israeli perceptions of Israel's victory in 1948 as miraculous and of all culpability for Palestinian departure as lying in the hands of regional Arab leaders and Palestinians themselves. For summaries of the evolving political stakes of the debate over memory within Israel, see Shapira, "Politics and Collective Memory"; Hirsch, "From Taboo to the Negotiable."

5. Daniele, "Mizrahi Jews and the Zionist Settler Colonial Context."

6. Turner, "The Significance of the Frontier in American History," 34. Cited in Altenbernd and Young, "Introduction," 130.

7. Trofe, *Reshit*, 19.

8. Israeli leaders and Hebrew writers during the 1950s acknowledged this dispossession, which they sometimes associated with the devastation of the Holocaust. In the 1960s, Palestinian writers began to associate the Nakba with the Holocaust. Bashir Bashir and Amos Goldberg identify an "associative space common to both events," which does not necessarily imply a sense of causality or culpability for those who made these linkages. Bashir and Goldberg, "Introduction."

9. Binyamin, "Nokhahim nifkadim," 85.

10. Eyal, *The Disenchantment of the Orient*, 103.

11. The moshavot celebrated their contribution to the Haganah in several locally published volumes. Kadman, *Erased from Space and Consciousness*.

12. Shmuel Alman testimony, recorded by Uri Sharfman, November 14, 1966, Haganah Historical Archive, Testimonies 234.00005.

13. Hayim Margalit Kalvarisky Interview, n.d., Haganah Historical Archive, Testimonies 120.00033.

14. Nahum Horovitz Interview, n.d., Haganah Historical Archive, Testimonies 17.00021.

15. Yisrael Shochat Interview, n.d., Haganah Historical Archive, Testimonies 132.29.

16. Dinur, Slutzky, and Avigur, *Sefer toledot ha-haganah*, Part A Volume A, 74–75, 92.

17. Ben-Zvi et al., *Sefer ha-Shomer*, 4.

18. "Self-defense, like agricultural settlement and the revival of the Hebrew language, were the products of the Jewish will to live and fight for life." Gilead and Megged, *Sefer ha-Palmach*, xvii.

19. Goldstein, *Ba-derekh el ha-ya'ad*, 8.

20. Yehiel Michael Pines, "Ten kavod leha-emet" [Respect the truth], *ha-Melitz*, Year 18: No. 19, May 30, 1882, 370–72, cited in "Shemirah, haganah u-vitahon ba-moshavah" [Guarding, defense, and security in the moshava], Rishon LeZion municipality [1990s], RLZ, Binder 51, Defense and Security.

21. Hayim Keller Testimony (n.d.), Haganah Historical Archive, Testimony 88.18.

22. Avner Davidson Interview Transcript, RLZ, Interviews on Defense and Security, Cassette 291a, 1.

23. Hayim Keller Testimony, n.d. Haganah Historical Archive, Testimony 88.18.

24. Barukh Ben Ezer Testimony, August 20, 1954, Haganah Historical Archive, Testimony 9.00018.

25. Abramovich Yaakov, Albom ha-mishpahot Rishon LeZion [Rishon LeZion Family Album], http://www.gen-mus.co.il/person/?id=1934.

26. Theodor Herzl, *Der Judenstaat* (Jüdischer Verlag, 1920), 22.

27. Kressel, *Avraham Shapira*, 18.

28. Interview with Zerubavel Haviv, RLZ interviews. Folder: Zerubavel Haviv 1–1a, Interview with Zerubavel Haviv Cassette 118, Side A, December 10, 1984, Topic "Bitahon be-Rishon LeZion" [Security in Rishon LeZion], interview by Yoska Fein.

29. O'Brien, *Firsting and Lasting*.

30. Interview with Zerubavel Haviv, RLZ interviews. Folder: Zerubavel Haviv 1–1a, Interview with Zerubavel Haviv Cassette 118, Side A, December 10, 1984, Topic "Bitahon be-Rishon LeZion" [Security in Rishon LeZion], interview by Yoska Fein.

31. Mordecai Barkai, "'Alilot Sheikh Ibrahim Mikhah" [Adventures of Sheikh Ibrahim Mikha], *Davar*, December 29, 1965.

32. See Halperin, "Petah Tikva, 1886."

33. Dinur, Slutzky, and Avigur, *Sefer toledot ha-haganah*, Part A Volume A, 96.

34. Tidhar, "Sender Hadad (Kriniker)," in Tidhar, *Entziklopedyah la-halutze ha-Yishuv u-vonav*, 5:2319. See also Yisreeli and Grinboym, "Khawaja Skandar."

35. Halperin, "Petah Tikva."

36. Oren, *'Alilot rishonim*, 27.

37. Oren, *'Alilot rishonim*, 28–29.

38. Sorek, *Palestinian Commemoration in Israel*, 43–47; Morris, *Israel's Border Wars*, 145–47.

39. Shemuel Segev, "ha-Merutz li-Kafr Qasim: Mapai u-Mapam mitharot mi yasig et ha-pitzuyim la-nifga'im" [The race to Kafr Qasim: Mapai and Mapam are competing to see who will obtain damages for the casualties], *Maariv*, November 18, 1957, 2.

40. Robinson, "Local Struggle, National Struggle"; Abulafia, "Kafr Qasim be-zikaron ha-Yisre'eli."

41. Robinson, "Local Struggle, National Struggle," 404.

42. Lea Ben-Dor, "Marginal Column," *The Jerusalem Post*, November 22, 1957, 1.

43. Robinson, "Local Struggle, National Struggle," 402–4.

44. Winder, "Anticolonial Uprising and Communal Justice in Twentieth-Century Palestine," 77.

45. Rifkin, "The Frontier as (Movable) Space of Exception," 177–78.

46. Abner Cohen, cited in Khleif and Slymovics, "Palestinian Remembrance Days and Plans," 190.

47. "Sulha bi-Kafr Qasim" [Sulha in Kafr Qasim], *Davar*, November 29, 1957, 20–21.

48. See my article on these ambivalent dynamics as they played out around the aftermath of the 1902 murder of a Jewish colonist in Rishon LeZion: Halperin, "A Murder in the Grove."

49. Smilansky, *Rehovot*, 31.

50. On the incident, its context, and its aftermath see Ben-Bassat and Alroey, "The Zionist-Arab Incident of Zarnuqa 1913."

51. Amihud Nahmani, "Avraham Shapira bi-Rehovot" [Avraham Shapira in Rehovot], in *Dapei Rehovot* 11, 1966, 36–37. Getzel Kressel Archive, Yishuvim RA-RM, Folder: Rehovot.

52. Helman, "Place-Image and Memorial Day in 1920s and 1930s Petah Tikvah."

53. Testimony of Mr. Abraham Shapiro [sic] in Great Britain, *Palestine Commission on the Disturbances of August 1929*, 768–73.

54. "Yosef Teitelboym ve-shomer 'Aravi nirtzehu ba-derekh" [Yosef Teitelboym and an Arab guard were killed on the road], *Al ha-mishmar*, December 10, 1947, 4.

55. Yitzhak Yaakovi, "Bi-se'udat 'sulha' bi-Gvar'am" [At the 'sulha' feast in Gvar'am], *Davar*, January 2, 1947, 4.

56. Winder, "Policing and Crime in Mandate Palestine," 168–218.

57. Yaakovi, "Bi-se'udat 'sulha' bi-Gvar'am."

58. "Ketatot hamoniyot be-Yafo ben Yehudim ve-'Aravim" [Mass altercations in Jaffa between Jews and Arabs], *ha-Boker*, October 6, 1949, 4.

59. "Sulha le-hashkatat ha-ruhot be-Yafo" [A sulha to cool tempers in Jaffa], *Herut*, October 9, 1949, 4.

60. "ha-Shalom be-Yafo hushav 'al kano" [Peace has returned to Jaffa], *ha-Tzofeh*, October 9, 1949, 4.

61. "Sulha ba-'emek" [Sulha in the valley], *'Al ha-Mishmar*, October 30, 1951, 4. See also "Sulha ben moshevet Tamra u-kfar Na'ura" [Sulha between the Tamra moshava and the village of Ne'ura], *Davar*, November 9, 1951, 7.

62. Gad Yagol, "ha-Etmol 'odenu kan," [Yesterday is still here], *Davar*, October 7, 1960, 20.

63. Khleif and Slymovics, "Palestinian Remembrance Days and Plans."

64. "Nehenakh kevish gishah li-Kafr Qasim" [Access road to Kafr Qasim opened], *Maariv*, September 6, 1962, 14. The 49 figure used here includes the unborn child of the pregnant woman killed in the massacre.

65. "Beno shel Avraham Shapira metaken" [Avraham Shapira's son sets the record straight], *Maariv*, September 19, 1960, 2.

66. Baruch Oren, handwritten notes, "Pegishati 'im Avraham Shapira z"l" [My meeting with Avraham Shapira of blessed memory], n.d., PTA, 003.043.007/588, Baruch Oren manuscripts, 1947–1991, 3–4.

67. Nets-Zehngut, "Israel's Publications Agency and the 1948 Palestinian Refugees."

68. Amnon Horvitz, "Marar [Maghar]: kfar ha-meratzhim" [Maghar: the murderers' village], *Davar*, April 26, 1948, 2.

69. Horvitz, "Marar: kfar ha-meratzhim."

70. Horvitz, "Marar: kfar ha-meratzhim."

71. Horvitz, "Marar: kfar ha-meratzhim."

72. Halperin, "Petah Tikva, 1886."

73. Davis, *Palestinian Village Histories*, 179–80.

74. Morris, *The Birth of the Palestinian Refugee Problem, 1947–1949*, 203–11.

75. Y. Svorai, "Tze'etza'ei 'Wilad al-Mayit' kovshe al-Yahudiyya" [The descendants of the 'Children of Death' are the conquerors of al-Yahudiyya], *ha-Mashkif*, May 19, 1948, 3.

76. Svorai, "Tze'etza'ei 'Wilad al-Mayit' kovshe al-Yahudiyya."

77. See for example the discussion of contextual factors in A.P, "Divrei ha-yamim" [Chronicles], *ha-Tzefirah*, 8 Nisan / April 13, 1886, 3.

78. Harizman and Poleskin, *Sefer ha-yovel li-melot hamishim shanah le-yisud Petah Tikva*, 361.

79. Svorai, "Tze'etza'ei 'Wilad al-Mayit' kovshe al-Yahudiyya." The origin of the apparently widespread Zionist settler belief that Arabs called Jewish settlers "children of death" is not clear.

80. Svorai, "Tze'etza'ei 'Wilad al-Mayit' kovshe al-Yahudiyya."

81. Svorai, "Tze'etza'ei 'Wilad al-Mayit' kovshe al-Yahudiyya."

82. Vladimir (Zeev) Jabotinsky, "The Ethics of the Iron Wall," originally published in Russian in *Razswiet*, November 11, 1923, Jabotinsky Institute Archives 201/1923.

83. Svorai, "Tze'etza'ei 'Wilad al-Mayit' kovshe al-Yahudiyya."

84. Avishai Teicher, "Luah hantzahah be-kir ha-misgad bi-Yehud le-lohamot ha-Etzel Ruth Moritz u-Miriam Aharoni" [Commemorative plaque on the wall of the mosque in Yehud to the female fighters Ruth Moritz and Miriam Aharoni], 2008, distributed under a CC BY-SA 2.5 license, http://bit.ly/2gZvPti

85. Esther Lipka, "Agadat ha-pela'im" [Legend of wonders], Mamlakhti Bet School Rehovot [1961], RHA 1-4-8-95-8 4a 2 Yovel 70 Student Essays.

86. Bruyneel, "Creolizing Collective Memory," 38.

87. Yael Bern, "Mikreh be-Rehovot" [Incident in Rehovot], Grade 5, Rehovot, [1961] RHA 1-4-8-95-8 4a 2 Yovel 70 Student Essays.

88. n.n., "Ehad mi-halutze Rehovot mesaper," Grade 6, Rehovot, RHA 1-4-8-95-8 4a 2 Yovel 70 Student Essays.

89. Davis, *Palestinian Village Histories*, 152.

90. Kadman, *Erased from Space and Consciousness*, 71.

91. Stamp: Menashe Meirovitch—last of HaBiluyim, Jerusalem: Jewish National Fund, 1950. CZA Poster Collection, via Harvard Judaica Division, item olvwork689029.

92. "Nitan ha-peras 'al shem Menashe Meirovitch z"l" [the Menashe Meirovitch Prize awarded], *Haaretz*, December 19, 1950, 3.

93. In 1953, the essay was about "the period of Bilu and the building of the land" and the ceremony took place at the Haviv school. By 1958, the essay was given to an essay "connected to the period of the Bilu group." "Azkarah le-M. Meirovitch Z"l," *Herut*, June 25, 1953, 4; "9 shanim le-moto shel aharon ha-Biluim M. Meirovitch z"l" [Nine years since the death of the last of the Bilu group, M. Meirovitch], *ha-Boker*, June 30, 1958, 4.

94. "Hadar Bilu yukam ba-arkhiyon ha-Tziyoni" [A Bilu room will be established in the Zionist Archive], *ha-Boker*, November 9, 1965, 6.

95. State of Israel, *Shenaton ha-memshalah*, 1955, 225.

96. "Abu al-Fadl ('Arab al-Satariyya)," in Khalidi, *All That Remains*, 356–57.

97. Contract with the Arabs of Satariyya on the issue of their animals grazing in vineyards and fields, RHA Folder 1–1, document 1.97–2238.

98. Ziv-Av, *Shelanu 'ad olam*, 80.

99. Smilansky, *Rehovot*, 13.

100. Peleg, *Orientalism and the Hebrew Imagination*, 76–78.

101. Smilansky, "Sheikh 'Abd al-Qadir."

102. Oppenheimer, *Me-Ëever la-gader*, 32.

103. Fischbach, *Records of Dispossession*, 27–39.

104. "Ketatah ben mityashve 'Talme-Menashe' u-pekide ha-apotropos" [Quarrel

between the settlers of Talme Menashesh and the Custodian of Absentee Property], *ha-Boker*, December 28, 1953, 4.

105. "Yinata' ya'ar 'al shem Avraham Shapira" [A forest will be planted and named for Avraham Shapira], *Davar*, July 11, 1960, 2.

106. "Avraham Shapira 'orekh 'heshbon' 'im va'ad Petah Tikva mi-otam ha-yamim" [Avraham Shapira called the Petah Tikva Committee from those days to account], *La-merhav*, July 12, 1960, 4.

107. M. Sayar, "ha-Riv she-hetish et Giv'at Koah" [The quarrel that weakened Giv'at Koah], *Maariv*, December 5, 1960, 4.

108. Zerubavel, "Putting Numbers Into Space," 69–92. West Bank settlers today frequently name new settlement outposts for compatriots killed by Palestinian Arabs. See Getmansky and Sinmazdemir, "Settling on Violence," 243.

109. Kadman, *Erased from Space and Consciousness*, 113.

110. Mar, "Carving Wilderness," 81–86.

111. "Ya'ar 'al-shem Avraham Shapira zekan ha-shomrim—yinata' ha-shavua" [The forest in honor of Eldest of the Guards Avraham Shapira will be planted this week], *ha-Boker*, September 10, 1961, 20.

112. "Nit'u ha-'etzim ha-rishonim be-ya'ar Avraham Shapira be-Petah Tikva" [First trees are planted in the Avraham Shapira Forest in Petah Tikva], *La-merhav*, September 15, 1961, 8.

113. "Nita' ya'ar 'al shem Avraham Shapira" [The Avraham Shapira Forest is planted], *ha-Tzofeh*, January 24, 1962, 4.

114. "Qula," in Khalidi, *All That Remains*, 408–9.

115. "Ka-agadah hayah mithalekh ha-ish ha-zeh: yinata' ya'ar li-khvodo shel ha-shomer Avraham Shapira" [The man would walk around like a legend: a forest will be planted in honor of the guard Avraham Shapira], *Maariv*, September 17, 1961, 8.

116. "Nita' ya'ar Avraham Shapira" [The Avraham Shapira Forest has been planted], *ha-Boker*, September 25, 1961, 10.

117. "Ka-agadah hayah mithalekh ha-ish ha-zeh."

118. Gertz, *Myths in Israeli Culture*.

119. Refael Bashan, "Boker ehad amar Weizman: Avramaleh, holkhim etzel ha-Lord Balfour" [One morning Weizmann said: Avramaleh, we're going to see Lord Balfour], *Maariv*, June 5, 1964, 10, 21.

120. Yosef Ben-Meir, "Ta'arukhat zikaron le-Avraham Shapira z"l" [Memorial exhibition for Avraham Shapira], *ha-Tzofeh*, December 26, 1966, 4.

121. "Alfe dunam ya'ar 'alu ba-esh le-yad Petah Tikva" [Thousands of acres of forest went up in flames near Petah Tikva], *Al ha-Mishmar*, May 19, 1968, 3.

122. Yehoshua, *Mul ha-ye'arot*.

123. Kadman, *Erased from Space and Consciousness*, 189, 192.

124. Email communication between the author and Yardena Tubol, Director of Human Resources, KKL-JNF, December 21, 2020.

125. Gad Yagol, "ha-Etmol odenu kan" [Yesterday is still here], *Davar*, October 7, 1960, 20.

Chapter 5

1. "Hagigot yovel 'irkha matai ve-ekh" [Your city's anniversary celebrations: when and how], in Dov Goldstein (ed.), "Yovel ha-75 shel Rishon LeZion" [The 75th anniversary celebration of Rishon LeZion], *Yedi'ot Rishon LeZion*," vol. 1, August 1957, RLZ, 3.

2. Mayor Hannah Levin, "Davar rosh ha-'iriyah" [Mayor's message], in Goldstein, "Yovel ha-75 shel Rishon LeZion," 2.

3. Eitan Belkind (Vice Mayor), "Rishon LeZion 'arisat ha-'arakhim ha-le'umiyim: devarim be-yeshivat mo'etzet ha-'iriyah ha-pumbit" [Rishon LeZion: cradle of national values: remarks at the public session of the municipal council], in Goldstein, "Yovel ha-75 shel Rishon LeZion," 15–16.

4. "Michael Levin," in Tidhar, *Entziklopedyah le-halutze ha-Yishuv u-vonav*, 9:3261; "Asefah hagigit li-ftihat Bank ha-Ikarim" [Gathering to celebrate the opening of the Farmers' Bank], *Do'ar ha-yom*, October 11, 1934, 5.

5. "Zichron Ya'aqov bat shemonim: hirhurim" [Zichron Ya'akov at 80: reflections], Zichron Ya'aqov Historical Archive, ZY-00175-1, folder: Yovel 80.

6. Gonen, "Mi-mivneh shel gal'in ve-shulayim le-pasifas meguvan ba-'arim ha-vatikot be-Yisra'el," 76.

7. Gonen, "Mi-mivneh shel gal'in ve-shulayim le-pasifas meguvan ba-'arim ha-vatikot be-Yisra'el," 76.

8. M. Gefen, "Ma'abarot bi-tehum ha-moshavot" [Transit camps in the vicinity of the moshavot], *'Al ha-Mishmar*, February 5, 1952, 2, 3.

9. Hakohen, *Immigrants in Turmoil*, 194–95.

10. Gefen, "Ma'abarot bi-tehum ha-moshavot"; "Havtahat rezervot karka'iyot ba-moshavot timana' herpat shekhunot 'oni" [Assuring land reserves in the moshavot will prevent the disgrace of poor neighborhoods], *Davar*, January 25, 1952, 8.

11. Gonen, *Between City and Suburb*, 65; Bashkin, *Impossible Exodus*, 59.

12. Kemp, "'Nedidat 'amim' o 'ha-be'erah ha-gedolah'," 38–39, 49.

13. Advocates for transit camps complained that thousands of dunams near Ramat ha-Sharon had been bought by foreign Jewish investors, leaving none for the transit camps. "Karka'ot ba-moshavot hulku beli tokhnit uve-nigud le-tzorkhei kelitat 'aliyah: Shafrir" [Tracts of land in moshavot were distributed without a plan and contrary to the needs of Aliyah: [Dov] Shafrir, *'Al ha-Mishmar*, January 25, 1952, 1. Later, the next generation of owners would sell off agricultural land closer to the center and within the municipal boundaries and immigrant Jewish workers would fill this intermediate space. Graiczer, "Spatial Patterns and Residential Densities in Israeli 'Moshavot' in Process of Urbanization," 535.

14. Gonen, "Mi-mivneh shel gal'in ve-shulayim le-pasifas meguvan ba-'arim ha-vatikot be-Yisra'el," 74–77.

15. Gonen, *Between City and Suburb*, 85.

16. "Hagah shel Petah Tikva" [Petah Tikva's holiday], *ha-Boker*, November 9, 1948, 2.

17. Goldstein, "Who Represented the Israeli Middle Class?"

18. Hakohen, *Immigrants in Turmoil*, 177–79, 194–95.

19. Rozin, *The Rise of the Individual in 1950s Israel*, 117–18.

20. Hakohen, *Immigrants in Turmoil*, 194–95.

21. Hakohen, *Immigrants in Turmoil*, 190.

22. Bashkin, *Impossible Exodus*, 107.

23. Avraham Levy, "Demuyot min ha-'avar u-min ha-'atid ha-mithaveh" [Personalities from the past and the future that is coming into being], in Dov Goldstein (ed.), "Yovel ha-75 shel Rishon LeZion" [The 75th anniversary of Rishon LeZion], *Yedi'ot Rishon LeZion*," vol. 1, August 1957. RLZ, 8–9.

24. Halperin, *Babel in Zion*, 222–24.

25. Levy, "Demuyot min ha-'avar u-min ha-'atid ha-mithaveh," RLZ, 9–10.

26. Asher [full name not provided], "Heseg le-fo'ale 'Gamish'" [An achievement for Gamish Workers], *Kol ha-'am*, July 19, 1945, 4. Rishon LeZion factory owners, including the owner of Gamish, had signed a mutual defense agreement in 1941 to protect against "unfair" strikes. "Heskem hitgonenut hadadi shel yatzrane Rishon LeZion" [Mutual Defense agreement of Rishon LeZion manufacturers], *ha-Mashkif*, July 24, 1941, 4; "Yitzhak Grinboim, "ha-Sokhnut mesarevet le-ganot ma'ase alimut neged ha-ta'asiyah" [The Jewish Agency refuses to condemn acts of violence against industry], *ha-Mashkif*, September 6, 1944, 4.

27. "Be-'Gamish' be-Rishon LeZion" [In the Gamish factory in Rishon LeZion], *Al ha-Mishmar*, July 12, 1950; "Shevitah be-vet haroshet 'Gamish' be-Rishon LeZion" [Strike at the Gamish Factory in Rishon LeZion], May 23, 1954, 4.

28. Avraham Levy, "Demuyot min ha-'avar u-min ha-'atid ha-mithaveh" [Personalities from the past and the future that is coming into being], in Dov Goldstein (ed.), "Yovel ha-75 shel Rishon LeZion," *Yedi'ot Rishon LeZion*," vol 1, August 1957. Rishon LeZion Archive, 9–10.

29. Cited in Goldstein, "'We Have a Rendezvous With Destiny,'" 40.

30. "Hag ha-telem ha-rishon-yuhag be-PT" [The holiday of the first furrow will be celebrated in Petah Tikva], *ha-Boker*, October 15, 1958, doc 101. PTA, 001.002.002/158, 80th Anniversary planning.

31. Protocol, Meeting of the Agricultural Union [Histadrut ha-hakla'im] council, PT #39, October 4, 1958. PTA, 001.002.002/158, Document 144, 80th Anniversary planning.

32. Protocol, Meeting of the Agricultural Union [Histadrut ha-hakla'im] council.

33. Yeshiva shel va'adat ha-pirsum veha-hazmanot [Meeting of the committee for

publicity and invitations], October 9, 1958, doc 142. PTA, 001.002.002/158, 80th Anniversary planning.

34. Letter from E[frayim] Gissin to Mr. Dagan, general manager of Nesher beer factory, Rishon LeZion, October 17, 1958, PTA, 001.002.002/158, doc 124, 80th Anniversary planning. On the Nesher beer company, see "Derekh hadashah le-mashkia'" [A new way for the investor], *Maariv*, July 21, 1959, 3.

35. Letter from E[frayim] Gissin to the Macabbi Avshalom Association, October 17, 1958, doc 123. PTA, 001.002.002/158, 80th Anniversary planning.

36. Letter from E[frayim] Gissin to David Novick, October 17, 1958, Doc 121. PTA, 001.002.002/158, 80th Anniversary planning.

37. Tokhnit hagigat ha-yovel ha-shmonim le-telem ha-'Ivri ha-rishon [Program for the 80th anniversary of the first Hebrew furrow], Oct 21, 1958, doc 112. PTA, 001.002.002/158, 80th Anniversary planning.

38. Notes about the reception for "the remnants of the generation of the founders, the descendants of the founders of Petah Tikva, and all the agriculturalists of Petah Tikva" went out to *Herut, ha-Boker, Haaretz, Davar, ha-Tzofeh, Maariv, Yedioth Ahronoth,* Israel Radio, Avraham Shapira, and the Petah Tikva Farmers' Association; dated October 16–20, 1958, PTA, 001.002.002/158, doc. 115, 80th Anniversary planning.

39. "Tekhunah rabah le-hagigot ha-telem ha-rishon" [Great quality at the celebrations of the First Furrow], *ha-Boker*, October 16, 1958, PTA, 001.002.002/158, doc. 102, 80th Anniversary planning.

40. Letter from Hayim Broz, Petah Tikva, to "Chairman of the Village Council" [*Yoshev rosh mo'etzet ha-kefar*], October 20, 1958, Handwritten doc 47. PTA, 001.002.002/158, 80th Anniversary planning. Broz was using an outdated term, as Petah Tikva had a municipal council by this point.

41. "Hirhur kal hispik kedei siluf" [A small reflection was enough to distort (the past)], *ha-Boker*, October 21, 1958. PTA, 001.002.002/158, doc 95, 80th Anniversary planning.

42. "Hashmatzat rishonim" [Defamation of the First Ones], *Yedioth Ahronoth*, October 20, 1958. PTA, 001.002.002/158, doc. 97, 80th Anniversary planning.

43. Letter from Efraim Gissin to Minister of the Interior Bar Yehuda, October 21, 1958, PTA, 001.002.002/158, doc 38, 80th Anniversary planning.

44. Letter from Moshe Lipkis to Efraim Gissin, head of the Agricultural Union, October 20, 1958, PTA, 001.002.002/158, doc. 46, 80th Anniversary planning.

45. "Melekhet siluf akrobatit" [A work of acrobatic distortion], *La-merhav*, October 21, 1958, PTA, 001.002.002/158, doc. 33, 80th Anniversary planning.

46. Letter from Y. Bar-Yehuda, Minister of the Interior, to Efraim Gissin, head of the Agricultural Union, October 22, 1958, PTA, 001.002.002/158, doc 99, 80th Anniversary planning.

47. Rozin, *A Home for All Jews*, 157.

48. Aharon Megged, *Living on the Dead*, trans. Misha Louvish, cited in Zerubavel, "The Historic, the Legendary, and the Incredible," 112–13.

49. Anat Helman describes ongoing local commemorations of this incident in Petah Tikva, arguing that these ceremonies emphasized Petah Tikva's commitment to national ideals: Helman, "Place-Image and Memorial Day in 1920s and 1930s Petah Tikvah."

50. Ben-Ezer, *Jeda'*, 220.

51. Ben-Amotz and Hefer, *Yalkut ha-kezavim*.

52. Eliram, *Bo, shir 'Ivri*, 39.

53. Ben-Amotz and Hefer, *Yalkut ha-kezavim*, 119.

54. Ne'omi Ya'aran, "Atem no'ar atem?" [You, are you youth?], *Herut*, March 13, 1959, 6.

55. M[ordechai] Avishai, "Atem no'ar atem?" [You, are you youth?], *'Al ha-mishmar*, June 5, 1959, 5–6.

56. Article by Nahum Slouschz, "Mishnato shel Menashe Ben-Zvi Meirovitch" [Menashe Ben-Zvi Meirovitch's Doctrine], November 1936, Tel Aviv, review of "Mihashevil el ha-derekh" [From the path to the way] (manuscript), RLZ A5/6/1 Folder 15.

57. Shapira, *Yehudim hadashim, Yehudim yeshanim*, 133–36.

58. Gamzu, *Atem no'ar atem?*, 4–5.

59. "Mo'etzet 'iriyat Tel Aviv danah be-matzav hof ha-yam be- Tel Aviv" [Tel Aviv municipality discusses the situation on the Tel Aviv beach], *She'arim*, July 21, 1952, 1.

60. "Ukhshe-Avrum Shapira kevar enenu" [And with Avrum Shapira already gone], in Gamzu, *Atem no'ar atem?!* 6.

61. Dan Giladi, "ha-Kol hogegim be-Rishon LeZion," *Maariv*, August 6, 1952, 2.

62. Mayor Hannah Levin, "Ma ta'aseh 'iriyat Rishon LeZion bi-shnat ha-75 le-kiyum ha-makom" [What will the Rishon LeZion municipality do in its 75th year], in Dov Goldstein (ed.), "Yovel ha-75 shel Rishon LeZion" [The 75th anniversary of Rishon LeZion], *Yedi'ot Rishon LeZion*," vol 1, August 1957. RLZ, 4–6.

63. Mayor Hannah Levin, "Ma ta'aseh 'iriyat Rishon LeZion bi-shnat ha-75 le-kiyum ha-makom."

64. Rachel Lipkin, "Zikhronot shel bayit" [A house's memories], 8th-grade school essay, 23 Shevat [February 9] 1961, RHA 1-4-8-95-8 4a 2 Yovel 70 Student Essays.

65. Yael Bern, "Saba mesaper" [Grandfather tells], 8th-grade school essay, Bet Sefer Mamlakhti Aleph, n.d. [1961], RHA 1-4-8-95-8 4a 2 Yovel 70 Student Essays.

66. Yael Hochberg, "Rehovot ba-'avar uva-hoveh" [Rehovot past and present], 6th-grade school essay, Mamlakhti aleph school, n.d. [1961], RHA 1-4-8-95-8 4a 2 Yovel 70 Student Essays.

67. Katriel, *Performing the Past*, 10.

68. Hakohen, *Immigrants in Turmoil*, 165.

69. Yehuda Dominitz, "Kakh tzadim et nefesh ha-yeled: ketzad mithankhim ye-

ladim be-Yisra'el" [How the soul of the child is hunted: how the children in Israel are educated], *ha-Tzofeh*, October 25, 1949, 2.

70. Tzila Dorfman, "Rehovot 'ir he-hadarim" [Rehovot, city of citrus], Grade 6, n.d. [1961], Rehovot, RHA 1-4-8-95-8 4a 2 Yovel 70 Student Essays.

71. Avital Weinstock, "Darko shel tapuah [zahav] ehad mine rabim" [The journey of one orange among many], 7th-grade school essay, Mamlakhti vav school. 30 Shevat [February 16] 1961, RHA 1-4-8-95-8 4a 2 Yovel 70 Student Essays.

72. Orit Bashkin noted that mizrahim in transit camps near moshavot were often drawn into illegal labor, "with farmers being eager to take advantage of the situation by paying very low wages." Bashkin, *Impossible Exodus*, 46.

73. D. Dyoknai [D. Lazar], "R. Alter Albert mevarekh shehehiyanu" [R. Alter Albert says the shehehiyanu blessing], August 8, 1952, Zichron Ya'aqov Historical Archive, 124-2 (70th-Anniversary Newspapers), 3.

74. D. Dyoknai, "R. Alter Albert mevarekh shehehiyanu," Zichron Ya'aqov Historical Archive, 124-2 (70th-Anniversary Newspapers), 3.

75. M. Meisels, "ha-Mitz'ad she-lo yitz'ad" [The march that won't march], *Maariv*, January 27, 1950, 7.

76. M. Meisels, "Masa' na'eh, kahal karir: 'adeleyada ha-yovel nitkalah be-kir adishut" [A nice parade, a cool crowd: the anniversary Purim parade runs into a wall of apathy], *Maariv*, March 25, 1955, 2.

77. "ha-Gederatiyim katzru mehiyot kapayim be-Tel Aviv" [The people from Gedera got rounds of applause in Tel Aviv], *ha-Boker*, March 10, 1955, 2.

78. M. Meisels, "Masa' na'eh, kahal karir."

79. Y. G., "Si nehefakh le-shefel: ahare ha-'adeleyada'" [The high became a low: after the Purim parade], *'Al ha-mishmar*, March 11, 1955, 3.

80. Shaul Ben Hayim, "ha-'Adaleyada' tza'adah!" [The Purim parade marched!], *Maariv*, March 9, 1955, 2.

81. "Milyon ish hazu be-masa ha-'adeleyada bi-rehovot Tel Aviv" [A million people watched the Purim parade in the streets of Tel Aviv], *Davar*, March 25, 1959, 1.

82. Herzl, *Complete Diaries*, 742.

83. M. Meisels, "Dr. Ben Gurion mofia' be-'televisyah' be-'adeleyada" [Dr. Ben Gurion appears on 'television' at the Purim parade], *Maariv*, March 14, 1960, 10.

84. This story is relayed, for example, in Anner, *Sipure batim*, 184.

85. Gad Yagol, "ha-Etmol 'odenu kan" [Yesterday is still here], *Davar*, October 7, 1960, 20.

86. Goffman, *The Presentation of Self*, 18-20.

87. Dan Giladi, "ha-Kol hogegim be-Rishon LeZion," *Maariv*, August 6, 1952, 2.

88. Aaronson House Nili Museum website, https://www.nili-museum.org.il/, accessed October 18, 2019.

89. "Hilufei binyanim tziburiyim be-Gedera" [An exchange of public buildings in Gedera], *ha-Boker*, July 29, 1962, 6.

90. Yeshayahu Aviam, "Petah Tikva metzigah taʿarukhah mi-reshit yemei ha-moshava: me-sof ha-meʾah sheʿavrah" [Petah Tikva presents an exhibit from the first days of the moshava from the end of the last century], *Maariv*, May 4, 1965, 16.

91. Letter from Pinhas Rashish to Amiran and Gutstein, Tel Aviv, February 19, 1963. PTA 003.043.001/40.

92. "Yeshivat vaʿadat ha-mikhraz livtzor agaf rishonim" [Meeting of the tender commission to support the First Ones wing], April 30, 1963. PTA 003.043.001/40.

93. Contract, dated December 2, 1963, between Petah Tikva municipality and Z. Amiran and D. Gutstein, Weizmann 123 Tel Aviv, PTA 003.043.001/40.

94. "Taʿarukhat ʿiriyat PT niftahat ha-yom" [The Petah Tikva municipal exhibition opens today], *Sheʿarim*, July 13, 1955, 4.

95. "Taʿarukhah benleʾumit le-safrut yeladim niftehah be-PT" [International children's literature exhibition opened in Petah Tikva], *Kol ha-ʿam*, March 1, 1961, 4.

96. "Mekhalim tovim ve-zolim yoter" [Cheaper and better containers], *ʿAl ha-mishmar*, June 1, 1956, 5.

97. "Havharat ʿekronot ha-tokhnit le-taʿarukhat ha-rishonim be-vet yad levanim" [Clarifying the principles for the First Ones exhibition at the Yad La-Banim memorial site], n.d. Around 1963. PTA 003.043.001/40.

98. "Homer gelem le-taʿarukhat ha-rishonim mi-misradam shel Amiran-Gutstein" [Raw material for the First Ones exhibition from the office of Amiran-Gutstein], PTA, Barukh Oren Collection, 003.043.001/225.

99. Furniss, *Burden of History*, 70–75.

100. Invitation to the opening of the permanent exhibition, PTA 003.043.001/200.

101. Miriam Shir, "Haytah gevurah Yehudit be-khol ha-dorot" [There was Jewish heroism in every generation], *Davar*, August 15, 1966, 4. On the pervasive place of Masada in Zionist commemoration, see Zerubavel, *Recovered Roots*, 114–37.

102. Baruch Oren, "Pegishati ʿim zekan ha-shomrim R. Avraham Shapira" [My meeting with the Eldest of the Guards Mr. Avraham Shapira], undated, PTA 003.043.007/588, 6–7.

103. Natali Mesika, *Tik teʿud murhav: Beit Shapira, Herzl 20, Petah Tikva* [Extended documentation file: Shapira House], prepared for the Petah Tikva municipality, November 3, 2016, Courtesy of PTA, 3.

104. Mesika, *Tik teʿud murhav*, 1–6. Courtesy of PTA.

105. Mendel had studied at a school for the deaf in Berlin but was sent back to Palestine via Damascus during World War I. Locals remembered him as a tragic figure and a kind of village idiot who harassed girls and was bullied himself. Ben-Ezer, *Jedaʿ*, 114, 140–41, 227, and many thanks to Marco Di Giulio for sharing insights from his unpublished research.

106. Yosef Ben Meir, "Mah ya'aleh be-goralo shel Beit Avraham Shapira" [What will be the fate of the Avraham Shapira house], *ha-Tzofeh*, October 10, 1967, 2.

107. "Beit Avraham Shapira—nekhes tziburi" [The Avraham Shapira house, a public asset], *Maariv*, December 4, 1967, 8.

108. Israel Feinberg, "Petihat Beit Avraham Shapira z"l" [Opening the Avraham Shapira house], May 3, 1978. National Library of Israel, Ephemera Collection, item 997001081160405171.

109. Bell, "Total History and Microhistory"; Levi, "On Microhistory"; Ginzburg, "Microhistory."

110. Uri Kesari, "Historiya ve-historiya ketanah" [History and small history], *Maariv*, September 30, 1960, 2.

111. Letters from David Ben-Gurion to Yitzhak Ziv-Av, July 22 and July 26 1962, CZA A483/74.

112. Letter from David Ben-Gurion to Yitzhak Ziv-Av, August 1, 1962, CZA A483/74

113. Y. Lapid, "Matanah la-nasi" [A gift for the president], *Maariv*, December 7, 1962, CZA A483/74.

114. Y. Lapid, "Matanah la-nasi."

115. Ahad ha-'Am, "Sakh ha-kol."

116. Y. Lapid, "Matanah la-nasi."

117. Israel Coins and Medals Corporation, "Medaliot shenat ha-rishonim 5723" [Year of the First Ones Medallions, 1962–3], n.d., CZA A483/74.

118. B[erl] Katznelson, "Shlomo Lavi Ben 70" [Shlomo Lavi turns 70], *Davar*, December 21, 1953, 2.

119. David Ben-Gurion, "Al ha-'avar ve-'al he-'atid," 268–70.

120. Ben-Gurion, "Rishonim," ii–iv.

121. Letter from A. Herzfeld, on the letterhead of Histadrut ha-po'alim ha-hakla'iyim [the Union of Agricultural Laborers], to Y. Ziv-Av, Farmers' Federation, Tel Aviv, September 13, 1963, CZA A483/74.

122. Tamir Sorek writes about the delicate navigation that Palestinian citizens of Israel were forced to perform during these years, while they remained under the administration of the military government and were asked to show loyalty to Zionist history and institutions. Sorek, *Palestinian Commemoration in Israel*, 4–6.

123. Aryeh Kinarti, "Shenat rishonim be-kaitanot" [Year of the First Ones in the summer camps], *La-merhav*, August 16, 1963, 4, 8.

124. "By encouraging campers from many different ethnicities to don a shared identity that they could all shed at will, playing Indian helped create a shared sense of whiteness among European American children." Van Slyck, *A Manufactured Wilderness*, 212.

125. Paris, *Children's Nature*, 216.

126. "Mitz'ad leli shel Tzahal be-Petah Tikva yesayem ha-yom 'Shenat Rishonim'" [A nightime IDF parade in Petah Tikva today will conclude the 'Year of the First Ones'], *La-merhav*, September 4, 1963, 6.

127. "Yeshivah hagigit shel ha-Knesset le-tziyun Shenat Rishonim" [Festive meeting of the Knesset in order to mark the year of the First Ones], *Divre ha-Knesset* 35 (December 7, 1962): 353–66.

128. Aba Sirka [Ahimeir], "ha-Shomer," *Herut*, May 31, 1957, 3.

129. Aba Sirka [Ahimeir], "Hiyuv u-shelilah ba-'Aliyah ha-Sheniyah" [Positives and negatives in the Second Aliyah], *Herut*, December 24, 1954, 3.

130. A. Guy [Abba Ahimeir], "'Im aharon ha-Biluim" [With the last of the Bilu members], *Herut*, July 11, 1949, 2.

131. "Yeshivah hagigit shel ha-knesset le-tziyun Shenat Rishonim," 359.

132. Ibid., 361.

133. Mirsky, *Rav Kook*, 32.

134. Kaniel, *Hemshekh u-temurah*.

135. Rozin, *The Rise of the Individual in 1950s Israel*, 47–50, 75.

136. Carmin, *The General Zionist World*, 83–84.

137. Neumann, "General Zionism," 3.

138. Mendilow, *Ideology, Party Change, and Electoral Campaigns in Israel, 1965–2001*, 40.

139. Untitled pamphlet in English, by the Farmers' Federation of Israel, 1967, CZA A483/74, 14–19.

140. Dan Horowitz, "Petihat 'Shenat Rishonim' ba-Knesset" [Opening of the 'Year of the First Ones' in the Knesset], *Davar*, December 5, 1962, 2.

Conclusion

1. Taharlev, "ha-Balada 'al Yoel Moshe Solomon u-shloshet re'av."

2. Yaniv, *ha-Baladah ha-'Ivrit bat-zemanenu*, 216–18, 221. Along with the "Ballad for Yoel Moshe Solomon," there is also "The Ballad for Yitzhak Sadeh" (1972), by Hayim Gouri, celebrating the "oldest of the Palmach commanders," Yitzhak Sadeh (1972). It closes with a reference to the "end of the legend." "The Ballad About Aharon David" (1976) by Yehonatan Geffen, imagines the Socialist Zionist A. D. Gordon as an old man in 1915 "looking out over the valley." Hayim Gouri, "ha-Baladah le-Yitzhak Sadeh"; Yehonatan Geffen, "ha-Baladah 'al Aharon David."

3. Yosef Lang, "Sefarim ve-yovlot."

4. Aharon Friel, "Aharon ha-tzerifim shel ha-Biluim be-Gedera mitmotet—ve-ein matzil" [The last Bilu cabin in Gedera is collapsing—and there is no one to save it], *Maariv*, June 4, 1973, 21.

5. Avraham Rotem, "ha-Bayit be-Abu Kabir she-mimenu yatzu ha-Biluim leyased

et Gedera: shuv horsim historiyah" [The House in Abu Kabir that the Biluim left from to found Gedera: destroying history again], *Maariv*, August 28, 1979, 18.

6. Davidovitz and Lavi, "Tik ti'ud: beit Anton Ayub (Bet Ha-Biluim)."

7. Zvi Lavi, "Rosh Pinna einah nimtzet 'al ha-mapah" [Rosh Pinna is not on the map], *Maariv*, August 23, 1962, 10.

8. Aviezer Golan, "Rosh Pinna: even ma'asu ha-bonim" [Rosh Pinna: the stone the builders refused], *Yedioth Ahronoth*, *7 Yamim* supplement, January 10, 1969, 6–7.

9. Ben-Porat, *Divided We Stand*, 28.

10. Sorek, *Palestinian Commemoration in Israel*, 49–59.

11. Bruyneel, "Codename Geronimo," 353.

12. Ann Mosely Lesch compiled a detailed survey of this period of settlement in 1977. It connects specific areas of settlement development to ongoing geopolitical circumstances and concludes that settlements are "designed to prevent territory from returning to Arab rule." Lesch, "Israeli Settlements in the Occupied Territories, 1967–1977," 35.

13. Kimmerling, *Politicide*, 38.

14. "Yeshivah meyuhedet be-yom kinun ha-Knesset le-tziyun me'ah shenot hityashvut ba-aretz" [Special Knesset session to mark 100 years of settlement in the Land], the 55th session of the Tenth Knesset—Second Sitting, Monday 15 Shevat / February 8, 1982, Jerusalem, 16:02. CZA A483/74, 7.

15. On the linkages between the Egypt-Israel peace treaty and the expansion of settlements in the West Bank and Gaza, see Anziska, *Preventing Palestine*.

16. "Yeshivah meyuhedet be-yom kinun ha-Knesset le-tziyun me'ah shenot hityashvut ba-aretz," 2–3.

17. "Yeshivah meyuhedet be-yom kinun ha-Knesset le-tziyun me'ah shenot hityashvut ba-aretz," 6, 16–17.

18. "Yeshivah meyuhedet be-yom kinun ha-Knesset le-tziyun me'ah shenot hityashvut ba-aretz," 21.

19. "Yeshivah meyuhedet be-yom kinun ha-Knesset le-tziyun me'ah shenot hityashvut ba-aretz," 18.

20. Yitzhak Ziv-Av, "Bnei banim be-'ikvot rishonim" [Grandchildren in the footsteps of the First Ones], Israel Department of Education; Jewish National Fund Teachers Movements, 1985. In CZA A483/74, 2–15.

21. Amir Ben-Porat, *Divided We Stand*, 28; Portugali, *Implicate Relations*, 75; see also Azoulay and Ophir, *The One-State Condition*, 44–46; Farsakh, *Palestinian Labour Migration to Israel*, 16.

22. Tamari, "Normalcy and Violence," 51.

23. Benvenisti, *The West Bank Data Project*, 62–63.

24. Lewis, "Israel's Bitter West Bank Harvest."

25. Gazit, *The Carrot and the Stick*, 171.
26. Morton-Jerome, "Palestinian Labor in West Bank Settlements," 53.
27. Berda, *Living Emergency*.
28. Morton-Jerome, "Palestinian Labor in West Bank Settlements," 50, 80, 88–91.
29. Hirschhorn, *City on a Hilltop*, 79.
30. Hirschhorn, *City on a Hilltop*, 167.
31. Hirschhorn, *City on a Hilltop*, 163.
32. Hirschhorn, *City on a Hilltop*, 171.
33. Hirschhorn, *City on a Hilltop*, 132.
34. Weizman, *Hollow Land*.
35. Booth and Taha, "Jewish Settlers Invited Palestinians Over for the Holidays"; Amos, "Bonim sukkat shalom: bekhirim Muslemim bikru be-Efrat."
36. Harari, "ha-Reshut ha-Falastinit ʿatzrah ʿAravim she-hitarhu ba-sukkah"; Breen-Portnoy, "Head of Major West Bank Jewish Community Calls on PA to 'Immediately Release' Palestinians Arrested After They Visited His Sukkah."
37. Siegman, "Super-Israel," 15.
38. Morton-Jerome, "Palestinian Labor in West Bank Settlements," 227.
39. Leonard and Benmeleh, "How SodaStream Makes—and Markets—Peace."
40. Rubenstein, "Soda Stream to Open Factory in Gaza."
41. Maidhof, "Settlement Secularism," 30.
42. Maidhof, "A House, a Yard, and a Security Fence," 30.
43. Morton-Jerome, "Palestinian Labor in West Bank Settlements," 50.
44. Siegman, "Enemies in the Aisles," 3.
45. David Goldenberg, "Sikum ve-hemshekh peʿulot ha-hantzahah veha-zikaron la-rishonim: mekime u-vone Petah Tikva ve-khen poʿali ba-nadon" [Summary and ongoing commemorative and memorial activities for First Ones: founders and builders of Petah Tikva, and also my action on the subject], February 1991. PTA 03.68–11.
46. Ran Aaronsohn, "Atare ʿavar ba-moshavot ha-rishonot," 249.
47. Mahveh le-Avraham Shapira: 135 shanah le-huladeto—40 shanah le-moto" [A gesture to Avraham Shapira: 135 years since his birth—40 years since his death], December 18, 2005, PTA 002.010.003/16.
48. Speech by Reuven Rivlin, event to mark 135 years since the birth of Avraham Shapira, Petah Tikva, December 18, 2005, PTA 002.010.003/16.
49. Scheindlin, "Israeli president's apology offers a rare hope for coexistence."
50. Yizhar, "About Uncles and Arabs," 322.
51. Dean, "Tales of the Apolitical," 458.

BIBLIOGRAPHY

Archives

Beit Aaronsohn Archive: Nili Museum, Zichron Yaʿaqov
Beit Rishonim Ness Ziona: Historical Archive
Central Zionist Archive, Jerusalem (CZA)
Gedera and Biluim Museum: Historical Archive
Getzel Kressel Archive, Leopold Muller Memorial Library, University of Oxford
Haganah Historical Archive, Tel Aviv
Jabotinsky Institute Archives, Tel Aviv
Khan Museum for the History of Hadera: Historical Archive (KMHH)
National Library of Israel (Jerusalem), Ephemera Collection
Netanya Municipal Archive
Oded Yarkoni Historical Archives of Petah Tikva (PTA)
Pinhas Lavon Institute for Labor Movement Research Archives, Tel Aviv (PL)
Rehovot Historical Archives (RHA)
Rishon LeZion Museum: Historical Archive (RLZ)
Tel Aviv Municipal Archive
Zichron Yaʿaqov Historical Archive

Newspapers and Periodicals

ha-Ahdut
ʿAl ha-Mishmar
Ba-Mahaneh
ha-Boker

Bustenai
Davar
Do'ar ha-yom
Filastin
Haaretz
Haqiqat al-'amr
Herut
ha-Herut (Jerusalem)
The Jerusalem Post
Kol ha-'am
La-merhav
Maariv
ha-Mashkif
Mirat al-sharq
ha-Or
Palestine Review
ha-Po'el ha-tza'ir
She'arim ha-Tzefirah
ha-Tzofeh
Yedi'ot Rishon LeZion
Yedi'ot Tel Aviv
Yedioth Ahronoth
ha-Zvi

Published Sources

Aaronsohn, Ran. "Atare 'avar ba-moshavot ha-rishonot: gesher tarbuti la-hoveh" [Historical sites in the first moshavot: a cultural bridge to the present]. In *Lesoheah tarbut 'im ha-'Aliyah ha-Rishonah* [Talking culture with the First Aliyah], 248–64. Tel Aviv: Ha-Kibbutz Ha-Me'auhad, 2010.

Aaronsohn, Ran. *ha-Baron veha-moshavot: ha-hityashvut ha-Yehudit be-Eretz Yisra'el be-reshitah 1882–1890* [The Baron and the colonies: early Jewish settlement in the Land of Israel 1882–1890]. Jerusalem: Yad Yitzhak Ben-Zvi, 1990.

Aaronsohn, Ran. *Rothschild and Early Jewish Colonization in Palestine*. Israel Studies in Historical Geography. Lanham: Rowman & Littlefield Publishers; Jerusalem: The Hebrew University Magnes Press, 2000.

Abulafia, Yodfat. "Kafr Qasim be-zikaron ha-Yisre'eli: hitmodedut ha-hevrah ha-Yisre'elit 'im 'avar ba'ayati" [Kafr Qasim in Israeli memory: Israeli society's coping with a problematic past]. Master's thesis, Ben Gurion University, 2014.

Ahad ha-ʿAm, Ahad [Asher Ginzburg]. "Emet mi-Eretz Yisraʾel" [Truth from the Land of Israel]. In *Kol kitve Ahad Ha-ʿam* [Collected writings of Ahad Ha-ʿam], 23–34. Jerusalem: Hotzaʾah ʿIvrit, 1956.
Ahad ha-ʿAm, Ahad [Asher Ginzburg]. "Sakh ha-kol" [All in all], *ha-Shiloah* 26:3 (Nisan 1912). Available online at Project Ben-Yehuda: http://benyehuda.org/ginzberg/Gnz_127.html#_ftn1.
Ahlbäck, Anders. *Manhood and the Making of the Military: Conscription, Military Service and Masculinity in Finland, 1917–39*. Farnham, UK: Routledge, 2014.
ha-ʿAliyah ha-Hamishit: 60 shanah la-ʿaliyah mi-merkaz Eropah [The Fifth Aliyah: 60 years of immigration from central Europe]. Tel-Aviv: Irgun ʿole Merkaz Eropah, 1994.
Almog, Oz. *The Sabra: The Creation of the New Jew*. Berkeley: University of California Press, 2000.
Alon, Yoav. *The Shaykh of Shaykhs: Mithqal al-Fayiz and Tribal Leadership in Modern Jordan*. Stanford: Stanford University Press, 2016.
Alroey, Gur. *Bread to Eat and Clothes to Wear: Letters from Jewish Migrants in the Early Twentieth Century*. Detroit: Wayne State University Press, 2011.
Alroey, Gur. "Halutzim ovdei derekh? sugiyat ha-hitʾabdut ʿal seder yoman shel ha-ʿAliyot ha-Sheniyah veha-Shelishit" [Pioneers who have lost their way? The issue of suicide in the Second and Third Aliyot]. *Yahadut zemanenu* 13 (1999): 209–41.
Alroey, Gur. "The Jewish Emigration from Palestine in the Early Twentieth Century." *Journal of Modern Jewish Studies* 2, no. 2 (2003): 111–31.
Alroey, Gur. "Mesharte ha-moshava o rodanim gase ruah? meʾah shanah le-agudat ha-Shomer, perspektivah historit" [Servants of the colonies or rude dictators? Centennial of ha-Shomer, a historical perspective]. *Cathedra* 13 (2009): 77–104.
Alroey, Gur. "Two Historiographies: Israeli Historiography and the Mass Jewish Migration to the United States, 1881–1914." *Jewish Quarterly Review* 105, no. 1 (Winter 2015): 99–129.
Alroey, Gur. *An Unpromising Land: Jewish Migration to Palestine in the Early Twentieth Century*. Stanford Studies in Jewish History and Culture. Stanford: Stanford University Press, 2014.
Altenbernd, Erik, and Alex Trimble Young. "Introduction: The Significance of the Frontier in an Age of Transnational History." *Settler Colonial Studies* 4, no. 2 (2014): 127–50.
Amichal Yeivin, Ada. *ʿEn-Ganim: sipuro shel moshav ha-poʿalim ha-rishon be-Eretz Yisraʾel* [Ein-Ganim: the story of the first Workers Colony in the Land of Israel]. Sidrat rishonim ba-aretz. Jerusalem: Yad Yitzhak Ben-Zvi, 2005.
Amos, Hofi. "Bonim sukkat shalom: bekhirim Muslemim bikru be-Efrat" [Building a sukkah of peace: Muslim elites visited Efrat]. *NRG/Makor Rishon*, October 19, 2016. https://www.makorrishon.co.il/nrg/online/1/ART2/841/870.html.

Anderson, Charles W. "State Formation from Below and the Great Revolt in Palestine." *Journal of Palestine Studies* 47, no. 1 (November 1, 2017): 39–55.

Angell, James Rowland. "Radio and National Morale." *The American Journal of Sociology* 47, no. 3 (November 1941): 352–59.

Anner, Zeev. *Sipure batim: sipuram shel shiv'im batim be-toldot ha-hityashvut.* Tel Aviv: Israel Ministry of Defense, 1988.

Anziska, Seth. *Preventing Palestine: A Political History from Camp David to Oslo.* Princeton: University Press, 2018.

Applegate, Celia. *A Nation of Provincials: The German Idea of Heimat.* Berkeley: University of California Press, 1990.

Ari, Nisa. "Orientalism Repeated: Shifting Time in Jumana Manna's A Sketch of Manners and the Politics of Photography in Palestine." *Third Text* 30, no. 5–6 (2016): 331–45.

Aryeh-Sapir, Nili. "'Sefer Gedera' le-Amnon Horvitz: ha-mityashev ke-historyon" [Amnon Horvitz's "Gedera Book": the settler as historian]. In *Lesoheah tarbut 'im ha-'Aliyah ha-Rishonah* [Talking culture with the First Aliyah], edited by Yafah Berlovitz and Yosef Lang, 176–97. Tel Aviv: ha-Kibbutz ha-me'uhad, 2010.

Aviv, Yoni. "Ma'avak 'al hashpa'ah be-'itonut miflagtit: Abba Ahimeir u-Zeev Jabotinsky ba-'iton Do'ar ha-yom" [Struggle over influence in partisan journalism: Abba Ahimeir and Zeev Jabotinsky at *Do'ar ha-yom*]. *Kesher* 37 (2008): 93–98.

Azaryahu, Maoz. *Tel Aviv: Mythography of a City.* Syracuse, NY: Syracuse University Press, 2007.

Azmon, Yael. *Historyah basar va-dam: ha-Tziyonut mi-nekudat re'utam shel manhigei moshevet rishonim* [Flesh and blood history: Zionism from the perspective of the directors of the First moshava]. Jerusalem: Ha-Sifriyah ha-Tziyonit, 2005.

Azoulay, Ariella, and Adi Ophir. *The One-State Condition: Occupation and Democracy in Israel/Palestine.* Palo Alto: Stanford University Press, 2012.

Barnett, Zerach. *Zikhronot Zerach Barnett* [Memoirs of Zerach Barnett]. Jerusalem: Moriah, 1928.

Barker, Adam J. "Deathscapes of Settler Colonialism: The Necro-Settlement of Stoney Creek, Ontario, Canada." *Annals of the American Association of Geographers*, 20180122, 1–16.

Bartal, Israel. "'Al ha-rishoniyut: zeman u-makom ba-'Aliyah ha-Rishonah" [On firstness: time and place in the First Aliyah]. In *Lesoheah tarbut 'im ha-'Aliyah ha-Rishonah* [Talking culture with the First Aliyah], edited by Yaffa Berlovitz and Yosef Lang, 15–24. Tel Aviv: ha-Kibbutz ha-Me'uhad, 2010.

Bartal, Israel. *Galut ba-aretz: Yishuv Eretz-Yisrael be-terem Tziyonut: kovetz mehkarim u-masot* [Exile in the Land of Israel: settlement in the Land of Israel before Zionism: a collection of studies and essays]. Jerusalem: ha-Sifriyah ha-Tziyonit, 1995.

Bartal, Israel. "Hanukkah Cossack Style: Zaporozhian Warriors and Zionist Popular Culture (1904–1918)." In *Stories of Khmelnytsky: Competing Literary Legacies of the 1648 Ukrainian Cossack Uprising*, edited by Amelia M. Glaser, 139–52. Stanford: Stanford University Press, 2015.

Bartal, Israel. "Petah Tikva: ben shorashim ra'ayoniyim le-nesivot ha-Zeman" [Petah Tikva: between conceptual roots and circumstances of the time]. *Cathedra* 9 (October 1978): 54–69.

Bartal, Israel, and Yehoshua Ben-Arieh, eds. *Shelhe ha-tekufah ha-'Othmanit*. Historiyah shel Eretz Yisra'el. Vol. 8. Jerusalem: Keter, 1983.

Bashir, Bashir, and Amos Goldberg. "Introduction: The Holocaust and the Nakba: A New Syntax of History, Memory, and Political Thought." In *The Holocaust and the Nakba: A New Grammar of Trauma and History*, edited by Bashir Bashir and Amos Goldberg, 9–12. Religion, Culture, and Public Life. New York: Columbia University Press, 2019.

Bashkin, Orit. *Impossible Exodus: Iraqi Jews in Israel*. Stanford Studies in Middle Eastern and Islamic Societies and Cultures. Stanford: Stanford University Press, 2017.

Beenstock, Michael, Jacob Metzer, and Sanny Ziv. *Immigration and the Jewish Economy in Mandatory Palestine: An Econometric Exploration*. Jerusalem: Maurice Falk Institute for Economic Research in Israel, 1993.

Beeri, Eliezer. *Reshit ha-sikhsukh Yisra'el-'Arav, 1882–1911* [The beginning of the Israel-Arab conflict, 1882–1911]. Tel Aviv: Sifriyat Po'alim, 1985.

Bein, Alex, *Toldot ha-hityashvut ha-Tziyonit mi-tekufat Herzl ve-'ad yamenu*. 3rd ed. Tel Aviv: Masada, 1953.

Beinin, Joel. "Knowing Your Enemy, Knowing Your Ally: The Arabists of Hashomer Hatza'ir (MAPAM)." *Social Text*, no. 28 (January 1, 1991): 100–121.

Belkind, Eitan. *Rishon LeZion: ha-medinah ba-derekh la-medinah: 90 shanah le-Rishon LeZion, 1882–1972* [Rishon LeZion: the state on the way to the state: 90 years of Rishon LeZion, 1882–1972]. Rishon LeZion municipality, 1972.

Bell, David A. "Total History and Microhistory: The French and Italian Paradigms." In *Companion to Western Historical Thought*, edited by Lloyd S. Kramer, 262–76. Malden, MA: Blackwell, 2002.

Ben-Amotz, Dan, and Hayim Hefer. *Yalkut ha-kezavim* [The pack of lies]. Tel Aviv: ha-Kibbutz ha-Me'uhad, 1956.

Ben-Arieh, Yehoshua. *'Ir bi-re'i tekufah: Yerushalayim ha-hadashah be-reshitah*. Sifriyah le-toldot ha-yishuv ha-Yehudi be-Eretz-Yisra'el. Jerusalem: Yad Yitzhak Ben-Zvi, 1979.

Ben-Arieh, Yehoshua. "ha-Nof ha-yishuvi shel Eretz-Yisra'el 'erev ha-hityashvut ha-Tziyonit." In *Toldot ha-yishuv ha-Yehudi be-Eretz Yisra'el me-'az ha-'Aliyah ha-Rishonah: ha-tekufah ha-'Othmanit*, edited by Israel Kolatt, 1:75–141. Jerusalem: Mosad Bialik; Israel Institute of Sciences, 1990.

Ben-Artzi, Yossi. *Early Jewish Settlement Patterns in Palestine, 1882–1914.* Israel Studies in Historical Geography. Jerusalem: Magnes Press, Hebrew University, 1997.

Ben-Artzi, Yossi. "Have Gender Studies Changed Our Attitude toward the Historiography of the Aliyah and Settlement Process?" In *Jewish Women in Pre-State Israel: Life History, Politics, and Culture,* edited by Ruth Kark, Margalit Shilo, and Galit Hasan-Rokem, 18–32. Waltham, MA: Brandeis University Press. 2008.

Ben-Artzi, Yossi. "ha-Hityashvut ha-Yehudit be-Eretz Yisra'el 1900–1917: me'afyenim ge'ografiyim-yishuviyim" [Jewish settlement in the Land of Israel, 1900–1917: geographic and settlement characteristics]. In *Toldot ha-Yishuv ha-Yehudi be-Eretz Yisra'el me-'az ha-'Aliyah ha-Rishonah: ha-tekufah ha-Othmanit* [The history of the Jewish community in the Land of Israel since the First Aliyah: the Ottoman period], edited by Israel Kolatt. Vol. 2. Jerusalem: Mosad Bialik; Israel Institute of Sciences, 1990.

Ben-Bassat, Yuval. "The Challenges Facing the First Aliyah Sephardic Ottoman Colonists." *Journal of Israeli History* 35, no. 1 (2016): 3–15.

Ben-Bassat, Yuval. *Petitioning the Sultan: Protests and Justice in Late Ottoman Palestine, 1865–1908.* Library of Ottoman Studies 42. London: I. B. Tauris, 2013.

Ben-Bassat, Yuval. "Proto-Zionist–Arab Encounters in Late Nineteenth-Century Palestine: Socioregional Dimensions." *Journal of Palestine Studies* 38, no. 2 (2009): 42–63. https://doi.org/10.1525/jps.2009.38.2.42.

Ben-Bassat, Yuval, and Gur Alroey. "The Zionist–Arab Incident of Zarnuqa 1913: A Chronicle and Several Methodological Remarks." *Middle Eastern Studies,* June 1, 2016, 1–17.

Ben-Ezer, Ehud. *Jeda': sipuro shel Avraham Shapira shomer ha-moshava* [Jeda: the story of Avraham Shapira, guard of the colony]. Jerusalem: Yad Izhak Ben-Zvi Press, 1993.

Ben-Gurion, David. "Al he-'avar ve-'al he-'atid" [On the past and the future]. In *Hazon va-derekh* [Vision and path], vol. 5, 267–96. Tel Aviv: 'Am 'oved, 1951.

Ben-Gurion, David. "Be-hag hatzi ha-yovel (Devarim ba-'atzeret hag hatzi ha-yovel)" [On the celebration of the 25th anniversary (Remarks at the 25th anniversary assembly)]. In *Sefer ha-'Aliyah ha-Sheniyah* [The Second Aliyah], edited by Bracha Habas and Eliezer Shochat, 15–19. Tel Aviv: 'Am 'Oved, 1946.

Ben-Gurion, David. *Mi-ma'amad la-'am: perakim le-virur darkah vi-yi'udah shel tenu'at ha-po'alim* [From class to nation: reflections on the methods and goals of the workers' movement]. Tel Aviv: Davar, 1933.

Ben-Gurion, David. "Rishonim" [First Ones]. In *Shenaton ha-memshalah* [Government Yearbook], *1962–3,* edited by Reuven Alkalai, i–li. Jerusalem: Government Printer, 1962.

Ben-Porat, Amir. *Divided We Stand: Class Structure in Israel from 1948 to the 1980s.* New York: Greenwood Press, 1989.

Ben-Porat, Amir. *Hekhan hem ha-burganim ha-hem? toldot ha-burganut ha-Yisre'elit* [Where are those bourgeois people? The history of the Israeli bourgeoisie]. Jerusalem: Magnes Press, 1999.

Ben-Uzi, Yaniv. "Tenu lihyot ba-aretz ha-zot: mifleget 'Tziyonim Kelaliyim' 1949–1952" [Let us live in this land: the General Zionist Party]. *Cathedra*, no. 127 (2008): 141–68.

Benvenisti, Meron. *The West Bank Data Project: A Survey of Israel's Policies*. Washington, DC: American Enterprise Institute for Public Policy Research, 1984.

Ben-Yehuda, Hemda. *ha-Lohem ha-me'ushar: haye Eliezer Ben-Yehuda* [The happy fighter: the life of Eliezer Ben-Yehuda]. Jerusalem: Tziyon, 1931.

Ben-Zeev, Nimrod. "Foundations of Inequality: Construction, Political Economy, Race, and the Body in Palestine/Israel, 1918–1973." PhD diss., University of Pennsylvania, 2020.

Ben-Zvi, Yitzhak, Yisrael Shochat, Matti Megged, and Yohanan Tabersky, eds. *Sefer ha-Shomer: divre haverim* [Ha-Shomer book: members' remarks]. Tel Aviv: Devir, 1957.

Berda, Yael. *Living Emergency: Israel's Permit Regime in the Occupied West Bank*. Stanford: Stanford Briefs, an imprint of Stanford University Press, 2017.

Berlant, Lauren. *The Anatomy of National Fantasy: Hawthorne, Utopia, and Everyday Life*. Chicago: University of Chicago Press, 1991.

Berlovitz, Yaffa. *Le-hamtzi eretz le-hamtzi 'am: tashtiyot sifrutiyot ve-tarbutiyot ba-yetzirah shel ha-'Aliyah ha-Rishonah* [Inventing a land, inventing a people: literary and cultural foundations in the creation of the First Aliyah]. Tel Aviv: ha-Kibbutz ha-me'uhad, 1996.

Bernstein, Deborah. "Challenges to Separatism: Joint Action by Jewish and Arab Workers in Jewish-Owned Industry in Mandatory Palestine." In *The New Israel: Peacemaking and Liberalization*, edited by Gershon Shafir and Yoav Peled, 17–41. Westview Press, 2000.

Bernstein, Deborah. *Constructing Boundaries: Jewish and Arab Workers in Mandatory Palestine*. Albany: State University of New York Press, 2000.

Bernstein, Deborah. *Nashim ba-shulayim: migdar u-le'umiyut be-Tel Aviv ha-mandatorit* [Women on the margins: gender and nationalism in mandatory Tel Aviv]. Jerusalem: Yad Yitzhak Ben-Zvi, 2008.

Bhandar, Brenna. *Colonial Lives of Property: Law, Land, and Racial Regimes of Ownership*. Global and Insurgent Legalities. Durham: Duke University Press, 2018.

Bialik, Hayim Nahman. *Shirim be-Yiddish, shire yeladim, shire hakdashah: mahadurah mada'it be-livyat mevo'ot ve-hilufe nosah* [Poems in Yiddish, children's poems, dedicated poems: scholarly edition with introductions and alternate versions]. Edited by Dan Miron. Vol. 3. Collected poems. Tel-Aviv: Katz Center for the Study of Hebrew Literature; Devir, 2001.

Binyamin, Shlomit. "Nokhahim nifkadim: ha-mikre shel Qubeyba/Kfar Gvirol" [Present-Absentees: the case of Qubeyba/Kfar Gvirol]. *Te'oriyah u-vikoret* [Theory and Criticism] 29 (Fall 2006): 81–102.

Booth, William, and Sufian Taha. "Jewish Settlers Invited Palestinians Over for the Holidays. All Went Well until the Guests Headed Home." *The Washington Post*, October 20, 2016.

Borneman, John. *Death of the Father: An Anthropology of the End in Political Authority*. New York: Berghahn Books, 2004.

Breen-Portnoy, Barney. "Head of Major West Bank Jewish Community Calls on PA to 'Immediately Release' Palestinians Arrested After They Visited His Sukkah." *The Algemeiner*, October 21, 2016. https://www.algemeiner.com/2016/10/21/head-of-major-west-bank-jewish-community-calls-on-pa-to-immediately-release-palestinians-arrested-after-they-visited-his-sukkah/

Breuilly, John. *Nationalism and the State*. University of Chicago Press, 1994.

Brown, Wendy. *Undoing the Demos: Neoliberalism's Stealth Revolution*. Cambridge, MA: Zone Books, 2015.

Bruyneel, Kevin. "Codename Geronimo: Settler Memory and the Production of American Statism." *Settler Colonial Studies* 6, no. 4 (20161001): 349–64.

Bruyneel, Kevin. "Creolizing Collective Memory: Refusing the Settler Memory of the Reconstruction Era." *Journal of French and Francophone Philosophy* 25, no. 2 (2017): 36–44. https://doi.org/10.5195/JFFP.2017.822.

Cameron, Emilie. "Indigenous Spectrality and the Politics of Postcolonial Ghost Stories." *Cultural Geographies* 15, no. 3 (2008): 383–93.

Campos, Michelle U. "Between 'Beloved Ottomania' and 'The Land of Israel': The Struggle over Ottomanism and Zionism among Palestine's Sephardi Jews, 1908–1913." *International Journal of Middle East Studies* 37, no. 4 (2005): 461–83.

Campos, Michelle U. *Ottoman Brothers: Muslims, Christians, and Jews in Early Twentieth-Century Palestine*. Stanford: Stanford University Press, 2011.

Carmin, Itzhak. *The General Zionist World: A Four-Year Report on the World Confederation of General Zionists*. New York: World Confederation of General Zionists, American Office, 1951.

Cohen, Hillel. *Army of Shadows: Palestinian Collaboration with Zionism, 1917–1948*. Berkeley: University of California Press, 2008.

Cohen, Michael J. *Britain's Moment in Palestine: Retrospect and Perspectives, 1917–1948*. New York: Routledge, 2014.

Confino, Alon. *The Nation as a Local Metaphor: Württemberg, Imperial Germany, and National Memory, 1871–1918*. Chapel Hill: University of North Carolina Press, 1997.

Currivan, Gene. "Two Worlds Meet in Tense Palestine." *New York Times Magazine*, November 18, 1945, 9, 43.

Dallasheh, Leena. "Troubled Waters: Citizenship and Colonial Zionism in Nazareth." *International Journal of Middle East Studies* 47, no. 3 (2015): 467–87.
Daniele, Giulia. "Mizrahi Jews and the Zionist Settler Colonial Context: Between Inclusion and Struggle." *Settler Colonial Studies* 10, no. 4 (2020): 461–80.
Davidovitz, Lihi, and Tamir Lavi. "Tik tiʿud: beit Anton Ayub (Bet Ha-Biluim)" [Documentation file: The Anton Ayub House (the house of the Biluyim)]. Preservation Studio 2006–7, School of Architecture, Tel Aviv University, available via website "Batei ha-beʾer: ha-armonot ha-neʿelamim shel Yafo" [Well houses: disappearing palaces of Jaffa], https://bit.ly/2H2T8iB, under the auspices of Tel Aviv University and the Municipality of Tel Aviv-Yaffo, built by Dionysus design.
Davis, Rochelle. *Palestinian Village Histories: Geographies of the Displaced*. Stanford Studies in Middle Eastern and Islamic Societies and Cultures. Stanford: Stanford University Press, 2011.
Dean, Jonathan. "Tales of the Apolitical." *Political Studies* 62, no. 2 (2013): 452–67.
Degani, Arnon Yehuda. "The Decline and Fall of the Israeli Military Government, 1948–1966: A Case of Settler-Colonial Consolidation?" *Settler Colonial Studies* 5, no. 1 (2015): 84–99.
Dinur, Ben-Zion, Yehuda Slutzky, and Shaul Avigur. *Sefer toledot ha-haganah* [History of the Haganah]. Jerusalem: ha-Sifriyah ha-Tziyonit, 1954.
Dizengoff, Meir. "Le-susati" [To my horse]. In *Li-yedidai mi-noʿar: sipurim ve-zikhronot* [To my friends since youth: stories and memories]. Tel Aviv: A. Y. Shtibel, 1936. http://benyehuda.org/dizengoff/lesusati.html.
Dolbee, Samuel, and Shay Hazkani. "'Impossible Is Not Ottoman': Menashe Meirovitch, ʿIsa Al-ʿIsa, and Imperial Citizenship in Palestine." *International Journal of Middle East Studies* 47, no. 2 (May 2015): 241–62.
Dowty, Alan. *Israel/Palestine*. 3rd ed., fully rev. and updated. Cambridge, UK: Polity, 2012.
Dowty, Alan. "'A Question That Outweighs All Others': Yitzhak Epstein and Zionist Recognition of the Arab Issue." *Israel Studies* 6, no. 1 (2001): 34–54.
Dreisbach, Daniel L. "The 'Vine and Fig Tree' in George Washington's Letters: Reflections on a Biblical Motif in the Literature of the American Founding Era." *Anglican and Episcopal History* 76, no. 3 (2007): 299–326.
Dror, Yuval. *The History of Kibbutz Education: Practice into Theory*. Europäische Hochschulschriften. Reihe XI, Pädagogik. Vol. 802. Bern: P. Lang, 2001.
Drori, Yigal. *Ben yamin li-smol: ha-hugim ha-ezrahiyim bi-shenot ha-ʿesrim* [Between right and left: the Citizens' Circles in the 1920s]. Tel-Aviv: University Publishing Projects, 1990.
Drori, Yigal. "ʿEmdatav shel ʿDoʾar ha-yom me-hivasdo ve-ʿad sof 1924" [Doʾar ha-yom's stances from its founding until 1924]. *ha-Tziyonut* 12 (1987): 141–64.
Drori, Yigal. "Hishtakfutam shel ha-ʿAliyah ha-Sheniyah veha-maʾavak le-ʿavodah

"Ivrit' ba-'itonut ha-eretzyisre'elit ha-kelalit." [Reflections of the Second Aliyah and the struggle for Hebrew Labor in the general press in the Land of Israel]. *Cathedra* 2 (November 1976): 69–80.

Druyanow, Alter, ed. *Ketavim le-toldot Hibat Tziyon ve-yishuv Eretz Yisra'el* [Writings on the history of Hibat Zion and the settlement of the Land of Israel]. Odessa: Ha-va'ad le-yishuv Eretz Yisra'el, 1919.

Edelstein, Yehuda. *Avraham Shapira (Sheikh Ibrahim Mikhah)*. 2 vols. Tel Aviv: Yedidim, 1939.

Edmonds, Penelope. "The Intimate, Urbanising Frontier: Native Camps and Settler Colonialism's Violent Array of Spaces around Early Melbourne." In *Making Settler Colonial Space: Perspectives on Race, Place, and Identity*, edited by Tracey Banivanua Mar and Penelope Edmonds, 129–54. London: Palgrave Macmillan, 2010.

Eidson, John R. "German Local History as Metaphor and Sanction." *Anthropological Quarterly* 66, no. 3 (July 1, 1993): 134–48.

Eliav, Mordechai. *Eretz Yisra'el vi-Yishuvah ba-me'ah ha-19, 1777–1917* [Eretz Israel and its Yishuv in the 19th century, 1777–1917]. Jerusalem: Keter, 1978.

Eliav, Mordechai. "Yihudah shel ha-'Aliyah ha-Rishonah: mavo" [The uniqueness of the First Aliyah: introduction]. In *Sefer ha-'Aliyah ha-Rishonah* [The First Aliyah], edited by Mordechai Eliav, ix–xix. Sifriyah le-toldot ha-yishuv ha-Yehudi be-Eretz-Yisra'el. Jerusalem: Yad Yitzhak Ben-Zvi, Israel Ministry of Defense, 1981.

Eliram, Talila. *Bo, shir 'Ivri: shirei Eretz Yisra'el, hebetim muzikaliyim ve-hevratiyim* [Come, thou Hebrew song: the songs of the Land of Israel: Musical and social aspects]. Haifa: University of Haifa, 2006.

Epstein, Yitzhak. "She'elah ne'elmah" [A Hidden Question]. *ha-Shiloah* 17 (July–December 1907), 193–206.

Ever Hadani [Aharon Feldman], ed. *Me'ah shenot shemirah be-Yisra'el* [One hundred years of guarding in Israel]. Tel Aviv: Y. Chechik, 1954.

Eyal, Gil. *The Disenchantment of the Orient: Expertise in Arab Affairs and the Israeli State*. Stanford: Stanford University Press.

Farsakh, Leila. *Palestinian Labour Migration to Israel: Labour, Land, and Occupation*. New York: Routledge, 2005.

Fischbach, Michael R. *Records of Dispossession: Palestinian Refugee Property and the Arab-Israeli Conflict*. New York: Columbia University Press, 2003.

Fischer, Elli. "The Prenumeranten Project and Other Good News." *HaMapah: Quantitative Analysis of Rabbinic Literature* (blog), September 12, 2019. https://blog.hamapah.org/prenumeranten/the-prenumeranten-project-and-other-good-news/.

Fish, Rachel. "Bi-Nationalist Visions for the Construction and Dissolution of the State of Israel." *Israel Studies* 19, no. 2 (2014): 15–34.

Foster, Robert, Amanda Nettelbeck, and Rick Hosking. *Fatal Collisions: The South Australian Frontier and the Violence of Memory*. Kent Town, S. Australia: Wakefield Press, 2001.

Frankel, Jonathan. *Prophecy and Politics: Socialism, Nationalism, and the Russian Jews, 1862–1917*. Cambridge, UK: Cambridge University Press, 1981.

Frenkel, Michal, Yehouda Shenhav, and Hanna Herzog. "The Ideological Wellspring of Zionist Capitalism: The Impact of Private Capital and Industry on the Shaping of the Dominant Zionist Ideology." In *The New Israel: Peacemaking and Liberalization*, edited by Gershon Shafir and Yoav Peled. Oxford: Westview Press, 2000. 43–69.

Furniss, Elizabeth. *Burden of History: Colonialism and the Frontier Myth in a Rural Canadian Community*. Vancouver: UBC Press, 2007.

Furniss, Elizabeth. "Timeline History and the Anzac Myth: Settler Narratives of Local History in a North Australian Town." *Oceania* 71, no. 4 (2001): 279–97.

Gamzu, Hayim. *Nahum Gutman: Paintings, Watercolors, Sculptures* (Jubilee Exhibition). Tel Aviv: Tel Aviv Museum, 1969.

Gamzu, Yossi. *Atem no' ar atem?!* [You, are you youth?!]. 2nd ed. Tel Aviv: Masadah, 1966.

Gazit, Shlomo. *The Carrot and the Stick: Israel's Policy in Judaea and Samaria, 1967–68*. Washington, DC: B'nai B'rith Books, 1995.

Geffen, Yehonatan. "ha-Baladah 'al Aharon David" [The ballad about Aharon David]. In Meir Noy, *Mahberet 'Ivrit 8* [Hebrew notebook 8], 201–3. Available through the National Library of Israel Digital Collection, http://bookreader.nli.org.il/NliBookViewer/?ie_pid=IE33524256#page/n200/mode/2up.

Gelvin, James L. *The Israel-Palestine Conflict: One Hundred Years of War*. Cambridge, UK: Cambridge University Press, 2014.

Gertz, Nurith. *Myths in Israeli Culture: Captives of a Dream*. Parkes-Wiener Series on Jewish Studies. London: Vallentine Mitchell, 2000.

Getmansky, Anna, and Tolga Sinmazdemir. "Settling on Violence: Expansion of Israeli Outposts in the West Bank in Response to Terrorism." *Studies in Conflict and Terrorism* 41, no. 3 (2018): 241–59.

Giladi, Dan. "Bitahon u-shemirah be-moshvot ha-'Aliyah ha-Rishonah" [Security and guarding in the colonies of the First Aliyah]. *Sekirah hodshit* [Monthly review] 27, no. 12 (1980): 35–42.

Giladi, Dan. "'Emdat ha-ikarim be-she'elat 'ha-'avodah ha-'Ivrit' be-moshvot ha-'Aliyah ha-Sheniyah (1904–1914)" [The farmers' stance on the question of Hebrew Labor in the Second Aliyah moshavot (1904–1914)]. *Ba-Derekh* 3, no. 9 (December 1970): 69–73.

Giladi, Dan. "ha-Moshavot she-lo be-hasut ha-Baron bi-shenot ha-90" [The colonies that were not under Baron Rothschild's sponsorship in the 1890s]. In *Toldot ha-Yishuv ha-Yehudi be-Eretz Yisra'el me-'az ha-'Aliyah ha-Rishonah: ha-tekufah ha-Othmanit* [History of the Jewish settlement in the Land of Israel since the First Aliyah: the Ottoman period], edited by Israel Kolatt, 1:503–37. Jerusalem: Mosad Bialik; Israel Institute of Sciences, 1990.

Giladi, Dan. "Rishon LeZion be-hasut ha-Baron Rothschild (1882–1900)" [Rishon LeZion under the patronage of Baron Rothschild]. *Cathedra* 9 (October 1978): 127–52.

Gilead, Zerubavel, and Matti Megged. *Sefer ha-Palmach*. Tel Aviv: ha-Kibbutz ha-Me'uhad, 1954.

Ginzburg, Carlo. "Microhistory: Two or Three Things I Know about It." In *Threads and Traces: True False Fictive*, translated by Anne C. Tedeschi and John Tedeschi, 193–214. Berkeley: University of California Press, 2012.

Glass, Joseph B., and Ruth Kark. *Sephardi Entrepreneurs in Jerusalem: The Valero Family 1800–1948*. Gefen Publishing House, 2007.

Goffman, Erving. *The Presentation of Self in Everyday Life*. New York: Doubleday, 1959.

Goldstein, Amir. "'We Have a Rendezvous with Destiny'—The Rise and Fall of the Liberal Alternative." *Israeli Studies* 16, no. 1 (2011): 26–52.

Goldstein, Amir. "Who Represented the Israeli Middle Class? The Crystallization of the General Zionists from 1948 to 1949." *Middle Eastern Studies* 54, no. 3 (2018): 400–414.

Goldstein, Yaakov. *Ba-derekh el ha-ya'ad: Bar-Giyora ve-ha-Shomer, 1907–1935*. Tel Aviv: Israel Ministry of Defense, 1994.

Goldstein, Yaakov, and Bat-Sheva Stern. "PICA: irgunah u-matarotah" [PICA: its organization and goals]. *Cathedra* 59 (March 1991): 103–25.

Gonen, Amiram. *Between City and Suburb: Urban Residential Patterns and Processes in Israel*. Aldershot: Avebury, 1995.

Gonen, Amiram. "'Iyur ha-moshavot ba-mishor ha-hof be-Yisra'el: gormim u-shelavim" [The urbanization of the moshavot on the Israeli coastal plain: causes and stages]. In *Nof moladetenu: mehkarim ba-geografiyah shel Eretz-Yisrael uve-toldotehah mugashim le-Yehoshua Ben-Arieh* [The landscape of our homeland: research on the geography and history of The Land of Israel: presented to Yehoshua Ben-Arieh], edited by Yossi Ben-Artzi, Israel Bartal, and Elhanan Reiner, 461–77. Jerusalem: Magnes Press, 2000.

Gonen, Amiram. "Ketzad kam 'merkaz ha-aretz' be-Eretz Yisra'el" [How the "Center" arose in the Land of Israel]. In *Kalkalah ve-hevrah bi-yeme ha-mandat, 1918–1948* [Economy and society during the mandate, 1918–1948], edited by Avi Bareli and Nahum Karlinsky, 439–88. Sede Boqer: Ben Gurion University Press, 2003.

Gonen, Amiram. "Mi-mivneh shel gal'in ve-shulayim le-pasifas meguvan ba-'arim

ha-vatikot be-Yisraʾel" [From a core and periphery structure to a varied mosaic in the veteran cities of Israel]. *Eretz Yisraʾel* 17 (1983): 74–82.
Gonen, Ehud. "ha-ʿIr Petah Tikva hi ha-yetzuʾanit mispar 1 be-Yisraʾel" [The City of Petah Tikva is the number one exporter in Israel]. Israel Foreign Trade Administration, Office of Economy and Industry, April 1, 2015. https://bit.ly/2XDbE8P.
Gordon, Alan D. *Making Public Pasts: The Contested Terrain of Montreal's Public Memories, 1891–1930*. Montreal: McGill-Queen's University Press, 2014.
Gorny, Yosef. *ha-Sheʾelah ha-ʿArvit veha-beʾayah ha-Yehudit: zeramim mediniyim-ideʾologiyim ba-Tziyonut be-yahasam el ha-yeshut ha-ʿArvit be-Eretz Yisraʾel ba-shanim 1882–1948* [The Arab Question and the Jewish Problem: Zionist political-ideological currents in relation to the Arab entity in the Land of Israel, 1882–1948]. Tel Aviv: ʿAm ʿOved, 1985.
Gouri, Hayim. "ha-Baladah le-Yitzhak Sadeh," *Davar la-yeladim,* August 21, 1972, 1514. In Meir Noy, *Mahberet ʿIvrit 6: milim u-lehanim le-shirim be-ʿIvrit* [Hebrew notebook 6: words and melodies for Hebrew songs] [no date or publication information], 22. Available through the National Library of Israel: http://bookreader.nli.org.il/NliBookViewer/?ie_pid=IE33654079#page/n2/mode/2up.
Graiczer, I. "Spatial Patterns and Residential Densities in Israeli 'Moshavot' in Process of Urbanization." *GeoJournal* 2, no. 6 (1978): 533–37.
Great Britain. *Palestine Commission on the Disturbances of August 1929*. Great Britain, Colonial Office, number 48. London: HMSO [His Majesty's Stationery Office], 1930.
Great Britain. *Report of the Commission on the Palestine Disturbances of August 1929*. Presented by the Secretary of State for the Colonies to Parliament by Command of His Majesty, March, 1930, League of Nations Documents and Publications, 1919–1945. London: HMSO [His Majesty's Stationery Office], 1930.
Green, E. H. H. *Ideologies of Conservatism: Conservative Political Ideas in the Twentieth Century*. Oxford: Oxford University Press, 2002.
Green, Reut. "Defuse hekerut ve-shidukhim ba-moshavot bi-tekufat ha-ʿAliyot ha-Rishonah veha-Sheniyah" [Dating and marriage patterns in the moshavot during the period of the First and Second Aliyot]. *ʿIyunim be-tekumat Yisraʾel* [Studies in the Rebirth of Israel] 25 (2015–2016): 179–213.
Green, Reut. "Meʿoravut vaʿade ha-moshavot u-vne ha-moshavot be-ʿinyane ha-perat ba-ʿAliyot ha-Rishonah veha-Sheniyah" [Involvement of moshava committees and residents in individual matters during the First and Second Aliyot]. In Moshe Rahimi (ed.), *Mi-mashber li-tzemihah* [From crisis to flourishing], 141–60. Rehovot: Orot College, 2014.
Greene, Ann Norton. *Horses at Work: Harnessing Power in Industrial America*. Cambridge, MA: Harvard University Press, 2008.

Gribetz, Jonathan Marc. *Defining Neighbors: Religion, Race, and the Early Zionist-Arab Encounter*. Princeton: Princeton University Press, 2014.

Gulst, Yoav. "Avraham Shapira: ben mizrah le-maʿarav be-Milhemet ha-ʿOlam ha-Rishonah." In *100 shanah li-frotz Milhemet ha-ʿOlam ha-Rishonah 1914–2014*, edited by Ezra Pimental, Yossef Charny, and Eran Tearosh, 108–17. Tel Aviv: Ariel, 2014.

Gurevich, David. *ha-ʿAliyah, ha-Yishuv veha-tenuʿah ha-tivʿit shel ha-ukhlusiyah be-Eretz Yisraʾel* [Aliyah, the Yishuv and the natural movement of population in the Land of Israel]. Jerusalem: Statistical Department of the Jewish Agency for Palestine, 1944.

Gvati, Haim. *Meʾah shenot hityashvut: toldot ha-hityashvut ha-Yehudit be-Eretz Yisraʾel*. 2 vols. Tel Aviv: ha-Kibbutz ha-meʾuhad, 1981.

Habas, Bracha, and Eliezer Shochat, eds. *ha-ʿAliyah ha-Sheniyah* [The Second Aliyah]. Tel Aviv: ʿAm ʿoved, 1947.

Hacohen, Mordecai ben Hillel. "Eretz Yisraʾel tahat shilton ha-tzava ha-Briti" [Palestine under British military rule. *ha-Shiloah* 41 (1923–24): 41–50, 141–48, 227–36, 335–41, 436–42.

Hakohen, Devorah. *Immigrants in Turmoil: Mass Immigration to Israel and Its Repercussions in the 1950s and After*. Modern Jewish History. Syracuse New York: Syracuse University Press, 2003.

Halbwachs, Maurice. *On Collective Memory*, edited by Lewis A. Coser. Heritage of Sociology. Chicago: University of Chicago Press, 1992.

Halperin, Liora R. *Babel in Zion: Jews, Nationalism, and Language Diversity in Palestine, 1920–1948*. Yale University Press, 2015.

Halperin, Liora R. "A Murder in the Grove: Conceptions of Justice in an Early Zionist Colony." *Journal of Social History* 49, no. 2 (December 2015): 427–51.

Halperin, Liora R. "Petah Tikva, 1886: Gender, Anonymity, and the Making of Zionist Memory." *Jewish Social Studies* 23, no. 1 (2017): 1–28. https://doi.org/10.2979/jewisocistud.23.1.01.

Halperin, Liora R. "Trading Secrets: Constructions and Contexts of Two Middle Eastern Jewish Guards in the Early Petah Tikva Agricultural Colony." *International Journal of Middle East Studies* 51, no. 1 (February 2019): 1–22.

Hameiri, Avigdor. "Mikhtav bimkom hakdamah" [A letter in place of an introduction]. In B. Havakuk, *ha-Retzah ha-mistori* [The mysterious murder]. Tel Aviv: Sifriyat ha-balash, 1931. Digitized by Beit Otzar, September 2016, https://books.treasure.co.il/product/balash1/

Harari, Orly. "ha-Reshut ha-Falastinit ʿatzrah ʿAravim she-hitarhu ba-sukkah" [The PLO arrested Arabs who were hosted in a sukkah]. *Arutz sheva*, October 16, 2016. https://www.inn.co.il/news/332169.

Harizman, Mordechai, and Jacob Poleskin, eds. *Sefer ha-yovel li-melot hamishim shanah le-yisud Petah Tikva: 1878–1928* [Anniversary volume to mark 50 years since the founding of Petah Tikva, 1878–1928]. Tel Aviv: Etan and Shoshani Press, 1929.

Healy, Chris. *Forgetting Aborigines*. Sydney: University of New South Wales Press, 2008.

Heller, Daniel Kupfert. *Jabotinsky's Children: Polish Jews and the Rise of Right-Wing Zionism*. Princeton: Princeton University Press, 2019.

Helman, Anat. *Or ve-yam hekifuhah: tarbut Tel Avivit bi-tekufat ha-mandat* [Light and sea surrounded her: Tel Aviv culture during the mandate period]. Haifa: Haifa University Press, 2007.

Helman, Anat. "Pardesim ve-hanuyot: haye yomyom be-Fetah Tikva bi-shenot ha-'esrim veha-sheloshim" [Orchards and shops: everyday life in Petah Tikva in the 1920s and 1930s]. *Tziyon* 70, no. 3 (2005): 355–82.

Helman, Anat. "Place-Image and Memorial Day in 1920s and 1930s Petah Tivkah." *Journal of Modern Jewish Studies* 5, no. 1 (2006): 73–94. https://doi.org/10.1080/14725880500510912.

Helman, Anat. *Young Tel Aviv: A Tale of Two Cities*. Hanover, NH: University Press of New England, 2010.

Hertzberg, Arthur. *The Zionist Idea: A Historical Analysis and Reader*. Philadelphia: Jewish Publication Society, 1997.

Herzl, Theodor. *Complete Diaries*, edited by Raphael Patai and translated by Harry Zohn. New York: Herzl Press, 1960.

Herzl, Theodor. *Der Judenstaat*. Berlin: Jüdischer Verlag, 1920.

Hever, Hannan. *Producing the Modern Hebrew Canon: Nation Building and Minority Discourse*. New Perspectives on Jewish Studies. New York: University Press, 2002.

Hirsch, Michal Ben-Josef. "From Taboo to the Negotiable: The Israeli New Historians and the Changing Representation of the Palestinian Refugee Problem." *Perspectives on Politics* 5, no. 2 (June 2007): 241–58.

Hirschhorn, Sara Yael. *City on a Hilltop: American Jews and the Israeli Settler Movement*. Cambridge, MA: Harvard University Press, 2017.

Histadrut ha-kelalit shel ha-'ovdim be-Eretz Yisra'el. *Hadera le-an?: li-ker'at ha-behirot ha-rishonot la-mo'atzah ha-mekomit be-2 be-Yanu'ar 1936* [Whither Hadera?: approaching the first elections to the local council on January 2, 1936]. Hadera: Si'at ha-po'alim ba-mo'atzah ha-mekomit, 1935.

Hubbell, Amy L. *Remembering French Algeria: Pieds-Noirs, Identity, and Exile*. Lincoln: University of Nebraska Press, 2015.

Israel Central Bureau of Statistics. "ha-Kibutzim ve-okhlusiyatam: temurot demografiyot ba-shanim 1961–2005" [The Kibbutzim and their populations: demographic changes in the years 1961–2005]. Jerusalem, June 2008. https://old.cbs.gov.il/publications/kibo5/pdf/h_print.pdf.

"Israel: Statistical Survey." *The Middle East and North Africa,1964–1965*, 11th ed, 265–69. London: Europa Publications, 1964.

'Ivri, Ish [Klausner, Josef]."Hashash" [Concern]. *ha-Shiloah* 17 (1907–8), 574–76.

Jackson, Kenneth T. *Crabgrass Frontier: The Suburbanization of the United States*. Oxford: Oxford University Press, 1987.

Jacobson, Abigail, and Moshe Naor. *Oriental Neighbors: Middle Eastern Jews and Arabs in Mandatory Palestine*. Waltham, MA: Brandeis, 2016.

Jacobson, Matthew Frye. *Whiteness of a Different Color: European Immigrants and the Alchemy of Race*. Cambridge, MA: Harvard University Press, 1998.

Kabha, Mustafa, and Nahum Karlinsky. "ha-Pardes ha-ne'elam: ha-pardesanut ha-'Arvit-ha-Falastinit 'ad shenat 1948." *Zmanim*, no. 129 (Winter 2015): 94–109.

Kadman, Noga. *Erased from Space and Consciousness: Israel and the Depopulated Palestinian Villages of 1948*. Bloomington: Indiana University Press, 2015.

Kaniel, Yehoshua. *Hemshekh u-temurah: ha-Yishuv ha-Yashan veha-Yishuv he-hadash bi-tekufat ha-'Aliyah ha-Rishonah veha-Sheniyah* [Continuity and change: the Old Yishuv and the New Yishuv during the periods of the First and Second Aliyah]. Jerusalem: Yad Yitzhak Ben-Zvi, 1981.

Kaniel, Yehoshua. "Ha-vikuah ben Petah Tikva le-Rishon LeZion 'al ha-rishoniyut ba-hityashvut u-mashma'uto ha-historit." *Cathedra*, no. 9 (October 1, 1978): 26–53.

Kaplan, Eran. *The Jewish Radical Right: Revisionist Zionism and Its Ideological Legacy*. Madison: University of Wisconsin Press, 2005.

Kark, Ruth. *Jaffa: A City in Evolution, 1799–1917*. Jerusalem: Yad Izhak Ben-Zvi Press, 1990.

Karlinsky, Nahum. *California Dreaming: Ideology, Society, and Technology in the Citrus Industry of Palestine, 1890–1939*. Albany: State University of New York Press, 2005.

Kasson, Joy S. *Buffalo Bill's Wild West: Celebrity, Memory, and Popular History*. Farrar, Straus and Giroux, 2015.

Katriel, Tamar. *Dialogic Moments: From Soul Talks to Talk Radio in Israeli Culture*. Raphael Patai Series in Jewish Folklore and Anthropology. Detroit: Wayne State University Press, 2004.

Katriel, Tamar. "Marking Time: Anniversary Celebrations and the Dynamics of Social Life," *Text & Talk* 25, no. 5 (2005): 719–21.

Katriel, Tamar. *Performing the Past: A Study of Israeli Settlement Museums*. Everyday Communication. Mahwah, NJ: Lawrence Erlbaum, 1997.

Katz, Adam, and Eric Gans. *The First Shall Be the Last. Re-Thinking Antisemitism*. Leiden: Brill / Martinus Nijhoff, 2015.

Katz, Yossi. *The "Business" of Settlement: Private Entrepreneurship in the Jewish Settlement of Palestine, 1900–1914*. Jerusalem: Magnes Press, Hebrew University; Ramat-Gan: Bar-Ilan University Press, 1994.

Katz, Yossi. *The Land Shall Not Be Sold in Perpetuity: The Jewish National Fund and the History of State Ownership of Land in Israel*. Berlin: Walter de Gruyter, 2016.

Kaye, Alexander. *The Invention of Jewish Theocracy: The Struggle for Legal Authority in Modern Israel*. New York: Oxford University Press, 2020.

Kemp, Adriana. "'Nedidat ʻamim' o 'ha-beʻerah ha-gedolah': shelitah medinatit ve-hitnagdut bi-sefar ha-Yisreʼeli" ["Human migration" or "The Great Conflagration": state control and resistance in the Israeli periphery]. In *Mizrahim be-Yisraʼel: ʻiyun bikorti mehudash* [Mizrahim in Israel: a critical observation of Israel's ethnicity], edited by Hannan Hever, Yehouda Shenhav, and Pnina Motzafi-Haller, 36–67. Tel Aviv: ha-Kibbutz ha-meʼuhad; Van Leer Institute, 2002.

Kesler, Yaela, and Yossi Goldstein. "Hiking as an Educational Tool of Zionist Youth Movements in Mandate Palestine." *Australian Journal of Jewish Studies* 29 (January 2015): 43–74.

Khalidi, Rashid. *Palestinian Identity: The Construction of Modern National Consciousness*. New York: Columbia University Press, 2010.

Khalidi, Walid. *All That Remains: The Palestinian Villages Occupied and Depopulated by Israel in 1948*. Washington, DC: Institute for Palestine Studies, 1992.

Khleif, Waleed, and Susan Slymovics. "Palestinian Remembrance Days and Plans: Kafr Qasim, Fact and Echo." In *Modernism and the Middle East: Architecture and Politics in the Twentieth Century*, edited by Sandy Isenstadt and Kishwar Rizvi, 186–217. Seattle: University of Washington Press, 2008.

Kimmerling, Baruch. *Politicide: Ariel Sharon's War Against the Palestinians*. London: Verso, 2003.

Klein, Menachem. *Lives in Common: Arabs and Jews in Jerusalem, Jaffa and Hebron*. London: Hurst & Company, 2014.

Klorman, Bat-Zion Eraqi. "Hityashvut poʻalim Temanim ve-Ashkenazim: me-Rishon LeZion le-Nahalat Yehuda uva-hazarah" [The settlement of Yemenite and Ashkenazi workers: from Rishon LeZion to Nahalat Yehuda and back]. *Cathedra* 84 (1997): 85–106.

Klorman, Bat-Zion Eraqi. *Traditional Society in Transition: The Yemeni Jewish Experience*. Brill Reference Library of Judaism. Vol. 39. Leiden: Brill, 2014.

Klorman, Bat-Zion Eraqi. "ha-Yahas el ha-ʻaher' be-tarbut ha-politit shel ha-moshava: mikreh Rishon LeZion" [The relationship to the "other" in the political culture of the moshava: the case of Rishon LeZion]. In *Lesoheah tarbut ʻim ha-ʻAliyah ha-Rishonah* [Talking culture with the First Aliyah], edited by Yaffa Berlovitz and Yosef Lang, 157–75. Tel Aviv: ha-Kibbutz ha-meʼuhad, 2010.

Kolatt, Israel. "Religion, Society, and State during the Period of the National Home." In *Zionism and Religion*. The Tauber Institute for the Study of European Jewry Series 30. Hanover, NH: University Press of New England, 1998.

Koltun-Fromm, Ken. *Imagining Jewish Authenticity: Vision and Text in American Jewish Thought.* Bloomington: Indiana University Press, 2015.

Kramer, Lloyd S. *Nationalism in Europe and America: Politics, Cultures, and Identities since 1775.* Chapel Hill: The University of North Carolina Press, 2011.

Kressel, Getzel. *Avraham Shapira: vatik ha-haganah veha-shemirah* [Avraham Shapira: Veteran of defense and guarding]. Petah Tikva: Petah Tikva municipality, 1955.

Lang, Yosef. "Hityashvut ha-Yarkonim: nisayon she-hikhziv" [The settlement by the Yarkon River: an attempt that failed]. In *Le-Fetah Tikva* [For Petah Tikva], 68–94. Petah Tikva: Oded Yarkoni Petah Tikva Archive, 2012.

Lang, Yosef. "Sefarim ve-yovlot: Petah Tikva mitmodedet ʿim ʿavarah" [Books and anniversaries: Petah Tikva deals with its past]. In *Le-Fetah Tikva* [For Petah Tikva], 10–50. Petah Tikva: Oded Yarkoni Petach Tikva Archive, 2012.

Laskov, Shulamit. *ha-Biluyim.* Jerusalem: ha-Sifriyah ha-Tziyonit ʿal yad ha-Histadrut ha-Tziyonit ha-ʿolamit, 1979.

Lehmann, Matthias. "Baron Hirsch, the Jewish Colonization Association and the Future of the Jews." *Jewish Studies Quarterly (JSQ)* 27, no. 1 (2020): 73–102. https://doi.org/10.1628/jsq-2020-0006.

Leket-Mor, Rachel. "Israpulp: The Israeli Popular Literature Collection at Arizona State University." *Judaica Librarianship*, no. 16–17 (2011): 1–53.

Leonard, Devin, and Yaacov Benmeleh. "How SodaStream Makes—and Markets—Peace." *Bloomberg Businessweek,* December 20, 2017. https://www.bloomberg.com/news/features/2017-12-20/how-sodastream-makes-and-markets-peace.

Lepore, Jill. *The Whites of Their Eyes: The Tea Party's Revolution and the Battle over American History.* Public Square (Princeton, NJ). Princeton: Princeton University Press, 2010.

Lesch, Ann Mosely. *Arab Politics in Palestine, 1917–1939: The Frustration of a Nationalist Movement.* Ithaca, NY: Cornell University Press, 1979.

Lesch, Ann Mosely. "Israeli Settlements in the Occupied Territories, 1967–1977." *Journal of Palestine Studies* 7, no. 1 (1977): 26–47. https://doi.org/10.1525/jps.1977.7.1.00p00037.

Levi, Giovanni. "On Microhistory." In *New Perspectives on Historical Writing*, edited by Peter Burke, 97–119. University Park: Pennsylvania State University Press, 1992.

LeVine, Mark. *Overthrowing Geography: Jaffa, Tel Aviv, and the Struggle for Palestine, 1880–1948.* Berkeley: University of California Press, 2005.

Levin-Epstein, Eliyahu Zeev. *Zikhronotai* [My memoirs]. Tel Aviv: Levin-Epstein Brothers and Co., 1932.

Levontin, Zalman David. "ha-Hityashvut be-Eretz Yisraʾel: emtzaʿeha ve-shitoteha" [Settlement in the Land of Israel: means and methods] [1924]. Republished in *Mida,* January 17, 2014. https://bit.ly/2Gc78rP.

Lewis, Anthony. "Israel's Bitter West Bank Harvest." *The New York Times*. July 22, 1984, A32.

Liebes, Tamar. "Acoustic Space: The Role of Radio in Israeli Collective History." *Jewish History* 20 (2006): 69–90.

Lissak, Moshe. *ha-Elitot shel ha-yishuv ha-Yehudi be-Eretz-Yisra'el bi-tekufat ha-Mandat: reka' hevrati u-defuse karyerah* [Jewish elites in the Land of Israel during the mandate period: social background and career patterns]. Tel-Aviv: 'Am 'oved, 1981.

Livak, Leonid. *The Jewish Persona in the European Imagination: A Case of Russian Literature*. Stanford: Stanford University Press, 2010.

Lockman, Zachary. *Comrades and Enemies: Arab and Jewish Workers in Palestine, 1906–1948*. Berkeley: University of California Press, 1996.

Low, D. A. *Eclipse of Empire*. Cambridge, UK: Cambridge University Press, 1991.

Maidhof, Callie. "A House, a Yard, and a Security Fence: Israel's Secular Settlers in the West Bank." PhD diss., University of California, Berkeley, 2016.

Maidhof, Callie. "Settlement Secularism." *Middle East Report*, no. 269 (2013): 30–34.

Mar, Tracey Banivanua. "Carving Wilderness: Queensland's National Parks and the Unsettling of Emptied Lands, 1890–1910." In *Making Settler Colonial Space: Perspectives on Race, Place, and Identity*, edited by Tracey Banivanua Mar and Penelope Edmonds, 73–94. Basingstoke: Palgrave Macmillan, 2010.

Matsuda, Matt K. *The Memory of the Modern*. New York: Oxford University Press, 1996.

Matthäus, Jürgen. *Approaching an Auschwitz Survivor: Holocaust Testimony and Its Transformations*. New York: Oxford University Press, 2009.

McNutt, Paula M. *Reconstructing the Society of Ancient Israel*. Library of Ancient Israel. Louisville, KY: Westminster John Knox Press, 1999.

Meirovitch, Menashe. *Minhat 'erev: zikhronot, mikhtavim, u-te'udot le-toledot Hibat Zion veha-Tziyonut, ma'amarim u-reshimot be-she'elot kalkaliyot ve-tarbutiyot shel ha-Yishuv* [Evening offering: memories, letters, and documents on the history of Zionism, articles and columns on the Yishuv's economic and cultural questions], edited by Hillel Isser Yanovsky. Rishon LeZion: Hotza'at yedidim ve-haverim, 1941.

Meiton, Fredrik. *Electrical Palestine—Capital and Technology from Empire to Nation*. Berkeley: University of California Press, 2019.

Melman, Billie. "Motah shel sokhenet: migdar, zikaron, ve-hantzahah." In *ha-'Ivriyot ha-hadashot: nashim ba-Yishuv uva-Tsiyonut ba-re'i ha-migdar*, edited by Margalit Shilo, Ruth Kark, and Galit Hasan-Rokem. Jerusalem: Yad Yitzhak Ben-Zvi, 2001.

Mendilow, Jonathan. *Ideology, Party Change, and Electoral Campaigns in Israel, 1965–2001*. SUNY Series in Israeli Studies. Albany: State University of New York Press, 2003.

Mikhail, Alan. *The Animal in Ottoman Egypt*. Oxford: Oxford University Press, 2014.
Mirsky, Yehudah. *Rav Kook: Mystic in a Time of Revolution*. New Haven: Yale University Press, 2014.
Morris, Benny. *The Birth of the Palestinian Refugee Problem, 1947–1949*. Cambridge Middle East Library. Cambridge, UK: Cambridge University Press, 1987.
Morris, Benny. *Israel's Border Wars, 1949–1956: Arab Infiltration, Israeli Retaliation, and the Countdown to the Suez War*. Oxford: Clarendon Press, 1993.
Morris, Wesley. "Why Do the Oscars Keep Falling for Racial Reconciliation Fantasies?" *New York Times*, January, 23, 2019, AR1 (print title "Friendship or Fantasy?"). https://nyti.ms/2AXKTAE.
Morton-Jerome, Ethan William. "Palestinian Labor in West Bank Settlements." PhD diss., University of Arkansas, 2018.
Moss, Kenneth B. *Jewish Renaissance in the Russian Revolution*. Cambridge, MA: Harvard University Press, 2009.
Moss, Mark Howard. *The Media and Models of Masculinity*. Lanham: Lexington Books, 2012.
Myers, David N. *Between Jew & Arab: The Lost Voice of Simon Rawidowicz*. Tauber Institute for the Study of European Jewry Series (Unnumbered). Waltham, MA: Brandeis University Press, 2008.
Nadan, Amos. *The Palestinian Peasant Economy Under the Mandate: A Story of Colonial Bungling*. Cambridge, MA: Harvard Center for Middle Eastern Studies / Harvard University Press, 2006.
Nadasen, Premilla. *Household Workers Unite: The Untold Story of African American Women Who Built a Movement*. Boston: Beacon Press, 2015.
Nelles, H. V. *The Art of Nation-Building: Pageantry and Spectacle at Québec's Tercentenary*. Toronto: University of Toronto Press, 2015.
Nets-Zehngut, Rafi. "Israel's Publications Agency and the 1948 Palestinian Refugees." In *The War of 1948: Representations of Israeli and Palestinian Memories and Narratives*, edited by Avraham Sela and Alon Kadish, 51–74. Israel Studies Book. Bloomington: Indiana University Press, 2016.
Neumann, Boaz. *Land and Desire in Early Zionism*. The Schusterman Series in Israel Studies. Waltham, MA: Brandeis University Press, 2011.
Neumann, Emanuel. "General Zionism as the Major Unifying Force in the Zionist Movement." Excerpts from the keynote address delivered at the opening session of the World Conference of General Zionists, Tel Aviv, December 26, 1964. New York: World Union of General Zionists, 1964.
"New American Economic Committee for Palestine Formed: Immediate Task of Stimulating Palestine Investment." *Jewish Telegraphic Agency*, June 9, 1932. https://www.jta.org/1932/06/09/archive/new-american-economic-committee-for-palestine-formed-immediate-task-of-stimulating-palestine-invest.

Niv, David. *Rosh Pinna bat me'ah (5642–5742)* [Rosh Pinna at 100, 1882–1982]. Rosh Pinna: ha-Moʿatzah ha-mekomit Rosh Pinah be-siyuaʿ ha-Agudah le-shihzur moshevet ha-rishonim [Rosh Pinna Local Council with the Support of the Association for the Restoration of the Colony of the First Ones], 1983.

Nora, Pierre. "Between Memory and History: Les Lieux de Mémoire." *Representations* 26, Special Issue on Memory and Counter-Memory (Spring 1989): 7–24.

Norris, Jacob. *Land of Progress: Palestine in the Age of Colonial Development, 1905–1948*. Oxford: Oxford University Press, 2013.

O'Brien, Jean M. *Firsting and Lasting: Writing Indians out of Existence in New England*. Indigenous Americas. Minneapolis: University of Minnesota Press, 2010.

Oppenheimer, Yochai. *Me-ʿever la-gader: yitzug ha-ʿAravim ba-siporet ha-ʿIvrit veha-Yisreʾelit (1906–2005)* [Barriers: the representation of the Arab in Hebrew and Israeli fiction, 1906–2005]. Ashkelon: ʿAm oved, Sapir Academic College, 2008.

Oren, Barukh. *ʿAlilot rishonim* [Tales of the First Ones]. Sifriyat Dan haskhan. Tel Aviv: ʿAm ʿoved, 1964.

Oring, Elliott. *Israeli Humor: The Content and Structure of the Chizbat of the Palmah*. SUNY Series in Modern Jewish Literature and Culture. Albany: State University of New York Press, 1981.

"Palestine Blue Book." British Mandatory Government, Print and Stationery Office, 1932.

Pappé, Ilan. *A History of Modern Palestine: One Land, Two Peoples*. 2nd ed. Cambridge, UK: Cambridge University Press, 2006.

Paris, Leslie. *Children's Nature: The Rise of the American Summer Camp*. New York: New York University Press, 2010.

Peleg, Yaron. *Orientalism and the Hebrew Imagination*. Ithaca, NY: Cornell University Press, 2005.

Penslar, Derek Jonathan. "Declarations of (In)dependence: Tensions within Zionist Statecraft. 1896–1948." *Journal of Levantine Studies* 8, no. 1 (2018): 13–34.

Penslar, Derek Jonathan. *Israel in History: The Jewish State in Comparative Perspective*. New York: Routledge, 2006.

Penslar, Derek Jonathan. "Radio and the Shaping of Modern Israel." In *Nationalism, Zionism and Ethnic Mobilization of the Jews in 1900 and Beyond*, edited by Michael Berkowitz, 61–82. IJS Studies in Judaica 2. Leiden: Brill, 2004.

Penslar, Derek Jonathan. *Shylock's Children: Economics and Jewish Identity in Modern Europe*. S. Mark Taper Foundation Imprint in Jewish Studies. Berkeley: University of California Press, 2001.

Penslar, Derek Jonathan. *Zionism and Technocracy: The Engineering of Jewish Settlement in Palestine, 1870–1918*. Bloomington: Indiana University Press, 1991.

Philips, Deborah. *Fairground Attractions: A Genealogy of the Pleasure Ground*. London: Bloomsbury Academic, 2012.

Pianko, Noam. *Zionism and the Roads Not Taken: Rawidowicz, Kaplan, Kohn.* The Modern Jewish Experience. Bloomington: Indiana University Press, 2010.

Pinsker, Leo. *Auto-Emancipation*, translated by D. S. Blondheim. New York: The Maccabaean Publishing Company, 1906.

Piterberg, Gabriel. *The Returns of Zionism: Myths, Politics and Scholarship in Israel.* London: Verso, 2008.

Portugali, Juval. *Implicate Relations: Society and Space in the Israeli-Palestinian Conflict.* Springer Science & Business Media, 2013.

Postman, Neil. *The Disappearance of Childhood.* New York: Vintage Books, 1994.

Raab, Yehuda. *ha-Telem ha-rishon: zikhronot ish Petah-Tikva, 1864–1930* [The First furrow: memoirs of a man of Petah Tikva, 1864–1930]. Tel Aviv: ha-Sifriyah ha-Tziyonit, 1956.

Rabin, Yitzhak. "Alfei kevarim: shelanu ve-shelahem" [Thousands of graves: ours and theirs]. Speech delivered at the signing of the Cairo agreement between Israel and the PLO, May 4, 1994. In Yitzhak Rabin. *Rodef shalom: neʾumei ha-shalom shel rosh ha-memshalah Yitzhak Rabin* [Pursuer of peace: the peace-related speeches of Prime Minister Yitzhak Rabin], 26–28. Tel Aviv: Zmora-Bitan, 1995.

Raz-Krakotzkin, Amnon. "A National Colonial Theology: Religion, Orientalism and the Construction of the Secular in Zionist Discourse." *Tel Aviver Jahrbuch Für Deutsche Geschichte* 30 (2002): 312–26.

Reicher, Mordecai. *60 shanah le-hakhrazat ha-herem ʿal poʿale Petah Tikva: Hanukkah 1905/6-Hanukkah 1965/6* [Sixty years since the boycott of Petah Tikva workers]. Petach Tikva: Beit Neta; Merkaz le-toldot kibush ha-ʿavodah ve-yedaʿ histadruti mi-yesodam shel ha-merkaz ha-haklaʾi u-moʿetzet poʿale Petah Tikva, 1965.

Rifkin, Mark. "The Frontier as (Movable) Space of Exception." *Settler Colonial Studies* 4, no. 2 (2014): 176–80.

Robinson, Shira. *Citizen Strangers: Palestinians and the Birth of Israel's Liberal Settler State.* Stanford Studies in Middle Eastern and Islamic Societies and Cultures. Stanford: Stanford University Press, 2013.

Robinson, Shira. "Local Struggle, National Struggle: Palestinian Responses to the Kafr Qasim Massacre and Its Aftermath, 1956–66." *International Journal of Middle East Studies* 35, no. 3 (August 1, 2003): 393–416.

Robson, Laura. *States of Separation: Transfer, Partition, and the Making of the Modern Middle East.* Oakland: University of California Press, 2017.

Roi, Yaacov. "Yahase Rehovot ʿim shekheneha ha-ʿArvim (1890–1914)" [Rehovot's relations with its Arab neighbors (1890–1914)]. *ha-Tziyonut* 1 (1970), 150–203.

Roi, Yaacov. "Yahase Yehudim-ʿArvim be-moshvot ha-ʿAliyah ha-Rishonah." In *Sefer ha-ʿAliyah ha-Rishonah*, edited by Mordechai Eliav, Yemima Rosenthal, and Chaya Har-El, 245–68. Jerusalem: Yad Izhak Ben-Zvi, 1982.

Ross, Kristin. *May '68 and Its Afterlives*. Chicago: University of Chicago Press, 2002.
Rovner, Adam. *In the Shadow of Zion: Promised Lands Before Israel*. New York: New York University Press, 2014.
Rozin, Orit. *A Home for All Jews: Citizenship, Rights, and National Identity in the New Israeli State*. Schusterman Series in Israel Studies. Waltham, MA: Brandeis University Press, 2016.
Rozin, Orit. *The Rise of the Individual in 1950s Israel: A Challenge to Collectivism*. Brandeis University Press, 2011.
Rubenstein, Sara. "Soda Stream to Open Factory in Gaza." *Jerusalem Post*, December 20, 2018. https://www.jpost.com/Israel-News/Sodastream-will-open-factory-in-Gaza-says-CEO-at-Globes-Conference-574925.
Rubin, Avi. "British Perceptions of Ottoman Judicial Reform in the Late Nineteenth Century: Some Preliminary Insights." *Law & Social Inquiry* 37, no. 4 (October 1, 2012): 991–1012.
Rubin, Avi. "Falastin bi-shenot ha-milhamah be-ʿenei shenei nosʿim Othmanim" [Palestine during the war in the eyes of two Ottoman travelers]. *Zmanim*, no. 126 (2014): 16–27.
Ruppin, Arthur. *Three Decades of Palestine: Speeches and Papers on the Upbuilding of the Jewish National Home*. Jerusalem: Schocken, 1936.
Ruppin, Arthur. *Zionistische Kolonisationspolitik, Bericht an den XI. Zionistenkongress*. Berlin: Jüdischer Verlag, 1914.
Samsonov, Aryeh. *Zichron Yaʿaqov: parashat divre yameha 5642–5702*. Zikhron Yaʿaqov: Zichron Yaʿaqov Colony Committee, 1943.
Saposnik, Arieh Bruce. *Becoming Hebrew: The Creation of a Jewish National Culture in Ottoman Palestine*. New York: Oxford University Press, 2008.
Saposnik, Arieh Bruce. "Exorcising the 'Angel of National Death'—National and Individual Death (and Rebirth) in Zionist Palestine." *Jewish Quarterly Review* 95, no. 3 (2005): 557–78.
Sauvage, Camille, dir. "ha-Lord Balfour be-Petah Tikva, 1925" [Lord Balfour in Petah Tikva], edited by Yaakov Gross. https://youtu.be/GwlVuH4TEkk. Accessed August 7, 2020.
Schama, Simon. *Two Rothschilds and the Land of Israel*. London: Collins, 1978.
Scheindlin, Dahlia. "Israeli President's Apology Offers a Rare Hope for Coexistence." *+972 Magazine,* October 27, 2014. https://www.972mag.com/president-commemorates-massacre-calls-for-equality-in-israel/.
Segev, Zohar. "Between Jerusalem and Tel Aviv: The Place of Jerusalem in the 'Weltanschauung' of Three American Zionist Leaders." *Israel Studies Forum* 22, no. 2 (2007): 28–52.
Schwartz, Regina M. *The Curse of Cain: The Violent Legacy of Monotheism*. Chicago: University of Chicago Press, 1997.

Schweitzer, Ivy. "Making Equals: Classical Philia and Women's Friendship." *Feminist Studies* 42, no. 2 (2016): 337–64.

Seikaly, Samir. "Christian Contributions to the Nahda in Palestine Prior to World War I." *Bulletin of the Royal Institute for Inter-Faith Studies* 2, no. 2 (Autumn 2000): 49–61.

Seikaly, Sherene. *Men of Capital: Scarcity and Economy in Mandate Palestine.* Stanford: Stanford University Press, 2016.

Seltenreich, Yair. *ha-Anashim mi-kan: Tziyonut, hityashvut u-vinyan ha-aretz* [The people from here: Zionism, settlement, and building the land]. Jerusalem: Yad Yitzhak Ben-Zvi, 2014.

Seltenreich, Yair. "Gavriyut, kavod, ve-guf be-moshvot PICA ba-Galil be-tekufat ha-yishuv" [Masculinity, honor, and body in the PICA colonies in the Galilee during the Yishuv period]. *Sotziyologyah Yisre'elit* 11, no. 1 (2009): 137–57.

Seltenreich, Yair. "Jewish or Arab Hired Workers? Inner Tensions in a Jewish Settlement in Prestate Israel." *International Review of Social History* 49, no. 2 (2004): 225–47.

Seltenreich, Yair. "Mifgashe tarbuyot? moshvot ha-Galil ha-Tahton be-'ene pekide JCA u-PICA" [Meeting of cultures? The colonies of the Lower Galilee in the eyes of JCA and PICA administrators]. *Cathedra*, no. 120 (2006): 107–34.

Shafir, Gershon. "Capitalist Binationalism in Mandatory Palestine." *International Journal of Middle East Studies* 43, no. 4 (2011): 611–33.

Shafir, Gershon. *Land, Labor and the Origins of the Israeli-Palestinian Conflict 1882–1914.* Berkeley: University of California Press, 1996.

Shafir, Gershon. "Revolutionary Pioneer: Manya Shochat and Her Commune." In *Struggle and Survival in Palestine/Israel,* edited by Mark LeVine and Gershon Shafir, 63–76. Berkeley: University of California Press, 2021.

Shafir, Gershon. "Zionism and Colonialism: A Comparative Approach." In *The Israel/Palestine Question: A Reader,* edited by Ilan Pappé, 78–93. 2nd ed. London: Routledge, 2007.

Shamir, Ronen. "Burganut Yehudit be-Palestinah ha-koloniyalit: kavei meta'er le-seder yom mehkari [Jewish bourgeoisie in colonial Palestine: outline for a research agenda]." *Israeli Sociology* 3, no. 1 (2000): 133–48.

Shamir, Ronen. *Current Flow: The Electrification of Palestine.* Stanford: Stanford University Press, 2013.

Shanes, Joshua. *Diaspora Nationalism and Jewish Identity in Habsburg Galicia.* New York: Cambridge University Press, 2012.

Shapira, Anita. *Herev ha-yonah: ha-Tziyonut veha-koah 1881–1948.* Tel Aviv: 'Am 'oved, 1992.

Shapira, Anita. *Israel: A History.* Waltham, MA: Brandeis University Press, 2012.

Shapira, Anita. *Land and Power: The Zionist Resort to Force, 1881–1948.* Stanford Studies in Jewish History and Culture. Stanford: Stanford University Press, 1999.

Shapira, Anita. *ha-Ma'avak ha-nikhzav: 'avodah 'Ivrit 1929–1939* [The disappointing struggle: Hebrew labor 1929–1939]. Tel Aviv: Tel Aviv University; ha-Kibbutz ha-me'uhad, 1977.
Shapira, Anita. "Politics and Collective Memory: The Debate over the New Historians in Israel." *History and Memory* 7, no. 1 (1995): 9–40.
Shapira, Anita. "Religious Motifs of the Labor Movement." In *Zionism and Religion*, 251–72. Hanover, NH: University Press of New England, 1998.
Shapira, Anita. *Yehudim hadashim, yehudim yeshanim* [New Jews, old Jews]. Tel Aviv: 'Am 'oved, 1997.
Shavit, Zohar, and Jacob Shavit. "Le-toldot sipur ha-pesha' ha-'Ivri be-Eretz Yisra'el" [The history of the Hebrew crime story in the Land of Israel]. *ha-Sifrut* 18–19 (1974): 30–45.
Shilo, Margalit. *Etgar ha-migdar: nashim ba-'Aliyot ha-rishonot* [The challenge of gender: women in the first Aliyot]. Tel Aviv: ha-Kibbutz ha-me'uhad, 2007.
Shilo, Margalit, Ruth Kark, and Galit Hasan-Rokem, eds. *ha-'Ivriyot ha-hadashot: nashim ba-Yishuv uva-Tziyonut ba-re'i ha-migdar* [The new Hebrew women: Women in the Yishuv and Zionism through the prism of gender]. Jerusalem: Yad Yitzhak Ben-Zvi, 2001.
Shiloah, Neomi. *Merkaz holekh ve-ne'elam: ha-hugim ha-ezrahiyim be-Eretz Yisra'el bi-shenot ha-sheloshim* [A disappearing center: Citizens Circles in the Land of Israel in the 1930s]. Jerusalem: Yad Yitzhak Ben-Zvi, 2003.
Shimoni, David. "Yovel ha-eglonim" [Jubilee of the wagon drivers]. In Benjamin Harshav, *Shirat ha-tehiyah ha-'Ivrit: antologyah historit-bikortit* [Poetry of the Hebrew revival: a critical historical anthology]. Tel-Aviv: Open University, 2000, 353.
Shochat-Vilbushevitz, Manya. "ha-Shemirah ba-aretz" [Guarding in the Land]. In *Kovetz ha-Shomer: Te'udot, zichronot ve-divre ha'arakhah* [The "ha-Shomer" Collection: Documents, Memories, and Appreciations]. Tel Aviv: Arkhiyon ha-'Avodah, 1937–38, 51–56.
Shoham, Hizky. *Carnival in Tel Aviv: Purim and the Celebration of Urban Zionism*. Israel: Society, Culture, and History. Boston: Academic Studies Press, 2014.
Shoham, Hizky. "Meha-'Aliyah ha-Shelishit la-'Aliyah ha-Sheniyah uva-hazarah: hivatzrut ha-halukah le-tekufot lefi ha-'aliyot ha-memusparot" [From the Third Aliyah to the Second Aliyah and back: the creation of the periodization according to numbered aliyot]. *Tziyon* 77, no. 2 (2012): 189–222.
Shoham, Hizky. "Tel-Aviv's Foundation Myth: A Constructive Perspective." In *Tel Aviv, the First Century: Visions, Designs, Actualities*, edited by Maoz Azaryahu and S. Ilan Troen, 34–59. Bloomington: Indiana University Press, 2012.
Shumsky, Dimitry. *Beyond the Nation-State: The Zionist Political Imagination from Pinsker to Ben-Gurion*. New Haven: Yale University Press, 2018.

Siegman, Jeremy. "Enemies in the Aisles: The Politics of Market Encounters on Israel's Settler Frontier." PhD diss., University of Chicago, 2018.

Siegman, Jeremy. "'Super-Israel': The Politics of Palestinian Labor in a Settler Supermarket." *Journal of Palestine Studies* 47, no. 4 (2018): 9–29.

Slotkin, Richard. *Regeneration through Violence: The Mythology of the American Frontier, 1600–1860.* Middletown, CT: Wesleyan University Press, 1973.

Smilansky, David. '*Im bnei artzi ve-'iri* [With the people of my country and city]. Tel Aviv: Masada, 1958.

Smilansky, Moshe. *Bnei 'Arav: sipurim* [The Arab people: stories]. Tel Aviv: Devir, 1964.

Smilansky, Moshe. "Meratzhim" [Murderers]. In *Havlagah o teguvah: ha-vikuah ba-yishuv ha-Yehudi, 1936–1939* [Restraint or response: the debate in the Jewish Yishuv, 1936–1939], edited by Jacob Shavit, 150–56. Ramat Gan: Bar Ilan University Press, [1939]-1983.

Smilansky, Moshe. *Perakim be-toldot ha-Yishuv* [Chapters in the history of the Yishuv]. Tel Aviv: Devir, 1943.

Smilansky, Moshe. *Rehovot: shishim shenot hayehah 650–710* [Rehovot: sixty years of life, 1890–1950]. Rehovot: Rehovot Local Council, 1950.

Solomonovich, Nadav, and Ruth Kark. "Land Privatization in Nineteenth-Century Ottoman Palestine." *Islamic Law and Society* 22, no. 3 (2015): 221–52.

Sorek, Tamir. *Palestinian Commemoration in Israel: Calendars, Monuments, and Martyrs.* Palo Alto: Stanford University Press, 2015.

Spurgeon, Sara L. *Exploding the Western: Myths of Empire on the Postmodern Frontier.* College Station: Texas A&M University Press, 2005.

Stanton, Andrea L. *This Is Jerusalem Calling: State Radio in Mandate Palestine.* Austin: University of Texas Press, 2013.

State of Israel. *Shenaton ha-memshalah* [Government yearbook], 1954–55. Jerusalem: Government Printer, 1955.

Stein, Rebecca L. "Travelling Zion: Hiking and Settler-Nationalism in Pre-1948 Palestine." *Interventions* 11, no. 3 (November 2009): 334–51.

Sternhell, Zeev. *The Founding Myths of Israel.* Princeton: Princeton University Press, 1998.

Tadmor-Shimony, Tali. "Shaping Landscape Identity in Jewish State Education during the 1950s to 1960s." *Paedagogica Historica* 49, no. 2 (April 1, 2013): 236–52.

Taharlev, Yoram. "ha-Baladah 'al Yoel Moshe Solomon u-shloshet re'av" [The ballad about Yoel Moshe Solomon and his three friends]. Music by Shalom Hanoch. Performed by Arik Einstein. In *Ein kevar derekh hazarah: shirim ve-sipurim 'al Yisra'el* [There's no way back: songs and stories about Israel], 10. Tel Aviv: Israel Ministry of Defense, 2004.

Tamari, Salim. "Normalcy and Violence: The Yearning for the Ordinary in Discourse

of the Palestinian-Israeli Conflict." *Journal of Palestine Studies* 42, no. 4 (2013): 48–60.
Tidhar, David. *Be-sherut ha-moledet (1912–1960): zikhronot, demuyot, te'udot u-temunot* [In service of the homeland (1912–1960): memories, images, documents, and pictures]. Tel Aviv: Hotza'at yedidim, 1961.
Tidhar, David. *Din ve-heshbon 'al hotza' at zikhronot Avraham Shapira bi-shenei kerakhim: 15 August 1938–10 Yuli 1939* [Report on the publication of Avraham Shapira's memoirs in two volumes: August 15, 1938–July 10, 1939]. Tel Aviv: H. Tzipkin, 1939.
Tidhar, David. *Entziklopedyah le-halutze ha-Yishuv u-vonav: demuyot u-temunot* [Encyclopedia of the pioneers and buildings of the Yishuv: personalities and photos]. Tel Aviv: Sifriyat Rishonim, 1947.
Troen, S. Ilan. *Imagining Zion: Dreams, Designs, and Realities in a Century of Jewish Settlement*. New Haven: Yale University Press, 2003.
Trofe, Eliezer. *Reshit: li-melot 70 shanah le-Fetah Tikva (638–708)* [Beginning: on Petah Tikva's 70th anniversary (1878–1948)]. Petah Tikva: Petah Tikva Municipality, 1948.
Trouillot, Michel-Rolph. *Silencing the Past: Power and the Production of History*. Boston: Beacon Press, 1995.
Turner, Frederick Jackson. "The Significance of the Frontier in American History (1893)." In John Mack Faragher. *Rereading Frederick Jackson Turner*, 31–60. New Haven: Yale University Press, 1994.
Turner, Victor W. *The Ritual Process: Structure and Anti-Structure*. Transaction Publishers, 2011.
Tzahor, Zeev. "ha-Mifgash ben ha-ikarim le-fo'ale ha-'Aliyah ha-Sheniyah be-Petah Tikva." [The meeting between the farmers and the workers of the Second Aliyah]. *Cathedra* 10 (January 1979): 142–50.
Tzur, Muky. *Le-lo ketonet passim* [Without a coat of many colors]. Tel Aviv: 'Am 'oved, 1976.
Vadasaria, Shaira. "Necronationalism: Managing Race, Death and the Nation's Skeletons." *Social Identities*, 20150603, 1–15.
Van Slyck, Abigail Ayres. *A Manufactured Wilderness: Summer Camps and the Shaping of American Youth, 1890–1960*. University of Minnesota Press, 2006.
Veracini, Lorenzo. "The Imagined Geographies of Settler Colonialism." In *Making Settler Colonial Space: Perspectives on Race, Place and Identity*, edited by Tracey Banivanua-Mar and Penelope Edmonds, 179–97. Basingstoke: Palgrave Macmillan, 2010.
Veracini, Lorenzo. "Settler Colonial Expeditions." In *Expedition into Empire*, edited by Martin Thomas, 51–64. New York and London: Routledge, 2014.
Veracini, Lorenzo. "Suburbia, Settler Colonialism and the World Turned Inside Out." *Housing, Theory and Society* 29, no. 4 (2012): 339–57.

Weizman, Eyal. *Hollow Land: Israel's Architecture of Occupation.* London: Verso, 2007.
Winder, Alex. "Anticolonial Uprising and Communal Justice in Twentieth-Century Palestine." *Radical History Review* 2020, no. 137 (May 1, 2020): 75–95.
Winder, Alex. "Policing and Crime in Mandate Palestine: Indigenous Policemen, British Colonial Control, and Palestinian Society, 1920–1948." PhD diss., New York University, 2017.
Winter, Jay M. "War, Memory, and Mourning in the Twentieth Century: Notes on the Memory Boom." In *The Merits of Memory: Concepts, Contexts, Debates*, edited by Hans-Jürgen Grabbe and Sabine Schindler, 97–118. American Studies (Munich, Germany). Vol. 143. Heidelberg: Winter, 2008.
Wolfe, Patrick. "Purchase by Other Means: The Palestine Nakba and Zionism's Conquest of Economics." *Settler Colonial Studies* 2, no. 1 (2012): 133–71.
Wolfe, Patrick. *Settler Colonialism and the Transformation of Anthropology: The Politics and Poetics of an Ethnographic Event.* London: Cassell, 1999.
Yaniv, Shlomo. *ha-Balada ha-ʿIvrit bat-zemanenu: masoret ve-hidush* [The contemporary Hebrew ballad: tradition and innovation]. Haifa: Haifa University Press, 1999.
Yavneʾeli, Shmuel. *Sefer ha-Tziyonut: tekufat Hibat-Tziyon, mekorot u-teʿudot, be-tosefet mevoʾot, heʿarot, beʾurim u-temunot* [Book of Zionism: the period of Hibat-Zion, sources and documents, with the addition of introductions, comments, explanations, and pictures]. 2nd ed. Jerusalem: Mosad Bialik, 1961.
Yehoash. *Fun Nyu-York biz Rehovot un tsurik* [From New York to Rehovot and back]. Vol. 1. Nyu-York: Farlag oyfgang, 1917.
Yehoshua, Abraham B. *Mul ha-yeʿarot: sipurim* [Facing the forests: stories]. Tel Aviv: ha-Kibbutz ha-meʾuhad, 1968.
Yellin, David. *Yerushalayim shel temol* [Jerusalem of yesterday]. Vol. 1. Kitve David Yellin; Jerusalem: Committee to publish the works of David Yellin, Hotzaʾat R. Mas, 1972.
Yerushalmi, Yosef Hayim. *Zakhor: Jewish History and Jewish Memory.* Samuel and Althea Stroum Lectures in Jewish Studies. Seattle: University of Washington Press, 1996.
"Yeshivah hagigit shel ha-knesset le-tziyun Shenat Rishonim" [Festive meeting of the Knesset to mark the Year of the First Ones]. *Divre ha-Knesset* 35 (December 7, 1962).
Yisreeli, Oded, and Yoskeh Grinboym. "Khawaja Skandar: ish ha-barzel" [Mr. Skandar: man of iron]. *Eretz ve-teva*, no. 116 (August 2008): 32–35.
Yizhar, S. [Yizhar Smilansky]. "About Uncles and Arabs," translated by Steven Bowman. *Hebrew Studies* 47 (January 1, 2006): 321–27. Hebrew original published in 1993.
Yizrael, Rami. "Le-vikoret ha-historiyografyah shel shenotehah ha-rishonot shel

Petah Tikva" [To critique the historiography of the first years of Petah Tivka]. *Cathedra* 9 (October 1978): 95–126.

Zahra, Tara. *The Great Departure: Mass Migration from Eastern Europe and the Making of the Free World*. New York: W. W. Norton & Company, 2016.

Zahra, Tara. "Zionism, Emigration, and East European Colonialism." In *Colonialism and the Jews*, edited by Maud S. Mandel, Lisa Moses Leff, and Ethan B. Katz. Indiana University Press, 2017. 166–92.

Zemach, Shlomo. *Sipur ḥayai* [Story of my life]. Jerusalem: Devir, 1983.

Zerubavel, Yael. *Desert in the Promised Land*. Stanford: Stanford University Press, 2018.

Zerubavel, Yael. "The Historic, the Legendary, and the Incredible: Invented Tradition and Collective Memory in Israel." In *Commemorations: The Politics of National Identity*, edited by John R. Gillis, 105–23. Princeton: Princeton University Press, 1994.

Zerubavel, Yael. "Memory, the Rebirth of the Native, and the 'Hebrew Bedouin' Identity." *Social Research* 75, no. 1 (2008): 315–52.

Zerubavel, Yael. "Putting Numbers into Space: Place Names, Collective Remembrance, and Forgetting in Israeli Culture." In *Taking Stock: Cultures of Enumeration in Contemporary Jewish Life*, edited by Michal Kravel-Tovi and Deborah Dash-Moore, 69–92. Bloomington: Indiana University Press, 2016.

Zerubavel, Yael. *Recovered Roots: Collective Memory and the Making of Israeli National Tradition*. Chicago: University of Chicago Press, 1995.

Zimmerman, Jonathan. *Whose America? Culture Wars in the Public Schools*. Cambridge, MA: Harvard University Press, 2002.

Ziv-Av, Yitzhak. *Shelanu ʿad olam* [Ours forever]. 2nd ed. Tel Aviv: Omanut ve-sefer, 1956. [Original publication, 1948.]

INDEX

Page references followed by *fig* indicate illustrated figures including photographs.

Aaronsohn, Aaron, 20, 53, 88–90, 91, 213, 217
Aaronsohn, Alexander, 50, 51, 88
Aaronsohn family, 34, 50, 53, 213, 215–17
al-Abbasiyya (was al-Yahudiyya) [later Yehud], 82, 173–74, 179, 191
Abu al-Fadl (al-Satariyya), 179–81
Abu Farid, Nasser Ghanem, 89–91, 102
"Abu Ibrahim" (Meirovitch's pseudonym), 99–100
Abu Kishk, Shaker, 166, 186
Abu Yusuf, Da'ud, 8, 97, 99
Agricultural Union (*ha-Histadrut ha-hakla'it*), 197
Agudat Yisrael party, 231
Ahad Ha-'Am (Asher Ginzburg), 40, 74, 221–22
Ahdut ha-'avodah party, 199
Ahimeir, Abba, 226–28, 229
aliyah (ascent), 17, 24
Alliance Israélite Universelle, 44
Allon, Yigal, 169
American Jews: investment in Zionist project by, 63; "Year of the First Ones" medal's appeal to, 222. *See also* Jewish population
Amishav transit camp, 191
Anglo-Palestine Bank, 19, 217
Apfelbaum, Meir, 103
apoliticism. *See* politics of apoliticism
Arab Awakening (Nahda), 7
Arab boycott (1936), 84–85
Arab Israelis. *See* Palestinian citizens of Israel
Arab labor: citrus industry employment of, 13, 41, 72–75, 77–78; Labor Zionists and, 4, 39, 40–53, 72–85; landless Muslim Arabs hired as, 10; lower wages paid to, 77; Meirovitch on mutual benefit of hiring, 80; private farming driven by, 26; role in evolution of modern hierarchical coexistence, 245–50; "stain of Boaz" on private farmers over, 221–22; workers in Rehovot citrus groves (1890), 73*fig*. *See also* Jewish workers; labor
Arab Palestinians: appeals made to Ottoman sultan by, 10;

celebrating Avraham Shapira's birthday (1940), 67–68*fig*; evoking memories of settlers' good relations with, 151; evolution of modern hierarchical coexistence with, 245–50; migrants from Mount Lebanon, 90; personal friendships between Jews and, 85–91; resistance to "First Aliyah" settlers by, 4; *sumud* practice of dedication to the land, 120. *See also* hierarchical coexistence; Palestine

Arab-perpetrated violence: Avraham Yalovsky murder, 108–9; fear of in light on Jews' historical experiences with violence, 29; Fishel Ferber murder, 171–73; in Kafr Saba (1910), 75; moshava commemoration of casualties of, 105–13; Nebi Musa riots (1921), 201; Shalom Yaakov Rosenzweig murder, 110–12, 129, 159; Stahl/Zohar murders, 129, 130, 132–41; student essays on Rehovot's seventieth anniversary mentioning, 176–77; al-Yahudiyya's attack (1886) against Petah Tikva, 160, 174–76. *See also* settlement guards

"Arab Question": Revisionist platform (1920s) on the, 71–72; Zionists' internal debate over the, 86

Arab Revolt (1936–1939), 77, 84, 85, 87–88, 94, 145–46, 266n.20

Arabian horses, 100–105

Arabic language and culture: Avraham Shapira on acquiring, 98–99, 137; *chizbat* (satirical anecdote) on Jewish farmers and, 93; discourse on coexistence and shared, 92–100; in Hebrew detective fiction, 129–41; Labor Zionists and, 75–85, 91–93; lack of fluency by Jewish immigrants, 91; of Middle Eastern Jews, 11, 97, 195; study encouraged by various Jewish organizations, 91–92. *See also* language

Ariav, Hayim, 65, 150, 194

Ashkenazi Jews: agricultural settlement (late nineteenth-century) by, 7; Arabic language and, 92–100; Bedouin nicknames given to, 100; class division between new immigrants and established farmers, 192–96; commonalities between Sephardi Jews and, 96; connections between "First Aliyah" settlers and "Old Yishuv," 13; and "Old Yishuv," 7, 24; Orientalist dress style adopted by guards among, 166; tensions between Yemenite Jews and, 73–74; young "sabra" Jews mocking the old guard, 200. *See also* moshava elites; private farmers

Association of Vinegrowers (*Agudat ha-kormim*), 91

Axelrod, Nathan, 124

Ayub, Anton, 239

Balfour Declaration (1917), 16–17, 35, 54–55, 59, 81

Balfour, Lord Arthur James, 54, 55–57, 124

Bar-Giyora, 159

Bar Kokhba, 30, 147

Barnett, Zerach, 65, 144

Bar-Yehuda, Yisrael, 198–200

Bat Shlomo, 9

BDS (Boycott, Divestment, Sanctions) campaign, 248

Bedouins: displacement of the Satariyya tribe, 179–81; evidence of opposition to settlers by, 71; hired as settler guards, 75; identified as Stahl/Zohar murderers, 139–41; Jewish adoption of horsemanship of, 33, 100–105; Jews with personal relationships

with, 70, 89, 97–98; nicknames given to Ashkenazi Jews by, 100; Shapira's "waving a staff left and right" at, 212; symbolism of the Hebrew Bedouin, 69; thief image of, 27
Be'er Yaakov, 179
Beitar, 64, 145, 146
Belkind, Eitan, 50, 81, 189, 190
Belkind, Israel, 44, 65, 81, 109
Belkind, Shimshon, 81, 190
Ben-Ami, Oved, 51, 53, 132, 140
Ben-Amotz, Dan, 201
Ben-Avi, Itamar, 50, 133
Bendel, Yaakov, 86–88, 100
Ben-Ezer, Ehud, 200–201
Ben-Ezer. *See* Raab (Ben-Ezer), Baruch
Ben-Gurion, David: approving "Year of the First Ones" recognition, 220–21; beginning leadership career in Petah Tikva, 41; "City to Village" movement spearheaded by, 179; on Hebrew Labor ideal, 84; marking Qula village for destruction (1948), 184; supersession ideology in "First Ones" (*Rishonim*) essay of, 222–24; unremembered by Alter Albert, 209; writing on Second Aliyah contributions, 43, 59–60. *See also* Mapai party
Ben-Shemen training farm (est. 1907), 79
Ben-Yehuda, Eliezer, 50
Ben-Zeev (Wolfensohn), Israel, 65
Ben-Zvi, Yitzhak, 134
Bialik, Hayyim Nahman, 102
Bilu/Biluim: Ahimeir's criticism of "firstness story" of, 228; becoming an imperiled relic (1970s), 238–39; Ben-Gurion's greetings at commemorative night for, 220; description and members of, 44–45, 65, 81; fiftieth anniversary of the arrival of, 61; "The First Biluim in the Land" lecture (1936) by Meirovitch on, 126–27; invoked by Zvi Horvitz in appeal for unity (1934), 49; Meirovitch on being one of the remnants of, 107, 114–15, 123*fig*

Binyamina, 51, 194
Bnei Binyamin, 50–56, 58, 132, 133, 138, 140
Borochov, Ber, 40, 227
Brandeis, Louis, 51
British Mandate government: criticized over Stahl/Zohar murder investigation, 134–35, 138, 140; Jews lobby for greater access to weapons, 134; Municipal Corporations Ordinance (1934), 192; Shapira on his preference for Ottoman police over, 138; Shaw Commission (1929), 82–83, 166; sulhas changed under the, 166–67. *See also* Great Britain
Brit Shalom, 21
built commemorative environment: Aaronsohn family museum (1956) in Zichron Ya'aqov, 213, 215; Avraham Shapira's house donated as educational site, 215–20; "The First Ones Wing" in Petah Tikva Museum (1963), 213–20, 250; Petah Tikva memorial site (*Yad la-banim*), 213; Rishon LeZion's public "museum" (1952), 213. *See also* First Aliyah commemorations
Buksheshter, Pesach Lieb, 100

capitalist plain, 14
Chancellor, John, 58–59
chizbat genre, 200–204
Citizens Circles, 21, 64, 131
citrus industry: Arab labor used in the, 13, 41, 72–75, 78; Avital Weinstock's student essay on oranges, 207–8; economics of, 11–13; Karlinsky's history of the private,

14; Mizrahi immigrants working in the, 208; Pardess (marketing cooperative), 12; workers in Rehovot citrus groves (1890), 73*fig*
Civic Union (*Ihud ezrahi*), 21
civilization: American frontier myth on wilderness and, 29–30; attacks on "First Aliyah" colonies as intrusions on, 106–7; documentation as symbolizing, 31
class divisions: British Municipal Corporations Ordinance (1934) and, 192; inner and outer urban spatial patterns reflecting, 192; between new immigrants and established farmers, 192–96
Cohen, Geula, 242
colonies. *See* moshavot ("colonies")
commemorations. *See* built commemorative environment; First Aliyah commemorations
confiscated Palestinian lands: annexed into Israeli municipalities (1950s), 191–92; Beit Nehemia built on site of Bayt Nabala (Palestinian village), 187; immigrant camps and transit camps placed on, 190, 193*fig*, 194, 285n.13; Palestinian citizens of Israel uniting around threat of, 240; Qula (later Giv'at Koah), 182; Satariyya tribe displacement and, 179–81; Shapira Forest planted on, 182–87. *See also* Nakba (1948); Palestinian citizens of Israel
Cooper, James Fenimore, 105
Custodian of Absentee Property, 181

Damari, Shoshana, 205
Detective fiction. *See* Hebrew detective fiction
Dinaburg, Ben-Zion (Dinur), 121
Dizengoff, Meir, 89, 102, 133, 140, 210, 217
Druyan, Avraham, 130, 132, 138–39
"dual society" paradigm, 72

Eastern European Jewish migration, 6–7
East European Haskalah (Jewish Enlightenment), 7, 13
East Jerusalem, 240
Edelstein, Yehuda, 136–37, 139
education. *See* youth education
Ein Ganim, 42
Einstein, Arik, 237
Eisenstadt, Shmuel Noah, 42, 72
Ekron (later Mazkeret Batya), 9
Elenberg, Shmaryahu, 121
Elmaleh (Elmaliach), Avraham, 94
Epstein, Yitzhak, 78–79, 93, 247
Erlich, Simha, 242–43, 244
Ettinger, Hayim, 49–50

fantaziya (horsemanship competition), 33, 251
Farmers' Federation: advocating for "mixed" labor force, 77; and apoliticism, 21, 64, 65, 234; *Bustenai* journal of, 27, 35; Farmers' Bank (Bank Ikarim) arm of the, 65, 189; "nationalist farmers" faction of, 84; on new generation of immigrants (1932), 116; supporting Petah Tikva citrus labor practices, 150; Talmei Menashe founded by representatives of, 181
Ferber, Fishel, 171–73
First Aliyah: Abba Ahimeir on honoring, 226–28; becoming an aging and neglected icon (1970s), 238–39; Ben-Gurion's essay undermining primacy of, 222–24; brief history of the, 6–16; celebrating living exemplars of the, 117–18; creating the "firstness" of the, 13, 16–20, 24–25, 37; the ex post facto twentieth-century conception of,

252; financing of Jewish purchasers during the, 7–8; historiography of, 13–14, 257n.51; Jewish settlers of the, 19; rarity of Jewish-Arab violence during, 171; Labor Zionist remaking of the, 18, 25–26, 45, 59–63, 66, 222–24; mapping the, 31–32; as religiously traditional, 142–43, 229–31; Second Aliyah's achievement over the, 20; Tiomkin Migration (1890s) during the, 19; as twentieth-century history, 32–38.

First Aliyah commemorations: directed towards new immigrants (1950s and 1960s), 204–13; fiftieth anniversary of the arrival of Bilu (1932), 61; Hadera's fiftieth-anniversary, 124–26; local quality of, 32–33; modern martyr figures and ancient heroes in, 117–18; one hundredth anniversary event (1982), 241–45; Petah Tikva's eightieth-anniversary, 197–200; reflecting cognitive dissonance after the Nakba (1948), 153; Rishon LeZion's agricultural exhibition (1952), 204; Rishon LeZion's seventy-fifth-anniversary (1957), 205; Rishon LeZion's fiftieth anniversary (1932), 59; in student essays (Rehovot's seventieth anniversary, 1961), 176–77, 205–8; The Year of the First Ones celebration (1962–1963), 37, 220–26. *See also* Zionist memory, Petah Tikva commemorations

First Aliyah colonies: Ahad Ha-'Am's visits to, 40; competing narratives of security and violence in, 154–59, 234; first Jewish immigration to Palestine and, 18; Hajj Tawfiq Hammad's perception of the, 83–84; Jewish populations living in modern cities of the, 23; "moshava/moshavot" terminology for, 3, 254n.7; as sites of memory and symbolism, 4–5, 12, 23–28; weaknesses challenging the early, 40; youth education curricula on history of, 119–24, 244–45; Zionist "cult of the fallen" in, 105–13; Ziv-Av on historic importance of the, 221. *See also* Israeli historiography; Jewish settlement process; Palestine; settlement guards; Yishuv

First Intifada (late 1980s), 246, 247

firstness/firsting: "ancestor veneration" through naming as act of, 182; creation of the First Aliyah, 16–20; description of, 23–28; Knesset session (1962) and postures of, 37, 226–35; performing for the British, 53–59; Petah Tikva's "First Ones" (*rishonim*) claims of, 19; supersessionist Second Aliyah discourses on, 18, 25–26, 45, 59–63, 66, 222–24; The Year of the First Ones celebration (1962–1963) as claim to, 37, 220–26. *See also* settler societies / settler colonialism

founder figures. *See* moshava elites

Freiman, Mordechai, 194

friendship. *See* Jewish-Arab friendship

frontier: Anglo-American myth of the, 29–30, 33, 104, 117–18, 222; as apolitical space, 37, 104, 110, 135, 163; as contact zone, 70–71, 163; settler casualties on the, 105–113; as site of heroism, 1, 36, 104, 108, 113, 118, 151, 241, 245; as site of survival, 30, 33; as "structure of feeling" beyond the state, 163–64, 220; as wilderness, 119, 206. *See also* security, settler societies / settler colonialism

Frumkin, Gad, 85

Gahal party, 5, 232

Galilee, 240
Gamzu, Yossi, 201–4
Gaza Strip: Palestinian unskilled labor from the, 245–46; post-1967 Israeli settlement in the, 233, 240; SodaStream factory planned in the, 249
Gedera, 9, 44–45, 213, 228, 238
Gedera historical museum (1962), 213
Gei Oni (later, Rosh Pinna), 7, 8
General Zionist party: championing capitalist ideology and individual freedom, 232, 233; Conference of Moshava Youth (1940) delegates from the, 64–65; *ha-Boker* (periodical) of the, 35, 86, 89, 94; immigrant workers' distrust of, 196; Joseph Sapir's leadership in, 64; Liberal Party (1961) merger of Progressive Party and, 232–34; as "non-political," 21, 232; Talmei Menashe (Menashe's Furrows) established (1953) by, 179, 181; victories during 1950 municipal elections and 1951 Knesset elections, 193–94
Geulah Land Development Committee (Odessa), 50
Gissin, Aryeh Leib, 52
Gissin, Efraim, 52, 152, 197–99
Givʿat Koah (was Qula), 182
Glickson, Miriam, 92
Glickson, Moshe, 136
Golan Heights, 233, 240
Goldenberg, David, 250
Gordon, Aaron David, 40
Grabovsky, Menahem, 100
Grayevsky, Pinhas, 144–46
Great Britain: Balfour Declaration (1917) by, 16–17, 35, 55–56, 59, 81; League of Nations Mandate for Palestine (1922) and, 4, 17, 53, 82; performing "firstness" for, 53–59; support for Jewish investment in Palestine by, 53–59. See also British Mandate government
Gush Emunim movement, 230–31

Hacohen, Mordechai ben Hillel, 47, 48, 55
Hadad, Sender, 158–61, 171–76
Hadera: anniversary committee, 124; citrus growers of, 77–78; in the discourse of Bnei Binyamin, 52; establishment of, 9–10; fiftieth-anniversary celebration and radio broadcast (1941), 124–26; Histadrut workers' candidates (1935) in, 116; immigrant demonstrations (1950s) in, 194; population living in modern, 23; post-1948 population growth of, 16; as religiously traditional, 142–43; "Yom Kippur in the Khan" play (1941) in commemoration of, 143–44
Haganah oral history project, 154–58
Haifa, 54
Halbwachs, Maurice, 120–22
halukah (charitable donations) system, 51, 158
Hameiri, Avigdor, 129–30, 132, 135, 145
Hammad, Hajj Tawfiq, 83–84
Hankin, Yehezkel, 41
Hankin, Yehoshua, 9
Hanoch, Shalom, 237
Hanotea (The Planter), 51, 140
Hartuv, 12
Haskalah (Jewish Enlightenment), 7, 13
Haviv, Zerubavel, 65, 93–94, 158–59
Hayutman, Herzl, 89–91
Hebrew detective fiction: Ashkenazi Jews deploying knowledge of Arab society in, 129; "Detective Library" publication, 129–30, 136, 145; evolution and impact of, 129–32; real-life Stahl/Zohar murders

investigation, 129, 130, 132–41; Shapira's stories modeled on, 128–29
"Hebrew Labor" principle, 4, 39, 76, 77, 80, 84
Hebrew literature: *chizbat* genre (satirical anecdote), 201–4; "Detective Library," 129–30, 136; evolution of detective fiction, 128–41, 145; Hameiri on need for popular, 132; memoirs of the moshava heroes, 141–48; translated European popular fiction, 131–32
Hebrew University, 85
Hefer, Hayim, 201
heritage elites, 32
heroism. *See* frontier heroism discourse
Herut party: Abba Ahimeir on honoring first Aliyah history, 226–28; Esther Raziel-Naor speaking at Knesset session (1962) on behalf of, 228–29; General Zionists' legacy legitimizing the, 232–33; Zionist politics of, 226, 232
Herzl, Binyamin Zeev (Theodor), 11, 50, 52, 101, 212
Herzliya, 23, 52, 194
hierarchical coexistence discourse: changed nature following Nakba (1948), 164; Epstein's "The Hidden Question" (1907) and, 78–79; evolution in twenty-first century of, 245–50; First Aliyah settlers and, 67–105, 113, 171; Hadad as figure in, 161; hierarchical friendship element of, 85–91; labor arrangements and, 39–40; language politics component of, 91–100; nostalgia coexisting with new enmity and destruction after 1948, 171–77; politics of apoliticism and rhetoric of, 245; racial aspects of, 26–28; Shapira as figure in, 161, 165–66, 169–70, 186; in Shapira's

Shaw Commission testimony (1929), 82–83; in Smilansky's "Sheikh 'Abd al-Qadir," 180–81. *See also* Arab Palestinians; Jewish-Arab coexistence; labor; settlers
Hirsch, Maurice de, 12
Histadrut (General Federation of Labor), 41, 91, 116, 196
Histadrut Labor archive (now Lavon Institute for Labor Movement Research), 42–45
history: constructed quality of historic "First Aliyah" paradigm of, 13; First Aliyah as twentieth-century, 32–38; German practice of teaching *Heimatkunde*, 119; the job of memory makers to interpret, 37–38; Labor Zionists' *kibush ha-historyah* (conquest of history), 42. *See also* the past
Hod HaSharon (originally Magdiel), 23
Holocaust: European diaspora after, 152; *shoah* terminology of, 175; teaching students about bravery as well as the, 215; testimonies of survivors of, 120
Hoofien, Siegfried (Eliezer), 217
Horvitz, Amnon, 172, 173
Horvitz, Zvi, 49, 172

Ichilov, Ezra, 64, 194
Ichilov, Moshe, 107
Ichilov, Nehemiah, 197
Ikar, Alexander, 145–47, 278n.116
Israel Defense Forces (IDF), 161, 162, 172, 174, 179, 187, 228, 239, 247
Israeli border police: Kafr Qasim massacre (1956) by the, 162, 168; Palestinians killed (1949–1956) by, 161
Israeli Chamber of Commerce, 140
Israeli Communist Party, 162
Israeli Department of Education, 244
Israeli historiography: "capitalist plain"

defeat by "socialist [Jezreel] valley" in, 14; constructed quality of "Aliyot" paradigm in, 13; on the "First Aliyah," 3; national commemorations of "firsts," 5–6; on Second Aliyah discourse on private farmers, 43–44. *See also* First Aliyah colonies
Israel Radio, 198
Israel. *See* State of Israel

Jabotinsky, Vladimir Zeev, 95, 131, 132, 136, 226
Jaffa Fruit Company, 81
Jamal Pasha, 57
Jerusalem: Arabic in, 97–98; as an "Old Yishuv" community in, 7, 97; the Ottoman court system in, 110, 112; students visit Petah Tikva from, 121
Jewish Agency: immigrant and transit camps funded by, 190–91, 192, 193*fig*, 194, 285n.13; letter sent to Petah Tikva on Shapira about, 68; memo on loss of Jewish-Arab contact (1942) by, 92; offering immigrants work, 192; promoting national land ownership, 134
Jewish-Arab coexistence: claims of moshava elites regarding, 67–72; discourse on shared Arabic language and culture as path to, 91–100; evolution in modern times of, 245–50; farmers' claim of representing model of, 36; features of moshava accounts of, 113; Jews on horseback as symbol of, 100–105; Labor Zionists promoting labor separation and education for, 75–85, 91–92; racialized hierarchies of early, 26–28; rarity of violence during First Aliyah period, 171; "relational paradigm" of, 266n.23; Rishon LeZion's approach to, 76–77. *See also* hierarchical coexistence; settlers

Jewish-Arab friendship: of Aaron Aaronsohn and Abu Farid, 88–91; Avraham Yalovsky murdered in spite of, 108–9; hierarchical, 86–91; in light of Western conceptualization of, 85–86; of Yaakov Bendel and Abu Hamdan, 86–88
Jewish Colonial Trust, 19
Jewish Colonization Association (JCA): moshava farmers criticized for dependency on, 51; Rothschild colonies turned over to, 12
Jewish immigrants: class division between established farmers and, 192–96; gravitating towards Labor parties (1930s), 115–16; immigrant and transit camps for, 190–92, 193*fig*, 194, 285n.13; State of Israel's Law of Return (1950), 190; youth education in response to numbers of, 118–24; Zarnuga Transit Camp photograph, 193*fig*
Jewish immigration: *aliyah* (ascent) concept of, 17, 24; Balfour Declaration (1917) tied to increased, 17; climbing after Hitler's rise to power (1933), 115; "First Aliyah" Jewish settlers (1880s), 19; following 1948 War of Independence/Nakba, 15–16; marked through numbered aliyot, 16–17; numbered waves (1882–1948) of, 18–19; prewar twentieth century, 6; swelling the mandate and early statehood-era Yishuv, 35–36; Tiomkin Migration (1890s), 19; from Yemen, 11, 73–74, 77;
Jewish National Council, 134
Jewish National Fund: Ben-Shemen training farm of, 79; film for Rehovot's fiftieth anniversary sponsored by, 124; "First Furrow" curriculum written by, 244; issuing

stamp in honor of Meirovitch, 178; lands acquired by the, 14, 18, 19; on nationally owned land as leased not sold, 257n.58; promoting national land ownership, 134; Shapira Forest sign moved to office of, 187; Zionist Organization coordination with, 19

Jewish-only guarding: Avraham Shapira criticized for refusing, 80–81; debate over hiring Arab labor vs., 70–71, 74–75; "Hebrew Labor" principle of Labor debate over, 4, 39, 76, 77, 84; hiring Arabic-speaking Jews for, 11

Jewish-Palestinian relations in Israel: Kafr Qasim as symbol of, 171; Shapira's predictions for future of, 187–88. *See also* Palestinian citizens of Israel

Jewish population: living in Palestine (1900), 6; in modern moshavot and kibbutzim, 23; within Palestine's population, 115; in pre-World War I colonies, 12; Yemenite Jews, 11, 73–74, 77.

Jewish settlement process: 1948–1967, 240; defining the future borders of Israel, 233–34; in the Occupied Territories, 233, 240–45; Zionist settlement project (pre-1948), 14, 240. *See also* First Aliyah colonies, Yishuv

Jewish workers: differences between private farmers and, 43; farmer "boycott" (1906) against organized, 41; Hacohen's description of the newer (1904), 47–48; "Hebrew Labor" principle of Labor Zionists, 4, 39, 75–77, 84; Labor Zionists' support of, 4, 39, 40–53; poor immigrants hired as, 10; Rishon LeZion winery strike (1907) by, 40–41; "stain of Boaz" on private farmers over disputes with, 221–22;

Yemenite Jews, 11, 73–74, 77. *See also* Arab labor; labor

Judaization (*Yihud*), 229, 240

Kafr Qasim: massacre (1956) in, 162, 168; Rivlin's visit (2014) and apology for massacre, 251; sulha (1957) presided over by Shapira, 161–64, 168–70, 251
Kalischer, Zvi Hirsch, 229–30
Katznelson, Berl, 45, 223
Kaufman, Menachem Mendel, 158
Kesari, Uri, 145, 216–20
Kfar Aharon, 53
Kfar Malal, 124
Kfar Saba, 11–12, 23
kibbutzim: early establishment of, 41; ideas of cooperation defining the, 234; population living in contemporary, 23; Refael on Mitzpe Gilboa (now Ma'ale Gilboa), 230; school group field visits to, 119–20; as symbol of the Second Aliyah, 18
Kiryat Shemona, 239
Klausner, Joseph, 42, 92
Knesset: elections (1951), 193–94; special session (1962), 37, 226–35; special session (1982), 241
Kook, Rabbi Abraham Isaac, 230
Kressel, Getzel, 158

labor: in citrus industry, 13, 41, 72–75, 78; ethnic hierarchies of, 11, 26–28, 36, 39–40, 67–105; Gamish's reactionary labor practices after 1948, 195–96; Hadera labor practices report (1935) on, 77; hierarchical coexistence and, 11, 26–28, 36, 39–40, 67–105; Labor Zionists' support of Jewish, 4, 39, 40–53, 75–85, 91–93; private farming driven by native Arab labor, 26; Rishon LeZion winery strike

(1907) by, 40–41; role in evolution of modern hierarchical coexistence, 245–50; wages for, 40–41, 77; workers in Rehovot citrus groves (1990), 73*fig*. *See also* Arab labor; hierarchical coexistence; Jewish workers

Labor Zionist Alignment (Maarakh) party, 243

Labor Zionists: Abba Ahimeir's criticism of the, 226–28; archives of, 42–45; criticism of Tel Aviv Purim parade (1935) by, 149–50; discourse on private farmers among, 43–44; First Aliyah criticisms of, 4, 13; "Hebrew Labor" principle of, 4, 39, 40–53, 72–85; *kibush* (conquest) rhetoric used by, 41; *kibush ha-historyah* (conquest of history) by, 42; "New Hebrew Man" association with, 69; opposition to private land acquisition by, 19–20, 39–45; political right criticism of restraint policy of, 146; promoting labor separation and education for coexistence, 75–85, 91–93; "pure settlement" model of, 15; rejection of Arab labor by, 13, 41; Second Aliyah activism by, 12; supersession of First Aliyah by, 18, 25–26, 45, 59–63, 66, 222–24; "Zionist culture" equated with, 20–21. *See also* private farmers

language: Avraham Shapira on acquiring Arabic, 98–99; discourse on Jewish-Arab coexistence and shared, 91–100; First Aliyah settlers marked by multilingualism, 121–22, 165, 194; Palestine Radio's Hebrew language service, 125; Yiddish as marker of First Aliyah, 17, 93, 122. *See also* Arabic language and culture

League of Nations Mandate for Palestine (1922), 4, 17, 53, 82

Lehrer, Reuven, 53, 108
Levin-Epstein, Eliyahu Zeev Levin, 63, 151
Levin, Hannah, 189, 205
Levontin, Zalman David, 11, 19, 205, 242
Liberal Party (1961), 232–34
Liberal Party (Pioneers of the East), 94–95
Likud Party, 5, 37, 232, 250
Lovers of Zion (Hovevei Zion), 6, 9, 11, 102
Lubman (Haviv), Dov, 58, 93
Lubrani, Eliezer, 124–25, 126, 127
Luz, Kaddish, 226

Maccabi Avshalom sport club, 197–98
Machnes, Gad, 51, 132, 140
Mafdal (National Religious Party), 229–31
Magdiel (later part of Hod HaSharon), 84, 121
al-Maghar, 171–72
Magnes, Judah, 85
Makoff, Batya, 50
Makoff, Yohanan, 74
Mapai party: efforts to encourage Arabic study by, 91; increasing tolerance of private enterprise by, 39, 50; Kafr Qasim sulha committee members from, 170; laborers and low-wage earners supporting, 192, 196; propaganda during the 1961 election by, 196; Zionism as developed under tutelage of, 5. *See also* Ben-Gurion, David
Mapam party, 92
martyrs. *See* frontier heroism discourse
Masada fortress, 30, 215
Megged, Aharon, 200
Meirovitch, Menashe: Ahimeir's reflections on death of, 228; as "apolitical Zionist," 20;

correspondence between Lubrani and, 126; discussed in Zionist memory books, 178; his frustration with the youth, 202; honors received following death (1949) of, 178; as a Bilu member, 107, 115; on benefit of hiring Arab workers, 80, 99; photographed with grandson in *ha-⊠Olam ha-zeh* (1947), 123*fig*; radio lectures by, 126–28; as Rishon LeZion landowner, 34, 58, 59; students' visits to and correspondence with, 114–15, 120, 121, 122–24; Yellin writing in praise of, 99–100, 110; *yeridat ha-dorot* principle and defense of founders, 48–50

memory: American frontier myth and, 29–30; ethnonational, 28–29; local quality of memory found in moshavot ("colonies"), 32–33; memory books (Palestinian and Israeli), 177–78; on removing Rehovot's Arabic name *Duran* from, 151. *See also* Zionist memory

Metulla, 10–11, 89–90, 93

Mikhlin, Yaakov, 96

Mikveh Yisrael, 44

Mishmar ha-Yarden, 9

Mitzpe Gilboa (now Ma'ale Gilboa), 230

Mizrachi party, 145

Mizrahi Jews (from Arab and Islamic lands), 28, 152, 191, 192, 196, 208. *See also* Sephardi Jews

moshava elites: as agriculturalist "ruling class" under the British mandate, 4; Ben-Gurion's essay undermining primacy of, 222–24; challenges from immigrants and newer generations (1930s–1940s) to, 116–17; *chizbat* genre about, 201–4; claims of coexistence with Arab Palestinians by, 67–72; class divisions between new immigrants and, 192–96; discourse about the non-ideological, 48–50; discourse on relationship between Arabs and, 67–105; elderly settlers as collective grandparents, 120–24; growing ambivalence toward (1960s) the, 198–204; intergenerational strife over honoring the, 200–204; memoirs of the moshava heroes, 141–48; as "natives of the land," 28, 88–89; Petah Tikva eightieth-anniversary squabbles over, 197–200; politics of the apoliticism (1920s–1960s) of, 20–23, 35–36, 64–66; second generation defending historical legacy of, 50; settlers' good relations with Arabs evoked by, 151; Stahl/ Zohar murder investigation reflecting features of, 129, 130, 132–41; Yisrael Bar-Yehuda's controversial remarks on, 198–200. *See also* Ashkenazi Jews; private farmers; settlers

moshavot ("colonies"). *See* First Aliyah colonies; private farmers

moshavot commemorations. *See* built commemorative environment; First Aliyah commemorations

Mustaqim, Ali, 68

Nahalat Reuven (later Ness Ziona), 9

Nakba (1948), 14–15, 32, 120, 152–53, 161, 171–77. *See also* State of Israel

National Religious Party (Mafdal), 229–31

Nebi Musa riots (1921), 201

Ness Ziona: immigrant demonstrations (1950s) in, 194; murder of Avraham Yalovsky in, 108–9; pioneer legacy of, 53; population living in modern, 23; post-1948 population growth of, 16; workers' neighborhood called Tel Aviv in, 222

Netanya, 23, 50–51, 140

Neumann, Emanuel, 232
"New Hebrew Man" ("New Jew") image, 53, 69
"New Yishuv," 96–97, 229–30
Nili, 50, 88, 90, 146, 217
Novemeysky, Moshe, 84
Novick, David, 111, 198

Occupied Territories: Palestinians as unskilled labor force in, 245–47; settlements in the, 241–45
Odessa Committee, 9, 19
"Old Yishuv": connection between "First Aliyah" settlers and, 13; differentiating between "New Yishuv" and, 96–97; opposition to Jewish land settlement, 255n.21; Petah Tikva's connection to Jerusalem, 7
Oren, Baruch, 121, 160, 161, 169–70, 213–216
Oriental Jews. See Mizrahi Jews (from Arabic and Islamic countries); Sephardi Jews
Orlovsky, Rabbi Aharon, 110
Ormsby-Gore, William, 88
Or Yehuda, 191
Oslo Accords (1990s), 246–47
Ossovitsky, Joshua, 109
Ottoman Empire: court system in Jerusalem, 110, 112, 272n.156; delegations to the Yishuv during World War I, 57; Land Law (1858) of, 8; peasant appeals against Jewish colonies sent to the, 10; Shapira on his preference over British authority, 138; Tanzimat reforms of the, 8

Pale of Settlement. See Russian Pale of Settlement
Palestine: Arab Revolt (1936–1939) in, 77, 84–85, 87–88, 145–46, 266n.20; Balfour Declaration (1917) regarding, 16–17, 35, 55–56, 59, 81; Balfour's visit (1921) to, 54, 55–57, 124; British support of Jewish investment in, 53–59; Jewish migration by turn of twentieth century, 6; League of Nations Mandate for Palestine for, 4, 17, 53, 82; Muslims as majority in, 24; nineteenth-century European Christian interest in, 8; United Nations Partition Plan (1947) for, 84–85, 233, 260n.125. See also Arab Palestinians; First Aliyah; First Aliyah colonies
Palestine Broadcasting Service, 125
Palestine Electric Company, 84–85
Palestine Liberation Organization, 108
Palestine Office of the World Zionist Organization, 19–20, 41
Palestine Potash, 84
Palestinian Authority, 248
Palestinian citizens of Israel: Kafr Qasim massacre (1956) of, 162, 168; Kafr Qasim sulha (1957) held following massacre of, 162–64, 168–70; united around threat of land confiscations, 240; work in Jewish-owned enterprises by, 170–71. See also confiscated Palestinian lands; Jewish-Palestinian relations in Israel
Palestinian displacement (1948): See Arab Palestinians; confiscated Palestinian lands; Nakba
Palestinian Police (British Mandate government), 134–35, 138, 140
Palmach force, 155, 201
Pardes Hanna, 65
Pardess Citrus Cooperative, 12, 50
Parush, Menachem, 231
the past: the job of memory makers to interpret, 37–38; as something created, 32. See also history
Peel, Lord William, 84

Peres, Shimon, 243–44
Petah Tikva: Ahimeir on honoring settlers of, 228; Arab attack (1921) on, 166; avenging the killing of an Arab worker (1910) in, 75; Balfour's visit (1921) to, 54–57, 124; "The Ballad of Yoel Moshe Solomon" (Taharlev) about, 237–38; citrus growers of, 78; as crucible of Second Aliyah, 41; current population and exports of, 23; establishment and significance of, 1–3; *fantaziya* (horsemanship competition) in, 33, 251; financial stability of oldest settler families of, 33; "First Ones" (*rishonim*) debate within, 19, 31; former Palestinian areas annexed by, 191; Gamzu's poem conveying nostalgia about early, 202–3; *ha-Boker* on functional capitalist relations in, 192; immigrant demonstrations (1950s) in, 194; Jamal Pasha's visit accompanied by Shapira to, 57; Jewish workers in, 47; as "The Mother of the Colonies," 3, 7, 8, 12, 23; murder of Shalom Yaakov Rosenzweig (1895) in, 110–12, 129, 159; "non-political" parade controversy (1935) and riders from, 149–50; photograph of Balfour's visit to, 56*fig*; planting a forest (1960–61) in honor of Avraham Shapira, 182; post-1948 population growth of, 16; reflections on the cemeteries of, 107; as rural idyll, 148–49; Spektor's labor archive account on, 42–43; status as municipality (1937) of, 115; student field trips (1948) to, 121–22; al-Yahudiyya as origin of first major attack (1886) on, 174; Yisrael Bar-Yehuda's controversial remarks about founders of, 198–200
Petah Tikva commemorations: Avraham Shapira's house donated as educational site, 215–20; Avraham Shapira's 135th birthday (2006), 250–51; celebrating birthdays of Avraham Shapira (1940, 1945), 67–68, 169, 187; city exhibition (1955), 214; "First Furrow" in, 244–45; honoring heroic deaths, 55; nighttime IDF parade (1963) in, 225–26; partisan squabbles (1958) over eightieth-anniversary events, 197–200; Petah Tikva memorial site (*Yad la-banim*), 186, 213; Remembrance of the First Ones wing in Petah Tikva Museum (1963), 214–20, 250; *Reshit* (First/Beginning) commemorative volume (1948) on, 25. *See also:* First Aliyah commemorations
Petah Tikva Museum, 169, 213–20, 250
Petah Tikva Workers' Council, 198
Pinsker, Leo, 100–101
Plumer, Lord Herbert, 57–58, 100
Poʻalei Agudat Yisraʼel party, 231
politics: language politics, 91–100; of commemoration, 196–200; nationalism described as form of, 22–23. *See also* Labor Zionists, politics of apoliticism
politics of apoliticism: in Avraham Shapira memoirs, 145, 148; during British Mandate era, 64–66; First Aliyah settlers as apolitical cohort, 20–23, 35–37, 39, 45–50, 55, 128–29; moshava anniversaries reinforcing, 61–63; "non-political" parade controversy (1935), 149–50; rhetoric of hierarchical coexistence and, 245; Rishon LeZion's anniversary (1957) and, 189; of Sephardi and Oriental Zionists, 95
private farmers: accusations of disrespect against, 48–49; apoliticism of

the early, 20–23, 35–36, 64–66; "boycott" (1906) against organized Jewish workers by, 41; British support of Jewish investment by, 53–59; on "capitalist plain," 14; differences between Jewish workers and, 43; as *effendis*, 198; Labor Zionists' opposition to, 19–20, 39–45; resistance to Jewish-only guarding by, 81; and responses to labor organizing, 45–53; "stain of Boaz" on, 221–22; tensions between Yemenite workers and, 73–74; Zionist historiography about, 43–44. *See also* Ashkenazi Jews; Labor Zionists; moshava elites

private farming. *See* Arab labor; Labor Zionists; moshava elites

Progressive Party, 232

al-Qasim, Salim bin Amin, 110–12
Qastina (later Beer Tuvia), 9
Qula (later Givʻat Koah), 182

Raab (Ben-Ezer), Baruch, 51–52, 156–57, 160
Raab, Eliezer, 97
Raab, Yehuda, 7, 8, 97, 105, 121, 201
Raanana, 84, 194
Rabin, Yitzhak, 108
radio, 124–27
railroad, 15, 54, 101, 103
Ras al-ʻAyn (Rosh HaAyin), 54, 112, 191
Rashish, Pinhas, 164, 170, 194, 197, 213, 215
Raziel-Naor, Esther, 228–29
Refael, Yitzhak, 229–30
Rehovot: Ahimeir on honoring settlers of, 228; Ben-Ami on the pioneer legacy of, 53; establishment of, 9, 10, 12; film produced for fiftieth anniversary of, 124–25; "Hatikva" (national anthem) written in, 222; Herzl's visit (1898) to, 101, 212; Moshe Smilansky of, 27, 34; population living in modern, 23; post-1948 population growth of, 16; as religiously traditional, 142–43; on removing its Arabic name *Duran* from memory, 151; student essays (1961) to honor seventieth anniversary of, 176–77, 205–8

religious Jews: of First Aliyah moshavot, 142–43; Tidhar's fund-raising among, 141–42, 144, 147, 230

religious parties: Agudat Yisrael party, 231; on the "First Ones," 229–31; National Religious Party (Mafdal), 229–31; Poʻalei Agudat Yisraʼel party, 231

Revisionist movement. *See* Zionist Revisionist movement

Revivi, Oded, 247

Ringold, Hannah, 205

Rishon LeZion: Ahimeir on honoring settlers of, 228; Bilu move to, 44; anniversary (1957) of, 189, 194, 205; Arabic language teacher in, 91; agricultural exhibition (1952), 204; Balfour's visit (1921) to, 54, 124; class divide (1950s) in, 189–90; current population of, 23; establishment of, 9, 11–12, 27; fiftieth anniversary celebration (1940) of, 59; Jewish-Arab relationship in, 76–77; local Haganah oral history project in, 158; Menashe Meirovitch of, 20, 34; Menashe Meirovitch prize for essay contest, 178; Plumer's visit (1917) to, 57–58, 100; post-1948 population growth of, 16; public "museum" (1952) organized in, 213; Smilansky's memory revealing racialized hierarchies in, 27–28; winery strike (1907), 40–41; student

visits to, 114–15, 119, 122–124; Zalman David Levontin as founder of, 19
Rivlin, Joseph Joel, 97
Rivlin, Reuven, 97, 250–51
Rokach, Israel, 194
Rokach, Yitzhak, 210
Rosenzweig, Shalom Yaakov, 110–12, 129, 159
Rosh Pinna: Balfour's visit to, 54; decay and neglect of, 239–40; establishment of, 7; "First Furrow" curriculum on establishment of, 244–45; firstness claim of founders of, 19; Jewish-Arab friendships in, 86–87, 156; "Old Yishuv" role in founding of, 224; Ottoman officials visiting (1917), 57; population growth by 1900 of, 10; reconstituted in early 1880s, 8–9; religious commitments of founders of, 231
Rothschild administration: criticism of moshava farmers' dependency on, 51; Gedera managed by the, 44; Smilansky on errors in agricultural policy of, 80
Rothschild, Baron Edmund James de, 9, 50, 89, 102, 144
Rothschild, James de, 12
Rovina, Hannah, 149
Ruppin, Arthur, 15, 43, 217
Russian Pale of Settlement: Avraham Shapira's immigration from, 97; Bilu established following anti-Jewish violence in, 44; Jewish migration to Palestine from, 6–7
Rutenberg, Pinhas, 84–85

Safed, 7, 9
Sapir, Joseph, 60, 64, 194, 233
al-Satariyya (Abu Fadl) (Talme Menashe built on site), 177, 179–81
Sauvage, Camille, 54, 124

Savidor, Menahem, 241–242, 244
schools. *See* youth education
Schwartz, Shalom, 145
Second Aliyah (1904–5): Abba Ahimeir's criticism of, 226–28; achievements over the First Aliyah by, 20, 43; Ezra and Nehemiah leading ancient, 17; Labor Zionist activism during, 12; settlements, 41; twenty-fifth-anniversary celebration (1929) of, 59–60; use of Arab workers disputed by, 10
Second Aliyah discourse: Christianity/ Judaism metaphor of "firstness," 25–26; influencing "First Aliyah" commemorations, 30; labor archives accounts contrasting First Aliyah to, 42–45; Labor Zionists efforts to canonize "Second Aliyah," 18, 25–26, 45, 59–63, 66, 222–24; on private farmers, 43–44; Yisrael Bar-Yehuda's remarks (1958), 198–200
security: displacement of Arabs and discourse around, 161; in Haganah testimonies, 154–157; Sapir on moshavot's ethos of, 234; Zerubavel Haviv on First Aliyah idea of, 158–59. *See also* frontier heroism discourse; settlement guards
Sejera, 12, 159, 254n.7, 256n.49
Sephardi Jews: commonalities of Ashkenazi Jews and, 96; connections with "First Aliyah" settlers, 13; discourses about Jewish-Arab coexistence among, 94–100; Hartuv founded by Bulgarian, 12; historic and ideological diversity (1880) of, 24; land purchase among, 11; Pioneers of the East organization, 94; self-perceived apolitical position of, 95. *See also* Mizrahi Jews (from Arab and Islamic lands)
settlement guards: Arabic-speaking

INDEX

Jews hired as, 11; Avraham Shapira as "The Oldest of the Guards," 55–56, 67; competing narratives of security and violence in history of, 154–59; debate over hiring Arabs as, 70–71, 74–75, 80–81, 84; defeating attack on Petah Tikva (1921), 166; exaggerated accounts of, 159–61; *ha-Ahdut* mourning death of "hero," 106; Orientalist dress style adopted by Ashkenazi, 166; solving Stahl/Zohar murders, 129, 130; student field trips to visit old guards, 121–22. *See also* Arab-perpetrated violence; First Aliyah colonies; security

settlements (post-1948): authorized by Custodian of Absentee Property, 181; in Occupied Territories after 1967, 241–45. *See also* Yishuv

settlements (pre-1948). *See* Yishuv

settlers: *See* First Aliyah colonies, hierarchical coexistence, Jewish-Arab coexistence, moshava elites, settlements (post-1948), settler societies / settler colonialism, Yishuv

settler societies / settler colonialism: Anglo-American case, 30–34; emigrant colonization discourse among Central Europeans, 30–31; national parks and, 182–84; "partnership" discourse in, 70–71; private property, 14–15; "pure settlement" model, 15, 70; racialized hierarchies and, 26–28; settlers as "natives of the land," 28, 88–89. *See also* firstness/firsting, frontier heroism discourse

Shadmi, Issachar, 168

Shapira, Avraham: ambivalence toward First Aliyah figures like, 200–204; birthday celebrations for, 67–68*fig*, 169, 187; *chizbat* (satirical anecdote) on adventures of, 112–13, 201–4;

contributions to the frontier heroism discourse, 128–29; criticized for refusing Jewish-only guarding, 80–81, 84; display case of weapons belonging to, 218*fig*; as exemplar of "hierarchical coexistence," 161, 165–66, 169–70; expiration of his weapons permit (1964), 151; family members of, 33, 97, 216–17, 290n.105; forest (Shapira Forest) planted in honor of, 182–87; his home donated to Petah Tikva as educational site, 215–20; immigration from Pale of Settlement by, 97; involvement in the "Year of the First ones" (1963), 225–26; Kafr Qasim ceremony (1957) sulha committee led by, 162–65, 168–69, 251; as "last of the Mohicans of Yishuv veterans," 105; on learning Arabic language, 98–99, 137; life and death in Petah Tikva, 2–3, 23, 33, 36, 59, 105, 204; memoirs of, 136–45, 147–48; memory of racing a train on horseback, 103; on the murder of Shalom Yaakov Rosenzweig, 110–12; as "The Oldest of the Guards," 55–56, 67, 164, 169–70; Old Patron's Brandy celebrating (1960), 1–2*fig*, 34; 135th birthday of, 250–51; personal contacts with rural Arab Muslims, 98–99; photographs of, 56*fig*–57, 219*fig*; predictions about Israeli-Arab relations by, 187–88; presiding over Kafr Qasim sulha (1957), 162–64; as propaganda tool for Labor Zionists, 69; Shaw Commission of inquiry testimony (1929) by, 82–83, 166; on solving the Stahl/Zohar murders, 129, 130–41; students' visit with, 121–22, 124; in Tel Aviv Purim parade, 149–50, 209, 210–13; Uri Kesari's critique of, 216–20

Shaw Commission (1929), 82–83, 166

Shertok (Sharett), Moshe, 92
Shimoni, David, 102
Shochat, Eliezer, 41
Shochat, Manya (Vilbushevitz), 75
Shochat, Yisrael, 41
ha-Shomer, 75, 76, 81, 101, 159
ha-Shomer ha-Tza'ir, 92, 141
Simkin, Mordechai Shalom, 197
Six-Day War (1967), 37, 233, 240, 243
Slouschz, Nahum, 49, 52, 201–2
Smilanksy, Moshe, 27, 34, 64, 79–80, 84, 108, 165, 180, 251–52
Smilansky, David, 49–50, 117
Smilansky, Zeev, 47–48, 49
SodaStream boycott, 248–49
Sokolow, Nahum, 55
Solomon, Yoel Moshe, 7, 230, 237–38, 242
Stahl/Zohar murders, 129–41
State of Israel: establishment (1948) of, 3, 152; inheriting pre-1948 national settlement project, 14; investment from American Jews in, 63; Law of Return (1950), 190; relationship to its Palestinian or Arab "other," 26; War of Independence (1948), 15. *See also* Nakba (1948), Israel Defense Forces (IDF)
sulhas: during British Mandate period, 166–67; Hebrew press reporting (1949) on Jewish-Arab, 167; leading to resolution of a Zarnuqa 1891 incident, 165; after Kafr Qasim massacre (1957), 36, 162–64, 168–70, 251; settler narratives on history of, 164–65; Shapira's role at Kafr Qasim in, 165–66; for restorative justice and conflict resolution, 162, 164–65
Sultz, Alexander, 139
sumud practice (post-Nakba Palestinian), 120
supersessionist ideology: Ben-Gurion's essay reflecting the, 222–24; Labor Zionists,' 18, 25–26, 45, 59–63, 66, 222–24

Taharlev, Yoram, 237
Talmei Menashe, 179–81
Tel Aviv: Balfour's visit (1921) to, 54; exports from, 23; foundation myth of, 270n.109; joke about moshava resident going to, 148; Purim parade, 209–13; The Year of the First Ones summer camp activities in, 224–25
Tel Hai, 30, 106, 278n.122
testimonies, Jewish practice of, 120
"Third Aliyah," 17
Tiberias, 54
Tidhar, David: commemorating First Aliyah figures, 34, 90–91, 141–48; fund-raising appeal for Shapira memoir project by, 141–42, 144, 147, 230; name used for fictional detective, 135–36; Shapira's memoirs published by, 136–45, 147–48; support of emerging detective literature by, 129, 131
Tiomkin, Vladimir, 9, 19
Tolkowsky, Sami (Shmuel), 81, 136
transit camps (*ma'abarot*), 190–91, 192, 193*fig*, 194, 285n.13
Trans-Jordan, 161, 174
"The Triangle" (region), 161–62, 169, 258n.63
Trumpeldor, Joseph, 44, 146, 147, 278n.122
Turner, Frederick Jackson, 104, 152
Tzidkuni, Yaakov, 42

Umlebes (site of Petah Tikva), 2, 10–11, 107, 214, 237
Union of Sons of the Yishuv, 65, 90, 96–97
United Nations Partition Plan (1947), 84–85, 233, 260n.125

Valero, Haim Aharon, 11
Vilkansky (Volkani), Yitzhak, 79
Vinegrowers' Association (*Agudat ha-kormim*), 12

Wadi Musrara (renamed Nahal Ayalon), 203, 239
Washington, George, 14, 257n.55
"wasteland" (*shemamah*), 27, 98–99, 114, 128, 177–78, 185, 242
Wedgwood, Josiah, 134–35
Weizmann, Chaim, 55, 136
West Bank: evolution of hierarchical coexistence in the, 245–50; Palestinian unskilled labor from the, 245–46; post-1967 Israeli settlement in, 233, 240
wine industry, 58–59
winery strike (1907), 40–41912
World Union of General Zionists, 232. *See also* General Zionist party

Yad la-banim memorial site (Petah Tikva), 186
al-Yahudiyya (later al-Abbasiyya), 82, 173–74, 179, 191
Yalovsky, Avraham, 108–9
The Year of the First Ones celebration (1962–1963), 37, 220–26
Yehoash (Solomon Blumgarten), 91, 92–93
Yehud (was al-Abbasiyya), 191
Yellin, David, 99, 100, 110, 121
Yemenite Jews: difficulty of settling on nationally owned land, 267n.26–68n.26; immigrating following Nakba (1948), 191; immigration during First Aliyah by, 11; lesser wages paid to, 77; tensions between Ashkenazi farmers and, 73–74
yeridat ha-dorot principle, 48
Yesud HaMaʻala, 9, 10
Yishuv: Arab boycott (1936) of the, 84–85; Balfour's visit (1921) to, 54, 55–57, 124; defining the future borders of Israel, 233–34; Jewish immigration (mid-1920s to 1960s) to, 35–36; "Old Yishuv," 7, 13, 96–97; Ottoman visitors (World War I) to, 57; "settling the land of Israel" (*yishuv Eretz Yisraʼ el*), 7; wine industry of, 58–59; youth education curricula on history of the, 119–24, 244–45. *See also* First Aliyah colonies
Yizhar, S. (Yizhar Smilansky), 251–52
Yizkor (Jewish memorial prayer), 105
Young Turk Revolution (1908), 35
youth education: in the built commemorative environment (1950s–1960s), 213–20, 250; field visits to biblical and historic sites, 119–20; "First Furrow" curriculum (1985), 244–45; "The First Seeds I Planted" (Meirovitch) used in, 127–28; in General Trend schools, 207; Hebrew literature as means of, 131–32, 137; increased Jewish immigration (1930s) motivates investment in, 118; "knowledge of the land" and "love of the homeland" curricula, 119–24; settler elders presented as collective grandparents, 120–24; student essays (Rehovot seventieth anniversary, 1961), 176–77, 205–8; tree planting as form of, 51; The Year of the First Ones summer camp activities, 224–25
Yudilovitz, David, 194, 205

Zarnuga Transit Camp, 193*fig*
Zarnuqa (Palestinian village), 193
Zichron Yaʻaqov: Aaronsohn family museum (1954) in, 213, 215; the Aaronsohn family of, 34, 50, 53, 88, 89, 90, 213, 216–17; Ahimeir on honoring settlers of, 228; Alter

Albert featured at seventieth-anniversary (1952) of, 208–9; eightieth-anniversary (1962) of, 37–38, 190; mentioned at dedication ceremony (1923) of Binyamina, 51–52; establishment and growth by 1900 of, 9–10; historical mystique and rural imaginary of, 149; immigrant demonstrations (1950s) in, 194; Nili espionage organization founded by colonists in, 146; Romanian Jewish founders of, 19

Zionist Executive, 133

Zionist labor movement. *See* Labor Zionists

Zionist memory: competing narratives of "First Aliyah" security and violence, 154–59; "cult of the fallen" in, 105–13; efforts to supersede "First Aliyah" with "Second Aliyah," 18, 25–26, 45, 59–63, 66, 222–24; elderly settlers as collective grandparents in, 120–24; elderly settlers as collective grandparents in, 120–24; emphasizing survival over heroic death, 30; First Aliyah agricultural colonies as site of, 4–5, 12, 23–28; "First Ones" complaining of exclusion from, 33; growing ambivalence toward (1960s), 198–204; invoked by Avraham Shapira riding in Tel Aviv Purim parade, 209–13; mapping the "First Aliyah," 31–37; memoirs of the moshava heroes, 141–48; performing firstness, 53–59; practice of testimony in, 120; settler "remnant" as guardians of, 107; texture and multiplicity within, 234–35; as variant of modern ethnonational memory, 28–31; Zerubavel's study (1995) of, 22, 30. *See also* First Aliyah commemorations; memory

Zionist Organization, 11, 15, 19, 41, 44, 55, 217

Zionist Revisionist movement: appeal of Shapira memoirs to, 145; ethos of the, 227; Herut party evolving from the, 226; opposing class-based Labor Zionist rhetoric, 227–28; Sephardi and Oriental Jews' support for, 95; studies on intellectual histories of, 21; Vladimir Jabotinsky's leadership of, 131

Zirmati, Ya'qub, 97, 99, 101–2

Ziv-Av, Yitzhak, 34, 180, 213–14, 220–21, 226, 244–45

Stanford Studies in Jewish History and Culture
David Biale and Sarah Abrevaya Stein, Editors

This series features novel approaches to examining the Jewish past in the form of innovative work that brings the field into productive dialogue with the newest scholarly concepts and methods. Open to a range of disciplinary and interdisciplinary approaches, from history to cultural studies, this series publishes exceptional scholarship balanced by an accessible tone, illustrating histories of difference and addressing issues of current urgency. Books in this list push the boundaries of Jewish Studies and speak compellingly to a wide audience of scholars and students.

Samuel J. Spinner, *Jewish Primitivism*
2021

Sonia Beth Gollance, *It Could Lead to Dancing: Mixed-Sex Dancing and Jewish Modernity*
2021

Julia Elsky, *Writing Occupation: Jewish Émigré Voices in Wartime France*
2020

Alma Rachel Heckman, *The Sultan's Communists: Moroccan Jews and the Politics of Belonging*
2020

Golan Y. Moskowitz, *Queer Jewish Sendak: A Wild Visionary in Context*
2020

Devi Mays, *Forging Ties, Forging Passports: Migration and the Modern Sephardi Diaspora*
2020

Clémence Boulouque, *Another Modernity: Elia Benamozegh's Jewish Universalism*
2020

For a complete listing of titles in this series, visit the Stanford University Press website, www.sup.org.

The authorized representative in the EU for product safety and compliance is:
Mare Nostrum Group
B.V Doelen 72
4831 GR Breda
The Netherlands

www.ingramcontent.com/pod-product-compliance
Lightning Source LLC
Chambersburg PA
CBHW031846220426
43663CB00006B/517